# The Growth of the Mind

# The Growth of the Mind

## An Introduction to Child Psychology

**Kurt Koffka**

With a New Introduction by
James A. Schellenberg

Transaction Books
New Brunswick (U.S.A.) and London (U.K.)

Library of Congress Catalog Number: 80-50103
ISBN: 0-87855-360-6 (cloth), 0-87855-784-9 (paper)
Printed in the United States of America

**Library of Congress Cataloging in Publication Data**
Koffka, Kurt, 1886-1941.
  The growth of the mind.

  (Social science classics series)
  Translation of Die Grundlagen der psychischen Entwicklung.
  Reprint of the 1924 ed. published by Harcourt, Brace, New York.
  Bibliography: p.
  Includes index.
  1. Child psychology. 2. Learning, Psychology of. 3. Gestalt psychology. I. Title.
II. Series. [DNLM: 1. Child psychology.
2. Psychological theory. WS105 K78g 1925a]
BF721.K62     1980     155.4'13     80-50103

ISBN: 0-87855-360-6
ISBN: 0-87855-784-9

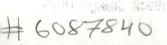

# Introduction to the Transaction Edition

*James A. Schellenberg*

## I

If a time and place are to be given for the origin of Gestalt psychology, it must be about the beginning of 1911 at Frankfurt am Main, Germany. Shortly after completing his doctoral degree at the University of Berlin, Kurt Koffka went to Frankfurt in 1910 to become an assistant at the Psychological Institute. That fall Wolfgang Köhler joined the Institute as another assistant, and during the following winter Max Wertheimer also came to Frankfurt. Thus the three founding fathers of Gestalt psychology were brought together, and the close relationship which immediately developed between them laid the foundations for the Gestalt movement.

Koffka, Köhler, and Wertheimer remained the dominant triumverate of Gestalt psychology for the rest of their lives. Although they went their separate ways from Frankfurt, each generously acknowledged the contributions of his colleagues as they built upon their common foundations.

In a real sense, however, Max Wertheimer provided the primary inspiration at the very beginning. Using

# INTRODUCTION

a stroboscope to study the visual perception of movement, he was obtaining experimental results which
could not be readily assimilated into the principles of
psychology as then understood. He demonstrated
that the perception of visual movement follows patterns which differ from those of the visual stimuli.
Wertheimer's paper on this research, published in
1912, is sometimes considered as the beginning of the
Gestalt movement. By this time, however, Koffka
and Köhler, as well as Wertheimer, were thinking
about the more general implications of this research.
They proposed nothing less than a revolution in the
basic structure of the science of psychology.

To understand the nature of this proposed revolution, we must have some idea of the kind of psychology which was dominant early in the present century. Today we identify it as the particular school
called "structuralism," but at the time it was considered—especially in Germany, where most of the
great nineteenth century psychologists had worked—
as essentially identical with psychology as a scientific discipline. The main goal of psychology was
considered to be the identification of forms of consciousness that reflected patterns of sensory stimulation. It was assumed that to be scientific about the
study of mind, consciousness must be broken up into
the smallest units possible. It was furthermore assumed that patterns of sensation directly reflected
the physical stimuli. Both of these assumptions were
called into question by the young Gestaltists. They
held, in contrast, that the unit for analysis must be
more meaningfully determined on the basis of the
evidence of psychological functioning. Affirming
that the whole is not simply the sum of its parts, they
chose the term "gestalt"—which is probably best
translated by the English word "configuration"—as
a label for their approach. It is a particular configuration of stimuli, they held, that is characteristically

responded to by the organism, and the way this configuration is identified does not simply reflect the physical nature of stimuli.

An early statement of the Gestalt views was made by Koffka in 1915. His colleague Köhler later summarized the main import of this presentation as follows (Köhler, 1942, p. 99):

1. An atomistic interpretation of human experience in terms of ultimate and simple elements is incompatible with the very nature of this experience. The primary data of perception, for instance, are typically specific structures or Gestalten.
2. Functional concepts must follow descriptive facts. In perception, therefore, it is misleading to correlate stimuli with sensations. Rather patterns of stimuli are to be correlated with those specific structural entities which are the essential content of perceptual fields.
3. With these premises the problem of psychophysical relationships appears in a new light. In place of the traditional view that brain processes are aggregates of elementary local excitations, it is postulated that brain function tends to assume the form of specific molar events which correspond to the structures found in experience.

The early research of the Gestaltists, including experimental work by Koffka and his students at the University of Giessen (where he went from Frankfurt in 1911), was primarily in perception. By the early 1920s, Gestalt psychology had begun to be recognized as deserving of a place in the science of psychology, but that place was seen as essentially limited to the area of perception. Köhler and Koffka, however, had begun efforts to change this situation by extending the application of Gestalt principles. Köhler's studies of apes in the Canary Islands (where he was isolated during World War I) extended Gestalt ideas to the study of learning. Although not reported

# INTRODUCTION

to English readers until *The Mentality of Apes* appeared in 1925 (except for Koffka's summary in *The Growth of the Mind*), Köhler's studies soon were recognized as demonstrating the central role of insight in learning.

Kurt Koffka was also intent on showing some of the broader implications of Gestalt psychology. This endeavor was to take the form of an introduction to child psychology, first published in 1921 as *Die Grundlagen der Psychlschen Entwicklung.* Although originally intended especially for German educators —to give them a more useful psychology than they had been taught in the course of their training—this book also was the first attempt to bring Gestalt ideas to bear upon the full range of psychology: upon developmental psychology, motivation, learning, memory, and social psychology, as well as the psychology of perception. The first English edition of this work appeared in 1925 as *The Growth of the Mind.* A second, slightly revised, edition followed in 1928. The original (1925) edition is the work now being made available again.

Although Koffka later presented even broader and more ambitious elucidations, *The Growth of the Mind* was the first really general work of Gestalt psychology. For the general reader it also remains the most easily understood of all of Koffka's works and one of the most persuasive statements of the Gestalt position.

## II

Kurt Koffka was born in Berlin on March 18, 1886, the eldest of three children. His father was a distinguished lawyer, and there were expectations that Kurt would continue in the legal field. His interest, however, was more whetted by broader subjects, and when he entered the University of Berlin in 1903 it was as a student of philosophy. After a time, however, he changed to psychology.

Koffka's first published paper, a study of his own color blindness, appeared in 1908, the same year in which he received his doctoral degree. His dissertation, with a title best translated into English as "Experimental Investigations of Rhythm," was published in 1909. By then he had done additional work in the psychological laboratory at Freiburg and had moved on to work with Oswald Külpe at Würzburg. Külpe and others at Würzburg were investigating such topics as "imageless thought" and perceptual "determining tendencies"; their conclusions, while not breaking with the main body of psychological principles then dominant, did suggest at least some significant modifications. It was within the Würzburg tradition that Koffka wrote his first book, published in 1912 as *Zur Analyse der Vorstellungen und ihrer Gesetze* ("Regarding the Analysis of Images and their Laws") and dedicated to Külpe. By the time this book was published, however, Koffka had moved to the influence of Wertheimer and Köhler at Frankfurt, where he was already developing a far more radical reformulation of the psychology of perception.

In 1911 Koffka moved to the University of Giessen, where he remained (except for two brief periods as a visiting professor in the United States) until 1927. At Giessen he embarked on a series of laboratory studies to identify the primary organizing principles of perception; this work is still considered as among the most important basic research contributions in the field of perception. At Giessen he also participated in clinical studies of aphasics and in military research of sound localization. And it was also at Giessen that several important works—most notably, *The Growth of the Mind*—were written.

Koffka moved to the United States in 1927 to

become William Allan Neilson Research Professor at Smith College. Although that particular appointment expired in five years, he continued to teach and do research at Smith until his death in 1941. The most important work of this period was his *Principles of Gestalt Psychology,* published in 1935. This was an ambitious attempt to systematize fully Gestalt contributions into a single culminating work.

Little has been reported about Koffka's private life. It is known that he was married four times, but that he had only two wives (each married twice). He was always generous in acknowledging the contributions of other scholars, without in any way reducing his painstaking pride in his own work. He was active almost up to the final day of his life, when a coronary thrombosis cut short his career at the age of fifty-five.[1]

## III

As I have indicated above, *The Growth of the Mind* was the first really general work of Gestalt psychology. Sub-titled "An Introduction to Child Psychology," this work included a review of the most important literature in that field. But this is no ordinary child psychology textbook. As the author makes clear in his 1928 revision, "This book stands for a cause" (Koffka, 1928, p. xiii). This cause is to demonstrate the wide application of the principles of Gestalt psychology, and the materials used are systematically brought together from the Gestalt perspective.

The central theme is well stated in the book's final sentence: "The nature of mental development as it has been revealed to us is not the bringing together of separate elements, but the arousal and perfection of more and more complicated configurations, in which both the phenomena of consciousness and the functions of the organism go hand in hand" (p. 356). The concept of mental growth is thus presented not in terms of the addition of new ideas or habits but in terms of increasingly complex organizations of behavior, organizations which are cognitively focused but which also depend directly on the biological functioning of the organism.

In his opening pages Koffka makes clear the breadth of the task which he is attempting: "to discover the evolutionary principles of child psychology" and to interpret them in such a way that we may improve our aims and methods of education and "better understand the product, which is the human adult" (p. 3). The problem of psychological development is cast first in an evolutionary perspective, requiring attention to animal studies as well as those of humans, but Koffka also makes clear that the task of interpretation requires careful attention to the peculiarly human characteristics of the child.

The problem of method is also discussed in Chapter I. Koffka here distinguishes between three approaches: a purely objective method, a purely subjective method, and a combination of objective and subjective methods. He, of course, prefers the third approach, which he calls the "psycho-physical method." It includes both the objective (or, as Koffka prefers to call it, "functional") analysis of observed events and the subjective (or, in Koffka's terminology, "descriptive") analysis of how these events are experienced. Koffka clearly rejects the behavioristic approach as being too limited because of its neglect of what is most peculiarly human (in terms of the physiological functioning of the brain as well as subjectively perceived events). Objective methods, however, are in no way rejected; it is rather held that understanding is strengthened by the combination of methods. Furthermore, we must be aware that "we can not use the same procedure in approaching the mental life of a child that we are accustomed to employ with adults" (p. 34) because we must be open to pre-logical patterns and other ways that children may organize their experience differently from their elders.

The "General Facts and Points of View" in Chapter II deal primarily with the evolutionary significance of individual development and the interplay of the forces of heredity and environment. Koffka avoids any sweeping assumptions about the manner that the development of the individual may reflect that of the species (or "race"); we should be alert to empirical evidence of parallels in development without being "led into the dogmatic construction of uniformities and dependencies" (p. 49). Koffka is also cautious about any advance theoretical commitment concerning the relative roles of heredity and environment. He points out that "learning is essentially a type of development, and learning involves the reaction of the individual to a definite situation wherein the reaction is certainly not unequivocally tied up with inherited dispositions" (pp. 51-52); but mental development also involves more than learning, as it proceeds "hand in hand with the development of the bodily organism" (p. 52).

The interplay of heredity and environment continues as a key theme in Chapter III. The original experience of the child is characterized from the first by a certain order which grows out of both his nature as an organism and the nature of his environment. This order consists fundamentally of *"qualities upon a ground"* or *"mental configurations"* (p. 131). In other words, the most primitive phenomena are configurative. This Gestaltist conclusion about the nature of the newborn infant's experience comes after a detailed examination of reflexes and instincts. The inherited base for these reflexes and instincts in humans is considered much less specific

than most previous writers assumed. What we in-
herit, according to Koffka, is not a repertory of
particular reactions, but a set of internal conditions
for response, which, together with external conditions, helps to determine our behavior.

Chapters IV and V are both titled "Special Features of Mental Growth." Both deal with what we
broadly call learning. Koffka's division here is primarily between new learning (or what he calls
"achievement"), dealt with in Chapter IV, and the
persistence of learned responses (or "memory"), dealt
with primarily in Chapter V. These two chapters
include some rather detailed discussions of the work
of others. Thorndike's work is discussed in detail (pp.
153-74) to refute the basic model of trial-and-error
learning. More appreciatively reviewed are Köhler's
studies of chimpanzees (pp. 179-230).

Chapter V is organized primarily around four
different kinds of learning: motor learning, sensory
learning, sensori-motor learning, and ideational
learning. The data of all of these areas are shown to
be broadly consistent with Gestalt principles. Regarding motor learning, for example, Koffka concludes that "in learning a more or less complicated
movement a movement-melody must be composed;
that is to say, a formation after the manner of our
'configuration' takes place, which does not consist of
independent parts, but is an articulate whole" (p.
261). Thus even for motor learning an ordered perception of the goal to be attained seems necessary; much
more clearly does the evidence seem to support this
Gestaltist interpretation for other, more obviously
cognitive, forms of learning.

Koffka's final chapter, "The World of a Child,"
appears different from the rest of the book in both
content and style. Its content is, literally, child's
play; this is (or at least was when Koffka wrote the
book) less traditionally an area for scholarly analy-

INTRODUCTION

sis than is the rest of the book. Koffka's style is here also less restricted by technical details and more broadly free-flowing. This provides a surprisingly effective capstone for the book. Rather than laboriously repeat in a concluding chapter the points already developed earlier, Koffka examines mental development from a completely new perspective. However, this turns out to be also a general restatement of the perspective present in the earlier chapters. The play of the child provides, therefore, a chance to sum up what Koffka sees as central in the psychological world of the child.

The world of the child, as seen by Koffka, is much less differentiated by conventional distinctions than is the world of adults; or, more accurately, the conventions used to make distinctions are used with much greater freedom. The world of play is therefore much less set off from the rest of reality than it is for adults; it can therefore more easily become the child's central reality.

The child's world must, however, also be partly the world of adults. "The world of the adult makes itself gradually felt by the child through the unpleasant consequences of certain acts of behavior. In the adult's world the child is not free, but instead meets with compulsion and opposition which are lacking in his own world" (p. 345). For a time these two worlds, of adult and child, co-exist in the child's experience; in the end, however, the adult world must become dominant. In a particularly lucid passage, Koffka sums up the different natures of these two worlds as follows:

> The adult's world ... soon forces itself to be comprehended as a *totality*, so that the independence of individual actions, one from another, gradually disappears; it is quite different in the other world where, to-day, the child may be a

coal-heaver and to-morrow a soldier; and where a stick of wood that has just been cuddled may the next minute be thrown into the fire. Yet these different actions do not interfere with one another, because they have no more connection with one another than they have for us when we are at play. The jack of diamonds may be a tremendously important card—"the right bower"—when I am playing euchre, but it is only a relatively unimportant card when I am playing bridge. With us adults, of course, there is always a conformity to the "rules of the game," which are fixed and valid in each kind of game; whereas a child's play is not bound by any such extraneously determined rules. Yet the lack of connection between plays is the same in both cases. The fixed and rigid connections that pervade our world are but a result of the domination of our non-play life; whereas to a child this domination is not originally present, and only gradually introduces itself (pp. 345-46).

## IV

*The Growth of the Mind* was written more than a half century ago. How well have its main ideas stood up in subsequent research and critical analysis?

Empirical investigations of child development have multiplied since the 1920s, and *The Growth of the Mind* can no longer claim to review the most important lines of research. Still, the over-all approach of the book bears a rather striking resemblance to the theoretical work which has been most widely used by child psychologists. I refer here to the work of Jean Piaget. Although Piaget was only generally familiar with the work of the Gestalt psychologists and has not claimed Koffka as a fundamental influence, the main outlines of Piaget's work are quite consistent with the methodological approach and theoretical position set forth in *The Growth of the Mind.* Of course Piaget and other child psychologists have elaborated on particular kinds of cognition and levels of development far beyond anything attempted by Koffka. Nevertheless, if we take Koffka's last chapter and ask what might clash with later research or the most widely received current theory, the answer must be "very little." "The World of a Child" as described by Koffka is still generally the same world as that characterized by our most contemporary child psychologists.

It is more difficult to characterize the status of *The Growth of the Mind* in relationship to psychology in general. Too much work has accumulated in learning, perception, and memory for Chapters IV and V to be considered particularly relevant today. In addition, Koffka sometimes uses his own special terminology, which is not that of most contemporary psychologists. Still, there are many parts of the book which deserve the continued attention of psychologists. Although his refutation of Thorndikes's connectionism would not precisely apply to all modern behaviorism, much of Koffka's discussion (such as especially pp. 163-174) can profitably be reread in relationship to some of the more mindless models of learning which are widely used today. And Koffka's analysis of Köhler's work with apes—though superceded by the more complete reports of Köhler (1925)—is still perhaps the best relatively brief review of this timeless piece of research.

The status of this book within psychology in general today depends primarily upon how Gestalt psychology is evaluated. *The Growth of the Mind* was admittedly written as a "cause," and this cause was to show the wide applicability of Gestalt principles. But does the Gestalt perspective deserve all that Koffka claimed for it? Many psychologists would see Gestalt psychology as a useful corrective for the

INTRODUCTION

excesses of structuralism and, later, of behaviorism. Some would go farther (as would the present writer) in recognizing the general validity of the Gestalt perspective, but would still hold back from full identification with the Gestalt school. It may be held that *The Growth of the Mind* carries the gospel of Gestalt beyond the range of empirical science when Koffka insists that the original nature of experience must be configurational. Koffka makes a plausible case for this doctrine (see especially pp. 130-42), but a reader can be forgiven if he fails to see the need to affirm what the ultimate or original nature of human experience must be like. Perhaps John Locke's *tabula raza*, Koffka's primitive figure-ground configuration, and the "blooming, buzzing confusion" of William James all are useful metaphors for extending their respective points of view to an ultimate beginning. But the confirmation of any such idea seems, at least to this writer, beyond the reach of empirical science.

So far as social science in general is concerned, or social psychology in particular, the contribution of *The Growth of the Mind* is mostly indirect. That is, there is little direct attention to the forms of social influence, the nature of human groups, or the impact of particular social institutions. Nevertheless, Koffka's social psychological assumptions are quite compatible with most of the social psychological and sociological work of the last half century. "The development of perception depends upon the total environment, the milieu, and above all, upon the sociological conditions of this milieu" (p. 339); and "man's entire development, including, of course, his perceptions, is dependent upon society" (p. 340)— such statements could have come from George H. Mead as easily as from Kurt Koffka.[2] The full expansion of Gestalt ideas into social psychology and social science was left to others—such as Kurt

Lewin (1951) and Solomon Asch (1952)—but the psychological basis was well prepared by Koffka's work in the present book.

Today *The Growth of the Mind* deserves the attention of a new generation of psychologists and social scientists. The interest is partly historical, for this was the first attempt to apply the principles of Gestalt psychology to the full range of psychological processes. But it is a classic also in a continuing sense. Many passages, especially in the final chapter (which may be read by the nonspecialist without reading the more difficult materials of the rest of the book), are of a relatively timeless character. This is true because the fundamental issues of psychology today have really not changed so drastically from what they were in the 1920s. Koffka's book, at least, well indicates issues that have been at the heart of the science of psychology throughout the present century.

## Notes

1. The above biographical summary is based primarily upon articles by Harrower (1973), Heider (1968), and Köhler (1942).
2. Some contemporary social scientists may be dismayed by Koffka's insistent discussion of "instincts" in humans and of his parallels between the thought of primitive man and that of children. Careful attention to the central points of such discussions, however, will show that Koffka's "instincts" are quite limited in content, and that his references to primitive societies represent in part a somewhat awkward way of acknowledging the importance of cultural differences.

## References

Asch, Solomon. *Social Psychology.* New York: Prentice-Hall, 1952.
Harrower, Molly. "Koffka, Kurt." *Dictionary of*

# INTRODUCTION

*American Biography, Supplement Three,* 1941-45. New York: Scribner's, 1973.

Heider, Grace M. "Koffka, Kurt." *International Encyclopedia of the Social Sciences,* v.8, pp. 435-438. New York: Macmillian, 1968.

Koffka, Kurt. *The Growth of the Mind: An Introduction to Child Psychology,* second edition. New York: Harcourt, 1928.

Koffka, Kurt. *Principles of Gestalt Psychology.* New York: Harcourt, 1935.

Köhler, Wolfgang. *The Mentality of Apes.* New York: Harcourt, 1925.

Köhler, Wolfgang. "Kurt Koffka." *The Psychological Review,* 49 (1942), 97-101.

Lewin, Kurt. *Field Theory in Social Science.* New York: Harper, 1951.

# CONTENTS

# CONTENTS

# CONTENTS

# CONTENTS

# CONTENTS

# AUTHOR'S PREFACE TO THE ENGLISH EDITION

WHEN I was invited to write a new treatise upon the Psychology of Childhood, the aim of the book, as it developed in my mind, was twofold. In the first place, I felt that I might be able to give a new and wider application to certain principles of psychological theory and research which have recently been advanced under the name of the *Gestalt-Theorie*, and thus might demonstrate their significance in the interpretation of childhood. In the second place, it was my belief that the teachers in the German elementary schools, for whom the book was intended, were in need of a psychology both modern and alive to the problems of the Educator. I believed it of urgent necessity that the psychological instruction usually given to teachers should be so modified as to set aside certain antiquated notions which, instead of promoting educational aims, often pervert them to such an extent that psychology is apt to become totally disregarded in educational circles. I was bold enough to believe that our new psychological principles would also serve this useful purpose.

And hence what I have tried to write is not so much a compendium of facts as an exposition of principles. In short, I have tried to work out some of the chief principles of genetic or comparative psychology, laying special emphasis upon the evolution of the child's mind. By keeping this object in view I hoped to avoid a rivalry with two other recent works upon Child - Psychology which have been written by William Stern and Karl Bühler.

But I have addressed myself not to teachers alone, but also to my scientific colleagues, and to all students of psychology. In so doing I have not always found it easy to satisfy the claims of any one group of readers. To some the book will in many places seem too elementary, while to others certain passages, at least, will seem much too difficult. The first objection may be readily overcome by simply skipping the elementary passages. But the second is not so readily set aside; for true scientific knowledge can not be taken in like a spoonful of honey; it can be acquired only by intellectual effort, just as science itself is advanced only by strenuous research. For this reason a mere collection of scientific facts is never a true presentation of the scientific spirit and insight. To obtain these one must comprehend how the facts have been discovered, and what position they occupy in the comprehensive system of scientific knowledge. The principles upon which this knowledge rests should therefore be treated exhaustively, even though, in the end, they should have to be given up as false or barren; for otherwise the reader would not know why these principles can not persist, wherein their weakness lies, and how the explanation of the facts can now be bettered. In writing this book nothing has been further from my thought than a wish to engage in polemic for its own sake. The criticism of divergent opinions has been undertaken solely in order that the reader might become acquainted at first hand with the way a science like psychology has grown and is growing. Every science grows amidst a lively conflict as to the precise nature of its foundations, and in this struggle the book before you is intended to take its place.

I have adopted the plan of gathering all the notes together at the end of the book, so that the text might have a rounded form, and also that the reader might not be disturbed in following the train of thought. The notes comprise a series of supplementary comments in addition to the textual references therein contained.

Though I have made but little use of abbreviations, I may here remark that to indicate age I have employed the method suggested by the Sterns in 1907, which has since come into general use : for example, 2·10 means the age of 2 years and 10 months.

The text and notes will give evidence of the unusual debt I owe to the available works on child-psychology. But since it is impossible to refer specifically to the source of every inspiration that has come to me, I wish here to make general acknowledgment of my indebtedness.

The translation of the book, for which I am greatly indebted to my friend Professor R. M. Ogden of Cornell University, was a difficult task because of the new terminology employed, for which English equivalents had to be coined. The difficulty was increased by the fact that one of the chief terms employed, namely, *Struktur*, could not be retained as " structure," since, as a result of the controversy between *structuralism* and *functionalism*, this term has a very definite and quite different meaning in English and American psychology. For want of a better term, we have chosen to follow a suggestion originally made by Professor E. B. Titchener, and have translated *Struktur* as "configuration," although I can not say that it has completely satisfied me. This, however, is but one of the many difficulties which have confronted the translator.

Since the publication of the German edition several important contributions to the topics treated in the book have either appeared in print or come for the first time to my hands. This new material I have endeavoured to work into the text so far as time has permitted.

KURT KOFFKA

GIESSEN, *October* 18, 1924

# THE GROWTH OF THE MIND

# CHAPTER I

## PROBLEM AND METHOD

### § 1—*The Concept of Development in Psychology*

WHEN we set out to make a psychological study of the world in which we live, we continually come upon facts that can be understood only after we conceive them as products of evolution. For a long time psychological theory was dominated by the question: How much of any observed fact can be explained as a process of development? And even to-day no agreement has been reached between the rival theories of *empiricism* and *nativism*, the first of which emphasizes the influence of environment, and the second the influence of heredity. With this situation before us it is surprising to learn—though historically not difficult to understand—that psychology—and German psychology in particular—has made so little use of the general principles of development. Indeed, from the point of view of experience, the problem of development has been dealt with in a very specialized way, which is mechanistic rather than truly biological. This period seems, however, to be drawing to a close; for the need is now felt of introducing the facts of psychology into a larger sphere, embracing other facts of life, from which our science has already departed too far. We must therefore try to envisage the problems of mental growth as they really are; we must seek to understand the peculiarities of mental evolution, and must endeavour to discover its laws.

I

# PROBLEM AND METHOD

In the accomplishment of this task we should not forget that the subject of a psychological investigation is usually the mature and cultured "West European" type of man; a living being—biologically considered—at the highest level of development. In the first place, we are dealing with the human being as opposed to the animal. Since Darwin's time, the conception of the descent of man has become common property, and we assume that what is valid in morphology and physiology must also have its significance in psychology. In the second place, we are dealing with representatives of a highly differentiated, as opposed to the members of a primitive, civilization. The world appears otherwise to us than it does to a negro in Central Africa, and otherwise than it did to Homer. We speak a different language from each of these, and this difference is a fundamental one, inasmuch as a real translation of their words into our own is impossible, because the categories of thought are different. In the third place, we are dealing with the adult as opposed to the child, though each of us was once a child, and has become an adult only by having outgrown his childhood.

We must not forget, then, that without a comparative psychology, without animal-, folk-, and child-psychology, the experimental psychology of the human adult is and must remain defective. For this reason the psychology of the human adult has not infrequently and in various respects been unable to define its problems correctly, to say nothing of arriving at serviceable hypotheses. For instance, the error has often been committed of trying to explain a fact by merely referring to its evolution, thus building up a theory of evolution instead of first investigating the facts by comparative methods. Whenever one has had a genetic problem to deal with, the danger has always been great that one would accept the old hypotheses and apply them to his new facts, instead of first giving his facts an unprejudiced consideration.

2

We might think that in child-psychology the process of development would be obvious to every one;
for we know the end-product to be an adult, with whom
experimental psychology can deal, and the origin of
the adult can be traced continuously from infancy. Yet
this procedure is not so simple as it might seem; for
as a matter of fact there is no principle of mental
development which we owe directly to child-psychology[1]
and, in so far as child-psychology makes use of any
principles at all, they have originated either in experimental or in animal-psychology. And yet there must
be a genetic psychology; for the child-psychologist
can follow the growth of a human being who in a
relatively brief period of time changes from a simple
inefficient individual into a highly complex and efficient
man. It ought therefore to be possible to study this
development in such a way that we can better understand the product, which is the human adult. Furthermore, if we could but understand this development,
we ought to be far better able than we now are to
promote, to check, and to direct the course of human
life.

This, therefore, is our problem: To discover the
evolutionary principles of child-psychology. But although we must depend for assistance upon comparative psychology, we must not confine ourselves
merely to transferring the principles of comparative
psychology to our own field; instead, we must first
test the value of these principles, and where necessary
we must be ready to recast them.

§ 2—*A Provisional Consideration of the Problem of
Psychology as applied to Child-Psychology.
Mother and Child. Points of View "from
within" and "from without"*

Let us now try to formulate the problems of child-
psychology more precisely. As a provisional defini-

tion of psychology, we may say that its problem is the scientific study of the behaviour of living creatures in their contact with the outer world. If we apply this definition to child-psychology, the thought immediately occurs to us that every mother is constantly doing just this; for no one knows the child so well, or understands his reactions and his impulses so thoroughly, as does his mother, by virtue of her unique and intimate relation to him. What need, then, of a child-psychology, if every mother knows her child better than the wisest psychologist can ever hope to know him? Without disputing this assumption the fact remains that psychology is scientific knowledge, in that it employs a method which brings knowledge into conceptually formulated propositions. Psychology must have definite concepts; its statements are not made about "Infant X" or "Infant Y", but rather about those features of babyhood common to all ordinary infants. The mother may know that her child is now in such and such a mood, that he desires this, that in giving utterance to a certain sound he means a certain thing, etc.; but she can not transcribe her knowledge in scientific terms. In the first place, she usually knows nothing about scientific terms; and, as we shall soon see, if we wish to secure scientific knowledge a different attitude is requisite from that which the mother finds most natural. In order to become a scientist the mother must suddenly become an "observer"; she must tear herself away from the intimate relation in which she lives with her child, so that she may replace each intuitive bit of knowledge— unreasoned, though undoubtedly certain—by a critical analysis of the facts. She must, therefore, learn to distinguish her interpretation from the simple facts of the behaviour itself. But this implies that she must maintain a "distance" from her child, and must, at least during the period of any scientific observation, cut herself off from the intimacy of her maternal relationship with him. Mothers are naturally unsympathetic

4

towards this procedure, and have, indeed, a primitive disinclination to allow their children to be thus practised upon by others. They can therefore be readily brought to oppose child-psychology in the fear that such observations and investigations may harm their children. On similar grounds an artist will often refuse to discuss the technique of his art. The mother has, of course, a right to protect her child from any injury that science might inflict, and in so doing she not only safeguards her child, but science as well; for an investigation which can injure the mental development of a child must almost certainly be a wrong method of securing psychological knowledge. If one could reassure the mother on this point, much of her hesitation would disappear. Many mothers could even be won over to child-psychology, if it were made clear to them that they might thus benefit their children; for although the mother's knowledge is intimate, it is, for the most part, a momentary knowledge, and if psychology could impart a knowledge of the chief characteristics of development, the mother would be far better able to guide and watch over her child.

Furthermore, if the mother can be reconciled to child-psychology she can render an invaluable service. We have already pictured the procedure of the scientific worker in contrast with that of the mother; we must now emphasize the disadvantages of the scientist when he proceeds alone. The scientist has his ready-made concepts with the aid of which he seeks to understand the facts as he observes them. From the outset his gaze is directed through spectacles fitted to his scientific view. Yet who knows but these glasses may be coloured, or else ground so as to produce a badly distorted image? To give a concrete example: Since the child-psychologist has a genetic interest, he is inclined to regard each childlike expression, from an adult point of view, as an incomplete or preliminary step in the direction of a later and more mature end. Yet this view fails to note the individual significance of the child's expression *per se*, which can not be seen at all through such glasses. Here the mother can and must assist. She knows her child from immediate personal experience, without preconceptions; she knows him and loves him as he appears to her at the time, nor does she ever try to think of her suckling babe as an immature student of life. Each of the child's stages in life is of equal worth and importance to her, and she tries to understand each one of them in the same unprejudiced way. If she is successful in making her immediate knowledge available to others, she will have rendered the investigator a service not otherwise to be had; for she is able to furnish first-hand material which no scientific observer can obtain. This, to be sure, is a difficult task; for in its accomplishment she must be a good psychologist in the common-sense meaning of the word, just as a poet must be a good psychologist. Yet the mother need not necessarily exchange her attitude for the objective point of view of the scientist. If she is capable of thus uniting the two points of view, she is indeed a true child-psychologist, since both attitudes constantly promote and supplement each other. In order to understand the behaviour of a child in his contacts with his surroundings, one must undertake a great deal of troublesome special study, involving detachment and a thoroughly critical attitude of mind. In this way it is possible to arrive at a view of the child "from without"; but we must not forget that every act of behaviour is the expression of an individual, depending more or less upon his entire constitution, and that we never can understand his behaviour completely unless we know him as a whole. In order to comprehend him thus, we must assume a different point of view, because a true knowledge of child-life can only be derived "from within." The reciprocal supplementation and furtherance of understanding supplied by these two considerations, "from within" and "from without,"

6

may perhaps be expressed half-paradoxically in this way: In order to understand the child, we must know his reactions; but in order to understand his reactions, we must also know the child.

§ 3—*Functional and Descriptive Concepts. Natural-Scientific and Experiential Observations. The "Descriptive" Side of Behaviour*

We can now go a step further, and raise the question : What is this point of view "from without"? This brings us to the problem of psychological method.

When we describe the behaviour of mankind, we use two quite different kinds of concepts. The difference can be made clear by a few simple, commonplace examples. I observe a wood-chopper, and find that the performance of his task gradually decreases without his giving me any impression of indolence. I can control this observation by determining how many blocks he splits in a minute, and from this I find that as the time is prolonged the number decreases. I attribute this phenomenon, this decrease in his efficiency, to *fatigue*.

Or, to take another example, I see a stranger lose something in the street, and I recover it for him. Next day I meet him again, and he greets me; that is, he reacts towards me otherwise to-day than he did yesterday, apparently as a consequence of yesterday's occurrence. I therefore say that he has *recognized* me, and I refer this fact to his *memory*.

Any one can reach these two conclusions concerning *fatigue* and the operations of *memory* who is able to observe these situations, for this is the general characteristic of a class of concepts where in any given case any one to whom the factual material is available will be able to decide whether a certain concept of the class is appropriate or not. We call this class of concepts *functional concepts*, and they are of the same kind as all natural-scientific concepts.

7

In order to acquaint ourselves with the second class
of concepts we may again refer to our two examples.
Whereas in the first example either I or any one else
can determine the fatigue of the wood-chopper by his
decreased efficiency, the wood-chopper himself is able
to make quite a different observation. He may find,
for instance, that at the beginning of his work, "It went
easy," and that later "It went hard." Or he may say :
"At first I felt fresh, but now at the end I feel tired."
Likewise, the man who greets me in the street, thus
leading me or any one else present to infer an operation
of his memory, may express himself by saying, "Your
face, which yesterday was strange to me, now looks
familiar."

These expressions attributed to the wood-chopper
and to the man in the street are quite different in
content, yet in contrast with observations of the first
sort, made with the help of functional concepts, they
have this in common, that the report of the wood-
chopper can be made only by the wood-chopper, and
the remark of the man in the street only by himself.
No substitution is possible, for no one but the wood-
chopper can say whether the work is tiring him or not,
and no one but the man in the street can decide
whether my features are familiar to him.

Facts which any one can determine are called *actual*
or *real* things or processes. For instance, that the
wood-chopper becomes fatigued, or that the person to
whom I was yesterday a stranger now greets me, these
are *real* processes. But we must also introduce a term
for those facts which can be established only by a single
person ; these we shall call *experiences*, or *phenomena*.
In order to define *real* processes we shall use *functional*
concepts, whereas the concepts we apply to experiences
we shall call *descriptive* concepts. In our examples we
have employed the descriptive concepts "feeling fresh,"
"feeling tired," "strange," and "familiar." We can also
refer to the experience of freshness, of fatigue, of

8

familiarity, of strangeness, or, to introduce a much-used word, the *impression* of any of these.

The consideration of this point may be carried a step further, because it is of especial importance to an understanding of psychology. To some, what has been said will seem obvious. Naturally, no one can get out of his own skin into the skin of another ; my tooth-ache does not hurt my neighbour, however much I might wish it upon him. But it may be remarked by others that there is something quite artificial in all this discussion, for if any one greets me he must, of course, know me, and I can readily assure myself of this without hearing what he has to say about it. In everyday life my assurance is that when one laughs he is gay, when one weeps he is sorrowful, and I can know all that without his telling me.

Both parties seem to be right, and yet they contradict one another, and so we may infer that perhaps the matter is not after all so simple. Of course it is true that in everyday life we act as though we could our-selves determine what kind of experiences another person is having, but we must not forget that in so doing we often fall into error, and sometimes are de-ceived by impostors. A person may weep, and arouse our sympathy, when the real cause of his weeping is not sorrow but the onions he has just eaten. With certainty all we are able to determine is the fact of his tears, but not how he may feel about them. Turning to our examples, if the man in the street greets me to-day he must have recognized me, provided that one means by recognition a functional concept, a term to express a certain operation of his memory. But that I appeared to him as some one he knew, who looked familiar to him, is a thing I can not be sure of from the mere fact of his greeting me ; because it is also possible that, sunk in thought, or deep in conversation, he may have greeted me quite "automatically." Whether or not this was the case, he alone can say. Likewise in our first

9

example, the investigation of the facts of fatigue has taught us that actual fatigue and "feeling tired" do not need to run parallel.[2] And hence we must differentiate the two classes of functional and descriptive concepts according to the criteria of their application. For the first kind, any one, but for the second, only one person is in a position to decide whether the application in a certain instance is right or wrong.

We remarked above that functional conceptions are of the same sort as any other concepts of natural science. On the other hand descriptive concepts are a unique characteristic of psychology. We noted tentatively that the problem of psychology was the study of the behaviour of living beings in contact with their surroundings. Having discovered that psychology employs not only functional concepts, but also the specifically psychological descriptive concepts, we can now make this definition more precise. Limiting ourselves for the present to the behaviour of mankind, we can attribute to it not only whatever may be determined with the aid of functional concepts, but also the fact that man can make reports of a "descriptive" nature; that man has experiences—or, as we commonly say, that man has a consciousness. This attribution implies, not merely that man can make these reports on his experience, but also the kind of reports he makes, and the nature of the experiences he has. And this side of behaviour is no less important than the other; to psychology, it is, indeed, of the utmost significance; because of the fact already emphasized, that the possession of descriptive concepts constitutes the peculiarity of this science. When the psychologist studies behaviour he always does so with reference to its descriptive side, in contrast, for instance, to the physiologist, who for the most part does not bother himself with anything but the functional aspects of behaviour.

Along with the natural-scientific methods of investigation, psychology has, therefore, a method of observation all its own, dealing, not with the determination of real things and processes, but with experiences. We shall refer to this method as *experiential observation*, or perception, and thus avoid the commonly used, though unfortunately chosen, terms: "inner perception" and "introspection." To enter at this juncture on the very important but controversial problem of the perception of experience would be too much of a digression,[3] yet it should be noted that the method of perceiving experience is something that has to be learned and practised to an even higher degree than any other kind of scientific observation.

As to the relative nature of these two kinds of observation a few words will be appropriate. The best means of investigating facts with the aid of functional concepts are *measure* and *number;* mensuration and calculation can be understood or learned by any one. The concepts of the most highly developed natural science, Physics, are for this reason, quantitative concepts. Physical reports' are always quantified, and it is the ideal of Physics to reduce all qualitative to quantitative differences.

The same can not be said of the facts of description, that is, of experience; for measurement is a typically functional method. Measuring with a scale supplies data that can be attained by any one. But in this sense experiences are not mensurable. Being only qualities they are at the opposite pole from the objects of pure Physics. The quantitative, in a natural sense, is altogether lacking in them.[4] Indeed this is the reason why the word "quality" is so often applied in psychology as though it were synonymous with "experience."

The results of these considerations may be summarized as follows: In addition to the natural-scientific method, psychology makes use of a form of observation peculiarly its own, namely, experiential observation, for the objects of psychology embrace not only real things and processes, but also experiences.[5]

# PROBLEM AND METHOD

§ 4—*The Psychology of the Behaviourist.   Criteria of Consciousness*

In opposition to this conception of psychology loud voices have latterly been raised, notably in America, where a tendency has arisen to set aside the differentiation which our theory of psychology accepts.   It is the tendency to maintain that psychology is a natural science like any other, and, therefore, has no justification for the use of any peculiar method or of any distinctive facts. Consequently experiential observation and all descriptive concepts are banned, leaving only the functional concepts which are subject to general control.   Behaviour being merely that which any one can observe and report of an individual, the psychologist need concern himself only with those reactions of an individual which can be determined by any one.   The observation of experience affords no real data, because it can not be controlled ; a conclusion which seems to gain support from a wider view when the behaviourist insists that, biologically considered, man can not be separated from other living beings.   And is it not, indeed, an error that traditional psychology should tend to concern itself exclusively with adult human beings, thus giving them a peculiar status, whereas man is but one of the many possible and equally important subjects of psychological investigation ?   In animal-psychology one must necessarily do without descriptive concepts ; for, since the animals are unable to communicate with us, no criteria of this sort can there be employed.   Likewise in the psychology of early childhood, we can do no more than determine how the infant behaves under definite conditions.   All else being uncontrollable must, therefore, be unscientific fantasy.   If then normal psychology has no right to claim special privileges, it follows that we must limit ourselves to real facts, and translate the results of psychology from the older terms of conscious contents into the newer terms of behaviour.   This means that, instead of reporting about experience, we may only admit reports about behaviour in certain situations where both the behaviour and the situation can be controlled by natural-scientific methods.

The advocates of this view call themselves *Behaviourists*, and, instead of psychology, they speak of the Science of Animal Behaviour or the Science of the Behaviour of Organisms. Since it is our purpose to treat also of Comparative Psychology, we must face this issue at once. In one important point the behaviourists are undoubtedly right. As soon as we leave the normal field of human adult psychology, the method of experiential observation has to be abandoned, and so long as we maintain a point of view " from without," we shall have no criteria of experience, nor any use for descriptive concepts. The mother may be ever so sure that her smiling baby is in a state of contentment ; she may be able to read ever so clearly the beaming happiness in its face, but from an objective point of view these phenomena are uncontrollable. Whether science should abandon these reports altogether is, however, quite another question, and one to which we shall presently return. Speaking strictly from an objective point of view, the behaviourist is right, and the principle is sound, that outside of adult psychology there are no criteria for the existence of consciousness.[6]

And yet attempts have often been made to find such criteria.[7] Two of the most important are these : First it has been said that, so long as the behaviour of living beings can be explained in purely physiological terms, we should avoid the hypothesis of consciousness ; this hypothesis being permissible only in case a purely physiological explanation is impossible. From our point of view such a procedure would be fundamentally false. Quite apart from the fact that there is no permanent criterion for such an inference—since a physiological explanation which to-day seems impossible may to-morrow be accepted—the hypothesis rests upon the fallacy of supposing that a physiological explanation can ever be replaced by one of a psychological nature. To explain always means to determine the connections between, and to formulate the laws applicable to, facts. Laws, however, are formulæ that can be controlled by any one; their objects must therefore, in the last analysis, be real things and processes. To explain the manifest behaviour of an organism by reference to an experience which can not be observed by any other person is to renounce all explanation in natural-scientific terms. We have already shown that, without some reservation, it is illegitimate to infer a phenomenal or conscious state from facts of a functional order. It is equally fallacious to make an inverse inference from descriptive phenomena to functional processes. For example, in a certain investigation the observer reports that during the whole time he has steadily fixated a point without moving his eyes. What does this report signify to the experimenter? Only that the observer has had the same experience as if his eyes had remained unmoved; not, however, that no eye-movements have taken place; for whether the eyes have moved or not must be determined by the experimenter, and often enough he finds that, as a matter of fact, they have.[8]

At some point every so-called psychological explanation contains an inference of this sort. In comparative psychology, where experiential observation is lacking, fallacious inferences lead also from functional to descriptive concepts. The facts are easily obscured, because our language does not always possess separate words for descriptive and functional concepts. Our everyday concepts, of course, are not at all scientific. Many typically functional concepts are often called mental, and one forgets that the everyday meaning of " mental " is not what the psychologist means by " consciousness." *Intelligence*, for instance, is a " mental " term. One may say that intelligence is requisite in such and such an achievement; and conclude that the animal thus behaving must have been conscious. Here the error is quite patent. When one observes a performance which merits the term " intelligent "—such, for instance, as an appropriate discovery on the part of an animal— the inference is clear that the animal must possess a capacity for this achievement, and this capacity may quite properly be called intelligent. But it does not follow that the animal must, therefore, have been conscious of what it was about ; nor is it permissible to call upon consciousness to furnish the explanation of an act of intelligence upon the assumption that this act could not otherwise have taken place. One sees the disjunction of this argument in the passage from intelligent behaviour to conscious behaviour. From the facts of a certain observed activity I can not with any assurance infer what experience, if any, may have attached to it ; and it is altogether without warrant to consider experiences as interrupting a chain of *real* processes. The behaviour of an animal as it takes place is something to be determined as a natural-scientific event. To explain this behaviour means to bring it into relation with other similarly conditioned natural-scientific events. So many observations must be made, and so many experiments performed, as are necessary to furnish the foundation for an assured inference, which, in principle at least, is always possible. To assume consciousness, however, and to refer the animal's achievement to it, is to abandon altogether the grounds of a scientific explanation.[9]

But the matter takes on quite a different aspect when one adopts the following point of view. In order to explain the animal's performance it may be necessary to assume brain-processes such as accompany what for us human beings are experiences, and by approaching the problem in this way it may be possible to justify the assumption of consciousness in the animal. At least the error is not committed of treating consciousness and functional processes on the same level ; for the explanation remains in the realm of natural science. It must be admitted that we do not know what peculiarity it is that distinguishes those brain-processes which correlate with consciousness from any others, and hence this line of thought does not lead to an actual criterion of consciousness. But, even so, we may in time be able to bridge the gap between human and animal-psychology if we continue to work with descriptive concepts in human psychology.

At least it is clear that we can draw no conclusions as to a criterion of consciousness by giving up the physiological explanation of behaviour ; and a physiological explanation is obviously indicated for every mode of behaviour, even where a consciousness of the highest order is involved.

The second attempt which has been made to determine the existence of consciousness may be dismissed in a few words. It has been said that consciousness may be assumed wherever memory is involved in an animal's performance ; but here again the fallacy of passing from functional to descriptive concepts is found in the same form in which we have discussed it with reference to the concept of intelligence.

§ 5—*A Denial of the Behaviourist's Point of View. The Significance of Descriptive Behaviour for Physiological Theory*

The behaviourist is right in denying the existence of conscious criteria wherever the method of experiential observation is inapplicable, but in spite of this we shall refuse to accept his position, for the simple reason that there is a consciousness, reports of which can only be made by the experiencing individual, and which is therefore not subject to the control of others. Science can not refuse to evaluate factual material of any sort that is placed at its disposal. Furthermore what appear to be two cases of the same objective behaviour may prove to be fundamentally different when the accompanying phenomena of consciousness are taken under consideration. A completely conscious action and an automatic action may seem to be identical, yet they may be widely different, while acts which are objectively quite different may be very similar when one considers the likeness of their attendant phenomena, and hence, were we to leave experiential observation out of account we should often reach false conclusions. If the behaviourist answers that some natural-scientific method should be sought in investigating these differences, our rejoinder is that we are quite ready to leave that task to him ; but at the same time the remark is permissible that it would never have occurred to him to search for such methods, had he not first become aware of these differences through his own conscious experience.

Finally, the bare fact that I am able to make a descriptive report is one of extraordinary significance. To me, it is at least as characteristic as that I breathe, or that I digest my food. A stick of wood can not do this, neither can an amœba ; and when I am dead I shall no longer be able to do it. Were I not able to make a descriptive report of my behaviour, I should be unable to make any record of it at all. Paradoxically expressed, if one had only the capacity to make such responses as others can observe, no one would be able to observe anything.

It is therefore impossible to remove this aspect of behaviour from science, not merely because of its immanent significance—since whatever we are, and of whatever we are proud, our culture, art, and religion, would otherwise be incomprehensible—but also because of the intimate connection which experience has with the objective side of behaviour.[10]

The last point needs to be emphasized in order that what has been said may not be misunderstood. We have declined to accept a psychological explanation, and have advocated in its place a thorough-going physiological explanation, but we must nevertheless insist that our physiological hypotheses shall be appropriate to the complete behaviour of the organism, which includes also its experiential aspect. It follows that in the construction of functional concepts we must constantly give heed to the data of experience. Indeed, it is so often our first task to secure accurate and significant descriptive concepts that in this respect a psychological theory is indispensable. The formation of a new descriptive concept often leads to important consequences both in research and in theory, and as I have elsewhere shown [11] the criterion of a good descriptive concept is just this, that new facts and their functions are revealed by it. Functional adequacy always determines whether a new descriptive concept finds acceptance or rejection, a fact which in itself meets many of the objections raised by the behaviourist against the scientific evaluation of " facts " of experience.

In thus relating functional and descriptive concepts to each other we are only following the universal method of science. Yet we are making an assumption which should be explicitly understood, for in the relation between "outer" and "inner" behaviour as here conceived, the two are not " casually " linked together, but on the contrary are assumed to be *essentially alike* and *materially related*. Reverting to our earlier illustration of the wood-chopper, what we assume is that when the man feels tired and his efficiency decreases, these two aspects of his behaviour are fundamentally united. Otherwise a feeling of freshness might as readily accompany fatigue as does the more natural state of feeling tired.[12] While this correspondence is not invariable, it will be found that functional and descriptive concepts coincide in their general aim and outcome, though they are less closely related in their origin. The importance of this general problem of correspondence is merely referred to at this point ; but we shall later attend to one of its special aspects, and shall see the weakness of a theory which allows the behaviourists to believe there is nothing to be gained from a description of experience.[13]

But, though we insist on holding fast to "experience," must we not approve the behaviourists when they criticize human psychology on the ground that it is made to occupy a position quite apart from all other branches of psychology? We have already admitted that animal-psychology has not supplied us with a criterion for the existence of consciousness. What, then, are the consequences to be drawn from this failure? We observe a dog whose master holds a morsel of food beyond the dog's reach. The animal assumes a very characteristic attitude, with its head stretched forward and upwards, the muscles of its body tense, and its ears pointed. We might continue the description in this manner, even supplementing it with pneumographic, sphygmographic, and other measurements. But is it forbidden us to summarize this description in a statement that the dog appears to be intent upon the hand of its master? Indeed, does not the enumeration of these details obtain its meaning from such a statement? Let us take another example from the work of Wolfgang Köhler upon the intelligence of primates.[14] In one place Köhler describes the affective expression of these apes. Referring to an outbreak of rage on the part of a female ape, Köhler writes: "If her coverlet is at hand, she will on such occasions strike the ground with it furiously; otherwise she will begin to pull and throw grass. These outbreaks always have a noticeable component which, both in a physical and in a physiological sense, indicate a direction of the behaviour towards her enemy." Or again: "In any strong emotion without solution the animal must do something in that direction of space in which the object of its desire is to be found"[15]. Köhler also observes that the same behaviour is characteristic of young children.

Descriptions of this sort do not merely tell us that

an animal will throw things in a direction which is later found to be approximately that of its enemy; they show us, rather, that the animal is *directed upon its enemy*, and that every action arising from an emotion is controlled by this direction. Not only do the acts have this direction, but the animal is itself thus directed. No unprejudiced observer can doubt that a description of this sort is not only permissible, but desirable, and indeed necessary, in order to understand the animal's behaviour.

The behaviourist's argument can now be turned against himself, for suppose we were to observe an outbreak of rage on the part of a negro in Central Africa whose speech we do not understand. Must we confine ourselves to an enumeration of details concerning his external behaviour? Are we not justified in saying that his anger was directed upon an object, upon a person? If we may and must say this, then we have grounds for denying that the psychology of man occupies a special position among the sciences and are fully justified in describing a behaviour similar to that of man in the same terms that we would use in describing man's own actions.

Descriptions of this order refer to objective matters of fact, and our contention is that the animal's behaviour (both "inner" and "outer") is actually reproduced in these descriptions. In other words, we deny that a description of this sort endows the behaviour in question with mental properties which do not rightfully belong to it. Although a natural-scientific observation is commonly supposed to be strictly analytic, the application of strict analysis to an animal's behaviour at once reduces it to mere mechanics of limb, and physiology of muscle and gland—a *reductio ad absurdum* which even some of the younger behaviourists have begun to realize. Yet the difficulty of maintaining a scientific point of view disappears when we allow ourselves to assume that animals possess certain characteristics that can not be thus reduced to terms of analysis. It is freely admitted that this assumption carries with it very important implications for the whole theory of natural-scientific observation, which, unfortunately, we can not here pursue. But one of its outstanding implications is this : that an essential connection and a true correspondence do exist between our "total impression" of a certain type of behaviour and the real constituents of the behaviour itself. The way in which we must conceive the nature of this connection, and the special conditions under which it becomes effective, are as yet unsolved problems, but they embrace the foundations of any adequate theory concerning our knowledge of the mental life of the "other man."[16]

Nor is it because the question of consciousness is itself of such outstanding importance that we must follow this course, but because this course furnishes the one possibility of *understanding the behaviour of the animal in a scientific way ;* which, after all, is the only thing that really matters. We can agree with the behaviourists that whether consciousness is actually present or not we do not know, nor are we concerned to find out. But we can not agree to be uninterested in finding out whether the behaviour is of such a nature that the consciousness which would go with it, if there were any, would necessarily be of a definitely corresponding nature. For this reason the behaviour in question must be explained in the same way in which we would explain any type of behaviour that a consciousness of this particular kind has been observed to accompany.[17] But if certain brain-processes must be assumed for every observable fact of consciousness, may we not with equal right assume the presence of consciousness upon the presumption of like brain-processes even in cases where no descriptive reports are available? If we are justified in answering this question in the affirmative, as it appears that we are, we need have no further anxiety about the application of descriptive concepts to animal-behaviour. This answer, however, is not to be taken as a defence of the anthropomorphism common to the older animal-psychology, which consisted more in pretty anecdotes than in scientific facts. To have made the attack upon this uncritical attitude is to the lasting credit of the American investigators ; but they have gone too far, and in their desire to be " objective " they have relinquished much of their best material.

The same point of view that is valid in animal-psychology is likewise valid in the psychology of childhood ; for naturally the problem whether consciousness is present or not plays a much less important rôle in infancy than it does in animal-behaviour. During the first days of life only can the presence of consciousness be questioned ; furthermore, another criterion aids us in certain cases to decide whether or not the infant is conscious.

§ 6—*Consciousness and the Nervous System*

In order to understand the aid rendered by consciousness we must first take a glance at the anatomy and physiology of the nervous system. The complete behaviour of the higher animals is controlled by their nervous systems. The central apparatus receives all the nervous pathways that make the reception of stimuli possible. This we call the central nervous system, which is stimulated both by processes that take place in the surrounding world and also by those of the organs of the body itself. The central system likewise issues in nervous pathways by means of which all movements are aroused. Processes of the first kind involve the sensory, afferent, or receptive nerves, their connection with the outer world taking place either in specially constructed organs called sense-organs, or else in the free nerve-endings of the skin. The second class are called motor or efferent nerves; which end in muscles or in glands and thus control the bodily movements and secretions. Among the various parts of the central apparatus we are concerned only with the central nervous system, for we can not here enter upon a study of the autonomic system, whose importance, however, becomes every day more apparent.

According to Edinger [18] we can differentiate two parts of the central nervous system; one of these, found in all vertebrates,[19] fulfils the function of the central apparatus to which we have already referred, in that it receives sensory impulses, and sends out motor impulses. This apparatus consists of the long and extended spinal cord (*medulla spinalis*), which continues into the *medulla oblongata*, and also of a series of brain parts among which the cerebellum, the hind brain, the mid-brain, and the olfactory lobes may be named. This organ, when taken altogether, is termed by Edinger, the "old" brain (*Palæ-encephalon*). To this original apparatus there is added, in the developmental series from the shark upwards, a new apparatus, called the *cerebrum*, which constantly increases its size until in man the original apparatus is completely covered by it. Edinger calls this the "new" brain (*Ne-encephalon*). The "new" brain is in the closest connection with the "old" brain, receptive pathways leading from the "old" to the "new," where they terminate at the surface, or cerebral cortex. Motor pathways likewise lead from the cortex into the "old" brain, so that this later, yet far more effective, organ is capable of influencing the "old" brain, and thereby the behaviour of the entire organism.

We shall return to these matters again. For the present it is of interest to note that in man, an organism which, as we shall see, is more dependent than any other animal upon the functions of the cortex, those phases of his behaviour which take place through the functioning of the "old" brain alone, without any co-operation of the cortex, appear to be unconscious. Since the "old" brain gives rise to no experiences, man knows as little by way of it as he does of what is happening on the moon. A chance-observation of Edinger furnishes us a crude illustration of this fact: "I observed the case of a woman in the act of labour, whose spinal cord, as a result of spinal caries, was totally incapable of carrying afferent impulses to the cortex. Consequently she went through all the characteristic movements of childbirth without in the least sensing these otherwise painful processes. Indeed, she discovered only by chance when some one came to the bed to render her assistance that she was in the act of giving birth. This patient has repeatedly assured me that she was altogether unconscious of this entirely palæ-encephalic reaction."[20]

If we were to assume the same dependence of consciousness upon the "new" brain of the suckling, we might infer that if there is a period of time in which the infant behaves in a purely palæ-encephalic manner, it is highly improbable that the child's behaviour is at that time accompanied by consciousness. In the course of our investigation of infancy we shall return to this question.

§ 7—*Division of the Psychological Methods*

We have already pointed out that psychology employs two kinds of concepts; for in addition to the natural-scientific method of observation, we also have recourse to experiential observations. Concerning both these methods, and especially with reference to their application in child-psychology, we shall soon have something more to say, but the two are so intimately connected with each other that psychology does not follow them separately. Indeed, the most important method employed in experimental psychology consists of natural-scientific observations combined with reports of experience. We come, therefore, to a division of psychological methods into three parts: First, the purely natural-scientific method; secondly, the combination of this with experiential observation, which is called the psycho-physical method, and thirdly, the purely psychological or descriptive method, which relies altogether upon the observation of experience.

1. The Natural-Scientific Method consists in observing the individual in a certain situation. An experiment can readily be constructed in this way by controlling the state of the organism—for instance, by depriving it of food—and likewise by controlling the situation in which the observations are to be made. Oftentimes an experiment of this kind involves measurements; for example, in the investigation of fatigue one can determine the quantity of work accomplished in a given unit of time. Or, again, one can measure the time taken by an individual in the solution of a problem. Such experiments are often referred to as *achievement-tests*.

2. The Psycho-Physical Method is distinguished from the first type in that a "description" of behaviour is also included as a part of its data. One includes not only the data observed by the experimenter, but also those reported as being the experience of the observing subject. This method also is employed, for the most part, in the form of an experiment. The situation is controlled by the experimenter so far as possible in mensurable terms. The behaviour of the subject is then studied while the situation is being altered in a pre-arranged manner so as to provoke corresponding changes in behaviour, which is understood to include the experiences reported by the subject. The aim of this method varies according as the emphasis is placed upon the descriptive, or upon the functional data involved.

25

This difference can be made clear by the following examples.

(*a*) The investigation of auditory perception may be referred to as emphasizing the descriptive aspect of behaviour. If I wish to find out what auditory experiences occur when an individual is stimulated by various kinds of sound, only the sound-processes are varied. These being the relevant factors in the situation, the procedure is much simplified. We call these variable elements of the situation, which have a bearing upon the experiences of the observer, *stimuli*, and they must be varied in a systematic way. For instance, the experimenter arranges simple sound-waves of variable frequency and intensity, and then replaces these with more complex waves. In short, such variations are introduced as may be necessary in the solution of his problem. It will at once be seen that, without the guidance of a descriptive point of view, the selection of an appropriate method in any psychological investigation is virtually impossible. That is why the above description is so vague, although it may suffice for the purpose at hand.

After hearing the sound, the observer proceeds to describe the effects of the different stimuli, and, generally speaking, this description involves certain kinds of behaviour. For instance, the observer may be called upon to judge whether two tones are equal or different; in what respect and in what direction they vary, etc. These judgments involve acts of behaviour which can be determined by natural-scientific means. In fact, we do not need the observer's report at all, since it can be replaced by other reactions, such as we are obliged to introduce in the tests of animals. We can, for instance, *train* the individual to make a certain response whenever the higher of two tones is sounded. If the training is successful under conditions which make it possible to ascertain that the response was not based upon a difference of intensity, or some other factor than pitch, we

26

may conclude that the frequency-number has been the effective agent in producing the observer's reaction. Yet this fact can be determined much more quickly, and much more easily, by simply asking the observer whether the two tones were alike or different.

It is, however, quite true that the report is only a convenient and abbreviated type of behaviour, and that in so far as the report refers exclusively to behaviour it can be replaced by a mensurable reaction. But, as our last example clearly shows, this in no way justifies the behaviourist in assuming that the observer's report is altogether negligible. The training-tests, introduced as a substitute for the psychological report, may indeed show that an organism is capable of reacting differently to two sound-waves of different frequencies. But this result, as we know, is psychologically insufficient. For instance, suppose I test two observers, A and B, with the tones of 500 and 600 v. d., and suppose that the test has in each case been successfully administered. If we examine the reports of A and B, A may say " the two test-tones constituted a minor third, and I reacted to the higher," while B may express himself quite differently; perhaps he does not know what a minor third is, nor when one tone is *higher* than another. Instead B may describe his experience by saying that one tone was *duller*, and the other *brighter*, and that he reacted to the *brighter* tone. Although the training was successful, and the objective behaviour the same in both cases, yet so different are the descriptions given by these two observers that we must conclude the results of the training involve different types of behaviour. In fact, tests are certain to show that observer A is much more capable of auditory training than observer B ; yet, without knowing anything of their respective experiences, how could one find out wherein this difference lay, or upon what it depended ?

If, on the other hand, an observer can master the descriptive aspects of the situation so as to be able to

27

differentiate such attributes, for instance, as Köhler's "tone-body" and pitch, then tests of behaviour can be made which are calculated to determine the utility of these descriptive results. This example furthermore demonstrates that experiential observation is not so simple an affair, and that to be able to proceed from a certain observation of experience to the construction of an appropriate descriptive concept of it may itself be a highly significant performance. Köhler was the first to define the concept of "tone-body," as a description of certain auditory data already well-known to the psychologist, though never before formulated. Thus, sooner or later inadequate descriptive concepts act as a check upon investigation; but progress can never be made, even with the aid of this check, by such a total abandonment of descriptive concepts as the behaviourist proposed. Progress can and will come, however, with a continuous refinement of these concepts, as they are employed by investigators with constant reference to the overt response in connection with which the experience occurs. Both the response and the experience must be intimately correlated, as, indeed, they always have been in the psycho-physical methods. Whenever we succeed in setting up a new and useful descriptive concept, it is immediately apparent that the multiplicity of relations between stimulus and behaviour (both external and descriptive) become more distinct and intelligible. The relation itself is a natural-scientific fact which can not be reported by an observer with his incomplete information, because the observer reports now this experience and now that. The experimenter accepts his report as something to be studied in connection with the nature of the stimulus which, as a rule, is known to the observer. In this procedure the experimenter's selection of data is immaterial[21]; for after the results have been recorded anyone can do the work of determining what uniformities they show, and likewise anyone can criticize, and should be ready to criticize, the conclusions reached. The individuality of the observer, however, is always material, for we can not attribute to observer A an experience that has been reported by observer B.

The final outcome of the psycho-physical method is a law expressed in terms of a functional concept. But this outcome is not arrived at without the employment of descriptive concepts; and under certain circumstances the definition of a new descriptive concept may, indeed, be the most important result of a psycho-physical investigation.

(*b*) Emphasis upon the functional side of the psycho-physical method can be illustrated by the investigations of memory. A number of the important methods in the investigation of memory consist in impressing certain material (preferably nonsense-syllables in an ordered series) more or less firmly upon the observer and, after a definite interval of time, determining by various methods what the observer still retains; how quickly he can reproduce it; what errors are made, etc. So far we are dealing merely with certain types of behaviour. But memory-experiments are more than tests of behaviour; for the observer is also asked to make reports upon his experiences while learning. We ask him to describe the images he reproduces, and to state the degree of certainty with which the reproductions occur, etc. The compilation of these reports permits a fuller understanding of his behaviour which is more in focus here than it was in the investigations described under (*a*). Yet the principle is the same in both cases. The enormous significance of working the material over in the mind before it will be retained [22] can hardly be determined without the aid of descriptive data. Yet this comprehension of the material is a fundamental datum in any doctrine of memory.

3. The Purely Psychological Method renounces all claim to natural-scientific observation, and is satisfied with experiential observation alone. The method as such is of greater importance to the psychologist than

it is to psychology ; that is to say, a contemplation of psychological phenomena will often suggest to the psychologist that certain hypotheses which have been framed to embrace these phenomena are incorrect. The psychologist will then seek to test his hypotheses by other, and especially by psycho-physical, methods. For this reason the psychological method is not to be rejected, because it may be very useful as a beginning, or as a preparation for a scientific investigation, and it may even set new problems, and suggest new hypotheses, as well as lead to the formation of new descriptive concepts. On the other hand, we can never be entirely content with this method alone, since it ever stands in need of a substantiation and a supplementation which can only be had by employing other methods.[23]

## § 8—*Methods in Child-Psychology*

In the psychology of childhood, and especially in the first stages of the child's development, the observation of behaviour plays a leading part ; and not only in the pre-linguistic stage, but later also in the investigation of the linguistic performances themselves. Indeed, one can have no recourse to experiential observation until long after birth. What the child says in his early efforts to speak concerns the " actual world," and not the world of experience as we have defined this term. Our purely natural-scientific observations, however, require supplementation. Already in discussing the question of consciousness we have seen that it may be of the greatest importance, in a scientific understanding of the organism's objective behaviour, to be able to form a picture of what was being experienced while this behaviour was going on. We must therefore consider the psychological aspects of infantile behaviour, and be prepared to employ descriptive concepts without the aid of any direct report of the child's experience. In order to accomplish this end a " psychological talent " is requisite which constitutes a special form of our third, or purely psychological, method. With the aid of this "talent" we must try to put ourselves in the place of the child, with the same tasks before us which the child is expected to solve, and with only those means at our disposal which are available to the child. In this way we can endeavour to determine the characteristic phenomena occurring under these conditions [24]. As a working hypothesis we may therefore assume that similar phenomena are present in the mind of the child, though we have then to verify this hypothesis indirectly by means of objective tests of behaviour.

In most cases, however, the way is more direct; for the observation of behaviour supplies us not only with a description of muscular contractions and glandular secretions, but also with certain properties of behaviour that belong to the "inner" as well as to the "outer" responses. Thus the objective behaviour which is observed implies an "inner" behaviour which can not be observed. Such implications demand, of course, functional verification, but their discovery is a service which the mother is peculiarly qualified to perform.

Concretely, how must we proceed?

1. Most of the knowledge we now have we owe to diary-notes concerning the development of individual children. From the first days of the infant's life a mother, a father, or some one who is intimate with the child, observes what he does, and what happens to him. Needless to say, the child's natural development should be recorded as completely as possible; but strictly speaking, one can not record everything. A selection being necessary, all depends upon its appropriateness. In making his observations the observer must therefore assume a certain attitude. He must consider certain things, or his observations will be aimless, and many important matters will be overlooked. These diaries of child-life are therefore not uninfluenced by the character of the writer, by the problem with which he is concerned, and, indeed, by the level of his child-psychology. The

diaries we have often give no answer to certain questions arising in the study of infantile development. These questions therefore lead us to begin new diaries intended to record data that will answer these questions. What I wish to say is only this—that the collection of data is not a merely mechanical and receptive affair, since the greatest foresight and the strictest self-criticism are demanded of those who keep diaries of child-life for scientific purposes. In the diary itself only actual observations should be recorded, and nothing at all in the way of interpretation [25]. This, however, is easier said than done; for in order to describe a child's behaviour concepts are needed, the applicability of which can often be decided only by recourse to the behaviour that is being described. Such concepts, for instance, are "environment" and "reaction." If one understands by environment, not the physical surroundings of the child, but rather his biological surroundings, and even, under certain conditions, his phenomenal or psychological experiences, then the environment can be known only with reference to the reaction, and sometimes the reaction *qua* reaction can be understood only in relation to the environment.

2. The occasional observation of a noteworthy performance may also be valuable in the investigation of infancy. But one must know the exact conditions under which it occurred. The record of such observations must therefore be very accurate, and should include a description of the complete status of the child as well as an account of the special conditions under which the behaviour took place.

3. Experiment, which is the most important method of normal psychology, has not yet attained the position it should have in the investigation of childhood. This is because we must deal almost exclusively with achievement-tests which hitherto have fallen without the scope of experimental psychology, and for which no exact methods were available. The methods employed by the American animal-psychologists, which we shall discuss

later, could not properly be applied to a child. To be sure, experiment has not been altogether lacking. J. Mark Baldwin carried on experiments with infants to whom he presented objects which varied stepwise in certain directions. For instance, colours were shown, and the observation was made as to which would be grasped spontaneously. Other investigators have undertaken experiments upon children, which were copied from the training-tests of animals. But, generally speaking, one can say that experiments have not yet been adapted to the most important problems of child-psychology.

Recently, however, Köhler has succeeded in devising tests suitable for the investigation of the most important problems of behaviour, which he has applied to anthropoid apes, and which can readily be carried over into child-psychology. Indeed, Köhler has already conducted some experiments with children, and Bühler has followed him with others of like nature.

The chief condition which these experiments fulfil—and a condition which all good achievement-tests must fulfil—is that the demands of the investigation shall be accommodated to the level of the subject ; so that he is not placed in situations entirely artificial and of necessity unintelligible to him. But in addition—and this is of the utmost importance in child-psychology—Köhler's tests are of such a nature that the normal and healthy development of the subject experimented upon is in no wise disturbed by them. We may confidently expect that with the aid of this new method, which at the proper time will be described in detail, child-psychology will make a great stride forward.

In conclusion, let me refer to an investigation conducted by Alfred Binet. This investigator believed that one could replace the experiments upon children by experiments upon feeble-minded adult-individuals who might be considered as "stereotyped children" of a mensurable age, and who, just because of this stereotypy, ought to furnish precisely the kind of subjects needed for experimentation. But "no more than dwarfs can be considered children of suspended development, can the feeble-minded be compared mentally with certain ages of childhood "[26]. For this reason alone Binet's method must be rejected as totally unsuited to the investigation of the mental development of children.

It is a different matter when one makes use of retarded children for the investigation of a definite problem, because a certain process may stand out more clearly in their behaviour than it does in that of normal children; since retarded children learn with greater difficulty, they remain unstable for longer periods of time, and they acquire automatic responses less quickly than normal children. For these reasons investigation is sometimes more effective with retarded individuals than with normal children, and an experiment of this sort undertaken by Peters has brought good results.

No general rules for the treatment of the results of observation and experiment can be laid down. Claparède emphasizes the importance of two questions : (1) What is the present developmental status of a certain type of behaviour? For example, does the child still merely babble, or does he understand his words? Suppose one has observed a certain "reaction," and wishes to know what its significance may be as a "performance." This question leads to that much disputed and almost always misstated problem : Is the behaviour in question inherited or acquired, or, more precisely, what part of it is inherited, and what part acquired? (2) What is the present function of the behaviour? For example, we must ask : What process performs the same function in a child of a given age that conceptual thinking does in a man? On the other hand, we should not ask whether a child thinks in terms of concepts ; for although Claparède's question is right and sound, we can not use the same procedure in approaching the mental life of a child that we are accustomed to employ with adults. There are two reasons for this : In the first place we know very little about the thought-processes of adults—much less, indeed, than our own philosophy would warrant us in supposing. Having originated in logic, the concepts with which we work—for good or ill as the case may be—have lost all connection with living thought. In the second place, by asking such a question we block the way to anything which may be specifically different from that which an adult might expect to find. Whenever an ethnologist of an earlier period was satisfied with ascertaining that a people could count only up to five, the nature of his question destroyed every possibility of securing insight into the processes of calculation which these people may have employed as a substitute for counting. Against this kind of error in child-psychology we can not be too much on our guard.

### § 9—*Books on Child-Psychology*

We shall mention here only a few of the more important books on child-psychology. A list of the works frequently used in this volume will be found preceding the notes in the appendix. The remaining literature is listed in the notes themselves, while ready reference is facilitated by the arrangement of the index.

The standard book on child-psychology is the work of William Preyer, published in 1882. It is still a mine of observations and is really indispensable, although in theory it is long since out of date. A good characterization of the work may be found in Bühler's book on the same subject.

> W. Preyer, *The Mind of the Child* (translated by H. W. Brown). Part I. The Senses and the Will, 1888; Part II. The Development of the Intellect, 1889.

The most recent work of importance dealing with the problems of child-psychology in closest relation with those of general psychology, and at the same time doing justice to the point of view of comparative psychology, is by Bühler, while a briefer though equally commendable book by the same author brings the idea of development still more into the foreground.

> Karl Bühler, *Die geistige Entwicklung des Kindes.* 4th edition, 1924 (citations from the 2nd edition).
>
> Same author: *Arbiss der geistigen Entwicklung des Kindes.* In *Wissenschaft und Bildung*, Vol. 156. 1919.

Equally modern, and filled with his own abundant experience of the subject, is the work of William Stern, *Psychologie der frühen Kindheit bis zum 6 ten. Lebensjahre*, 1914, 2nd edition, 1921 (English translation, 1924).

Among older works should be mentioned the stimulating book of Karl Groos, *Das Seelenleben des Kindes*, selected lectures, 4th edition, 1913; and the little book by R. Gaupp, which also treats of the psychology of the school-child, *Psychologie des Kindes*, in *Natur und Geisteswelt*, Vol. 213, 3rd edition, 1912.

Among works not of German origin a book by Eduard Claparède is written from a pedagogical point of view—*Experimental Pedagogy and the Psychology of the Child* (translated from the 4th edition, by Louch and Holman, 1911; a 9th edition has since appeared in the original French, 1922).

> J. Sully, *Studies in Childhood*, New York, 1896.
>
> G. Compayré, *The Intellectual and Moral Development of the Child* (translated by Wilson, Part I. New York, 1896; Part II. *Development of the Child in Later Infancy*, New York, 1902).

These are two beautifully written older works which are stimulating, and contain much valuable material.

Finally, I wish to refer to the comprehensive work of Thorndike, which attempts to establish the principles of the science, many of which are criticized in this book. The work is not a child-psychology in the narrower meaning of the term.

> E. L. Thorndike, *Educational Psychology*, 3 Vols. New York, 1913-1914.

Some monographs on the development of individual children are specified in the list at the end of the book. Reference is here made to but two voluminous treatises of special subjects, by William Stern and his wife, and which, beginning with observations of their own children, led them to survey the whole field of investigation in child-psychology.

> Clara and William Stern, *Monographien über die seelische Entwicklung des Kindes.* I. *Die Kindersprache*, 1907. II. *Erinnerung, Aussage, und Lüge in der ersten Kindheit*, 1909.

CHAPTER II

GENERAL FACTS AND POINTS OF VIEW

*§ 1—Maturation and Learning*

WE speak of development whenever an organism or
any special organ becomes larger, heavier, more finely
structured, or more capable of functioning.  One must,
however, differentiate two types of development: development as growth or maturation, and development
as learning.  Growth and maturation are processes of
development which depend upon the inherited characteristics of the individual, just as any morphological
character like the form of the skull is determined at
birth.  To be sure, growth and maturation are not
altogether independent of the individual's environment.
Under-nourishment will check growth, and it may, in
exceptional cases, prove permanently harmful.  In the
forcing-house, one can accelerate growth and blooming,
but under "normal" conditions the course of these
developmental phases is primarily dependent upon the
laws of heredity.[27]  Likewise under "normal" conditions the environment may influence growth and
maturation by determining the selection of individual
types of behaviour.  Children who grow up out-of-doors
are stimulated by their surroundings to run, to jump,
to swim, etc., while children who are kept indoors are
more likely to use their fingers than their arms and
legs.  The mere fact that an organ, such as a muscle,
is frequently used will influence its growth quite apart
from the specific character of the response; think of

38

the many "systems" in vogue for strengthening the bodily muscles. A similar statement is applicable to the maturation of the sense-organs. By learning, however, we understand a change in ability resulting from quite definite individual activities. In learning to play cards it is not enough that one should grow up amid favourable circumstances, or that one's fingers should have attained a certain degree of technical facility; but, first of all, it is necessary to understand the significance of a pack of cards, and of each card for itself. When some one says that So-and-so is a born card-player, he does not mean that by merely glancing at a pack of fifty-two cards spread out on a table the "born player" could sit down with three other persons and without instruction be able to play a perfect game of "bridge." Nor does he even mean that such a person would at once be able to play the game somehow and would quickly master its intricacies by himself as, for instance, birds are able to fly as soon as they try to do so, and quickly attain the highest degree of perfection in this art. An ability to play cards is not thus laid down in the individual's inherited disposition. It need not develop at all in the whole course of a lifetime, and when it does develop, it is a new acquisition.

In any consideration of development we are confronted with this opposition of inherited and acquired traits. Whether this opposition can be bridged over, whether that which is inherited must first have been acquired by our ancestors in the course of racial development,[28] are questions we shall here leave out of consideration. Yet this opposition is found in the development of every individual; a fact which we can only note in passing without further explanation at present; since to explain it would require a detailed analysis of what learning actually is, and that is one main problem of our entire book.

Nevertheless, we should have this problem clearly in mind at the beginning of our inquiry, because capacities are controlled by laws, inherent in the organism, and are very loosely dependent upon the individual's achievements, whereas the abilities of an individual are chiefly determined by his experiences and achievements.

This double aspect of development makes difficult the solution of a problem to which reference was made at the beginning of the first chapter—the problem, namely, as to what part of any performance is inherited, and what part of it is acquired. In general, it has been thought possible to proceed as though whatever took place at birth, or upon the first appearance of a certain type of behaviour, could be differentiated from later forms of the same act—the former as being inherited, and the latter as being acquired. But even so, this differentiation is extraordinarily difficult. Furthermore, one need not regard every improvement in a performance as an acquisition of learning; neither are all complicated performances necessarily acquired or learned; for we must not neglect the part played by mere maturation in the refinement of behaviour, both in its motor and also in its sensory aspects.

§ 2—*The Function of Infancy*

A comparative study of behaviour leads us to conclude that the higher an individual stands in the animal-series, the more helpless he is at birth, and the longer will his period of "infancy" last. The human being constitutes the extreme in both respects; his almost complete dependency at birth being associated with an extraordinarily long infancy and youth, a period which, indeed, exceeds the whole lifetime of many mammals. At no time during the entire course of his maturation does the human being attain a complete mastery of any of his capacities, whereas such a mastery is attained much earlier by other animals, especially by organisms much farther down the scale—which in this respect are superior to man. Infancy must therefore have a peculiar

40

and a specific function, closely related to the superiority of the higher forms of life. For this reason Claparède raises the question: "Of what use is childhood?" The superficial facts of comparative biology show us in what direction the answer to this question must lie, since infancy is the period of greatest potentiality for development. During this period man changes from a very helpless creature into the best-equipped of all the species. In comparison, a chick can perform many acts correctly as soon as it breaks from the shell, and a full-grown hen can not do much more than a chick.

The development that takes place during infancy is also subject to conditions specifically different from those of embryonic development. The embryo's surroundings are constant, and its development is guided chiefly by a kind of immanent law, external conditions playing only the part usual in processes of growth and maturation. But all this is changed in the post-embryonic period, for the older the child becomes, the more specific is the influence which the world exercises upon his life. From this fact alone one may conclude that development becomes more and more a matter of "acquisitions"—in the sense of learning — and also, that certain stages of development are attained only after learning has been added to growth and maturation. Childhood is the period of learning *par excellence* which Claparède speaks of as the constructive period of life. Indeed, the efficiency that distinguishes the most highly-developed from all lower forms of life can not be attained simply through the fixed and inherited laws of development in growth and maturation. Learning is also essential to them; for efficiency depends upon functions that are not fixed in advance. When we reflect that learning, objectively considered, is an actual performance, we are better able to understand infancy, since both the extent and the intensity of learning that goes on at this time far exceed the amount of learning in all the later epochs of an individual's life-history.

## § 3—*Parallels in Developmental History*

A comparative method of treatment has gone still further in bringing ontogenetic and phylogenetic development—or, in other words, the development of the individual and of the race—into relation with each other. Many analogies have been drawn, of varying theoretical significance, in the explanation of which many different hypotheses have been constructed. Let me introduce this topic with a statement by William Stern concerning the development of a child.[29] " The human individual in the first month of his life is a ' suckling' whose lower senses preponderate. He enjoys but a dull instinctive and reflexive existence on the mammalian level. In the second half-year, however, the infant has attained a stage of development like that of the highest mammals—the apes [30]—furnished as he now is with the capacity of grasping, and also with a versatility in imitation. But he does not become a man until his second year when he has acquired an upright posture and the ability to speak. During the next five years of play- and dream-life he is at the level of primitive peoples. Then follows entrance into school, and a closer articulation with the social group, together with the imposition of definite obligations, involving a sharp distinction between work and leisure—all of which constitutes an ontogenetic parallel to the introduction of man into a civilized state with its political and economic organization. In the first years of school-age the simple situations of antiquity and of the Old Testament are most adequate to the youthful mind. The middle years bring with them the enthusiastic features of Christian civilization, while at puberty he attains for the first time the mental differentiation which corresponds to present-day civilization. The period of puberty has, indeed, often been designated as the ' Age of Enlightenment' for the individual."

I have reproduced this long quotation, not because I believe that all the analogies indicated are truly factual, but rather to make clear the purport of Stern's view. We find here epochs of childhood compared with stages in the developmental series of animals, both the lower and the higher mammals, and compared also with human epochs, stages of culture, primitive, antique, Christian, and modern. Stanley Hall, who for a generation has been pointing out the importance of these analogies, and who has devoted both time and effort in working them out, goes even further than Stern; for he finds traits amongst children which recall the aquatic ancestors of man, as, for instance, paddling movements and the rapture with which the infant beholds a body of water.

It should be expressly noted that actual and material grounds of connection which can be employed in the explanation of development are assumed for these analogies, and not mere similarities. Accordingly we shall now turn our attention to these theories; for without a doubt such analogies do exist. Typically infantile modes of behaviour, such as play, are obvious in other mammals. There are stages of child-development in which intelligent performances gradually become possible which, according to Köhler's investigation, are also typical of chimpanzees. Furthermore, the categories employed by the child in his apprehension of the world about him are quite similar to those of so-called primitive peoples. Yet these analogies are not at all limited to the age of childhood. Many adult forms of behaviour, especially when the inhibitions of education, custom, and convention fall away, are remarkably like the behaviour of apes. I may refer here to Köhler's description of the function of adornment among chimpanzees [31]. The question is, what conclusion may be drawn from these analogies? And before we proceed to an answer our material must first be tested in a strictly critical manner. In the use of analogies scientific stringency is all too readily replaced by fantastic excursions into the realm of fiction. It is easy enough to find analogies when one is looking for them, but to separate out of the abundance of material that which, properly speaking, is alone essential to the act, is a problem that has not always been rightly solved in this field of study.

1. The Theory of Recapitulation regards the development of the individual as an abbreviated and a more or less distorted replica of the development of the race. The theory assumes that every individual passes through all the stages of development through which his species has previously passed. This is taken to be an immanent law of development based upon inherited dispositions. One thinks at once of Haeckel's biogenetic law, which states of morphological embryonic development that ontogenesis is an abbreviated repetition of biogenesis. The connection of this law with the theory of recapitulation is strongly emphasized by its advocates. The distortion, which is apparent in ontogenesis when compared with biogenesis, is explained by the different conditions under which the two kinds of development take place. Every development is, indeed, dependent, not only upon immanent laws, but also upon external influences, and if these influences happen to vary a difference in development must also result.

The theory has many advocates, among whom Stanley Hall and his school have taken the greatest pains to formulate it in demonstrable terms. Their method is essentially this : to analyse modes of behaviour of the most general sort, and to point out those features which can not be explained as a product of learning or individual acquisition, but which may be found nevertheless in quite similar forms at earlier stages of development. In this way Stanley Hall has investigated the phenomenon of fear. As an instance, he takes the inexplicable *pavor nocturnus*—the fact that children often awake and cry out in the night with a terror from which it is hard to get them back to sleep again—which he explains as an atavism. The child reverts to a long-past epoch when man slept alone in the woods, exposed to danger, and was suddenly disturbed in his sleep. An important set of facts relevant to this general problem may be found in the play of children; for in play the child is supposed to re-enact the life of his remote ancestors. With the aid of Hall's questionnaire-method, one of his students has collected a large mass of material concerning children's play of the most various kinds. Plays of Indians and robbers, also constructive plays of building and digging, plays of adornment, such as tattooing and filing the nails, furnish material which Hall regards as a complete vindication of the theory, because the influence of environment, he thinks, would be quite insufficient to explain the details of these varied types of activity [32].

2. Instead of regarding individual development as a repetition of racial development, the Theory of Utility attributes both to the same causes. All development is said to result from the operation of two principles: accidental variation and the selection of appropriate responses. In the course of racial development certain types of response arise in accordance with these principles, and either survive or are again lost. If retained in any species, the moment for the appearance of such a trait in the ontogenesis of that species is determined as a joint effect of variation and selection, rather than by the law of recapitulation. For instance, nursing occurs very early in ontogenesis but very late in phylogenesis. The situation is reversed with respect to the sexual instinct, which appears early in racial development, but late in the development of the individual. This theory, which is vigorously upheld by Thorndike, is based upon the general theory of development associated with the name of Darwin, although Darwin and his immediate school did not restrict themselves within the limits imposed by the " Neo-Darwinism " which has been named after him, and which employs only the two principles of variation and selection [33].

If we examine a number of individuals of the same

45

species, we find that no two specimens are wholly alike. Individuals of the same species differ more or less from one another in the most varied ways. The uniformity of a species therefore is only an agreement of type within certain definite limits of variation. These limits of variation are assumed by Neo-Darwinism, and are considered to function in such a way that some individuals are better equipped to meet certain external conditions, while others are better equipped to meet other conditions. In the course of development those individuals better adapted to the essential features of their surroundings are much more successful in their struggle for existence. The traits of these surviving individuals are then passed on to their descendants, while those who lack these traits gradually die out. The same principles of variation and selection are again active in the offspring, so that the race is constantly becoming better adapted to its surroundings, and must therefore continue upon its course of development.

3. The third of these theories of development, which is known as the Theory of Correspondence, maintains that ontogenesis and phylogenesis are closely related processes. Since each has to do with the development of organisms, it is highly probable that certain general characteristics of development play a dominating part both in ontogenesis and in phylogenesis. In the concrete terms of Claparède[34], " Nature employs identical means for effecting the evolution both of the individual and of the race." One may expect, therefore, that all the beginning-stages in any course of evolution will actually be of a similar nature, and that this similarity will apply equally to primitive levels, to more progressive levels, and even to the highest levels of development. Dewey and his school have elaborated this theory for child-study[35], and a similar idea underlies Oswald Spengler's *Philosophy of History*.

The points of difference between these three theories may be made somewhat more precise in the following manner. According to the first theory the inherited disposition upon which the development of the individual rests is so constituted as to include everything that was ever inherited in the preceding generations of the race. All these tendencies become actualized in a serial order which is essentially determined by the order in which they arose in the ancestral series. The individual, therefore, possesses every single possibility of reaction to its environment ever possessed by the race, and the temporal order in which these different possibilities are realized is in the main determined by the original order of their succession.

According to the second theory the tendencies are so constituted as to include only those characteristics that have been selected because of their utility, while the serial order of their appearance is determined by the biological needs of the individual, and of the species. Consequently the individual possesses only a selection from among the various possible tendencies of the past with which to react upon its present environment, the temporal order of their realization depending altogether upon their utilization.

According to the third theory dispositional traits are so constituted that the individual indicates the history of his development from the most primitive beginnings by typical forms of reaction to his environment which appear at every stage in his career; and these reactions correspond in a general way to the stages of racial development. There are, therefore, primitive, more highly developed, and very highly developed forms of reaction, each of a uniform type, whether they be found in ontogenesis or in phylogenesis.

If we must declare ourselves with respect to these three theories, it is at once obvious that the third theory is far more cautious than either of the other two; its hypothesis being closer to the factual data, the way is left open to further theoretical constructions. This is a great advantage, because in general the current theories of development, and especially those of inheritance, are highly controversial and unsatisfactory. The third theory relieves us from the necessity of deciding for any one theory—a decision which at best would be arbitrary —and it thereby holds our interest in the discovery of further explanations of the facts. After investigations undertaken from this point of view have yielded concrete results, we can readily use them in the construction of further hypotheses. William Stern accepts this theory when, for instance, he speaks of "genetic parallels"[36], in a concrete investigation of speech.

The theory of recapitulation and its exaggerations, with which the reader is already acquainted from our discussion, has been frequently attacked[37], and most energetically in his larger work by Thorndike, who rightly points out the fragmentary data and the often contradictory inferences it employs. In its principal field, that of play, the theory has also been rejected by Stern, who agrees with it only to this extent: "that every mental development in the individual, as well as in the race, follows certain laws governing the change from primitive and cruder forms of life onwards to complicated and more highly differentiated forms; for which reason the play of the child reveals many analogies with behaviour at lower stages of human development"[38]. This admission, however, is nothing but an acknowledgment of the correspondence-theory[39].

The utility-theory is much too closely tied up with special hypotheses to warrant our acceptance of it, because it stands or falls with Neo-Darwinism. Consequently we can dismiss both the recapitulation- and the utility-theories, and urge instead the collection of as many facts as possible which may prove helpful in tracing the correspondence between individual and racial development. This means that one should constantly endeavour to support, to control, and to supplement the results of one branch of developmental investigation with results obtained in another branch; as, for instance, by comparing child-psychology with folk-psychology ; but one should never allow oneself to be led into the dogmatic construction of uniformities and dependencies. When material enough is at hand, one can then take up the problems of dependency which naturally arise [40], without being in any wise hindered by theoretical presuppositions.

§ 4—*The Tempo and Rhythm of Development*

Development, or the succession of its different stages, is conditioned primarily, though not altogether (see § 5), by an inherited disposition. This statement holds true both for the organism as a whole and also for its dynamics and rhythm ; because these, too, are conditioned by inherited disposition. What interests us here is the fact that disposition, and therefore development, may greatly vary in these respects. In point of fact, one is able to infer dispositional differences only on the ground that different individuals when placed in the same situation and amid the same surroundings exhibit quite different forms of development. Thus, for some individuals the rate of development is very rapid, while for others it is very slow ; furthermore, some individuals show a greater regularity of development than do others. A slow rate of progress at the beginning may be followed by a period of very rapid development, and, conversely, an accelerated development may suddenly be arrested, as illustrated by infant-prodigies who fail to live up to their early promise. In general, these differences may be attributed to inherited disposition, though an environment which constantly offers strange and unchildlike problems may also contribute to hasten a child's development and early maturation. On the other hand, an environment which offers no appropriate stimulation to activity may be a serious check to development.

What has been said about development as a whole—

its tempo and its variations which appear as individual differences—holds true for the individual ; because here, too, we find variations in tempo, and a developmental rhythm consisting of periods in which slight advancement is noticeable from without, alternating with other periods in which development seems to take more rapid strides. Let us note at once, however, that periods of relative quiescence are not necessarily periods of stagnation ; but may only be intervals in which development has taken another form. The astonishing advancement often observed in a succeeding period would be quite impossible if the child had not accomplished a considerable amount of preliminary work during the time when he was apparently quiescent. As an analogy, one can imagine a heaping-up of a great mass of potential energy during these rest-periods, which thereafter is transformed into kinetic energy. Finally, it should be observed that the rhythm of development in a single individual is not the same in all his varied functions. There are periods in which one functional complex is engaged in a particularly active state of development, while the rest are comparatively quiescent. Indeed, one might be able to characterize whole periods of life with reference to the preferment of certain achievements, if only we were in possession of more extensive and more definite data than the present status of investigation affords. We must note, too, that developmental rhythm is subject to great individual variations ; from which it is evident that the time of the appearance of any particular activity may greatly vary from individual to individual. All age-data have therefore but an approximate value for purposes of generalization ; relative statements, such as before and after, being, for the present at least, of much greater interest than absolute statements regarding the exact time at which a certain type of behaviour appears.

# HEREDITY AND ENVIRONMENT

*§ 5—Heredity and Environment*

We have had occasion to refer repeatedly to conditions other than those of inherited disposition but affecting development—namely, the conditions set by the outer world, or environment. The question now arises: How are these two sets of conditions related to each other? This question, since it involves philosophical, ethical, sociological, and pedagogical consequences, can not be answered off-hand; yet neither can we overlook the fundamental opposition of these two tendencies as they are embodied in the well-known theories of Heredity and Environment. According to the former theory, development is determined in all its important issues by an inherited predisposition; whereas, according to the latter theory, this determination comes chiefly from environment. The same opposition is found in psychology between the rival positions of Nativism and Empiricism, according to which the quality of our perceptions—and especially those of space—is taken to be either an inborn function or a product of experience.

In contrast to both these theories, Stern advances a point of view which he calls the "convergence-theory," and which plays an essential part in his philosophy of personality. "Mental development," he writes, "is not a mere passive unfolding of inborn traits, neither is it a mere reception of external influences; instead, it is a result of the convergence of both the internal opportunities and the external conditions of development. One should not ask, concerning any function or trait, whether it originates from within or from without; but rather, what part of it is derived from within and what part from without; for both are constantly co-operating in the work, though at times in varying degrees" [41].

It is at once apparent that we can not side with either of these extreme theories of heredity or environment; for we have already agreed that learning is essentially a type of development, and learning involves the reaction of the individual to a definite situation wherein the reaction is certainly not unequivocally tied up with inherited dispositions. But before we can proceed we must inquire into the nature of learning, and it seems to me that we can not arrive even at a clear statement of the question—much less at a final decision between psychological empiricism and nativism —so long as the problems of experience itself, and of learning, have neither been solved, nor, indeed, for the most part, accepted as definite problems.

Our aim, therefore, may be characterized by the statement that we are trying to investigate the facts which underlie the formation of all theories, and for this reason we must not allow ourselves to be hindered by the acceptance of any special theory. The concept of convergence advanced by Stern merely indicates a problem which, before it is solved must first be more clearly defined ; for at present we do not even know what is meant by saying that "a certain behaviour is conditioned from without."

## § 6—*Mental and Bodily Development*

Mental development naturally goes hand in hand with the development of the bodily organism. Let us, then, briefly consider the very general connection which obtains between these two aspects of development. A few anatomico-physiological observations may be useful to us in this connection. In the foregoing chapter (pp. 22-3) we gave a very crude description and classification of the central organ of the nervous system, explaining in particular the difference between the "old" and the "new" brain. We may now complete our sketch by going more into detail, and considering the microscopical structure of the nervous system. It is not our task, however, to furnish the reader with information upon this subject ; for that, reference should be made to other books[42]. We shall therefore confine ourselves to the most important facts needful in laying a basis for later considerations.

We find nerves acting as mediators between the sense-organs and the brain, and likewise between the brain and the muscles. These nerves are fibres of varying and sometimes considerable length, and also of variable thickness. They are surrounded by a protecting and insulating tissue. A nerve of this kind is not a uniform structure, but consists of a great number of separate, mutually isolated, fibres which are the real bearers of the process of conduction. These fibres may be strictly classified as *sensory* and *motor*, but not the whole nerves, since there are nerves containing both kinds of fibres ; as, for instance, the trigeminal nerve— the fifth cranial—which occasions the skin-sensitivity of the head and also innervates the jaw musculature ; or, again, the vagus nerve—the tenth cranial—which performs numerous functions involving, among others, the regulation of breathing, circulation, and digestion. Each fibre taken by itself has, however, but one function— sensory or motor; either it leads from the periphery to the centre, or from the centre to the periphery. In this way one distinguishes *centripetal* and *centrifugal* fibres. These, however, are not independent elements ; for each leads to a nerve- or ganglion-cell, and these ganglion-cells exhibit great variations both of structure and size. The common feature of all is a greater or lesser number of fibrous processes ; one of these processes, called the *axis-cylinder*, being the same structure we have just referred to as the nerve-fibre. At its end this neurite divides into a fine net-work which closely invests either the muscle-tissue or the tendrils of another ganglion-cell. Besides the axis-cylinder, the ganglion-cell sends out still other processes, much shorter and very numerous, often forming a net-work of the finest ramifications. With this plexus the arborizations of the axis-cylinders of other ganglion-cells are in close connection. It has been discovered that in many respects

53

the ganglion-cell with all its processes forms a unit, called a *neurone* by Waldeyer. So the whole nervous system can be conceived as an organization of number-less neurones knit together with one another. Whether the connection between two neurones results from a mere contact in the fibrous net-work, or whether the fibrils distinguishable in the microscopic structure of the fibres form a continuous connection from neurone to neurone, is a matter which, though it has been under discussion for a long time, has not yet been decided. Without prejudice to this decision, the neurone may pass with us for a unit.

We have already distinguished between centripetal and centrifugal fibres ; we must now add a third sort, namely, those which connect one part of the brain with another. "The last, the *fibræ propriæ* of the cortex, are very numerous in fully - developed brains, stretching everywhere from convolution to convolution, from the nearest to the farthest, binding whole lobes together" [43].

Likewise the two hemispheres are bound together through other collections of such fibres, called com-missures, the largest of which, the *corpus callosum*, is easily detected in each median section of the brain.

We now come to our particular theme, the rela-tion between physical and mental development, which we shall first discuss from a phylogenetic point of view.

*a.* "Whoever knows the structure of the brain in the animal-series will become convinced that the ap-pearance of new functions is always accompanied by the appearance of new parts, or by the enlargement of already existing parts, of the brain" [44]. Thus Edinger formulates as a principle of investigation the results of his long years of research. In the phylogenetic series of vertebrates, in which, as we have seen, the "old" brain gradually associates with itself a "new" brain, Edinger seeks to point out the functions which belong to the new organ, by tracing the changes in function which parallel its enlargement. In differentiating the "old" from the "new" brain, and their corresponding functions, Edinger remarks not only that the functional activity increases enormously, but also that it takes on a new and qualitative departure, in that the behaviour of the higher animals appears to become more and more "intelligent." Paralleling this change of activity, according to Edinger, morphological changes in the brain are indicated by an increase of the areas lying between and in front of the sensory centres, and also by the growth of intercortical pathways. The investigation of these parts of the fore-brain is easy, and, indeed, these parts "clearly increase in size as the animal increases in its capacity to guide its observation and activity by intelligence" [45]. Man is peculiarly characterized by the development of his frontal lobes, whereas an arrested development of these lobes goes hand in hand with idiocy.

There can be no doubt that Edinger discovered a valuable heuristic principle which he has been able to use successfully. In the course of this book, however, we shall be led to a quite different conclusion as to the nature of these activities, especially as regards intelligence, but also as regards the nature of the functions performed by various parts of the brain.

*b*. While the "new" brain and the ne-encephalic activities increase constantly in the ascending series of vertebrate evolution, the "old" brain is at the same time losing its independence. The higher an animal stands in the series, the less it can function without the "new" brain. Although the cerebrum has often been removed from living animals, so that their behaviour without it might be studied, there is scarcely a reported case of a human being born without a cortex which has survived the first day after birth.

A single instance is known of an infant lacking a cerebrum which lived, in fact, for three and three-

quarters years. This case is reported by L. Edinger
and B. Fischer [46], who have compared the behaviour
of this child with that of one of the dogs operated upon
by Rothmann, which lived also without a cerebrum
for more than three years. "The dog soon learned to
run and even to jump a hurdle, whereas the child lay
contracted and almost motionless for three and three-
quarters years, never making any attempt to sit upright.
Neither did he attempt to grasp or hold anything in
his hands. Only in his face could a certain mobility
be noted, when occasionally the features were painfully
distorted. Both the lips and the tongue were used
together in sucking and in taking nourishment from a
spoon. The dog, which at the beginning had to be
fed like a child, later learned to feed himself so well
that it was only necessary to put the dish before
his nose and he would empty it. Nothing of the
great restlessness which dominated the dog after the
restraint exercised by the cortex had been removed
by the operation, making him constantly run about,
was ever apparent in the child. Only a continual
crying was observed from the second year onwards, and
this could be stilled by patting him, especially on
the head.

"The acts of bodily excretion, which took place in
a normal manner in the dog, were accomplished by the
child without change of position; nor did he in any
way indicate when his napkin was wet. With the dog,
sleep alternated with waking, whereas the child seemed
always to be sleeping. The dog could not taste, smell,
or hear, nor could any evidence of vision be found.
This was likewise the case with the child; yet both
responded with optical reflexes, and at times the eyes
would close in a cramp-like manner under stimulation
from light. It was not possible to find a single mental
reaction in the child, or in any way to get in touch
with him, so as to teach him anything; but to a certain

degree the dog could be taught, and he also gave evidence of moods, fits of temper, and periods of contented quiescence "[47].

We shall return in the next chapter to the child without a brain, but the quotations already given show clearly enough how much more efficient are the same palæ-encephalic parts of the brain in dogs than they are in man, and how much man depends upon his "new" brain. We have but to compare the marked reduction in the dog's efficiency after operation with that of a fish which naturally subsists by means of the "old" brain alone, in order to have our previous thesis fully confirmed. Among all the animals man comes into the world the most helpless, and passes through the longest period of childhood. Between these facts and man's dependence upon his cortex some relationship must exist.

This leads us to *ontogenesis*. At birth the human brain is macroscopically ready ; but not so in its microscopic structure. For the most part, the fibres of the brain possess no sheathing at the time of birth, and are therefore incapable of functioning. The maturation of the fibres goes on throughout the first months of life. At the beginning medullation takes place principally in those fibres which extend downwards from the cortex, and upon whose functioning the voluntary motion of the limbs is dependent ; thence it extends to such fibres as connect the cortical areas with one another. The "new" brain of the newly-born child is consequently in a very unfinished state, and on the basis of the information acquired in the last chapter, we can now explain the helplessness of the child at birth by this fact. Yet the child, far more than the animal, is directly dependent upon the functioning of the "new" brain. Despite its unfinished state the human brain is relatively large and heavy even at birth ; for the weight of the brain is already over 300 gr., or nearly one-fourth the weight of the adult organ. In proportion to the weight of the body it is indeed heavier than in adult life, as the following figures will show:

Child $\dfrac{1}{6\ \text{to}\ 8}$ $\dfrac{\text{Weight of brain}}{\text{Weight of body}}$ $\dfrac{1}{30\ \text{to}\ 35}$ Adult

The weight of the brain increases very rapidly, being doubled after nine months, and tripled before the end of three years; but in the course of time the rate of

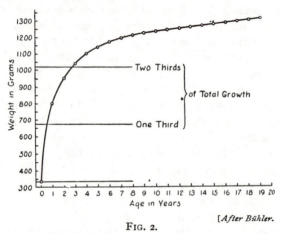

FIG. 2.

[*After Bühler.*]

growth decreases more and more, until the full weight has been attained at about the middle of the third decennium. (See Figure 2.)

Increase in weight parallels the development of behaviour. Weight is therefore a crude unit of measure for development, and rapid growth no doubt correlates chiefly with the first cultivation of bodily movements; although other functions also undergo their most rapid development at the beginning. A splendid example of the parallel development of organ and function is found in the cerebellum, the organ which controls bodily equilibrium. That all parts of the brain do not develop in the same rhythm, and that different parts have different epochs of particularly rapid growth, are facts or laws of mental development to which reference has already been made. Now the cerebellum grows very slowly in the first five months, then suddenly it begins to develop faster, until finally it attains its greatest rate of growth in the last half of the first and in the first half of the second year, reaching its full size towards the end of the fourth year. The time at which its greatest increase is indicated, at the end of the first year, is also the time when the child is learning to sit and to walk—activities requiring the effective regulation of bodily equilibrium which the cerebellum supplies.

CHAPTER III

THE STARTING-POINT OF DEVELOPMENT;
THE NEW-BORN INFANT AND PRIMI-
TIVE MODES OF BEHAVIOUR

§ 1—*A First Survey of Behaviour. Physiological
Correspondences*

BEFORE undertaking a consideration of development
we must know its starting-point. For us the starting-
point will be the human being who has just come into
the world. Embryonic development lies without the
scope of our inquiry, because the mental development of
a human being can not be studied until he has become
an independent individual. In this chapter, then, we
shall have to deal with the behaviour of the newly-born
child.

We must consider first of all the crude features of the
infant's behaviour, and ask: What are the first actions
of a human being who has just come into the world?
Aside from feeding, and the vegetative functions connected with it, of which we shall soon speak in greater
detail, we note a series of bodily movements, including
the extension and bending of the arms and legs (these
are often unco-ordinated, that is, the right and left sides
of the body act independently); the stretching of the
limbs upon wakening; movements made in a warm bath,
which movements may spread over the whole body;
eye-movements of all kinds; and the most striking of
all expressions—crying, whose immediate cause it is
frequently impossible to determine, though usually it

60

PHYSIOLOGICAL CORRESPONDENCES

can be connected with a situation in which the child
finds something painful to himself; as when he is in
need of nourishment, or when the environment acts
directly upon his body through pressure, temperature,
moisture, etc.  This enumeration is by no means complete, nor is it limited to the moment of birth, but it
may be considered as covering roughly the first two
weeks after birth.  The fact that the new-born child
spends twenty hours and more each day in sleep is at
least as characteristic of his kind as are any of the
movements mentioned.  His sleep is not one long
continuous slumber, but is divided into many short
periods broken by other short periods of waking.
Another general characteristic is that all movement of
the limbs takes place slowly.  Bühler likens this to the
movements of our fingers when they are half rigid with
the cold.

Both of these last-named peculiarities in the behaviour
of new-born infants are elucidated by certain physiological facts.  In a prolonged series of experiments,
Soltmann [48] stimulated the muscles and motor nerves
of new-born and adult mammals (dogs and rabbits) by
artificial electrical means, and found a characteristic
difference between the reactions of young and mature
animals.  In the new-born: (1) the irritability was much
less; in general, a much stronger current being needed
to produce a muscular response; (2) the form of the
muscular contraction was different, in the young the
contraction and release were slow instead of being sharp
and sudden; (3) the onset of fatigue was found to be
very rapid; (4) the muscles of the young were more
highly susceptible to tetany.  When a muscle is stimulated repeatedly by intensive shocks, unless the frequency
be too great, a contraction corresponds to each stimulation.  But as the frequency of stimulation is gradually
increased, a limit is reached at which the muscle no
longer responds to separate stimuli, but remains permanently contracted in a condition of tetanus.  This

limit lies between 70-80 stimulations per second for
the adult animal, but in the new-born it is as low as
16-18. We may without hesitation apply these results
to the human being. We can then understand the
slowness of the infant's movement from Soltmann's
second result; the great need of sleep from his third;
and the capacity to regain sleep so readily from his
first. We adults, on the contrary, find great difficulty
in falling asleep during the daytime, even when very
tired, because of the many stimuli constantly influencing our sense-organs. But in the case of infants, their
sensitivity being less, such inhibitions are much weaker.

Furthermore, I believe an analogy can be traced
between the conduct of the newly-born infant and
Soltmann's fourth result, though this analogy refers to
the sensory and not to the motor aspect of tetanus. By
stimulating sense-organs periodically one can obtain the
same kind of uniformity in the phenomenal effect that
is found in the tetanus resulting from recurrent muscle-
stimulation. Take the most familiar and thoroughly
investigated instance of this—the sense of sight. If
one casts light upon the eye by means of a rotating
disk, or colour-wheel, half white and half black, for
definite periods of time separated by intervals of complete darkness, a slow alternation between bright and
dark is observed when the rate of rotation is slow; but
if the frequency is increased a new phenomenon occurs:
the disk begins to flicker. A still further increase in
the frequency of rotation brings us to a limit beyond
which the rapidly revolving disk of black and white
sectors appears like a uniform gray, completely at rest.
The occurrence of this uniform impression is known
as *fusion*, and fusion corresponds to tetanus. But the
correspondence of these two results extends still further;
for the laws upon which these effects depend—the conditions influencing the limits of tetanus and fusion—
are the same [49]. Therefore, the inference may be drawn
that the critical frequency for fusion—that is, the lowest

frequency that will just produce it, which in the case of adults is about 50 periods per second [50]—might be very much lower for infants. This fact may be difficult to prove; but at all events nothing is now known to contradict such an inference.

The results of certain investigations which I conducted jointly with P. Cermak, showed that a close relationship exists between this phenomenon of fusion and the visual perception of movement. I will only indicate the fact that when a movement is made too rapidly it loses the phenomenal characteristic of seen-motion; and what we then perceive is a motionless streak of light, instead of a moving point [51]. The laws here involved are the same as those controlling fusion.

In conclusion, we may infer from Soltmann's fourth statement that in the perception of movement the limen at which movement disappears is more quickly reached (that is, at a lower speed), in the case of new-born infants than it is in adults, an inference which fits the known facts perfectly. Although authorities are at variance as to the time when a child begins to follow a moving object with his gaze, they are agreed that the child can accomplish this act only if the movement of the object *takes place slowly*. [52]  Up to the present, these observations have been referred chiefly or wholly to the development of the motor side of this performance—the arousal of the eye-movements which follow the moving object, and which are supposed to result from the successive stimulation of different points on the retina.  That is to say, the explanation was supposed to be furnished by a "connecting mechanism" operating between the sensory and the motor parts.  But perhaps the sensory performance itself should be included in the explanation In as much as we shall soon become acquainted with a conception of this "connection" which establishes a very close relationship between the sensory and the motor aspects of the optical apparatus, I, for my part, am ready to conclude that, as a matter of fact, infants do have far less capacity than adults to see movements, and that this deficiency is directly related to the more ready onset of tetanus in the young.

In this connection a question arises. If our assumption regarding the defective motor-vision of new-born infants is correct, it appears that we are dealing with a performance which improves during the course of life. Shall we then conclude that experience accounts for this change? By no means, for if our other assumption, which would bring this fact into relation with the facts of muscle- and nerve-physiology, is correct, it is not "experience" which accounts for the gradual increase of the limit from 15 to 80 periods of stimulation per second at which tetanus takes place, but, evidently, a physiological alteration of the organ which, in the preceding chapter, we have called *maturation.*

The process of maturation would then be the occasion for development in the perception of movement, and there is no reason to suppose that this development can be referred to experience alone.[53] Furthermore, we have here a most instructive example of the possibility mentioned in the last chapter of interpreting development in terms of maturation. We shall meet with this problem again, when we come to speak of eye-movements.

§ 2—*Is the New-Born Infant a Purely " Old-Brain " Type of Being ?*

We already know that most of the connections between the " old " and " new " brain of the new-born infant are neither medullated nor conductile. In addition, Soltmann obtained the following results: Until the tenth day after birth no sort of movement of the body- or head-musculature could be aroused by electrical stimulation of the puppy's cortex, though with older animals movements were readily produced in this way. Furthermore, destruction of the motor cortical areas,

64

which in older animals results in a severe disturbance of movement, produced no interruption or paralysis of the muscular apparatus during these first days of life. When one considers these facts and the points noted above with reference to human beings, one is tempted to infer that the new-born human being is also a purely palæ-encephalic creature. It has also been observed that the behaviour of children lacking a cerebrum (anencephalic) does not appear to differ in any important respect from that of normal children. For instance, children without a cerebrum cry at birth just as normal infants do. Yet the case described by Edinger and Fischer, to which reference was made in the foregoing chapter, does not seem to agree with such a conclusion.[54] " The child accepted the breast immediately, and from the first nursed in the right way ; but really, the child was awake only at the time of nursing, and before it would nurse it had to be wakened. Otherwise, it always lay as if 'in sleep.' It was never heard to cry during the first year, but only occasionally to utter a low tone." [55] From this account it appears that the behaviour of the Edinger child must have been somewhat different from that of a normal infant, even from the very first days of its life, because in normal infants a facial expression of contentment can at times be observed (Preyer), whereas Edinger's infant did not indicate the slightest facial expression during its entire life. It therefore seems probable to me that in healthy new-born children the " new " brain already plays some part in determining their behaviour, although we can not yet tell how. Soltmann's investigations with dogs thus furnish an inconclusive parallel, because, as we have seen, the human being is dependent upon his " new " brain to a much greater extent than the dog.

One can very soon discern the growing influence of the " new " brain in the course of normal development; which is but another instance of the process of *maturation*.

65

# THE NEW-BORN INFANT

## § 3—*Impulsive Movements*

When we consider the movements of the new-born infant described in § 1, we find that few of them are correlated with definite external stimuli or with determinable situations; hence they do not appear as reactions, but give one the impression of spontaneity. In this sense they are aimless or purposeless, in as much as they do not attain a recognizable end. These movements have therefore been distinguished as a group, termed by Preyer " impulsive movements." Their physiological origin is also implied by this distinction. Preyer regarded them as a continuation of embryonic movements, " which the fœtus already executes, and earlier than any others, at a time when, as it can not possibly be incited to movement by peripheral stimulus, its centripetal paths are not yet practicable, or not yet formed at all, and the ganglionic cells from which the excitations proceed are not yet developed.[56] " Since, however, no movement can occur without a stimulation of the motor nerves, he concludes that internal physiological processes, such as nourishment and growth, must occasion these impulsive movements; a conclusion in which Stern agrees[57]. This view is generally accepted in so far as it states the fact that these movements, unlike the spontaneous responses of adults, are aroused neither by external stimulation nor by excitations of the cortex. In their description, however, one must add, as both Stern and Thorndike have remarked, that objectively considered, they are by no means useless. On the contrary, their function has a considerable value to the individual in promoting the growth and maturation of their respective organs[58]. Stern calls this a *pre-practice* value, while Thorndike, in accordance with his Theory of Utility, which was discussed in the last chapter, regards this value as the explanation of their arousal and conservation in the development of the race. Thorndike proceeds, then, to argue against a sharp dis-

66

tinction between this group of movements and any other ; and, indeed, it is true that impulsive movements ought not to be regarded as though they were entirely independent of the situation, or purely arbitrary in their nature. If one could fully understand the total situation, which in instances like these mainly involves the conditions and processes of the nervous system, one would find that all impulsive movements are strictly regulated. This, of course, needs to be emphasized, but a certain distinction still remains, in as much as the impulsive movements are specifically attributable to inner situations, whereas other movements are expressly conditioned by external situations. Yet even when so considered the distinction is not very important ; for it matters little whether a child cries because it needs food or because its leg is being pinched. We shall pass on, therefore, to a consideration of the more significant behaviour which occurs in response to definite external stimuli, adding that in the course of development these so-called impulsive movements retreat more and more into the background.

## § 4—*The Reflex-System*

Into a second group we may place a type of behaviour which occurs in response to external stimuli. These movements have a number of peculiarities: (1) The reactions as well as the stimuli are relatively simple. This is not an exact description, because it is not easy to define what is meant by "relatively simple." But the statement will serve to distinguish these movements from a third group yet to be considered. (2) The movements of this group take place with extraordinary uniformity. That is, the situation remaining the same, identical stimuli always produce the same reaction, unless, indeed, the irritability of the organism deviates from its normal level, toward hypersensitivity on the one hand, or toward fatigue on the other. (3) Variation

67

of the stimulus in a certain direction, such as a gradual increase of intensity, does not always produce an alteration of the reaction in the same direction; for the reaction may suddenly become qualitatively different, sometimes because an organ hitherto quiescent has been called into action. (4) These movements belong to the inherited disposition of the individual, and do not have to be learned. (5) They are of the greatest utility to the organism, consisting, in general, of protective, defensive, or adjustive movements, as is obvious from any description of their separate types. (6) Still another uniformity may be mentioned. The reaction can be facilitated or inhibited when, in addition to the normal stimulus, another stimulus is applied at some other point. We call these movements reflexive, or, briefly, *reflexes,* and an example would be the contraction of the pupil when the eye is stimulated by light.

Before entering upon a discussion of the reflexes of the new-born infant, let us glance at some of the ideas which have been advanced in their explanation. We might ask the question: How must an organ be constructed whose function is destined to be reflexive? The usual answer to this question is very simple. We know two kinds of nerves, anatomically and physiologically—namely, sensory and motor nerves. Furthermore, we know that sensory nerves possess a terminal arborization which, either directly or through the mediation of other neurones, approaches the terminals of the motor nerves; and we know, finally, that an injury at any point of this more or less complicated series of neurones involved in the arousal of a movement interferes with the movement itself. The function of the reflex also indicates the double nature of the stimulation and response. The organ of the reflexes is therefore quite obviously a more or less complicated chain of neurones which, in the limiting case, may consist of but two neurones. Always beginning with a sensory neurone and ending with a motor neurone, this apparatus is called a *reflex-arc*. One should not overlook the fact, however, that these reflex-arcs are not isolated mechanisms, but are interconnected with other parts of the nervous system, as can be demonstrated both by the facts concerning facilitation and inhibition already mentioned, and also by the fact that many reflexes can be voluntarily influenced ; as, for instance, sneezing can be repressed voluntarily for a longer or shorter time.

Although investigators, perhaps, have not always been conscious of it, current theories of reflex-action have shaped their views concerning the reflex-organ in a very definite way. It has been customary to consider the reflex-arc as composed of a centripetal and a centrifugal branch, these being regarded as independent parts, while the characteristic feature of the apparatus was the *connection* that exists between them. A reflex-mechanism is then conceived as a *pre-determined, inherited connection* between afferent (receptor) and efferent (effector) pathways. Such a formulation of the original data is, of course, readily inferred. Anatomically the parts can be separated, and in accordance with the principles of the assumption, one can easily imagine a mechanical scheme of explanation. Such a scheme also satisfies our reasoning to a considerable extent, because it is readily comprehended and thus seems to be a good explanation.

But before we accept this hypothesis we should look more closely into the functional aspects of the mechanism involved. What happens in the reflex-arc when a reflex movement is made ? Obviously the energy arising from the external stimulus can not be simply transformed into a nervous process. Such an assumption would be untenable for any kind of nervous action. The effect— the movement of reaction—stands in altogether too loose a relation with the energy of the stimulus to warrant such an assumption. The only possibility is that the stimulus releases energy which lies stored up in the nerve-cells. At the same time the stimulus may co-operate very materially in determining how much and what kind of energy shall be released ; but the only energy available is the energy already present in the nerve-cells [59]. This conclusion holds true for the motor as well as for the sensory nerves. If I stimulate a motor nerve directly by electricity, it is not the electric shock itself which is conducted to the muscle, causing it to contract, for here again we have only a release of energy. Assuming, then, the independence of the centripetal and the centrifugal neurones, the reflex takes place as follows : The stimulus releases a certain amount of energy in the sensory neurone, which, passing along the neurone, acts in turn as a release for the energy stored up in the motor neurones ; the relation between the processes in the sensory and motor neurones being of the same order as that between the stimulus and the sensory process. At any rate, the stimulus can have nothing to do with the movement of reaction. While such an apparatus may be called a *mechanism*, the teleological character of reflex-movements is not accounted for until still further assumptions are made, which can be better understood after we have discussed a third group of movements.

To complete the picture of the reflex, we should add that reactions may in their turn stimulate sensory nerves, thus apprising the nervous system that a movement has been made, and what kind of a movement it was. This does not mean that we ourselves must become aware of it ; for many reflexes take place altogether without consciousness, just as other movements do when their reflex-arcs have been cut off from the " new " brain. An instance of this was described in the first chapter—the case of the woman who gave birth without being aware of it.

We have emphasized the strong points in the theory of the reflex-arc, and have also called attention to a deficiency in it. Further defects will become evident as we turn now to consider the reflexes evinced by new-born infants.

§ 5—*The Reflexes of New-Born Infants*

From the very outset, all manner of reflexes take place upon stimulating any of the infant's sense-organs. These reflexes have already been subjected to thorough investigation over a long period of time. We shall here limit ourselves to a few examples.

(a) *Eye-Reflexes.*—The pupillary reflex is bilateral from the very first; that is, when light is directed into one eye only, both pupils contract. The lids of the eyes also function from the beginning by closing whenever the eyes are stimulated with light; at first, however, they do not close when an object approaches the eye rapidly. A much disputed problem is that of the eye-movements which adapt the eyes in their position and adjustment with reference to the outer world, so as to provide the individual at all times with the most effective use of his organs of sight. In us adults these movements occur automatically, like reflexes, and they are co-ordinated; in the new-born infant, however, they are sometimes entirely unco-ordinated. Indeed, the infant can readily move one eye, while keeping the other one perfectly still. For the present it is well to separate the two problems here involved; first, the problem of the direction of the eyes toward a certain object, or *fixation* ; and secondly, the problem of co-operation, or the co-ordination of the two eyes. In fixation, the eye is turned until the fixated object falls upon the place of clearest vision lying at the centre of the retina (the *fovea cent-ralis*), while the lens assumes a degree of curvature such that a distinct image of the object is focused upon the retina (*accommodation*). Co-ordination, on the other hand, consists in keeping the accommodation and fixation always the same in both eyes (this is called *convergence*) [60].

Do eye-movements, then, belong among the inherited reflexes, or are they acquired? First let us consider co-ordination ; two diametrically opposed theories have

71

been here advanced. According to Hering, "the co-ordination of movements in the two eyes depends upon an inborn arrangement, and not upon exercise. So far as concerns their movements in the service of vision, both eyes may be taken together as constituting a single organ "[61]. It is not as though each eye moved by itself, because a single impulse suffices to occasion a reaction in both eyes, just as if the organs were a double-eye.

On the other hand, Helmholtz observes " that although the necessity of moving both eyes together . . . appears to be something which can not be overcome in normal vision . . . it can be shown, however, that the regularity of this connection is a result of practice "[62].

We have before us two opposed theories which have dominated the whole psychology of space-perception. From the one point of view the essential feature of behaviour—which is, in our case, eye-movements—is explicable on the basis of pre-determined, inherited dispositions. Individual life, practice, experience, all serve in the perfection, but introduce no new forms, of behaviour. In accordance with the other theory, however, the essential features of behaviour are conceived to be a result of practice. The first theory is called *nativism* and the second, *empiricism*.

Of the various arguments that have been advanced on both sides, we shall consider in the main only those that have a bearing upon our particular theme—the psychology of infancy. The chief argument of Helmholtz rests upon the fact that one can learn in some measure to destroy the co-ordination of the two eyes. The inference is then drawn that what can be altered by practice, must also have been acquired through practice. This argument, however, is not at all convincing; for it is unnecessary to suppose that an inherited co-ordination must involve an insurmountable compulsion towards behaviour. It is easy enough to demonstrate that other inherited modes of response are modifiable through practice. Hering, for instance, notes that one can train a four-footed animal to adopt a pace unnatural to its kind, as does the trotting horse.

The empiricist in his turn might seek to support his views by reference to the unco-ordinated eye-movements of the infant, were it not for the fact that co-ordination has been observed even in the first day after birth—a thing which could not happen if each eye were quite independent of the other in its reaction to light; because, apart from the fact that no adjustments of fixation take place during the first days after birth, one can screen one of the infant's eyes without interfering at all with its co-ordinated eye-movements [63]. This fact becomes even more convincing as a support of nativism, in as much as the new-born infant often moves both hands or both legs at once, and when these movements are co-ordinated at all they always take place symmetrically—that is, in opposite directions; never in the same direction. The hands, for instance, are moved towards one another or apart from one another, but never simultaneously to the right or to the left. Indeed, Hering calls attention to the fact that it is not easy even for an adult to move the hands quickly to and fro at the same time in the same direction [64]. Let the reader try this experiment for himself and he will be astonished to find how difficult it is. On the other hand, even infants can move their eyes in the same direction with the greatest ease at every turn of the gaze from right to left, or from left to right. Consequently the co-ordination of the eyes can not be altogether a result of practice, but must have its foundation in an inherited disposition. In support of this conclusion it may be added that unco-ordinated eye-movements usually occur under conditions favourable to impulsive movements, such as those observed when the child is placed in a warm bath. Likewise in older children, unco-ordinated eye-movements have been observed when they are asleep. Furthermore, an experiment with animals, involving direct stimulation of the *corpora quadrigemina,* a nucleus of the "old" brain, always results in co-ordinated eye-movements.

From this last fact, the inference may be drawn that co-ordinated eye-movements are called forth by the central organ of the brain, and that atypical, non-co-ordinated movements have a quite different origin, and have nothing specifically to do with vision [65]. If we recall what has already been said regarding impulsive movements, we shall find a warrant for adding the unco-ordinated eye-movements to this group of responses.

Our conclusion is that an extreme empiricism certainly can not be maintained, since inherited disposition must play a part in the co-ordinated movements of the eyes. So far, at least, agreement may be said to have been reached by all investigators. But the question remains unanswered as to how large a part inheritance plays in the co-ordination of the eyes, and to how great an extent practice and experience contribute their influence—a question which is apparently unanswerable at the present time [66].

Let us turn, then, to a consideration of the problem of fixation. Here the case is different, because ordinarily one finds no evidence of visual fixation in the irregular wandering of the newly-born infant's eyes. Only after the second week does the visual world appear to exercise a definite influence upon the infant's eye-movement.

If, at about this time, a glittering or lighted object is brought before the child's eyes, its gaze ceases to wander the moment the object is directly in the line of vision; the eyes become fixated and the child then *stares* at the object. This behaviour occupies the child profoundly. Under certain circumstances the infant can even be induced in this way to stop crying. This "passive" fixation—so-called because it is produced by an inter-ruption of movement—persists for several weeks, being followed by an "active" fixation which appears for the first time about a week after passive fixation. Active fixation can be demonstrated in two ways: (1) When

74

an impressive object is introduced into the periphery of the child's field of vision from a position where it was invisible, at once there occur movements of the eyes fixating the object. The eyes must then assume an entirely different position in order that the object may now be focused upon the fovea of each of them. Or (2) one can induce the child to stare, as described above, and then slowly move the object being stared at to one side. The child then follows the object with his gaze. I can not agree with Bühler that these two experiments amount to the same thing; for in the first one the stimulus is a stationary object lying at one side; while in the second it is a moving object in the centre of vision. Although it may be quite true that even adults follow a movement with the gaze by fits and starts, so that the eye is always following small displacements of the object from the middle toward one side or the other, still a moving object is never the same as an object at rest. The conditions of movement are therefore different in the two cases.

At any rate, an active fixation is now possible, although it may not be perfect at first. For instance, the eye-movements occasionally overshoot the mark, or fall short of it.

J. B. Watson has recently reported some experiments [67] in which about twenty infants were tested from the first day after birth by exposure to light in a dark room. The tests show that when conditions are favourable, the eyes turn towards the source of light whether it be at the right, left, above, or below. The test-light was moved upon the arm of a perimeter, whose radius was one-half a metre, in a room otherwise dark. Unfortunately, the description of the tests does not indicate whether the light was moved from an initial position at the centre, or was first exposed laterally.

The result was that only two of the twenty infants—one of which could not be kept awake—failed to give a positive reaction. All the rest reacted frequently,

75

though not always, even when the light was removed as far as 20° from the central position. It was noted, however, that lateral eye-movements were more complete than up-and-down movements. While Watson does not maintain that a true fixation is implied in these tests, it is obvious that his experiments deal with an early stage of this process.

Both nativists and empiricists can base arguments upon these facts in support of their respective points of view. The empiricist can refer to the gradual improvement of the act of fixation in comparison with its initial imperfection ; while the nativist can call attention to the fact that the time taken for learning this act would be much too short—considering the difficulty of the task—were there not already present some inherited foundation, such as appears to be indicated by Watson's tests. Thus, to the empiricist the observed development is regarded as a process of learning ; while the nativist regards it as a process of maturation.

Because of this conflict, investigators now tend to accept both factors and to admit that inheritance and acquisition are alike involved without attempting to limit the participation of either [68].

But what does it mean to say that the movements of fixation result from an inborn pattern ; or, in other words, that they are true reflexes ? The behaviour consists in turning the eye so that a stimulus anywhere in the field of vision will be brought to its centre ; or, stated differently, an image of a luminous point anywhere on the periphery of the retina acts as a stimulus for movement which brings the point to a focus upon the fovea. "When carefully examined, these processes reveal a complicated and finely differentiated system of interconnections between the impressions of light upon separate points of the retina and the specialized impulses of eye-movements. Strictly speaking, a different movement must arise from every retinal point ; *therefore, every fibre of the optical nerve must have a different*

76

*central connection with the motor nerves which innervate eye-movements*" [69]. This statement of Bühler agrees entirely with what we have already learned about the reflex-apparatus, but the conditions must actually be much more complicated, as the following consideration will show. Assume that the gaze of a child is first of all directed straight ahead upon a point A (see Fig. 3). There appears now in the same plane a point of light at B on the right. The eyes will then move so that this point falls upon the fovea. If now another point of light $B_1$ is introduced vertically above B, the eyes will move upward and fixate it. Let us assume that the eyes are again directed upon A, after which a point $A_1$ is flashed vertically above it. In passing from A to $A_1$ the same retinal position will be affected which received $B_1$ when the gaze was first directed upon B. Again there is an upward movement of the eyes to effect the fixation of $A_1$; but although in this case $A_1$ stimulates the same retinal point which in the case of the first retinal movement from B to $B_1$ was stimulated by the point $B_1$, yet the two movements are not at all the same, because the movement from A to $A_1$ and that from B to $B_1$ require different innervations of the eye-muscles. What is shown in this special case may be stated in general terms as follows: the innervations which the eye-muscles undergo in movements of fixation are determined, not only by the position of the retinal points which arouse the movement, but also by the pre-existing position of the eyes. It therefore follows that every sensory fibre must possess not merely one connection with the motor nerves, but as many as may be required for all possible positions of the eyes. This means an enormous multiplicity of connections, among which those that function in a special instance must always be determined by the position of the eyes.

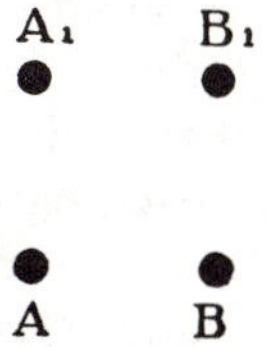

Referring again to our example, it appears that the

A₁    B₁
●     ●

●     ●
A     B

FIG. 3.

movements from A to $A_1$ and from B to $B_1$ are actually different. The optical, centripetal impulses which release the two pass through different connections, and yet each time the movement leads to the same end. In other words, as a result of both movements a point placed above the original point of fixation becomes itself the fixation-point. An internal connection between the same end and the different means whereby it is attained can not exist in the way the general theory of reflex-action has provided; for although the reaction is in each case linked with its stimulus, the sensory and motor processes involved are quite heterogeneous. Accordingly, the question arises in our minds whether any such system of connections can be assumed to be at all probable. And this question persists and, indeed, becomes more insistent when we attempt to explain the movements of fixation in purely empirical terms; for, as we shall see, according to current teaching learning is nothing more than the establishment of these specific connections between neurones. The difference between Nativism and Empiricism does not touch this point, since it refers not to the presence, but only to the establishment of connections, whereas our doubts are directed upon their very existence. Must we then give up any attempt to explain eye-movements? Not at all. We must, however, introduce a new and quite a different hypothesis. We have simply come to a point where modern psychology must relinquish some of its older views, and accept instead certain new principles to which we shall have occasion to recur again and again in this book. Among other things, these principles will also be found to have a significant bearing upon the theory of learning.

Going back to the older theory of eye-movements, we find in the optical sensorium and motorium (I believe these terms will be readily comprehended) two distinct types of apparatus which are bound together simply by a multiplicity of connections. Consequently sensory and motor processes in the optical field will have as much or as little to do with one another as would be the case with any other reflexes. This is the view which dominates to-day, but in opposition to it we find that eye-movements are determined to a very considerable extent by the characteristics of the visual phenomena which are involved. As a proof of this fact, the reflexes of fixation which we have described are merely one example. To mention another, eye-movements are dependent upon the contours of seen-objects. By means of accommodation, the fixation of a contour affords a sharp image upon the retina. These movements of co-ordination are so regulated that, apart from a few unimportant deviations, every position of the two eyes provides for the reflection upon corresponding points of the retina of the largest possible number of external points furnished by the stimulating object ;[70] so that, whatever position the eyes take, a horizontal line passing through the fixation-point will always fall upon a corresponding line on each retina.[71] Briefly stated, the principles according to which our eye-movements are regulated are so determined that our visual perception furnishes the clearest possible purview of surrounding space.

The "beautiful harmony" between the sensory and the motor functions of binocular vision has already been appropriately emphasized by Hering. But so long as all the functions involved were considered to be held together as a mere connection of individual elements, it was impossible to comprehend the significance of this harmony. Is there, then, no other possible conception whereby this harmony can be understood? According to the fundamental work which Wolfgang Köhler [72] has recently published, it appears that there is. But Köhler's conception is of quite a different order from Hering's, and agrees instead with certain ideas which Wertheimer has recently introduced into psychology. What these ideas are will be made clear in later chapters; here we must confine ourselves to the new explanation of eye-movements which they afford. First of all, the assumption is definitely renounced that the relation between sensory and motor functions in optics is a mere system of interconnections ; and with this renunciation go all the consequences of the previous assumptions which we have pointed out on p. 76 f. For instance, we can no longer assume that the sensory function serves merely to release the motor function without involving any *inner* or *material* connection between the two. Instead, the hypothesis is advanced that the specific pattern of the seen-object itself regulates the movements of the eye. From this it follows at once that the optical sensorium and motorium can not be regarded as two independent pieces of apparatus, since for many types of performance they constitute a *unitary organ*—a physical system—within which separate organic parts may react upon other parts. Accordingly, what happens at one point in the organism is never independent of, or without its influence upon, what is taking place at any other point in the organism. What this new conception means to psychology can be revealed only gradually in the course of this book.

Thus we have an entirely new explanation of eye-movements, according to which our optical organ, sensory plus motor, becomes a self-regulating apparatus. By operating upon the motor parts, the sensory event alters its own conditions. This regulation must take place according to exactly determinable and physically predictable laws ; and, indeed, the eye-movements do actually conform throughout with these laws. The alteration of conditions must therefore take place in accordance with the greatest possible simplicity and equilibration of forces ; and the principle of the greatest horopter (cf. p. 79 and note *70*) will be found in harmony with this requirement.

I can perhaps illustrate this self-regulatory process by a simple example. The centre of the field of vision,

80

which corresponds to the *fovea centralis*, is phenomenally as well as functionally a point of outstanding character and significance. Assume an infant lying on its back in a totally dark room, as described in Watson's tests, and allow a light to fall on the peripheral region of its retinæ. The infant's optical system will then be in a state of dis-equilibrium occasioning eye-movements which continue in a certain direction until equilibrium has been re-established. This will be the case when the light falls upon the fovea of each eye—that is, upon the centres of gravity, as it were, in each optical field, which condition the fixation of the light by the eyes.

To go into the matter on its physical side would take us too far afield; but the main point to be noted is this : that a connection between two different functions is possible without the provision of a special mechanism to account for it (cf. pp. 68-70) [73]. I repeat that the reader can not be expected at once to fully comprehend the significance and the importance of this new principle. But when the same ideas have recurred again and again in connection with different problems, this end will have been attained, and the reader can then turn back to these pages and review this section.

One concluding observation is here in place. Eye-movements may still be termed reflexes, although, as we have seen, they can be explained without the assumption of any special mechanism conceived as a system of mere interconnections, which leads us to question whether we can not apply this explanation of eye-movements to all reflexes. We shall only raise the question at this point, but will attempt something in the way of an answer to it in the next chapter.

This much, at least, is clear; that the question whether the empirical or the nativistic theory of eye-movements is right—whether these movements take place according to inherited laws, or whether they must each be learned by individual experience—now assumes an entirely different meaning. Since the visual phenomena themselves, or at least their physical correlates, regulate eye-movements by virtue of their specific qualities, it follows that in the course of development eye-movements must depend upon the phenomena which go with them. Progress in any performance, such as visual fixation which we have been discussing, will therefore be partly conditioned by the progress made in the act of seeing itself. Here again Empiricism and Nativism are opposed as bitterly as ever, but a decision between them can be reached only after we have taken up the problem of learning.

Returning now to the list of the reflexes found in new-born infants, a few more examples may be added.

(b) *Ear-Reflexes.*—In the beginning specific reactions to auditory stimuli are lacking (cf. p. 121), but during the third or fourth month—sometimes even in the second month—a response is developed that appears to be like the eye-movements of fixation, when the infant turns his head in the direction of a sound. In Preyer's son this reaction had attained "the regularity of a reflex-movement" in the sixteenth week. According to Miss Shinn's observations, turning the head towards a sound at the right or left is executed much more promptly and accurately than towards a sound located above or below; the latter adjustment being made with considerable difficulty by her niece even at the end of the second year. We now know that the localization of a sound to the right or left depends upon the time-sequence in which the sound-waves issuing from the source of sound strike the right and left ear, respectively. Since a sound coming from the median plane between the two ears strikes them simultaneously the act of turning the head has the effect of bringing about this condition which appears to be a simplification of the excitatory processes in the brain-centres where the separate excitations of the two auditory nerves are united. Again, as in the case of eye-movements, the system alters its own conditions in the direction of maximal simplicity. The advantages of this hypothesis are obvious, especially in view of the difficulty involved in constructing a satisfactory hypothesis in terms of bonds of connection ; for what would the bond connect ? An impulse to move with a difference in time ? According to our hypothesis the amount of the difference in time determines the magnitude of a movement requisite to abolish the difference, and to permit the two ears to hear the sound simultaneously.

The greater effectiveness of right-and-left over up-and-down localization lends support to this interpretation ; so also does another observation made by Miss Shinn that *continuous* sounds, such as playing on the piano (forty-fifth day), were the first auditory stimuli to cause the turning of her niece's head, whereas brief sounds like sneezing did not occasion this reaction until the ninety-second day.

Miss Shinn not only records the turning of the head, as Preyer does, but also the direction of the child's gaze. Further investigation is needed to elucidate this point; but even if Miss Shinn's observations are correct it is possible that the direction of the child's gaze was a visual effect secondary to, and dependent upon, the original adjustment of the head to sound. The observation of the child's turning her head at so early a date as the forty-fifth day, lends weight to such an interpretation, yet it is also possible that even at this time the visual and auditory sense-organs are so intimately connected that in turning the head in re-action to a sound the eyes are at the same time freed to look straight ahead.[74]

(c) *Skin-Reflexes.*—A considerable number of reflexes are aroused by stimulation of the skin. Among these, one that is typical of the new-born infant is the so-called Babinski-reflex, which after a few weeks is supplanted by the plantar reflex and does not again appear in the normal adult. If one touches the sole of a new-born infant's foot, the toes are stretched upwards and

# THE NEW-BORN INFANT

outwards. This is the Babinski-reflex. If the same stimulus is applied later in life it causes the toes to move downwards and press together, which is the plantar reflex.

The Babinski-reflex appears to have a protective, or flight, character. A similar reflex can be released in infants by touching the eyelids or lashes, which is immediately followed by closing the lids. In the sense of a positive adaptation, still another reflex is effective, even in the case of an infant without a cortex. If one touches the palm of an infant's hand, the fingers close about the object with which the hand has come in contact. In this connection one should also mention the remarkable reaction which the Americans call the "clinging" or grasping reflex. In the hand-closing reflex the child exercises an extraordinary force. In America, Robinson has made a special study of this reaction, and has found that a great many infants, not yet an hour old, will grasp a small stick so tightly with their fingers that one can raise them in the air. Twelve newly-born infants hung thus for half a minute, like gymnasts on a horizontal bar, and three or four held on for fully a minute.[75] As an addendum to these remarks, it may be noted that the vegetative processes take their normal course from the beginning, although breathing and the pulse-beat are much quicker and less regular in infants than in adults. Reflexes, such as sneezing and coughing, have also been observed during the first days after birth.

## § 6—*The Suckling Instinct, and the Primary Characteristics of Instinctive Movement*

We shall pass over further details concerning the reflexes and turn to a third group of movements. Up to the present we have not touched upon one of the most frequent, most important, and most characteristic of the infant's forms of behaviour: its mode of nourishment by suckling. Immediately after birth the child is

84

able to suckle and swallow its milk. When the nipple is placed between its lips this characteristic behaviour either begins at once, or within a few minutes, during which less appropriate movements are being made. Suckling is not so simple a reaction as it might at first seem; for it requires the exact co-operation of the muscles involved. The lips must surround the nipple so as to exclude air, and the movements of sucking must take place with a rhythm of the contracting and expanding muscles which is in time with the movements of swallowing; and yet "of all the movements of the 'suckling,' hardly any is so perfect from the beginning as that which gave him his name." [76]

The sucking movement is not continued indefinitely, nor until fatigue sets in; for when the infant has taken a sufficient amount of nourishment it refuses the breast and will no longer suck even if one places the nipple again in its mouth. When, on the other hand, a child is hungry or in want of food, sucking is induced not alone by the nipple, for the infant will also suck a finger or the cheeks of its mother or nurse whenever its lips come in contact with them; showing that it is not necessary to introduce milk into the mouth in order to stimulate the reaction. Not that any object placed in the mouth will necessarily be sucked; for, as Preyer has pointed out, the object must not be too large or too small, too hot or too cold, too bitter or too salty. It is likewise important that the milk should be of a proper consistency, otherwise the act of sucking is interrupted. Thus Preyer reports that on the fourth day his child refused cow's milk thinned with water, which on the second day he had taken without hesitation, and not until a small amount of sugar had been added could he be induced to receive the nourishment. This behaviour of suckling is likewise evinced in infants without a cortex. The child described by Edinger and Fischer also "took the breast at once and sucked properly from the beginning." A certain difference between normal

85

children and idiots, especially those lacking a cortex, seems to be indicated by the fact that normal children perfect the act in so short a time that, as Preyer reports, it takes place with machine-like regularity after about two weeks. According to the observations of Sollier, no improvement in the performance is observable in cases of congenital idiocy. The response appears, says Sollier, as though it were each time new to the infant.[77] As for the child without a cortex reported by Edinger and Fischer, it ceased to take the breast altogether during the sixth week of its life and thereafter had to be fed with a spoon. Feeding it in this manner, the attentive mother noticed during the fourth month that the child made slight movements of sucking, which suggested that she should try it with a bottle. This proved successful, moreover the child would suck the bottle only when there was milk in it.

Whether a normal infant seeks the breast from the start is uncertain. But it is unable to find the nipple without assistance, though it succeeds in doing so after a few days, probably with the aid of smell—at least this is the only cue one can think of in the case of congenitally blind dogs in which this capacity has also been observed. After approaching the breast, however, the tactual sensitivity of the lips probably also plays a part.

At first view, suckling seems to be a reflex action. It takes place, in the beginning at least, as a reaction to a stimulus ; its course is quite regular, it belongs to the congenital dispositions, and it is eminently useful in the preservation of the species. A closer consideration, however, reveals several important differences from the reflexes. In the first place, suckling, as already noted, is a relatively complicated act ; which, however, in view of the indefiniteness of the statement, is not a very important difference. But in the second place, the relation of the response to its stimulation is in several respects different from that usually found in reflexes.

(a) The movement depends upon the stimulus in

the sense of being adapted to it, not merely because the reaction proves to be objectively appropriate—as when the pupil contracts more to a strong light than it does to a weak light—but because the act of suckling is regulated directly by the formal characteristics of the stimulating object. Thus the position of the lips in sucking must be different according as it is the breast nipple, a rubber nipple, an adult's finger, or the child's own finger, which is being sucked.

(*b*) Fine differences in the stimulus-complex may lead to opposite reactions (sucking or rejecting the nipple), which are sometimes of biological importance— as, for instance, the proper constitution of the milk to be taken.

(*c*) Aside from fatigue, the operation of a stimulus alone is not a sufficient condition for the appearance of the reaction. In addition, there must be a particular state of the organism as a whole—in this case a want of food ; for we observe that the satiated infant no longer sucks, but rejects the nipple. Characteristic as are these differences, they would scarcely have sufficed to distinguish a special group of movements from the reflexes, were it not that certain modes of behaviour have been discovered in the study of animals which originate neither in experience nor in deliberation. These are called *instinctive* movements, and suckling can be assigned to this group.

It will serve our present purpose to mention a few typical instinctive actions of animals [78]. A chick which has just broken from its shell pecks at any small object in its neighbourhood. This action requires no example from the hen or from another chick. Chicks hatched in an incubator act in this respect like those hatched in the natural way. The chick pecks only at objects of a certain size, such as grain, caterpillars, etc., that chance to be within its reach ; otherwise it pecks without distinction and with surprising accuracy. This complicated movement is perfectly developed within a

87

short time, though at first the defect may be noticed of pecking a little to one side of the object—missing it, however, only by a hair's-breadth. On the whole, pecking affords an instance of an extraordinarily precise co-ordination of optical stimuli with impulses that control a large group of muscles.

Another example is this: Birds that have been reared in an artificial nest without parent birds commence building their own nests when brooding time approaches. For this purpose they employ every kind of suitable material, even including some which is not available under natural conditions, such as cotton wadding, coloured woollen, etc. The nest resulting from the use of these materials has, however, a form that is *typical for the species of bird*. Thus the swallow builds a different nest than the thrush. Without ever having seen a nest, and without an opportunity to imitate the nest-building activities of others of its kind, a swallow reared under artificial conditions constructs the same kind of nest built by swallows that have grown up in freedom. It is unnecessary to emphasize the fact that we are here dealing with a very complicated performance. The nests of birds are often true works of art, as is shown in the case of the reed-warbler which, building its nest in the reeds, must make it deep enough so that the eggs will not fall out even when the wind bends the supporting reed to the water's edge.

A third and final example may be given of a squirrel taken from its hole high up in a tree immediately after birth, and reared thereafter under artificial conditions. At first the animal was nourished with milk and biscuit, but one day it was offered a nut—the first it had ever seen in its life. The squirrel examined the nut attentively and then gnawed around it until the kernel was exposed and devoured. Afterwards, whenever the squirrel was freed in the room it was observed that if more nuts were about than the animal could eat at one time, a nut would often be seized and "cached."

88

The animal would first look carefully around the room, and then run to some protected place—behind a sofa leg, or to a cavity in the foot of a carved table—and place the nut in the chosen spot. This behaviour terminated with the movements characteristic of burying a nut, and also of pressing the earth firmly over it. The squirrel would then go about its usual affairs quite undisturbed by the fact that the nut would still be wholly exposed to view. In order to comprehend this behaviour one must know that under natural conditions squirrels do actually conceal nuts in this manner. They hide their nuts two or three centimetres under the ground, recovering them later by the aid of smell. But the animal whose actions we have been reporting had never in its life been upon the open ground [79].

These examples are typical of instinctive activities, and demonstrate that a living being can behave in a manner peculiarly suited to its own existence, or even necessary to the perpetuation of its species, without any relevant experience whatsoever. These acts are never quite simple—being for the most part extremely complicated—and the relation of the activity to its stimulus is not at all simple. As demonstrated by the nature of the behaviour when it takes place under conditions very different from those of the normal habitat, the result of the action must be entirely unknown to the animal, and yet the animal *works towards a definite end*, and ceases only when this end—in so far as the conditions will permit—has been achieved. For example, the hen stops pecking when it is satiated, and the squirrel stops scraping when the nut is buried. It is quite impossible to interpret these examples as evidence against the conclusion we have reached, by saying, for instance, that the squirrel is really quite unconcerned about the end, and merely performs a series of movements determined once and for all, which cease as soon as the series has run its course. That would be a quite unjustifiable generalization of behaviour under unnatural conditions applied to behaviour under normal conditions. Since the nut can not be buried in the room, the usual achievement is impossible. But in the open country it is certainly not one and the same series of movements that lead always to the same end. How the squirrel must dig depends upon the nature of the soil, and its scratching and scraping must be different in firm and in loose earth, in dry and in damp earth, etc.

None of these activities is simple, and all are extensive movement-complexes. Think how many and how varied are the movements requisite in nest-building; yet all are adapted to the surroundings just as suckling is adapted to the reception of nourishment. It is activities of this kind—found in their most complete form in insects—which we term *instinctive*. But we must be careful not to take this name as being an explanation of the behaviour itself. It is all too easy to believe that a real explanation can be avoided by merely labelling the action *instinctive*. Surely the term *instinct* removes from these activities nothing of the mystery or incomprehensibility which they arouse in the mind of an unprejudiced observer; and from this point of view science must admit that instinct is still an unsolved puzzle.

We now see why we did not classify suckling with the reflexes, but instead placed it among the instincts; for instinctive action furnishes criteria which differentiate suckling from the reflexes (p. 87), both in its relation to a previously unknown achievement, as indicated by seeking and rejecting, and by the presence of extensive movement-complexes.

### § 7—*Instincts as Chained Reflexes. Thorndike's Theory*

When we were trying to explain reflexes in the preceding paragraphs (p. 68), we asked ourselves how an organ must be constructed in order that its function might be reflexive. We now ask the same question in regard to instinctive movements. How can we conceive a mechanism for the instincts?

The answer to this question promises to be much more difficult than it was in the case of the reflexes, and, indeed, there is no universally accepted theory of instinct. Many investigators have given up attempting to explain it, finding in instinct an unsolved, and perhaps an insoluble riddle (Stern). One answer has been given to the question so frequently, however, that we must give heed to it. This answer is that instinctive action is nothing more than a series of reflex-actions; more specifically, instincts are chained reflexes. A stimulus excites a reflex-movement starting the instinctive action. This movement either acts as the stimulus for a new movement or else occasions new stimuli from without which act upon the individual and in turn excite new movements. So it goes until the instinctive action is complete. For example, the hungry lion sets out upon a hunt for prey. The organic processes of hunger touch off the movements of search for the prey. The lion begins to stalk the prey as soon as he is made aware of its approach by one of his sensory organs. He springs upon the hunted animal as soon as he comes near enough to it; and finally, he devours it as soon as his claws and teeth touch it. Thus each movement leads to the arousal of a new stimulus which in turn excites a new movement. We have taken this example from the vivid account of William James who, among psychologists, was one of the chief supporters of this point of view [80], which originated with Herbert Spencer. The view is supported to-day in comparative psychology by the behaviourists, as we have already seen. In Watson's book entitled *Behaviour* we read that "an instinct is a series of chained reflexes" [81].

The same view is presented with remarkable cogency by Thorndike, who applies it throughout in his psychology of human development. Our consideration may therefore be based upon his statement of the theory.

Thorndike teaches, as does the behaviouristic school in general, that every act of behaviour is a reaction to a situation, and that the act consists of three component parts: First the situation, within as well as without the body, which stimulates the individual; secondly, the reaction, a process within the individual which is a result of this stimulation; and lastly, the bond which makes this connection between the situation and the response possible. This, however, is nothing more nor less than the reflex-scheme as we already know it (see p. 68); though it has undergone a notable extension in the scope of its application so as to cover all acts of intelligence [82]. We shall consider this extension later; for the present we have only to deal with inherited modes of behaviour. These are characterized by the fact that the connection between situation and response is determined unequivocally by the order and arrangement of the neurones. One sees, therefore, that from this point of view there can be no form of inherited behaviour which is essentially different from the reflexes. With this in mind it is clearly inappropriate to describe the instincts by reference to the ends they serve. Instead, one ought to characterize them with reference to the stimuli which call them forth. When one attributes an instinct of self-preservation to an animal, this description is just as inappropriate as if one were to attribute to oxygen an instinct to produce rust.

The mechanism of an instinct is therefore regarded as a system of reflex-arcs (see p. 69), although it has not yet been explained why the instinctive acts have so close a relationship to the ends they serve; for it was precisely here that we found the chief characteristic which distinguishes them from reflex-movements.

We may now add a few words to the statement already made on this subject. When we compare different situations which give rise to the same instinctive activities, we find that the alterations of behaviour corresponding to differences in the situation are of such a nature as to secure the same result in a manner conformable to the changed conditions. In carrying a heavy stick of building material to its nest, a bird must make other movements than in carrying a lighter stick. Such modifications of behaviour may take place easily and immediately. On the other hand, it may be that the original movement is first carried out and, if it proves inappropriate to the new situation, it may then be altered and the alteration continued until the result is attained—excepting, of course, cases where attainment is impossible. An example of this method of procedure is found in the act of suckling; for if the milk-bottle is stopped up sucking becomes stronger and more energetic. This peculiarity of instinctive movement is of the greatest importance. Lloyd Morgan has termed it " persistency with varied effort."

Thorndike tries to construct his theory so that it will embrace this feature of instinctive behaviour. The chief problem, as he sees it, is to find out why the reactions vary in the same situation and cease only when an end is attained. But from the point of view of the reflex-arc theory, two different problems are here involved. One might explain variation by the application of Thorndike's hypothesis that the reflex-arc is not a simple mechanism, since the centripetal branch is connected in varying degrees of intimacy with numerous centrifugal branches, so that, in point of fact, different reactions corresponding to different connections function successively. Further assumptions are, of course, necessary to cover the serial order of the different movements; but the explanation is still incomplete, for why does the alteration of movement take place in the direction of a special consummation, or end?

Here Thorndike advances a new hypothesis. We might suppose that as long as the end is not attained, the stimulus persists and continues to be effective. It must be explained, however, why the stimulus does not always call forth the same reaction until exhaustion sets in, instead of which the animal's behaviour leads finally to a successful response. Thorndike assumes here, as a part of the inherited disposition of the organism, that certain conditions are tolerated without opposition, or are even actively supported and maintained, whereas other conditions are naturally avoided or modified [83]. These conditions he calls "original satisfiers" and "original annoyers." As examples of "original satisfiers," he cites: "To be with other human beings rather than alone"; "To rest when tired"; "To move when refreshed." As examples of annoyers, he gives, "Bitter substances in the mouth"; "Being checked in locomotion by an obstacle"; "Being looked at with scorn by other men."

Since a collection of examples, however complete, affords less understanding than a law from which these examples can be derived, Thorndike formulates his law in the following terms: "For a conduction-unit ready to conduct, to do so is satisfying and for it not to do so annoying," which, however, only brings us back again to our original problem; for the result it was intended to explain appears again in the explanation. Without arguing in a circle, this explanation is tenable only by recourse to the behaviour of the neurones. A situation may release a number of movements which are completely determined by inherited disposition. It is a function of this inherited disposition, however, not only to release movements, by conducting the nervous impulse over pathways, but also to set other pathways in readiness for conduction when their time comes. And hence, something is still wanting before James's example of the lion has been completely accounted for (cf. p. 91). If the lion is stimulated to stalk its prey by the scent of the animal, the chain of neurones that will later regulate the act of springing upon the prey must at the same time be set in readiness. Likewise, the system

94

of nervous pathways upon which the still later activities of rending and devouring are dependent must in some degree be aroused at the very beginning of the hunt. If the act is completed, these nervous pathways which are in a state of readiness actually become functional; but if the act is not completed, they remain inactive. Thus the conclusion is reached that a functioning of neurones in a state of readiness is satisfying to the system of neurones involved,—or, as Thorndike says, to the *conduction-unit*—whereas not to function, when in a state of readiness, is annoying. There is also the opposite state in which a pathway may be either unready to conduct, or in such an unfavourable condition that conduction meets with resistance, so that when forced to conduct, the act is likewise annoying.

Thorndike is now faced with the problem of applying these laws to all situations which are originally satisfying or annoying. We shall not follow him in his task, which involves many hypotheses, but will proceed at once to estimate what has been gained by his theory for a solution to the problem of instinct, and especially its characteristic "persistency with varied effort." A principle already mentioned aids Thorndike at this point; for the situation is supposed to release not one reaction alone, but a large number of different reactions. If the first act does not achieve the end but, instead, produces annoyance, then other possible reactions will be released by this failure and by what remains of the original situation, so that finally satisfaction is obtained; unless, to be sure, fatigue sets in and the animal abandons the attempt. This principle is found to be applicable in the explanation of "varied effort," because variation is attributed to the annoying situations, while cessation is attributed to the satisfying situations.

Two points are to be noted in this attempt to solve the problem of instinct. In the first place Thorndike's theory provides that so long as unsuccessful movements

95

are being made, they are always succeeded by others, determined by the situation and by the interconnections of the neurones, until finally an end is achieved. Yet the substitution of one movement for another is in no wise determined with reference to a goal, but altogether by the neurone-connections laid down in the organism. The theory is therefore *mechanistic*, in the sense explained above (p. 69). The question immediately arises: How can a movement follow upon another that is unsuccessful? According to Thorndike the answer would be this: The peculiar annoyance arising from an act, together with the remainder of the old situation, creates a new situation with a new set of reactions which it releases. But we have here the same difficulty we met with in the case of eye-movements; for apparently there must be an infinite number of connections. Let us see how Thorndike himself describes the behaviour of a hungry kitten confined in a small cage with food in sight outside the bars. Having never been placed in such a situation before, the kitten "tries to squeeze through any opening; it claws and bites at the bars or wire; it thrusts its paws out through any opening and claws at everything it reaches; it continues its efforts when it strikes anything loose and shaky; it may claw at things within the box. It does not pay very much attention to the food outside, but seems simply to strive instinctively to escape from confinement. The vigour with which it struggles is extraordinary. For eight or ten minutes it will claw and bite and squeeze incessantly." [84]

To ask what is the stimulus for this response, and to expect an answer in terms of the total situation, including the states of readiness in the neurones whereby the stimulus is supposed to release movements according to predetermined inherited pathways, seems a wholly inadequate statement of the case.

Erich Becher suggests other considerations. [85] The situation which releases the instinctive action is frequently of such a character that it may be resolved at different times into quite different stimulating elements, and yet, taken as a whole, the result remains the same. This is illustrated by the following example. Spiders of a certain kind possess an instinct which causes them to flee from bees, and they do so at the very first sight of a bee. Now Dahl has shown that no particular colour, odour, or size serves as an effective stimulus for these movements of flight on the part of the spider. Although the bee is unequivocally defined as a real object, it is not defined as a stimulus producing a definite retinal image; because the bee appears differently when seen from the front, from behind, or from the side, and also differently from above and from below. The effective elements of stimulation must therefore differ in accordance with the position the bee occupies with respect to the spider. Yet movements of flight are released even when the bee occupies the most unusual positions. Here we have an endless number of possibilities of stimulation by the same object; consequently, if the instinct-apparatus is conceived as a system of predetermined paths, these pathways must be almost infinite in number. Just how this problem can be solved is, of course, another matter, but the significance of this objection to the Spencerian theory of instincts can scarcely be denied.

On the other hand, Thorndike's theory is a positive contribution to the subject, in as much as his doctrine of satisfying and annoying situations furnishes the nucleus of a solution by the support it gives to a principle that can be expressed in the following terms: Physiological processes take place both in the form of "closed" and "unclosed" responses. This principle appears in Thorndike's work only in a special form which is closely interwoven with all his other assumptions, but it is a principle of the greatest significance in the explanation, not only of instinctive acts, but of behaviour in general.

§ 8—*A Contribution to the Theory of Instinct, Looking Towards the Abandonment of the Alternative Views of Mechanism and Vitalism. Instincts and Reflexes*

The Spencerian Theory, taken over by Thorndike, is entirely inadequate without a reinterpretation of behaviour in terms of "closed" and "unclosed" physiological systems; but even so it still has certain incurable defects. We must, therefore, try to understand instinctive action without the hindrance of any theoretical presuppositions. In order to do so we must distinguish between instinctive and reflexive actions even more closely than we have already done. We found reflex-action to be well adapted to the simple reflex-apparatus. Following Stout we can now supplement our earlier statements in three ways:

1. A chain of reflexes must consist of a number of separate part-activities determined in a purely objective manner by the order of the system of neurones laid down in the organism. If we name these single part-activities *a*, *b*, *c*, . . . then *b* is carried out because it is stimulated either directly by *a* or by a stimulus that becomes effective through *a*, and *c*, in turn, has the same relation to *b* that *b* has to *a*. In short, every successive part-activity stands only in relation to the immediately preceding activity, or to its effects. Moreover, if we accept Thorndike's hypothesis of readiness, the particular act may be conditioned by many or all of the preceding part-activities. Yet when we consider a typical instinctive action as it appears in the natural course of an animal's life, the impression is not at all that of a summation of part-activities which have in themselves nothing to do with one another. On the contrary, an instinctive activity takes a *uniform course*: it is a *continuous* movement; it does not appear as a multiplicity of separate movements, but as one articulate whole embracing an end as well as a beginning. Every member of this activity seems to be determined,

not only by its position with reference to what has gone before, but also with reference to all the members of the completed act,—especially to the last phase which leads to the result. An instinctive activity does not make the same impression upon us as does a succession of tones, for instance, which a playful child might produce by pressing the keys of a piano in irregular succession; but, instead, is like a melody. We can also describe the facts in this way: An instinctive reaction is *adapted* to its stimulus; it is not merely set off by it. And this truth applies not merely to the end, but to the reaction as a whole. We have already referred to the fact that an instinctive reaction directs itself upon the situation which arouses it. Under certain circumstances, obstacles interfering with its progression are set aside, while the tendency persists, with varied effort and by varying means, until the end is attained. Consider the building of a nest. One can not say at any particular stage in its construction that the bird will now make this or that movement; one can say, however, that the bird must now fulfil this or that requirement.

I wish it understood that these statements are intended as an unprejudiced description, without theoretical presuppositions. The truth of our description can therefore freely be admitted, even though one sees fit to maintain that in reality the behaviour is something quite different. It is also significant that descriptions of this sort are not only suitable for instinctive actions, but also for higher types of behaviour which we call acts of intelligence[86]. We shall, therefore, employ such descriptions frequently in what follows. Yet the reader need not hesitate to accept our description through fear of being led into a false theoretical conclusion; for, of course, one can not infer from this agreement between instinct and intelligence that an intelligent consciousness must participate in instinctive action—an inference which has been drawn, for instance, by Stout. On the other hand, it would be equally inadmissible to pass this similarity over and leave it out of consideration [87].

2. While reflexes are typically "passive" modes of behaviour, which depend upon the fact that some stimulation has taken place, instinctive behaviour is, by contrast, significantly "active" in its search for stimuli. The bird *seeks* the material for its nest, and the predatory animal *stalks* its game.

3. Instinctive activity is constantly controlled by the sense-organs. The situation which presents itself to the sense-organs, after a movement has taken place, determines the continuation of the movement; but success and error are differentiated, so that varied activities may lead to a single goal.

From all of which it appears that the instinctive activities are much more like voluntary activities than they are like pure reflexes. At any rate, they possess the same forward direction that is characteristic of voluntary action.

One might object that such a forward direction could only be given if the animal already knew the goal towards which he was striving. In the case of voluntary action this knowledge is presupposed, but not so in the case of instinct, where the animal must direct his course without any previous knowledge of the end. How, then, is it possible to strive for a goal of which nothing is known? To this question Stout gives the right answer. One can quite well be directed forward without knowing anything of the goal which one is approaching. One can wait, and yet know not what one is waiting for. The present situation appears, therefore, not as one that is constituted thus-and-so, but as one that is constantly undergoing change. It is not a *state*, but a *transition;* not a *being*, but a *becoming*. There is no difficulty in comprehending what this means. From the first scene of a drama one may feel that something terrible is going to happen, and thereafter all that transpires on the stage is merely a preparation for, or a delay in the tragic

*dénouement;* and yet one would not be able to tell what
it is precisely which thus hangs, as it were, in the air[88].
As a simple example, suppose you are listening for
the first time to an unfamiliar melody, which ceases
abruptly before its termination; you will then have
a very clear impression that the music should continue.
Or again, if some one taps the following measure:
. .— . .— . . , the last beat has no finality; the
rhythm ought to go on.  In this instance, the expectation is quite definite, but in the preceding case it is
not altogether indefinite, though the indefiniteness, may
under circumstances be greater than it could possibly
be in the case of a simple rhythmical succession.  Even
in the instance of the drama, the tragic end which hangs
over the audience is not altogether undetermined.  Indeed, expectancy consists, not only in a definite situation
which must change—including a specific change of its
parts—but also in the direction of the change itself,
however indefinite this may be.  For if the course of
action be interrupted in any one of our examples, we
have not merely stopped an external succession of independent processes, we have disrupted a unitary course
of events which, though incomplete at the moment
of interruption, yet bore within itself, and evolved as it
went along, its own law of progression.  Indeed, I
should go further than Stout does; for I think it quite
possible that this is a fair characterization of instinctive
behaviour, so that one might say that the nearer an
animal comes to the end of his instinctive action, the
more clearly and definitely will the directions of change
reveal themselves in the as-yet-incomplete present
situation.

In order to make clear this point concerning the
"inner" behaviour of an animal when it acts instinctively, let us consider the nature of a human instinct.
Suppose some one suddenly hears shrieks which be-
token agony and distress; at once he will move in the
direction from which the shrieks come, and if he finds

the victim who uttered the cries, he will endeavour to render him assistance in his trouble. What is a person's "experience" from the moment he hears the shrieks? One may feel both pity and courage, whereas another, instead of being drawn towards the sufferer, may be tempted to run away. The "inner behaviour" of the individual is therefore *affective*, and the phenomena which accompany his action are of the type called *emotional*. Furthermore, these emotions, or "inner behaviour," fit the external behaviour of the instinctive act perfectly, just as our general conception of behaviour requires that they should. This conception of the relation between instinct and emotion has been developed by William McDougall who writes that "instinctive activity is naturally accompanied by some degree of a general felt excitement; this felt excitement, accompanying the operation of any instinct, is specific in quality to that instinct." And hence, when we run away we feel fear, when we strike out we feel anger, when we spew out we feel disgust. In a recent paper, Lloyd Morgan has expressed similar views [89].

Taking this conception in conjunction with what has been said of the expectant attitude, it is possible to make several important inferences regarding the emotions. It follows, for instance, that the emotions are dynamic phenomena conditioned by time, and it also appears that there is no impassable gulf which separates the affective from the cognitive processes. But these are lines of thought which we can not here pause to follow out.

Returning, then, to our main topic we note the fact that, without starting from any hypotheses, the study of instinctive behaviour, itself, brings us to the same conclusion reached by Thorndike regarding the difference between a closed- or end-situation and a transitional situation. So long as the activity is incomplete, every new situation created by it is still to the animal a transitional situation; whereas when the animal has attained his goal, he has arrived at a situation which to him is an end-situation.

The examples we have given as analogies have nothing to do with Thorndike's theory, yet they indicate how and where we must seek for a true explanation of instinct.

At this point in the discussion we can only indicate the theory we have in mind. From what has been said, it appears that phenomena occur in connections determined by peculiar inherent laws of relationship which have to do with "closure" and "non-closure." To illustrate: Fig. 4 appears at once as an open triangle, although, being open, it does not have three angles. To bring this observation into relation with our terminology we might say that the figure exhibits "non-closure," yet indicates with a relatively high degree of certainty the direction in which "closure" is to be effected.

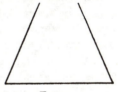

FIG. 4.

When we consider that our phenomena belong to our behaviour, just as all our behaviour is bound up with definite processes of the central nervous system, the conclusion to be drawn from the consideration of instinctive performances is that the characteristics of "closure"—as we shall call it—belong not merely to the phenomena themselves, but likewise to the behaviour taken as a whole, including all reactions made to the environment. Instinctive activity then becomes an objective mode of behaviour analogous to such phenomena as rhythm, melody, and figure.

Now the question arises: how shall we conceive the apparatus of these functions? As our later chapters will show, and as modern psychology is proving day by day, it is quite impossible to identify any scheme of chained neurones with the device needed. But at this point arguments directed against the explanation of instinctive activity in terms of reflexes meet their counterpart in arguments which would deny the whole issue as to an appropriate apparatus for these functions, by an assertion that the events of life can not in any way be traced back to the same laws that dominate the inorganic world. Accordingly, the conclusion has been reached that the operation of a specific "vital force" expresses itself in the events of life by means of energies which are either essentially mental, or, at least, are conceived as being directly related to mind.

This view is called *vitalism* or, in so far as vital and mental energy are identified, *psycho-vitalism*. Köhler has justly remarked that [90] "if one asks what phenomena of experience prompt the vitalists to accept this view, it may be answered that the motive of many can be found in what we have termed 'closure,' both in the organism and in its behaviour."

In the first chapter of this book various objections to a "psychological theory" were set forth; but despite all of these, if the choice lay between a mechanistic or a (psycho-)vitalistic explanation, we should feel obliged to choose the latter, if only in order to avoid the alternative of maintaining an entirely false attitude towards life. This alternative, however, is not forced upon us as Wertheimer was the first to make evident in his new theory of the brain-processes [91]; for if nervous processes correspond to such phenomena as rhythm, melody, and figure—and the pathological cases, in which an injury to the brain renders the creation of such phenomena difficult or even impossible, teach us that nervous processes must have a share in occasioning them—then these same nervous processes must embrace all the essential characteristics of the phenomena in question. Köhler, indeed, has demonstrated that formal qualities belong likewise to inorganic processes in quite the same way in which they are evident in the phenomena we have mentioned.

Again I must confine myself to a few suggestions relative to this subject. We are confronted with two separate problems: (1) Is there any such thing as "closure" in inorganic processes and, if so, (2) Does "closure" exist in such a form that we can regard it as analogous to our distinction between an end- and a transitional situation? The first problem is the more difficult of the two, and Köhler solves it first for processes which are independent of the time-parameter, by demonstrating that states of rest and stationary processes, that is, events which do not alter their characteristics with the passage of time—as, for example, a constant electric current, or the flowing of water in a tube—do, indeed, possess the features of "closure." The reader will not be able to correctly understand the meaning and significance of this proposition until he knows more exactly what is meant by "closure". The meaning, however, will become clearer in the course of further discussion, while, at the same time, the significance of the proposition as we have employed it in this connection will also become more evident.

A solution of the first problem leads at once to the second. Among an endless multiplicity of other conditions and events, stationary or rest-conditions represent those striking instances in which all happenings issue. The distinction of these particular instances may be characterized in two ways: (1) they satisfy certain conditions of energy, and (2) they possess a certain simplicity and compactness, which, in isolated cases, can be defined mathematically—though at present this can not be done in all cases. A concrete example will best explain what we mean. A soap-film is produced upon a wire-frame and upon it a little noose of thread is cast in whatever form it may take. If one proceeds carefully the thread will be supported upon the surface of the film, "but if one pricks the film *inside* the noose with a point, the surface will break apart and the thread will be pulled out by the surface-tension of the outer portion of the film, which seeks to give the area outside the thread the least possible surface, and the area circumscribed by the thread the greatest possible surface. As a result, the thread immediately assumes the form of a circle." In this example we can conceive of circularity as the " end-situation," puncturing the soap-film as the stimulus releasing the movement, and the movement itself as the " transitional situation." The same procedure holds true for all events, and especially for those that issue in the nervous system. Thus inorganic nature includes the possibility of " closed" events—at least in the case of events independent of time—and the distinction of the end- and the transitional situation is as appropriate here as it is in organic behaviour. This fact, to be sure, is not all that is necessary to explain instinct; because the uniformity of instinctive action very obviously suggests that with " closure" the whole temporal course of the activity is involved, and, so far, we have not referred to any dependency upon time. Yet this reservation raises no difficulty in principle; for the same hypothesis which is applicable to stationary events can also be carried over to the events of a dynamic series—although with much greater difficulty as regards details—so that even in the field of physics it can be demonstrated that dynamic processes also exhibit " closure." In psychology it was precisely the dynamic phenomena of seen-movement that furnished the starting-point from which this new hypothesis has developed.

An explanation of instinctive activity is therefore not called upon to discover an inherited system of connected neurones, but rather to investigate what kind of physico-chemical " closure" produces these astonishing types of behaviour, and under what conditions [92]. Although instinct is still a riddle, at least it is no longer one which forces upon us the acceptance of psycho-vitalistic principles [93].

Events which shape themselves toward a definite end are, however, not merely a characteristic of the instincts, but likewise of all truly intelligent actions.

# THE THEORY OF INSTINCT

When I am faced with a problem, I do not rest until I have solved it. The distinction between instinctive and intelligent behaviour must, therefore, be sought in the way in which one arrives at the end-situation from the beginning-situation. In the case of instinct, it is enough to present the beginning-situation to a living being, and at once an activity is started which continues until the end is attained. This, however, is not sufficient in the case of truly intelligent behaviour, whose specific peculiarity will be discussed later on [94].

As we proceed in our study of mental development, we shall constantly be learning more of this same type of process in its most variable forms. Let us now reconsider a result already mentioned. In the explanation of eye-movements we employed these principles which we have now developed in greater detail (see p. 79 f.), although at the time eye-movements were referred to as "reflexive." Think now of the instinctive action of a young chick in pecking. This, to be sure, is a more complicated performance than that of eye-movements. It has, however, this much in common with them—that the pecking - movement is regulated by the optical system, the reactions of which have an important bearing upon the chick's behaviour. When we draw the consequences of this connection, and reconsider pecking as an analogy of reflexive eye-movements, we find that it makes no difference in the result whether we regard pecking as reflexive or instinctive. In either case we must assume that the sensorium and motorium together constitute one system. Whatever takes place in the sensorium influences the motorium, and *vice versa*, because all instinctive activities possess the characteristics of "closure." Thus we have a bridge which carries us over from the instincts to the reflexes. And it is not only the example chosen which suggests this conclusion ; for everywhere one meets with instances concerning which one is in doubt whether they should be classified with the instincts or with the reflexes. For example, a pheasant just emerged from its shell, with its bill smeared with food, will at once proceed deliberately to wipe its bill on the ground.

But if, by emphasizing the common characteristics of both types of behaviour we can now close the gap which previously seemed so wide between the instincts and the reflexes (see p. 87), this does not signify a return to the point of view that instincts are chained reflexes. On the contrary, we have reversed the procedure; for it is no longer the reflexive mechanism which is the fundamental fact of behaviour, but the characteristics of "closure" as they appear most clearly in the instinctive activities. Instead of trying to explain instincts in terms of reflexes, as Spencer and his followers have done, we would explain reflexes as instincts. But the question, wherein the difference arises which leads one in an unprejudiced observation to distinguish so clearly between reflexive and typically instinctive acts, is still open. How do reflexes become fixed mechanical types of work which suggest a mechanistic theory? To this question we can only intimate a direction in which an answer may be found. In addition to the reflexes themselves there are many other modes of behaviour which possess reflexive characteristics in a high degree. These are the so-called automatic activities—habitual movements which have been termed "acquired reflexes," though originally they were not automatic but voluntary acts which only became automatic as a result of frequent repetition. Since their quasi-reflexive character was acquired in this way, we can perhaps assume a similar relationship between the true reflexes and the instinctive activities. If the so-called acquired reflexes can be conceived as fixed voluntary acts, perhaps the pure reflexes are likewise conceivable as a result of instinctive fixation. It is noteworthy that Erich Becher—who rejects a mechanistic theory of instinct, in favour of a psycho-vitalistic theory — adopts this interpretation of the reflexes, and tentatively employs for the reflexes the same principle which he has elaborated in explanation of the instincts [95].

One of the questions already raised has now been answered, in as much as we may assume that the mode of explanation applicable to eye-movements must in principle be applicable to all other reflexes. Yet it does not necessarily follow that the reflexive apparatus of the older theory with its system of neurones must in all cases disappear from the explanation; for it is still conceivable that the fixation of a function may go hand in hand with the fixation of an organ as it develops a system within which the process can take place in a relatively independent manner. But even so, the apparatus itself would not be the cause but the consequence of this kind of functioning. The existence of such an apparatus therefore lends no weight to any argument for the older theory, or against the newer one.

Finally, the problem of the utility of reflexive and instinctive activities must be attacked from quite a different angle than that indicated by the mechanistic theory; because if the beginning and the successful ending of an activity are no longer determined by external bonds, we shall have to conceive the physiological process in such a way that the conclusion of the activity involves a peculiar condition towards which, for physical reasons, the whole process is directed. Let us remember, however, that, as Köhler has recently been able to demonstrate, *physical* does not necessarily signify *mechanical*.

§ 9—*The Instincts of New-Born Infants, with some General Remarks upon the Instincts of Man*

After this lengthy theoretical discussion, we may now return to a consideration of the instinctive movements of new-born infants. The most striking thing to be noted is that the infant makes very few movements, and very few well-developed serial activities which can be called "instinctive." Stern [96] singles out from among the activities of new-born infants an instinctive "attraction" which draws the child towards different stimuli from the very first day of its life. Thus, an infant whose cheek is touched with the finger quickly turns its head in such a way that the finger is brought into contact with its mouth. Even upon the third day after birth, before any actual contact had been made, the nearness of the mother's breast exerted this attraction in the case of Stern's oldest daughter — the stimulus apparently being based upon sensitivity to odour. Similarly, intensive light-stimuli will cause the head to be turned in the direction of the light. As we have already seen, all these movements, and particularly the last one, are closely related to eye-movements.

In possessing a complete picture of the infant's first responses, it is of no great importance whether we follow Stern in accepting the instinct of attraction as being the only one besides suckling which asserts itself during the first weeks of life, or add to these two the movements of avoidance which Preyer observed in his son on and after the fourth day whenever the left breast, which he found it uncomfortable to nurse, was offered to him. Even the addition of other movements, with which we shall become acquainted in the following section of this chapter, affords as an inventory of the instincts functioning from birth only a very paltry list as compared with the instincts of many animals standing much lower in the scale of development. "The really pitiable helplessness of the new-born human being is accounted for by a dearth of ready-made instinct-mechanisms," says Bühler [97]; and this is quite true except that we should not employ the term "instinct-mechanism."

The conclusion that man, in a general way, possesses fewer instincts than any other animal has, however, been disputed. James in particular has tried to demonstrate the contrary. In order to understand how one can entertain James's position, it is necessary to consider briefly certain peculiarities of instinct which we have not yet discussed. In characterizing reflexes as stereo-typed instincts a very important difference between these two modes of behaviour is emphasized; for while typical reflexes, like the pupillary reflex, are not at all influenced by the rest of one's behaviour—if we except the facts of reflexive inhibition and facilitation (cf. above, p. 69)—just the opposite is true of instincts, which are greatly modified by individual experience during the lifetime of the animal. Chicks just hatched from the shell will peck at all sorts of objects within reach, pro-vided they are of a certain size. Hence, if one place before the chick a cinnabar caterpillar, which is readily distinguishable by vision on account of its alternating bands of black and gold, the chick will at once peck at it. But the caterpillar is immediately rejected, and the chick wipes its beak as a token of disgust. If the ex-periment is repeated after an interval of, say, one day, most chicks are already disposed to inhibit pecking before the caterpillar is attacked [98]. Lloyd Morgan has fully described this transformation of an instinct by ex-perience; a transformation which may take place after a single experience. The same investigator has also observed that young birds learn in this way to avoid pecking at their own fresh excrements.

Another example can be given from a much lower stage in the animal series. It is well-known that stereo-typed modes of behaviour, called *tropisms*, can be observed in lower forms of life. These may be char-acterized briefly as a positive or negative behaviour with respect to certain stimuli; that is, some stimuli are sought, while others are avoided. A cockroach possesses a negative photo-tropism, that is to say, it avoids the light and makes its abode in dark places. The experi-ment was made of stimulating a group of these insects, gathered together in the dark, by an electrical shock; the result was that the insects congregated thereafter on the lighted side of their cage. But the original tropism was not necessarily annulled on this account, any more

III

than a chick loses its pecking instinct after an unpleasant experience with a cinnabar caterpillar, and, indeed, when the insects were removed to another and a differently constructed cage, they again took up their position on the darker side [99]. Tropisms are, therefore, subject to modification even with organisms quite low in the scale [100]; but reflexes, such as our pupillary reflex, can not be thus altered.

Returning now to the instincts, an important inference can be drawn from this peculiarity. Since the instincts are influenced by the total behaviour of the organism, it becomes more difficult to recognize them the more numerous are the dispositions an organism may possess and employ other than instinctive. For under these more complicated circumstances a purely instinctive tendency can no longer assert itself, but must operate merely as one among many factors in the total behaviour of the organism. To maintain, therefore, that man is provided with a great abundance of instincts does not mean that we shall find in him, as we do in other animals, a series of relatively fixed courses of movement originally tending towards unknown goals. But it does mean that, despite the enormous individual differences determined by birth and environment, certain general tendencies are still discoverable in human behaviour. And although these tendencies appear in different ways under different conditions, they still give evidence of certain peculiarities common to all men. Needless to say we are not thinking of these tendencies in terms of innate connections between neurones, as Thorndike does in his discussion of all the original tendencies.

For the present this is about all we have to say of human instinct, although the problem of instinct and experience, to which Lloyd Morgan has dedicated an entire book, is overflowing with questions of detail which, if space permitted, could be profitably considered. The reader will find valuable data upon this subject in the works of Thorndike and McDougall, as well as in the book of Lloyd Morgan just referred to. In addition, what James has to say of instinct is so vividly expressed that, although the fundamental differences between his point of view and the one here supported are extreme, the reading of his chapter is, nevertheless, to be highly recommended.

One peculiarity of instinct should be mentioned, however, upon which James placed great emphasis. This is the so-called transitoriness of instincts. Many instincts would seem to have only a limited term of existence. They appear at one definite point of time and disappear at another, although their coming and going is not abrupt but gradual. If these instinctive dispositions are not allowed to function during the course of their existence—if they do not work themselves through the individual's behaviour so as to constitute habits, as we say—they will disappear, never to return. James derived his law from general observation, but it has since been tested by experiment. Yerkes and Bloomfield observed the behaviour towards mice of kittens that had been fed with milk, and with meat and fish, for the most part cooked. In the course of the second month all eight of their kittens, coming from two different strains, showed the normal type of behaviour towards mice—the one strain earlier and the other later—quite like any ordinary cats, although these kittens had never seen a cat react to a mouse. The investigators conclude, therefore, that the instinct to kill mice appears usually at the end of the second month, and sometimes even a month earlier. This investigation is of special interest because, a few years before, another experiment upon the behaviour of cats was carried out in the same laboratory by Berry who, among other things, dealt with this same problem. As a result of his experiments Berry reached the conclusion that, although kittens have an instinctive tendency to run after running things, they must nevertheless *learn* to kill mice, since their instinctive tendency does not carry them to this extent. The apparent contradiction in these results is explained, however, by the fact that Berry's animals were already five months old when they first came in contact with mice. It would seem, therefore, that the instinctive disposition noted by Yerkes and Bloomfield in the second month had by the fifth month disappeared, which gives us a very pretty example of the transitoriness of instincts [101]. Similar exact observations in the case of man are lacking, and whether they are possible, in view of the greater complication of human behaviour, we can not yet say.

It is not our intention to give a list of human instincts. Two-thirds of the first volume of Thorndike's comprehensive work is taken up with a consideration of man's original tendencies, and one may also refer to James for a discussion of this subject. For our part, we prefer to go into a few modes of behaviour appearing early in the course of human development, the instinctive character of which can hardly be doubted, since Köhler has also found them among the chimpanzees. I have in mind especially the instincts of cleanliness and adornment. We shall have to speak about walking as an instinct in the next chapter.

Regarding cleanliness, I will quote Köhler's vivid description [102]. " I have observed but a single member of the species in captivity that was not coprophagous (a fæces-eater), and yet whenever one of them steps into fæces his foot loses its firm hold just as a human being's would in a similar predicament; the animal then hobbles away until an opportunity is found to cleanse the foot, and in cleansing it the hand is never used, although but a moment ago the same substance was being conveyed to the mouth by the hand, the animal refusing to let go even under severe punishment. In cleaning his foot, however, the ape must have a stick or a piece of paper or cloth, and his gestures show unmistakably that the task is a disagreeable one. Indeed, there can be no doubt that the animal's behaviour is that of freeing himself from something nasty. This is also the case whenever any part of the body is dirtied. The dirt is removed as quickly as possible, and so far as my observation extends, it is never removed with the naked hands, but always with the aid of something else, including such methods as rubbing against a wall or upon the ground."

Concerning adornment, Köhler found his animals prepossessed of a tendency to hang all kinds of things upon their bodies, after which "the things hung upon the body functioned as *adornments* in the broadest sense." Köhler believes, indeed, "that primitive adornment does not depend upon its visual effect on others, but exclusively upon a curious heightening of the animal's own bodily feeling, pompousness, and self-consciousness, just as is the case with man when, for example, he drapes himself with a sash. . . ." [103]

It ought not to be difficult to observe similar tendencies in children; the existence of an instinct of adornment in particular might readily be determined with the aid of well-directed observations. [104] To make sure of inherited tendencies of cleanliness will doubtless prove more difficult, since education takes powerful hold upon the child in this respect from the very beginning. It is possible, however, that paradoxes like those observed by Köhler in chimpanzees might also appear in children, though of a less disagreeable nature.

### § 10—*Expressive Movements*

We turn now to a final group of infantile movements which occupy a unique position by virtue of the impression they make upon every one who has anything to do with children. These movements influence one's attitude toward the child, and give rise to the intimate relationship between the infant and the adults who attend him. Crying, laughing, and turning the head away, all of which have been previously mentioned, together with certain other responses we are about to describe, constitute what are commonly referred to as "expressive movements." In the infant these expressions are inborn, being conditioned by inherited disposition. Yet they seem to differ from other instincts, first of all, in that they do not stand in any direct relation to definite consequences. This distinction is not absolute, however, as we have seen in the case of turning the head described by Preyer, which was specified as being instinctive. One may say that crying continues until the child is relieved from a painful situation; but even so, the relation between this reaction and its consequence is a rather loose one, because crying is not of service to the child in the same way as suckling the mother's breast. In adults, most of the expressive movements seem to be entirely useless. Nevertheless the assumption is justified that at some earlier stage of life many of these actions have had significance for the organism. To-day they may have lost their original function, and yet still play an important part in their influence upon the behaviour of others. It is also quite possible that many of these expressions have always served a social purpose. Thus Ordahl observed that when birds feed their young the largest portion always goes to those that cry most and loudest.[105]

In calling these actions expressive movements, it is necessary to warn against a certain misunderstanding; for although the movements to which we refer do express something, so that we are able to observe whether a man is pleased or angry; yet, as a rule, the man himself does not make these expressive movements for the purpose of expressing anything at all. The idea that expressive movements are intentional—which in so crude a form would hardly be advanced by any one —is energetically opposed by Thorndike, who holds that the movements expressive of emotion may, on the one hand, be biologically more important and more original than the emotion itself, and that, on the other hand, while they tend to alter the situation for the reagent, they do not serve as a means of communication. Indeed, according to Thorndike, the social effect of expressive movements may be quite direct. One may be led to comfort a child without first considering that he is unhappy, and when the mother bird gives the most food to that young one that cries the loudest, this also takes place without any deliberation on the part of the parent-bird.

The questions before us are two : How to understand social influences, and what the relation is between emotion and expressive movements. If we are content to fall back upon external inborn connections, as Thorndike does, we find no better explanation than we did in the case of instinctive activity. Furthermore, if "outer" and "inner" behaviour are anywhere actually related, surely the expressive movements must be instances *par excellence*. Can we believe that the emotions have obtained their expressive movements, or that these movements have obtained their emotions, merely by selection based upon fitness?

Reverting to some previous suggestions (cf. p. 21), let us follow Köhler's discussion and try to indicate the nature of the hypothesis needed to fit this case. "If we were to represent behaviour graphically by means of a time-curve, the behaviour of fright might show an abrupt rise in the curve, followed by a gradual fall. The dynamics of the phenomenal or mental processes accompanying this behaviour would then be indicated by a curve of essentially the same character—and so would a purely electro-motor process in a photo-electric element when it is suddenly and briefly exposed to the light." Now let us assume that the terms "abrupt rise" and "gradual fall," used in these three cases, are not merely analogous, but are in some sense identical, " then, in principle at least, it is possible that a material relation exists between the mental processes of a living creature, and the total impression made by movements of the creature's limbs upon one who witnesses the movement." The connection between emotion and movement, including instinctive movement, is thus conceivable in a way which includes an understanding of the expressive movements.

In our first chapter it was noted that certain real entities of behaviour correspond to the total impression which an animal's behaviour makes upon us (cf. p. 21). In addition to other characteristics, no less important in solving this problem, every form of behaviour has a certain articulation or phrasing. This articulation issues from a similar articulation of the central nervous processes of the acting individual. This central articulation in turn corresponds to the individual's "experience" which is articulated in a like manner. Thus the perception in the mind of an onlooker, if it be so constituted as to embrace what is going on in the reagent, must itself possess a similar articulation. And hence the experience of the reagent A, and of the observant B must resemble each other.

Köhler elucidates this point with a striking example: When a pianist moved by his feelings articulates a series of muscular innervations with varying degrees of phrasing, fixed time-relations are determined in the series of sound-waves which constitute a sort of physical projection of the phrasing of his muscular innervations, thus conditioning in the mind of the listener an articulated auditory process which closely resembles the pianist's own nervous articulations [106].

Bühler distinguishes in the first weeks of life four different expressive movements; namely, crying, smiling, head-deflection as avoidance, and pursing the lips. Concerning the first of these it may be remarked that to screaming, which is the sole type of crying at birth, weeping is added after the third week, at which time a true smile likewise appears, although even before this an expression may be observed which Preyer has called "contentment."

"The pursing of the lips, finally, is a peculiar gesture which can be aroused in the first weeks of life by touching the lips of a hungry infant with an object which is immediately withdrawn. The mouth at once takes on the peculiar shape characteristic of sucking. Later on this pursing of the lips may be observed to accompany any kind of attentiveness"[107]. The movement clearly betrays its origin; for, in the first place, it is not an expressive movement, but one directed towards a goal. The lips continue, as it were, to follow the goal even after it has been withdrawn; in this respect the act is quite as instinctive as turning the head.

Lastly, facial grimaces occasioned by sours, bitters, and sweets, also belong to the characteristic expressive-movements which appear at birth.

## § 11—*The Sensitivity of Infants*

We have now surveyed the movements made by a new-born infant. What, then, is the nature of his sensitivity? In other words, what sort of stimuli provoke his reactions, and how do the different senses share in their reception? We have formulated the question of sensitivity very cautiously, because there is no other way of testing the sensitivity of a new-born infant than by observing whether or not a controlled stimulation is followed by a reaction. In experimenting with an adult we can secure direct information whether a certain stimulus has affected him or not—whether, for instance, he has heard something or not. We can ask directly if a certain stimulus has been phenomenally apprehended, and thus limit the reaction to the observer's "inner behaviour." In the case of an infant, however, we are altogether dependent upon the evidence of his external behaviour. We must, therefore, be careful not to confuse the problem of conscious phenomena with that of sensitivity.

# THE NEW-BORN INFANT

From the first all the sense-organs give rise to reflex-movements [108], and hence sensitivity can be attributed to all sense departments, yet the different senses exhibit a great variation with respect both to delicacy and to the differentiation of their response to stimulation. Stern has clearly described these relations [109] and we shall follow his division of the senses into three groups :

### (i) *The Senses of the Skin*

1. Touch shows the greatest differentiation of response, since different reactions take place according to the particular point at which the stimulus is applied. This fact is apparent from numerous reactions with which every one is familiar. A touch in the region of the eyes occasions closing the lids ; a touch on the lips gives rise to movements of suckling ; contact with the palm of the hand causes the hand to close, and contact with the sole of the foot causes a spreading of the toes.

But not all regions of the skin are sensitive in the same degree that they are in adults. According to Preyer, the mucous membranes of the lips and nose are hypersensitive in infancy, while the regions of the trunk, forearm and thighs, are hyposensitive.

2. The end-organs for temperature are to a considerable extent functional at birth. Bathing-water and milk must be of the right temperature or they are refused by the infant.

3. Sensitivity to pain, on the contrary, is subnormal.

### (ii) *The Chemical Senses and Sight*

1. Taste. Here again there are very distinct differences of reaction : sweet substances are swallowed ; while those markedly sour, bitter, or salty, are rejected ; at the same time we can readily observe a characteristic facial expression to sweets, sours, and bitters. Finer discriminations are not long delayed, as was evidenced in the case of Preyer's son who refused thinned cow's milk as early as the fourth day. The infant's preference

120

for sweet things grows continually, so that he may even refuse the breast if the bottle-milk is sweeter.

2. Attraction- and avoidance-reactions can also be aroused by the sense of smell. Turning towards the mother's breast has already been mentioned ; a positive avoidance of the breast can also be induced by smearing it with some evil-smelling substance.

3. We have previously discussed the important re-actions of the eyes, including the pupillary reflex, the closing of the lids upon the incidence of a strong light, and the direction of the eyes toward bright objects. It should be realized, however, that there are enormous differences between the optical adjustments of adults and those of new-born infants. We shall have occasion to refer to a special peculiarity in the visual sensitivity of infants when we come to consider the development of perception. This peculiarity has to do with a remark-able limitation of the field of vision with respect to its extension and depth.

### (iii) *Audition*

The observation of differentiated and specific reactions to auditory stimuli is quite impossible [110]. Intense sounds only provoke shuddering, raising of the eyelids, etc. On the other hand, the infant can be quieted by sound-stimuli (whistling) as early as the first week of its life. The human voice seems to affect the child very soon after birth, and, indeed, the first differentiated reactions to auditory stimuli seem to be aroused in this way.

When we survey these three main divisions of sen-sitivity (i-iii) we find that in general they correspond to a rank-order of capacities. With the exception of sensitivity to pain, the skin-senses stand at the top of the list with reference to differentiation, while hearing is at the bottom, and the others in between. This rank-order agrees very well with certain anatomical facts ; for Flechsig has shown that the nervous paths leading from the sense-organs to the cortex are not

121

medullated at the same time, those of the skin being completed first and those of hearing last. Thus, the development of the organs and their functions appear to be closely connected.

At the beginning of this section the manner in which we propose to consider the sensitivity of infants was defined, and thus far we have limited ourselves to objective behaviour. But now that we have answered the question of sensitivity under this limitation, we may proceed to consider the limitation itself and inquire if any features are to be found in the behaviour called forth by sensory stimulation which would warrant the assumption of a corresponding "inner" experience. In other words, we are now almost ready to take up the so-called question of consciousness, and shall do so in the last sections of this chapter. But before that, another problem confronts us.

## § 12—*Dispositional Plasticity*

Up to the present we have been trying to learn something of the new-born infant's motility and sensitivity. In each inquiry we have had to do with inherited modes of behaviour, or dispositions. But we have not yet exhausted the description of the infant's endowments; for many inherited reactions are not yet functional at birth, and only attain their maturity at a later time. Even this leaves us with a considerable gap in our knowledge; because development is not alone a matter of maturation, but also one of learning. The modes of reaction that differentiate the adult from the new-born child are quite unlike those that differentiate a grown hen from a chick. Human modes of response are only in small measure the result of innate reactions which, though characteristic of the whole species, are merely delayed in their maturation. On the contrary, the distinction between the development of a chick and the development of a human being is based upon individual acquisitions. Hen and man differ not only in their dispositions leading to definite types of reaction, but first of all in the fact that man acquires individual reactions of an incomparably higher type. And this capacity to learn is likewise an inherited disposition. In comparison with the rigid dispositions previously mentioned, the disposition to learn may be ascribed to plasticity, and a large measure of plasticity is one of the striking characteristics of man (cf. above Chapter II, p. 41). As Bühler remarks, plastic dispositions "do not completely determine what shall take place, since they are subject to modification by the activity itself"[111].

This conception of plasticity as dispositional may easily lead us into difficulties if we think of dispositions only as certain predetermined bonds of connection in the system of neurones; because from this point of view one is led to regard plasticity as nothing more than a lack of definite connections. Indeed, it has been argued that the fewer fixed connections an organism brings with it into the world, the less it is bound to employ definite reactions, and the more it can learn by experience. Thorndike seizes upon this explanation and traces its consequences with great thoroughness[112]. Yet the fact that an organism possesses no definite bond leading from a situation S to a certain reaction $R^1$, can not be assumed to explain at all why the reaction should be $R^2$ or $R^3$ with which S is no more definitely connected than it is with $R^1$. The mere fact that my sneezing-reflex does not function, would not of itself lead me to use my handkerchief, or to seek a physician who can remove some foreign body which has lodged in my nasal passages. Reactions such as these all demand a positive basis — *definite bonds*, as Thorndike conceives them — quite as much as does the sneezing itself. Neither can we say that a number of reactions which have no definite bonds with any particular situation are better suited to explain plasticity than just as many reactions, or even more, each of which is assumed to be definitely connected with a specific situation. Every connection must indeed be a connection of some definite kind ; consequently, indefiniteness can not furnish the explanation of plasticity. Plasticity, which Thorndike identifies with *multiple response to a single situation*, depends, according to his view, upon a fecundity of unlearned connections, providing as it does that a reaction which does not lead to an end is forthwith resolved into another and again into still another until finally the end is attained.

Thorndike makes no distinction between rigid and plastic dispositions. To him all dispositions are either simple or more complex bonds of connection between neurones. Consequently, the question of plasticity for him reduces itself to this : What kind of inherited bonds does man possess which other animals lack ; or, stated in reverse order, what bonds does man lack which make it possible for him to learn so much more than any other animal ?

Since we have refused to accept Thorndike's fundamental assumptions, the problem appears quite differently to us. Having found no reason for accepting a system of fixed bonds as the mechanism of *unlearned* functions, we are under no obligation to discover an apparatus of *learning* in any hypothetical system of bonds between neurones, whether inherited or acquired. A solution of this problem will be attempted in the next chapter, but this much may be said at once : If we abandon the view that learning is merely a matter of new combinations of connections already in existence, then plasticity becomes something more significant and more definite than even Bühler makes it out to be ; because the question is now before us whether anything new can take place in the behaviour of an individual which can not be referred to a re-combination of old elements. If this question is answered in the affirmative, a line will be drawn between those organisms that are capable of creative responses, and those that are not; or at least a distinction can then be made with respect to greater and lesser degrees of

124

creative capacity [113]. It would then follow that plasticity must be something more than memory—something more than the retention of an achievement by the simple means of effecting a new combination of reaction-pathways which the organism already possesses—and we could then rightfully say that by virtue of his plasticity man is superior to all other living creatures. A further inference is also possible, and one which gives us an outlook upon the progress of our investigation; for, apart from the reflexes, the distinction usually drawn between instinct and habit no longer exhausts the possibilities of behaviour. Provision is now made for a new and important type of response which has neither an instinctive basis nor has it yet become habitual.

In comparing Thorndike's explanation of behaviour with the one here being developed, we find that the two methods of approach are based upon quite different principles. Thorndike confines himself exclusively to the question *where* the act takes place; and since for him all acts are alike, the problem reduces itself to the bonds established between separate neurones. We, on the contrary, find ourselves faced with the question *what* it is that takes place. And hence, we are not interested in a nervous pathway which always affords the same kind of excitation, but in the specific form of excitation requisite for the behaviour under consideration.

§ 13—*The Infant's Phenomenal Experience. Methodological Considerations with Respect to the Question of Consciousness, and the Phenomena of Mental Configurations*

We come now to the last problem of this chapter. Thus far the infant has been described as an object of natural-scientific observation. We have noted what he does and what kind of stimuli determine his responses; but the question remains, how does his behaviour appear to the infant himself? Does he know anything of his behaviour? Does he have any experience when he is stimulated and reacts? Is there any "descriptive" side to his behaviour? Or, to employ the usual terminology, is the infant conscious of his behaviour? The problem may be divided into two parts. Has the infant any consciousness at all, and if so, how is this consciousness constituted in the beginning? The first question can be easily answered and is of relatively little importance. Since the infant certainly attains consciousness after a shorter or a longer period of time, it is relatively unimportant whether consciousness begins earlier or later, and we have no absolute criterion by means of which a decision can be reached. It has often been thought that one must deny consciousness to the new-born infant upon the assumption that he is, then, a purely palæ-encephalic being. If this were so the new-born child could not possibly have any experiences, but would live as a plant lives, without even hunger or satiety, pleasure or pain. But the behaviour of the brainless child reported by Edinger and Fischer indicated that in comparison normal children, even from the hour of their birth, differ from brainless children. The assumption that the cerebrum plays no part in early infancy is therefore unproved, and we are under no necessity of denying some form of consciousness even at birth. Against the hypothesis of an unconscious beginning, both the very early expressive movements as well as the "expression" upon the infant's features may be cited. Preyer [114] points out that even from the first day a contented facial expression can be differentiated from a discontented one, whereas Edinger and Fischer report that their anencephalic infant never showed the slightest trace of expression. We may therefore turn to our second question; namely, what kind of experiences can the new-born infant have?

Since the infant's consciousness is not directly accessible to us, the question we have raised calls for the exercise of what at the beginning of this book was referred to as a "consideration from within." We can not directly conjure forth the world of a new-born infant in our own minds, any more than we can see with the infant's eyes, feel through his sense of touch, or be told anything by him. Therefore we must reconstruct his situation for ourselves. Why we should not forgo this difficult task altogether, has already been indicated (cf. p. 15 f.); but how shall we begin it? The ordinary man, ignorant of psychology, assumes it to be self-evident that the world is essentially the same to every one; although to a new-born infant things must appear less complete, less distinct, and less familiar than they do to the adult. When such a person attributes a mental achievement to an infant—as, for instance, when he says that a child "thinks"—he really means that the child's thought is of the same order as his own, being merely an imperfect copy of what goes on in his own mind. A person somewhat better acquainted with psychology would perhaps turn up his nose at this naïve conception, but it may be doubted if the position he would take is necessarily a better one; for what he usually does is merely to apply to the suckling a theory derived from current psychology, which enables him to define mental "incompleteness" by attributing to the infant fewer sensations, no associations, etc. It need scarcely be repeated that a true psychology of childhood can not be achieved in this way. Indeed, we must begin with the "specific beginning-stage" of development whose peculiar nature it is our task to discover.

To those for whom psychological ways of thinking are unfamiliar, the following example may clarify the problem. Although two men are born into the same real world, its phenomenal aspects are not necessarily the same for each. It is often said that there is no use in quarrelling over tastes, because in the very same situation one person may find himself altogether dissatisfied, while another is charmed. It is the task of the psychologist to trace this difference in behaviour to its source. When this has been done it will often be discovered that, quite apart from feeling and evaluating, persons of conflicting tastes are actually experiencing quite different phenomena. For example, in looking at a picture one person sees nothing but a confusion of clashing colours, while another sees an admirable and expressive work of art; or, again, where one person hears only a chaos of clangs, another is being impressed by a richly ornamental musical theme. The examples chosen are as crude as possible, in order to make it quite clear to the reader that the same external situation may furnish phenomenal contents which are entirely different. In each example it can be said that the experience of the first-named person was less adequate than that of the second ; but it is obviously impossible to believe that this inadequacy rests upon fewer sensations or upon fewer associated ideas. Let us now apply these examples to the infant's consciousness. In asking how the world is reflected in the experience of a new-born infant, the fact that the world is reflected very differently, even in the phenomena of adult experience, permits us to make use of just such differences as our examples have furnished in arriving at a correct description of the "inadequacy" of an infant's mind.

The argument, which has previously been negative in trend, now becomes positive. The objective world does not suffice to determine the experience of an individual; to this must be added the constitution of the individual himself. The new-born infant *experiences* the world *differently* from us adults, just as an unmusical person *hears* a symphony *differently* from one who is musical.

But how can we find out the nature of this difference? How shall we proceed to reconstruct the phenomenal world of a new-born baby? Our previous considerations indicate that our reconstruction of the infant's consciousness must "fit" the observed facts of its "objective" behaviour, that is to say, the two must fit together in the same way in which the phenomenal world of the adult fits his objective behaviour. It ought, therefore, to be possible to turn the results of experimental psychology to account in the solution of our problem, without falling into any of the errors against which we have warned. If we find the behaviour of the infant to be but slightly differentiated, as compared with our own, then we must try to find some movements in our own behaviour which are also slightly differentiated as compared with other movements. When this has been done, we can compare the two with reference to the phenomena usually connected with more and with less differentiated movements, and if any characteristic distinction is found, we must then try to carry it over to the phenomena of infants. In a concrete case we shall have to examine each bit of infantile behaviour for itself, and work out its typical differences from the corresponding behaviour of adults, before we can proceed to reconstruct its phenomenal aspect. We must deny that "objective" and "subjective" behaviour have no inner connection, and are simply bound to one another like the obverse and reverse of a coin which might be stamped in any way; for if this were so, we might as well give up any attempt to reconstruct the infant's experience. But, on the contrary, we insist that behaviour can not be described in its entirety until we are acquainted with both its aspects, and that only then can we give it an adequate explanation. The position we have taken holds, not only for infants, but for the whole of child-psychology, in so far as it is concerned with the phenomena of mind. An older child is not a "little man"; and just as his behaviour differs from that of an adult, so also do his experiences differ.

How, then, shall we proceed to reconstruct the experiences of a human being during the first days of his life? First let us inquire, what are the most important features of his behaviour? Quite obviously, they are his gross bodily conditions, such as hunger, satiety, fatigue, freshness—all of which can be understood in a purely objective way. Let us consider these conditions as they seem to us. When we "feel fresh," there are no very definite reactions connected with this condition (as there are, for instance, when we drive a nail into the wall). Our feeling of freshness can be explained in all sorts of movements, so long as we move at all. The situation is reversed, but no more specific, when we feel tired, and seek quiet. Even when we are hungry, all that this phenomenon determines is that we should do something in order to obtain food. Whether we cut a piece of bread, seek a restaurant, or do something else, depends upon a thousand things which have nothing to do with the feeling of hunger. And when we are satisfied, we simply stop eating. In all these instances the objective behaviour of the infant appears to be essentially the same as our own. When he is refreshed, he moves about; when he is tired, he lies still; when he needs nourishment, he cries until he is offered the breast; and when he has had enough, he stops sucking. To be sure, his behaviour is very slightly differentiated, but so would ours be under similar circumstances. Nevertheless, his behaviour is of enormous biological significance, so that we may quite justly conclude that the states we recognize as hunger, etc., are among the first experiences an infant has; and that they are, in point of fact, phenomenally quite similar to our own.

But what can be said of those experiences which put us in touch with the outer world? How are the perceptions of an infant constituted? We find the new-born child capable of movement whenever external stimuli come in contact with his senses; that is, whenever the equilibrium of his condition is disturbed. For instance, a bright object appears in the field of vision and the eyes move; a contact is made with a certain place on the hand and the fingers close, etc.

In every case a state of rest is interrupted; into the already existing world wherein the child was at rest a new factor has been introduced which disturbs his quiescence. If we wish to reconstruct the phenomenal counterpart of this objective behaviour we must consider the child's state as a *whole*. Consequently, we ought not to say that the child sees a luminous point; but rather that the child sees a *luminous point upon an indifferent background;* or, in the case of touch, that pressure is felt upon the hand, otherwise untouched. Generally stated, *from an unlimited and ill - defined background there has arisen a limited and somewhat definite phenomenon, a quality.* Whether or not the background existed phenomenally even before the new factor emerged from it, will be discussed later. Here it is sufficient to note that when a quality appears, the "indifferent" ground must also be considered as more or less "uniform." We are presupposing that before the appearance of the stimulus the child was at rest, and not moving. Inferring phenomena of experience from behaviour, an undifferentiated phenomenon must correspond to the absolutely undifferentiated behaviour of quiescence. The reader should not forget that we are speaking of the earliest beginnings of consciousness; and that it is the very first experience of the child that we are attempting to characterize. Our characterization is, then, this: That the first phenomena are *qualities upon a ground.* Introducing at this point a new concept, they are the simplest *mental configurations.* The phenomenal appearance in consciousness divides itself into a given quality, and a ground upon which the quality appears—a level from which it emerges. It is, however, a part of the nature of a quality that it should lie upon a ground, or, as we may also say, that it should rise above a level. Such a co-existence of phenomena in which each member "carries every other"[115], and in which each member possesses its peculiarity only by virtue of, and in connection with, all the others, we shall henceforth call a *configuration*. According to this view, the most primitive phenomena are figural; as examples, the luminous point set off from a uniform background; something cold at a place upon the skin set off from the usual temperature of the rest of the skin; the too cold or too warm milk in contrast with the temperature level of the mouth-cavity. We attribute configurations, also, to such reactions as the rejection of milk when it is not of the right temperature; thus milk in the mouth may lead either to an " adequate " or to an " inadequate " configuration.

To many this view of the constitution of the most primitive phenomena will appear very odd indeed; for it assumes that a certain order dominates experience from the beginning, whereas we would be in much better agreement with current views if we were to assume that order comes only as a result of experience —a theory which has given rise to the view that the consciousness of the new-born infant is nothing but a confused mass of separate *sensations*, some of which are present earlier than others, because of the earlier maturation of their appropriate brain-centres. Upon the basis of such a theory the sense of vision would seem to supply the child with a chaotic mass of achromatic and chromatic impressions, like the colours upon a painter's palette, from which experience would proceed to choose the ones that are requisite to constitute his perceptual world. And this doctrine is founded upon one of the fundamental presuppositions with which psychology has long worked; namely, that single mental units called sensations are aroused in a simple manner by stimulation, and from them every other kind of experience is derived by a process of association [116]. The behaviour of the child, however, certainly does not of itself suggest any such presumption. A few arguments may also be added which directly contradict it, and at the same time support

132

our hypothesis of the configurative character of the first sensory phenomena.

1. Our principle of reconstructing the phenomena of infantile experience in such a way that they will fit the child's behaviour, would certainly not lead us to assume that a new-born infant possesses an abundance of mental phenomena. On the contrary, his behaviour seems to demonstrate that there are very few motives which can set him in action [117].

2. If the theory of original chaos were correct, one would expect "simple" stimuli to be the first to arouse the reaction and interest of the child; because simple stimuli ought to be the ones first to be singled out from the chaos for association with one another. This, however, contradicts all our experience. It is not the stimuli the psychologist takes to be simple, because they correspond to his elementary sensations, that are most influential in the behaviour of a baby. The first differentiated reactions to sound are aroused by the human voice whose stimuli (and "sensations") are very complicated, indeed. Nor is the interest of a suckling aroused by a single colour, but by human faces, as Miss Shinn has expressly reported to be the case with her niece after the child's 25th day. Think what sort of experience must parallel the process of distinguishing, among an infinite variety of chaotic images, the father's from the mother's face (and more than this, a friendly from an unfriendly countenance), the sensations of which are constantly undergoing change. On the other hand, "it may be observed occasionally even in the second month of life that a child does not remain indifferent to certain impressions which he has frequently had—the face and voice of the mother especially—for they cause him to laugh softly. By the second quarter-year this recognition has developed into 'discrimination,' and thereafter the child behaves quite differently toward familiar persons than he does toward strangers" [118]. As early as the middle of the first year of life an

133

influence of the parents' facial expression upon the child may be noted. According to the chaos-theory the phenomena corresponding to a human face can be nothing but a confused mass of the most varied light-, dark-, and colour-sensations, all in a constant state of alteration—changing with every movement of the person observed, or of the child himself, and likewise subject to every change of illumination. Yet the child recognizes its mother's face as early as the second month, and in the middle of the first year it reacts quite differently to a "friendly" face than it does to an "angry" face. Furthermore, this difference is of a kind which obliges us to conclude that "friendly" and "angry" faces are phenomenal facts to the infant, and not mere distributions of light and shade. It seems quite impossible to explain this behaviour by experience, upon the assumption that these phenomena arise from an original chaos of sensations in which single visual sensations combine with one another, together with pleasant or unpleasant consequences. One of Köhler's observations is here in point [119] : " By suddenly showing signs of the greatest terror, while staring at a certain spot as though possessed, it is not difficult to make all the chimpanzees in the station look at the same place at once. Immediately all the black company starts as if it had been struck by lightning and proceeds to stare at the same spot, even though there is nothing to be seen there. According to the usual view this involves an inference drawn by analogy from what is taking place in 'my consciousness.'" The animals understand this terror-stricken direction of the gaze *immediately*, and an inference by analogy from Köhler's consciousness of terror would be an altogether absurd explanation.

Is it not possible that phenomena, such as "friendliness" and "unfriendliness," are very primitive—even more so than the visual impression of a "blue spot"? However absurd this possibility may seem to a psychologist who regards all consciousness as being ultimately made up of elements, it ceases to be absurd as soon as one reconsiders the matter biologically, while bearing in mind that all psychological phenomena stand in the closest relation to objective behaviour. " Friendliness " and " unfriendliness " certainly influence behaviour, whereas it is not easy to understand how the behaviour of so primitive an organism as the human infant could be motivated by a " blue spot." On similar grounds Scheler concludes " that of all the external objects apprehended by man, ' expression' is the very first." [120] With this statement we are in full accord, if the connotation of the term " expression " is made sufficiently broad to include such behaviour as a response to light in darkness.

Referring again to what has already been said about the perception of "expression" (p. 117), we need only add one further remark upon this subject. If we accept phenomena such as " friendliness " and " unfriendliness " as primitive, we must maintain that primitive phenomena are indivisible into perceptive and affective elements, and that a " subjective" feeling does not exist alongside of, though apart from, " objective " perceptions, but that *qua* phenomenon, the primitive world of experience embraces affective determinations just as it does those we are accustomed to characterize as objective. Thus we find ourselves again in complete accord with many standard authors. [121] Folk-psychology teaches the same thing—namely, that for men of primitive culture the world is full of qualities which we are accustomed to characterize as emotional and which we consider purely subjective, egotistical, ingredients. [122] But, of course, what we imply is that the first perceptive phenomena already carry with them the characteristics of objectivity, which phenomena, such as freshness and hunger, lack. It goes without saying that one must not use the term " objectivity " in the sense in which it is employed by the philosophers. All we mean is that perceptive phenomena are something other than " organic feelings "; and that the distinction between subject and object is not learned, but is given, no matter in how primitive a form, in the very first phenomena of the infant mind.

3. Brod and Weltsch [123] advance the following argument in opposition to the view that mind is originally a mosaic of innumerable sensations. It happens sometimes, either intentionally or through inattention and fatigue, that the developed phenomena of adult life are "screwed down" in the direction of a less developed state. We have all experienced states of distraction in which our consciousness is transformed into an inarticulate unity. The world then appears, not variegated, but monotonous. The assumption of an original multiplicity would be untenable in the light of this experience; because we have here the inarticulate uniformity already described as the phenomenal ground from which a *quality* emerges. Imagine this modification, which our adult world of perception sometimes undergoes, carried to an extreme : May we not assume that we would then revert to the first and most primitive of conscious phenomena? The only question would be where to set a limit, for ultimately this limit appears to lead us to nought. In the end, with absolute monotony, have we any consciousness at all? Previously we left open the question whether the inarticulate ground - work upon which the quality of an experience appears is already there before the quality emerges, or whether it arises with the quality itself. To affirm the question asked above would be to accept the second alternative; namely, that the most primitive phenomenon of consciousness is not the inarticulate ground-work, but the configuration, or quality, which arises from this uniform background. This opinion seems to me the more tenable of the two, because the phenomenon of a uniform ground-work would be meaningless for behaviour, and therefore a pure luxury. Furthermore, this opinion is directly supported by certain marked disturbances of perception which involve organic changes of the brain; it having

been found that certain patients are quite unable to see a complicated figure when their condition prevents them from grasping its configuration [124].

Ground and quality, although phenomenally inseparable (cf. above), would seem therefore to arise together. A part of the world is thus differentiated and appears as a quality, whereas whatever remains may still appear as a uniform ground, though in reality it is extremely complex. I emphasize this statement in order to give point to the following fact: We can not construe the phenomenon corresponding to a given stimulus-pattern as though each particular stimulus had its own special phenomenon, such as can be discovered under the conditions of a psychological experiment which analyzes the stimulus-pattern into discrete stimuli, and studies their phenomenal correlates separately. Indeed, the assumption which is commonly made that sensation is determined once and for all by its stimulus, will simply have to be abandoned.

4. Finally, there is direct proof that simple configurations must be regarded as very primitive phenomena. It is customary in animal-psychology to perform the following type of experiment, known as "selective training." An animal is presented with two stimuli, such, for instance, as a lighter and a darker gray paper, and is trained to seek food with reference to one of them, but not with the other. It has been thought that in this way one could test two things, first, whether the animal experiences two phenomena, or sensations, corresponding to the two stimuli, and, secondly, how his memory operates with and after training. Leaving aside the second problem, let us consider the first one. It is usual to explain training in the following way: The animal learns to seek one sensation and to avoid the other. Each sensation, therefore, becomes connected with a different mode of behaviour. We may call the sensation the animal seeks the "positive" and the other the "negative," and apply these terms to their

corresponding stimuli. Köhler undertook the following
experiment: he first trained an animal to choose the
brighter of two grays. After the training had been
brought to a successful issue, "critical tests" were made
in which two gray papers were again presented to the
animal, so chosen, however, that the previously employed
brighter and positive stimulus was retained, while the
darker and negative one was replaced with a paper still
brighter than the positive stimulus of the training-series.
There had been no training with the new paper; it was
therefore neither positive nor negative. In Figure 5,
from which one can comprehend the entire scope of the
experiment, it is indicated as "gray o." What will the
animal do? The new gray is neither positive nor

FIG. 5.

[*After Köhler.*

negative, but neutral, while beside it lies a gray strongly
positive as a result of many repeated experiments. If
the theory of specific response to specific stimuli is
correct, we should expect the positive stimulus to be
selected in a majority of cases; there certainly would
be no reason to suppose that the neutral gray would be
more frequently chosen.

The experiment can be varied by making the darker
gray the positive colour of the training-series, and then
using a still darker colour instead of a brighter one in
the critical tests. Or again, one can retain the negative
rather than the positive stimulus in the critical tests,
and associate with it a gray which is still farther removed from the positive colour than it is from the
negative, though in the same direction. In the interest
of brevity, we shall confine ourselves to the first case.

Köhler carried out a long series of careful experiments

of all kinds with hens, with chimpanzees, and with a child nearly three years old. In order to give the reader an idea how these experiments were performed, I will briefly describe the tests with hens. A hen was placed in a cage, one of the sides of which was so wired that the fowl could easily thrust her head and neck outside. Before this side of the cage a horizontal board was placed from which the hen could eat. Upon this board, adjacent to one another, the two papers were laid which were to be employed in training, and upon each paper an equal number of kernels of grain were placed. If the hen pecked at the grains upon the positive paper, she was allowed to eat them all, but whenever she pecked at those on the negative paper, she was shooed away, and thus prevented from eating[125]. This procedure was continued on different days until the hen no longer attempted to peck at the negative paper. The position of the papers was frequently altered so that the positive stimulus lay now at the right, now at the left, in order that the fowl should not learn always to peck in the same positional direction. To complete the necessary training, four hundred to six hundred trials, and more, were requisite. When this training had been achieved, Köhler proceeded with the *critical tests* in which the fowl was allowed to eat without hindrance all the grains from whichever paper she might chose. The experiment was then at an end and could be repeated.

The results of these experiments on hens contradicted altogether the expectations based upon the sensation-theory. Among four hens, two of which had been trained to select the brighter, and two the darker gray, the newly introduced neutral paper was selected fifty-nine times out of eighty-five critical tests, whereas the original positive paper was selected only twenty-six times. On the basis of the sensation-theory, the opposite was to be expected; at least, the positive colour should have been chosen no less often than the neutral.

The presuppositions of this theory must therefore be false.

How then can we explain the outcome of these experiments? What can have remained over in the critical tests from the situation of the training-series except the objective presence of the positive stimulus? "In this special arrangement where two different colours are placed side by side in an otherwise symmetrical figure of a very simple form, introspection shows that what is characteristic of the experience is not the mere presence of one colour lying by itself, and another colour lying by itself, but the 'togetherness' of the two colours"[126]. Obviously this dark-bright pattern, this colour-figure, is retained when one passes from the setting of the training-series to that of the critical tests. It can therefore be inferred that, in the majority of cases, choice was determined by this pattern, rather than by the retention of the absolute positive quality of the training-series. If the behaviour of the fowls depends primarily upon the characteristics of a configuration, rather than upon the absolute constitution of the colours employed, the conclusion is justified that the phenomena involved in these experiments are configural. Furthermore, the fact that these experiments were carried out with hens, proves that such configurations are possible, not only in a developed state of intelligence, but that they must be regarded as a very primitive type of mental achievement.

In the experiments Köhler performed with a child, two boxes were placed before the child, one with a brighter and the other with a darker cover. The child was told to take one, and without further aid he soon learned to choose always the brighter box which contained candy, and to reject the other box which was empty. After two days (forty-five trials), when the child was able to make his choice virtually without error, the critical test was given; the result of which was the same as with the hens, though far more decisive. With reference to comparative brightness, and the rejection of the "absolute" colour, the child invariably and without hesitation chose the new and the brighter box.

We have noted that "absolute" choice sometimes occurred with the hens. In a special series of tests, Köhler modified the conditions in order to find out which were favourable to the operation of the "absolute" and of the configural factor. His results indicate that the operation of the "absolute" factor ceases to be effective with time, and is quickly forgotten. "The truly essential, lasting, and definite product of learning," he tells us, "is dependent upon the function of a configuration"[127]. This statement holds true in a measure for all the more primitive forms of life; but not for human beings. An adult's choice would not have been unhesitatingly in accordance with the configuration, as was the child's. There would have been a question in the adult's mind whether to behave with reference to the configuration, or with reference to the absolute grayness already known to him. Only when we adults are called upon to judge of colours that are qualitatively very like one another—that is, when a small enough interval has been chosen between the negative, positive, and neutral colours—do we likewise fall under the compulsion of a configurative choice. The difference between the behaviour of adult and child shows clearly that the "absolute" factor is not more primitive, but instead is a product of higher development; and hence it can not be identical with the "simple sensations" which, according to the older point of view, lie at the foundation of all training.

As a consequence of this observed difference, we may conclude that simple configurations are primitive modes of behaviour which in no wise presuppose the existence of absolute sensations. Our presumption that the very first phenomena of the infant mind are qualities of this figural sort is likewise supported by these results.

Again it should be emphasized that the configuration under discussion, which we have assumed to be the first phenomenon of mind, must be thought of as very simple indeed ; merely as a quality emerging from a uniform ground. We must, therefore, not think of these phenomena as being at all like the experiences we adults have. At the beginning, only the slightest degree of complexity and definiteness can be ascribed to them ; but in the following pages we shall become acquainted with configurations as they appear at a higher level, which will enable us to study their development.

CHAPTER IV

## SPECIAL FEATURES OF MENTAL GROWTH

### A. GENERAL STATEMENT OF THE PROBLEM. HOW NEW TYPES OF BEHAVIOUR ARE LEARNED

#### § 1—*Four Ways in which the Mind Grows*

WE now know how the new-born infant begins his journey through life, and how he is equipped to undertake the immense task of becoming an adult and entering the circle of human society as an independent member. Let us therefore accompany him on his way, in order that we may observe his growth and development, and at the same time learn something of the laws in accordance with which growth and development take place. The principles here involved will again occupy the foreground of our attention; because for our purpose the problem of development itself is of greater importance than the detailed facts of behaviour. Accordingly, our attempt will be to point out the nature of man's achievement in the course of his development.

With this end in view, the first questions to be asked are: What the infant has to acquire, and in what directions his behaviour must develop. To these questions we can answer that it is possible to differentiate roughly four different directions of mental development.

1. The first is concerned with purely motor phenomena. Movements and postures which appear at the beginning of life must be carried out with greater completeness; new movements must be built up and

brought to a higher degree of perfection. Beginning with the activities of grasping and locomotion, one attains in due course the ability to speak, to write, and to perform musically, gymnastically, in sport, in play, etc.

2. The second direction of mental growth is in the field of sensory experience. Here the magnitude of the task is even more obvious. We have already tried to show how simple must be the first perceptual phenomena of the human being; although this simplicity is, to be sure, of quite a different sort from that of the so-called "simple" sensations. Out of these rudimentary phenomena of dawning intelligence, our richly furnished, multi-coloured, and finely organized outlook upon the world must be developed. We have seen that amid a multiplicity of things supplied by the environment which might be operative upon the child, only a very few are at any time effective. In the course of his development, however, this multiplicity must be mastered. The requirements which the adult's life brings to bear upon his behaviour are so numerous that they can in no wise be satisfied by the primitive phenomenal configurations of infancy. Gradually, therefore, the phenomena of the child's mind must be adapted to the innumerable stimuli which arouse them. The nature of this task can be made clear by an example. Consider the processes involved in deciphering a puzzle-picture, where, out of a confusion of quite irrelevant lines, the figure of a cat suddenly springs forth. Think now of a puzzle-picture, constructed not merely to show a cat or some other figure, but consisting in a chaos of lines and surfaces, which, however, either suddenly, or by successive stages, make possible the recognition of a landscape or a group of human beings. This example is related to the subject under discussion at the close of the last chapter (p. 128), where we were concerned with pointing out differences in the phenomenal world as they appear to different

human beings who nevertheless observe the same actual world. The example is therefore chosen in order to indicate the problem which confronts man in the development of his sensory capacities. Briefly stated, the primitive, disjointed phenomenal patterns of infancy must be replaced by an integrated, membered, and effectively composed outlook upon the world.

3. But external and internal behaviour are not two opposed and isolated systems; for in truth the problem of behaviour is to carry out appropriate actions which involve the motorium in situations that are mediated to the individual through his sensorium. Along with purely motor and purely sensory acquisitions, we must, therefore, place those which are at once sensory and motor; meaning, thereby, the co-ordination of explicit with implicit forms of behaviour, and those adjustments of movements to phenomena without which an individual could never lead an independent life. To give a very elementary example of this, we may recall the saying that a burnt child fears the fire. Here the co-ordination of an avoidance-reaction with the phenomenon of fire is an acquisition that takes place after the original act of grasping has led to the painful experience of being burned. In this same connection we may recall the modification of instinct observed in the case of Preyer's boy, who preferred a bottle of sweet milk to the breast.

Having emphasized the close connection between the sensorium and the motorium, we must now point out that in reality all purely motor acquisitions, classified under the first heading, contain a sensory component. In such activities as those of speaking and writing, this component is quite obvious. Deaf persons learn to speak imperfectly at best. The same thing is true, however, in forms of behaviour which require special motor practice, as, for instance, playing tennis; for here, too, it is not merely a matter of repeating the same stroke, but of administering the right kind of a stroke whenever and wherever the ball is met.

# BEHAVIOUR AND LEARNING

Even in many quite early activities a sensory component enters, as can be understood by reference to walking, which is in no wise a stereotyped movement. Not only does the tempo of walking greatly vary according to the occasion for locomotion, but, in addition, walking-movements are directed in accordance with the characteristics of the ground, being adapted to its irregularities without our cognizance of this fact. The process is more or less automatic ; that is to say, the brain-centres which regulate walking must receive reports from the outer world regarding the nature of the ground passed over, and these sensory impulses regulate the movements made, though they need not lead to consciousness. To employ a striking example, consider how differently one walks when one has a sore foot, and how impossible it is under these circumstances to place one's feet normally even with the best of will. The nature of the connection between sensorium and motorium becomes still more evident when we consider another type of movement described in detail in the preceding chapter. If we chance to be gazing into the distance when suddenly there appears a striking object near at hand, this object will be fixated, and the eyes will accommodate to it. The reaction, especially the accommodation, is quite involuntary, and the sensory impulse thus released occasions a phenomenon in consciousness only after the movement has taken place, and the eyes have been directed upon the new object. The point of view from which we have found it desirable to consider this connection between sensory and motor behaviour, is that of regarding the whole procedure as an interconnected system in which the motor and the sensory processes are not independent of one another, as they would be if they were connected by external bonds. We shall retain this conception here ; for even acquisitions of a purely " motor " type presuppose an integrated, sensorimotor process. Every movement occasions a new sensory impulse in the brain-centres which in turn contributes

146

to the motor process. A proof of the important contribution made by sensory impulses to motor processes
is furnished in the disturbances of walking that occur
with locomotor ataxia (*Tabes Dorsalis*). In this disease
it is not the motor but the sensory centres that are
attacked, and yet a complete paralysis results. The
patient, however, may learn again to walk if he can
learn to make use of other sensory impulses than those
of the tactual field which he has lost. For instance,
optical impulses may be employed, but the patient
must then learn to regulate his walking by his eyes;
that is, he must constantly watch his feet. Since in
this manner a very considerable improvement in his
performance is possible, it appears that the disturbance
does not involve the motor centres; but it is also evident
that some sensory impulse is necessary for each movement. The same conclusion has been reached from the
physiological investigation of animals in which certain
sensory centres have been destroyed.

The converse of this proposition is also true; for a
"purely sensory" knowledge of the world as described
under our second heading also occurs in co-operation
with movement. Think, for instance, of grasping and
touching, and also of "the line of regard" in vision, and
of the movements of the head involved in spatial orientation. To understand in detail how the motor aspects
support the sensory is, of course, a problem for investigation; but at least we have passed the stage where we
must resort to the hypothesis of "eye-movements" whenever other current theories fail us.

We have tried to show that, strictly speaking, there
are no "purely motor" or "purely sensory" acquisitions,
and yet it is quite justifiable to distinguish the sensori-
motor group from the other two. The object of the
sensory and motor groups, taken separately, is to determine the acquisition, either of an external motor or of an
internal sensory mode of behaviour; whereas the problem
of the sensori-motor group includes the correlation of

these two. This third type of development has therefore to do with uniting phenomena and movements, either of which can exist apart from the other, in one total form of behaviour; for instance, a hen can run, and it can see black and yellow striped caterpillars, but it acquires the tendency to run away *when* it sees these caterpillars.

4. From the third type of development we pass directly to the fourth. When we are suddenly confronted with the problem of adjusting ourselves to a new situation we do not as a rule respond at once with an appropriate form of behaviour, but, instead, the reaction is checked while we consider the matter; that is to say, between the stimulating situation and the behaviour of reaction there occur certain phenomena which do not need to correspond directly with anything actually or objectively present. The following is a crude example of this. A child, finding itself alone, sees before him a tempting dish of sweets; then it occurs to the child that he has been forbidden to take sweets without permission; accordingly he hesitates as to what he shall do. Should he leave the dish untouched, his behaviour with respect to the stimulating situation would be determined by the phenomena which have intervened. In the course of development interventions of this sort play a constantly increasing part. Whereas originally the reaction follows directly upon the stimulus, intervening members become more and more numerous, and more and more important, as development progresses. Our most significant accomplishments rest upon their employment, and their acquisition is therefore an essential task of development. By means of these intervening members, we are able to disengage ourselves more and more from our immediate surroundings, and it is in this way that we are able to control nature to the degree that we do. Education finds one of its chief tasks in promoting this kind of development; for the best of what we learn at school is not the sum of positive knowledge acquired, but that we learn how to think, so that we can assume an independ-

ence which rests upon our ability to supplement the situations that confront us with appropriate intervening phenomena.

As to the importance of these phenomena, the following is worthy of consideration. We have seen that the simplest form of behaviour is a reaction to a situation, the most primitive type being reflexive. With reference to the conception of the reflex-arc—which we have modified to a certain extent—a type of development can be described in which the way from the stimulus to the reaction is being constantly prolonged so that more and more parts of the organism are being set in activity. This conception furnishes us with the physiological correlate for the intervening phenomenal members. However, as these new parts begin to function, the function may itself develop in a relatively independent manner, without it being always apparent that these intervening parts are indeed the members of a sequence established between stimulus and reaction. Now consider the matter from the psychological side. What we call mental work is for the most part work done with these intervening members. Art and science are thus carried on for their own sake; and yet finally they always lead back to some kind of external response, thereby demonstrating their origin.

We have previously selected our examples from what one pleases to call the intellectual domain, but ethical conduct belongs in the same category, and behaviour must also develop ethically, so that it need not depend upon environmental conditions alone.

We shall call this general field of behaviour *ideational behaviour*. Here again the definition is not actually so sharp as the classification suggests; for the ideational field depends most intimately upon the sensory, and any means that enable us to become independent of immediate perception find roots in perception, and, in truth, only lead us from one perception to another. This fact will become clearer when we come to discuss

149

in the next chapter certain categories which begin in the sensory field and lead out into the ideational field.

In our exposition we have been saying that a child must *acquire* this or that form of behaviour. We have selected this vague term "acquire" expressly because, as was pointed out in the second chapter, development may follow either of two paths—namely, maturation or learning. With reference to acquisition we must keep both of these in mind; for although learning is incomparably the more effective process of the two, and the one which therefore chiefly engages our interest, it would be a mistake to regard every acquired performance as necessarily one that has been learned.

§ 2—*Maturation and Learning. The Problem of Memory and the Problem of Achievement in Learning*

Maturation is noticeable in the first weeks of life, mainly through the growth of the "new" brain as it gradually becomes more effective in its functioning. Among other signs, this growth is indicated by a reflexive irritability which, though very slight at the beginning, increases until it attains its maximum within a few weeks, after which time it begins to decrease. The reason for this change is that as soon as the brain, and the connections between the brain and the spinal cord, have attained a certain stage of development, the cerebrum begins to exercise an inhibitive effect upon the reflexes. The transformation of the Babinski-reflex into the plantar reflex, for instance (cf. p. 83 f.), depends upon the maturation of these parts. When disease destroys the connections in the pyramidal tract between the brain and the spinal cord, the Babinski-reflex reappears in place of the plantar reflex. Similarly, the reflexive control of excretion depends upon a certain maturation of the cerebrum. In the brainless child previously described this control was never effected.

Behaviour of this type, however, can not be regarded altogether as a product of maturation, for learning is also involved.

Learning, however, brings before us an entirely new set of problems to which we must now give our attention. All learning depends upon *memory*—upon the fact that the past is not dead to us, but is preserved more or less in some form or other within our psycho-physical organism. Whenever we have adjusted ourselves to a new situation, or have once solved a new problem, we find that our behaviour is easier the next time we meet the same or a similar situation, or whenever we are called upon to solve the same or a similar problem. This aspect of learning has been especially favoured by investigation, and numerous experiments have been carried out by different methods with the object of determining the laws of memory. The problem of memory is, however, not the only problem of learning; for still another problem has at least an equal importance. We have just stated that memory makes it possible for the organism to preserve the effect even of a single performance. Consider, now, this single performance a little more closely. If it be of an inherited type, such as an instinctive action, it need be no easier, nor succeed any better, the second time than it did the first; because instinctive activities are already fairly complete at the start, and even if a certain improvement is noted, this need not necessarily be referred to memory, for it may be entirely attributable to growth. We shall see in the course of this chapter that, as a matter of fact, the maturation of a performance is promoted by its exercise.

The superiority of a second performance over the first is evident, however, when the activities in question do not belong to innate endowment, but are of a kind that involves more or less serious difficulties of acquisition. We may cite examples from each of the four types of development that we have distinguished. 1. Swimming is learned with considerable difficulty; once learned, however, we need never afterwards be quite helpless in the water. 2. Having once solved a puzzle-picture, the solution is very much easier the next time we see it; this facility applies also to other pictures similar to the first. 3. Having once succeeded in crossing a stream on a log, one is not likely to hesitate as to what to do the next time he finds himself in a similar predicament. The example of the burned child, which we have also referred to this type of behaviour, seems to be of a different sort, but we shall defer consideration of it until later. 4. After I am once able to understand a proof in some particular field of mathematics, I find myself much better prepared with respect to other problems in the same field.

These are all significant instances of learning, and in all of them the first performance contains the determining factor. The problem of learning, therefore, is not merely one of finding out how later performances depend upon earlier ones—which is essentially the problem of memory—but also involves the question: How does the first performance come about? Hereafter we shall refer to this as the *problem of achievement*.

The distinction here made is a fundamental one, although it has not usually been accorded the important position in psychology which it deserves. Often, indeed, the problem of learning has been identified with the problem of memory, while the problem of achievement, as a matter for separate consideration, has been more or less overlooked. Thus the criterion of an instinctive performance has frequently been found in the fact that it takes place without previous experience. Accordingly, whatever a living being does the first time it is placed in a certain situation is supposed to depend solely upon its inherited disposition [128]. This view we shall oppose by another which assumes all learning to be a non-heritable achievement. What this means, we must now endeavour to find out.

§ 3—*The Principle of Trial and Error. Thorndike's Investigations and the Mechanistic Theory of Learning*

We come now to one of the most significant problems of comparative psychology, the solution of which is supposed by some to have been reduced to a very simple formula, namely, the Principle of Trial and Error. This principle, however, instead of untying the knots of the problem, simply slips by them ; for according to its hypothesis there is no such thing as a "non-heritable" type of behaviour, nor are there any first performances in the sense of being new performances. It is important to bear this in mind when one is trying to understand the Principle of Trial and Error.

We shall begin by considering the concrete facts which have led to the formation of this principle. These facts may be found in typical experiments with animals, such as Thorndike was the first to undertake, and which have since been carried out very extensively in America [129]. A general idea of these experiments may be had from the following statement: Animals which have not been fed for a long time are confined in closed cages before which food is visible, or otherwise sensed. Observations are then made upon the behaviour of an animal in this situation, and especially how it finally succeeds in getting out of the cage to the food [130]. The cage is provided with a door or some arrangement which opens as soon as the animal has carried out a certain act, the animal being required to pull down a string, or turn a lock, or press upon a board, or by means of some other mechanical device, raise a latch so that the door can be pushed open or release secured in some other manner.

Fig. 6, taken from Thorndike's book, shows in a schematic way how such a cage is constructed. Among the many different locks pictured, a particular experiment may employ but one, or a combination of several, leading in a definite serial order to the release. Thus, for instance, it may be impossible to loosen lock C until B has first been unlocked, and lock B only after lock A.

Thorndike, whose experiments we shall now trace a little more closely, confined cats and dogs in such cages, always using each animal alone. He then observed what the animal did under these conditions, and measured the time from the beginning of the experiment up to the moment when the animal succeeded in getting out of the cage. Sooner or later, after the animal had eaten, it was again placed in the cage, and the experiment was

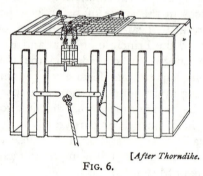

*[After Thorndike.*

FIG. 6.

begun anew. The repetitions extended sometimes over several days before the animal could at once release itself from the cage. Having measured the time of confinement in each separate test, a time-curve could then be constructed in which the several repetitions are indicated on the abscissæ, and the time required in each repetition on the ordinates (cf. Figs. 7 and 8, pp. 163, 165).

It may, of course, happen that the animal will never succeed in escaping from the cage, but as soon as it is confined the animal begins to show signs of distress and to strive for relief. Thorndike's description of this behaviour has already been given on p. 96. The procedure continues until the animal, in the course of its aimless pursuit, at length chances to make the movement which gives it freedom. Thus an animal striking

154

about at random may sooner or later fasten its claws upon the string, or upon the bolt, which affords a means of exit. The animal thus gains its freedom the first time by a movement in nowise new, being one that already belongs to its inherited repertory of reactions (cf. p. 96).

If the experiment is repeated again and again, the behaviour of the animal changes, in that the unsuccessful movements are gradually reduced in number, while the successful movement becomes constantly more perfect and more exact; both results having the same influence upon the time-curve, which shows that the animal gets out of the cage quicker and quicker.

These are the facts. How are they to be understood? American animal-psychology prides itself with having worked out a very simple hypothesis. This hypothesis has passed through different stages, some of which we shall here reproduce, but its nucleus was given at the start as a result of the following considerations. Since insight and intention play no part in determining the movements by means of which the animal frees itself the first time from the cage, these can be no more effective after the animal has learned to master the situation, and hence the modification of behaviour by the elimination of the useless and the perfection of the useful movements may be said to go forward *without any participation on the part of the animal.* The animal has not the slightest notion why its behaviour is being modified; the whole process, in which the successful acts are preserved and the unsuccessful acts gradually eliminated, is purely mechanical.

This is the Principle of Trial and Error, or Success and Failure. But the question remains: How does it happen that the successful movements rather than the unsuccessful ones are retained? The first answer given to this question was that a definite connection, or association, is gradually built up between the situation and the useful movements, in consequence of which

155

the perception of the situation is immediately translated into appropriate activities. An association is established between the situation and the appropriate, but not with inappropriate, movements, because the former are attended by pleasure whereas the latter are attended by displeasure. This, approximately, was the theory of Lloyd Morgan. But the further questions how pleasure and displeasure can be effective in establishing or hindering associations could be answered by Morgan only in these words : " I conceive," he says, " that there is but one honest answer to these questions. We do not know "[131].

For a long time the theory remained in this form, and quite recently Bühler, in his attempt to explain the principle of training, or drill—which we shall consider later—appears to accept this view when he remarks that the pleasure of success and the displeasure of failure suffice to establish " an unequivocally clear and definite association between certain sensory impressions and the movement-complex of the successful mode of behaviour."[132] This connection is assumed to be purely associative, that is, the sensory impression determines the movement without the animal's being conscious of an " I should ", or an " I will "[133]. Morgan's theory has therefore been modified to this extent, that the association is now supposed to be established directly between the perception and the movement without the mediation of any other conscious data. At first Thorndike accepted this view and then proceeded to verify it by experimentation. According to his first hypothesis, the association was supposed to take place only in the connection between the sensory impressions and the movement-impulse of the animal under investigation.[134] Let us see what is involved in the employment of this word, association. By association we understand a connection between processes not inherited but acquired in the course of life. The term has this meaning for Morgan, and also for Bühler, who writes that " there is an ' over-production of movements' and an 'aimless trying-out' involved in training. Consequently the range of possibilities is sufficient for the attainment of an end by chance. This range of chance is restricted, however, and finally set aside altogether by the building up of an unequivocal association."[135] If one understands by "over-production" the appearance of movements not connected by any inherited pathways with the situation at hand, it follows that new bonds of connection must actually be established.

Thorndike, however, sees the matter differently. "Over-production" to him is only the successive functioning of inherited modes of behaviour. As already remarked, the animal, according to Thorndike, does nothing at all to secure its freedom which is not already a part of its instinctive tendencies, and wholly dependent upon the predetermined inherited connections of its neurones. The connections established in learning are, therefore, in no wise new; the total effect consisting only in this, that among the numerous predetermined bonds existing between any situation and the many possible reactions to it, a few are retained and strengthened while the rest are eliminated. Although Thorndike does employ the term association, this function does not signify for him the establishment of any new connection in a physiological sense, but at most a facilitation in the functioning of nervous tracts already defined.[136]

The same view is advanced in its most extreme form by Watson, who is very emphatic in his statements that there is no such thing as building up a new course of action, and that to speak of association is therefore quite superfluous. We need not concern ourselves at all, he thinks, with the establishment of new connections, but only with a selection from among those already present, and this selection results from the mere fact that useless movements are gradually eliminated, whereupon the useful ones fall into their proper serial order.[137]

# BEHAVIOUR AND LEARNING

Learning could not be reduced more completely to mechanical terms. Even the questions how the selection among different ways of response is to become effective, and what factor gradually determines the elimination of the useless movements, have been answered by Watson in the simplest, but also in the crudest, and, as regards a natural feeling for living creatures, in the most un- sympathetic manner.[138] The movements retained he regards as being merely those most frequently carried out ; these being at the same time the successful move- ments for the simple reason that they are ones which must occur in every trial that does not end in failure. No such compulsion attaches to the unsuccessful acts, because the experiment ends as soon as the right act has been performed. If one assumes that all possible acts are equally probable at the start, and that one order of acts is as probable as any other, it follows that the right act has double the probability of any act that is wrong.

A simple example will clarify this relation. Suppose only two movements, A and B, are possible and equally probable, and that B leads to the result, while A does not. Then the series of trials may be something like this:

1. A *B*
2. *B*
3. A *B*
4. A *B*
5. *B*
6. *B*
7. A *B*
8. *B*

Whenever A comes first B must follow, but when B is the first member there can be no second, because B closes the experiment. We see that B occurs in the eight trials eight times, while A occurs but four times, although as the first member one is just as frequent as the other.

158

This *Law of Frequency* is for Watson and other American authors[139] the chief law of learning. Watson supplements it with the less important *Law of Recency*, according to which the act last performed has a certain advantage over the others which enhances the probability of the appearance of the successful act; being always the last act in every trial, it is at the beginning of each succeeding trial the one most recently performed. But the original principle of explanation, whereby the effectiveness of success and failure was referred to pleasure and displeasure, has altogether disappeared from the theory, and is no longer regarded as having anything to do with learning and habituation.[140]

This extreme point of view has not proved acceptable to the majority of investigators. Although all recognize the Law of Frequency, or, as Thorndike calls it, the Law of Exercise[141], it is not generally thought that this law alone is adequate to give a full explanation of the facts. Explanation in terms of the result itself, which Watson discards, is therefore retained by other investigators as a necessary addendum. Thus Bühler finds pleasure and displeasure the effective means by which infants and animals select their responses. "Success brings pleasure and pleasure determines the frequent repetition of any movement that was once successful, while frequent repetition gives it a fixed and enduring character. Failure, on the other hand, brings displeasure which does not prompt repetition. Thus unsuccessful movements are not retained, but eliminated."[142] The process of "stamping in" is therefore explained by frequency, but the frequency of the act is again referred back to pleasure. This seems very simple at first, but difficulties arise as soon as one considers a concrete case, as, for instance, that of the animal-experiments just described. The connection between movement and pleasure, for example, is not nearly so close as the hypothesis would have it be. A cat, while engaged in biting the bars of its cage, may gain its release by a chance-movement of its head which throws the lock. The subsequent pleasure in being free is supposed to be effective in determining a repetition of the same movement, but in order that this movement may again lead to success it must be repeated in exactly the same manner and in the same place ; otherwise the cat's head will not come in contact with the lock in such a way as to open the cage. But what causes the animal to assume this same position again? In point of fact, as Hobhouse in particular has observed, the animal does *not* repeat the same movement, but as a rule only the same general kind of behaviour. Thus a cat which has once freed itself by pulling a string with its foot, may upon another occasion pull the same string with its teeth [143]. The argument can be carried still further ; for if we accept Bühler's hypothesis and its consequences the movement, strictly speaking, must be exactly repeated just as it was made the first time success was achieved. But, of course, it is absurd to suppose that repetition will occur with any such exact or, as one might say, photographic fidelity to the original movement. An attempt to prove such a thesis must certainly fail. Indeed, so many elements of movement are present in the restless behaviour of the animal that the same succession of acts is quite impossible until the animal has learned its task, and the habit has been completely formed. In the case of the cat which secured its release by a movement of the head, the animal would certainly be found in a somewhat different position the second time the trial was made, and this would necessitate a somewhat different movement in order to slip the lock. The art of learning simply can not be explained by the mere repetition of a movement which leads to pleasure.

The theory of trial and error meets still another difficulty which its opponents have pointed out. The pleasure often follows much later than the movement, since a whole series of movements, some right and some wrong, may have to be made before the end is attained. For instance, when the cage from which the animal must release itself has more than one lock, the opening of the first lock can bring no pleasure, and before the other hindrances are set aside the animal may make many false responses. Yet even under these conditions the animal will learn to carry out the first act of such a series.

We have not as yet criticized the Law of Frequency, but it is not difficult to demonstrate that it is inadequate, and likewise that its derivation from the law of probability is unfounded. Thorndike refutes the law very simply [144] by pointing out that the entire deduction is based upon a false presupposition; namely, that the animal will perform each separate act once only, and must then proceed to a new and different act, which does not at all agree with the facts. Very often an animal will repeat an unsuccessful act many times before a change takes place in its behaviour. In these cases repetition would have quite a different result. Consider the previous illustration where there were but two possibilities of reaction, A, unsuccessful, and B, successful. B can be repeated but once in a trial because the first B solves the problem, whereas A can be repeated many times. With the same scheme used on p. 158, and allowing A to be repeated three times before the act is abandoned, we gain the following picture of the animal's behaviour in successive trials :

| | |
|---|---|
| 1. A A A *B* | 5. *B* |
| 2. *B* | 6. *B* |
| 3. A A A *B* | 7. A A A *B* |
| 4. A A A *B* | 8. *B* |

From this record it appears that A has occurred twelve times, while B has only occurred eight times. By the law of frequency A rather than B should be selected, which shows clearly the inadequacy of this law as an explanation of learning.

Thorndike attempts to overcome this difficulty by adding to the Law of Exercise, a *Law of Effect*[145]. If a reaction leads to a "satisfactory state of affairs," the connection involved in the reaction is strengthened, whereas if it leads to an "unsatisfactory state of affairs" the connection is weakened. This addition is nothing more than the old principle of the effects of pleasure and displeasure now reduced to an original innate tendency; but why the principle should be effective, we can understand no better than we did before. Thorndike, however, tries to set this question aside altogether, by basing the law of effect upon the individual's inherited tendencies.

The same objection already raised against Bühler's formula can, however, be applied to Thorndike's principle as soon as we take it up in detail, and trace its consequences as they are applied by Thorndike in explanation of the learning of animals. But before we follow this criticism further, I wish to point out that, to me at least, it seems as though Thorndike himself were not altogether satisfied with the dominating mechanistic tendency of his principles, and that he would like to overcome this implication by means of the Law of Effect. At any rate, he also considers the ethical aspects of development, and he clearly refers the possibility of ethical progress to this Law of Effect when he writes that "man is thus eternally altering himself to suit himself. His nature is not right in his own eyes. Only one thing in it, indeed, is unreservedly good, the power to make it better. This power, the power of learning, or modification in favour of the satisfying, the capacity represented by the law of effect, is the essential principle of reason and right in the world"[146]. Since we shall be obliged in what follows to criticize Thorndike's principles adversely, it seems only fair to note this tendency which he has seen fit to incorporate into his otherwise mechanistic hypothesis.

§ 4—*Thorndike's Hypothesis criticized by showing that the Behaviour of his Animals was not altogether stupid*

Let us now return to Thorndike's theory of learning, according to which acts "teach themselves," so to say, in as much as the animals never participate in what they are doing, and never know that a critical action will bring them freedom and food. Since this assumption of animal-stupidity is at the root of Thorndike's whole theory, we must first of all test it out. In the main,

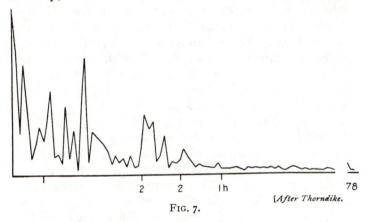

| | 2 | 2 | 1h | | 78 |

[*After Thorndike.*

FIG. 7.

Thorndike derives the proof of his radical thesis from two groups of facts: the time-curves of the animal's performances, and the errors they commit.

The time-curves, which have already been described (p. 154), are so constructed that one millimetre on the ordinate is equivalent to ten seconds, the small marks upon the abscissa indicating interruptions in the experiment. Unless otherwise noted, these interruptions involved a whole day. When several days elapsed before a new trial was made the number of days was indicated near the mark, or if less than a day the number of hours was indicated by the addition of a letter *h*. The curve here reproduced (Fig. 7) is typical of the performance of a cat which in order to secure its freedom had to turn a movable wooden bar-lock from a horizontal into a vertical position. (Locks of this kind are shown upon the door in the picture on p. 154.)

Thorndike argues that if the animal possessed a trace of intelligence it could not happen, as was often observed, that, after having already freed itself several times, the animal was still unable to repeat the act in a later trial. Furthermore, if the animal ever actually grasped the situation, it ought thereafter to be able to proceed immediately without delay to a correct and definite solution of its task. This result would then be indicated by a sharp descent of the time-curve without any recurrent rise; but on the contrary, the time-curves always indicated a gradual descent with numerous recurrent rises. So far as this argument is directed against the explanations offered by an "arm-chair" psychology, it is quite justified, for the animals in these experiments certainly showed no "consecutive thinking." Yet, in declining to accept an anthropomorphic explanation, we are by no means required to assume that all animals exhibit a complete lack of insight. In the first place, many of the curves do actually show the sharp descent demanded by Thorndike as a criterion of insight. Two such curves which relate to the same problem as the first curve are here reproduced (Fig. 8).

These curves show not only a sharp descent, but no recurrent rise even after a long interval of time; a result which also contradicts the law of exercise, since a long pause ought to weaken the bonds previously established (cf. p. 159, and note *141*). Why should we not proceed from cases like these, and lay our emphasis upon the suddenness rather than upon the gradualness of learning? The gradual type of learning, however, which Thorndike found in most of his experiments, impresses him so strongly that he dismisses sudden learning with the remark that "of course, where the act resulting from the impulse is very simple, very obvious, and very clearly defined, a single experience

164

may make the association perfect, and we may have an abrupt descent in the time-curve without needing to suppose inference" [147]. But the position he takes is open to objection, because the description of a solution as "simple," "obvious," and "clearly defined" can apply only to the experimenter and not to the animal. According to Thorndike's own presuppositions the animal does not participate at all, nor does it even understand the

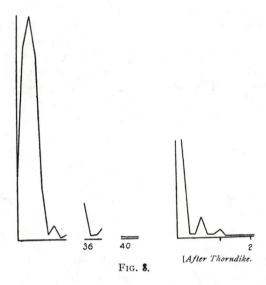

36    40        2

[*After Thorndike.*

Fig. **8.**

solution after it had been mastered; and hence there can be no point in saying that the solution is "obvious" to the animal. The time-curves we have reproduced will indicate how differently different animals behave in the same situation; yet Thorndike is unable to refer to individual differences, because the individual has been excluded from his theory. Therefore, whatever is "simple" or "obvious" can only include that which is "objectively" simple or obvious, and not at all that which is simple or obvious to the animal.

The fact that in these experiments a sudden fall in the time-curve ever should occur, and that it sometimes happens that an animal is able to master its task in a single trial, are matters that can not be simply brushed aside when they do not agree with the law of frequency, which requires a long and troublesome development even for the objectively easiest tasks. Since in the initial trial a single response must always be selected from among a large number of equally possible responses, the law of effect is, therefore, the only one upon which an explanation can be based, and we have already seen that this law is itself in grave need of elucidation.

As a matter of fact the ability of an animal to learn an act by performing it a single time is not at all unusual. Lloyd Morgan in his observation of fowls has reported instances like the following : He brought a chick seven days old to his study, and placed it in a pen made of a newspaper. The chick began to pick and scratch at one corner of the pen until it made an opening, and was able to come out into the room. When caught and replaced in the original position, the chick ran to the same corner, and again pulled down the newspaper, and came out into the room a second time. The chick was then placed on the opposite side of its pen, but it soon returned to the first corner, and released itself a third time in the same way as before [148].

In behaviour like this the inadequacy of Thorndike's principles is keenly felt. It seems quite too nonsensical to suppose that the breaking down of a certain corner of the pen should have nothing to do with the chick's release from the enclosure. Furthermore, the fact that on the third trial the chick ran back to its original corner can only be explained as a matter of chance by Thorndike ; since all that could have been learned in a blindly mechanical fashion was the movement of pulling down the paper, the procedure of the chick to a particular place in the pen not having been included in the original response.

To repeat, then, the conclusion that animals are altogether blind in their learning is not sufficiently assured from the evidence of the time-curves. Nor is the argument which Thorndike bases upon the errors committed by animals any more convincing. Animals which have completed a certain performance one or more times frequently fail in later trials, or act otherwise than they would if they really understood what they were about. "Stupid errors," as Köhler calls them, have often been reported in animal-experiments. Cats have been observed to strike at strings or at levers when the door of the cage was already open. They will also sometimes strike at a certain place after the device which once called for this action has been removed[149]. But must we accept a purely mechanical hypothesis because it can be shown that some acts are not fully comprehended? This question assumes greater importance when it is associated with another; namely: Has the experimenter selected the conditions of his experiment in such a way that the animal could possibly have understood what he was about[150]? A mere glance at the picture of the puzzle-box on p. 154 will suffice to answer this second question in the negative. Without possessing some technical experience, even a man placed inside of such a box would be unable to comprehend these mechanisms of release; for several essential parts are placed upon the outside, and are therefore invisible from within. Accordingly, the connection between the movement made and its effect upon the animal must necessarily be of a purely arbitrary sort. Even in the employment of the simple turning-bar lock which produced such good time-curves, the experimenter did not raise the question whether this lock could be understood by the animal tested. Yet, unless one knows this, one is quite unable to decide where the difficulties lie, and what actually constitutes the animal's achievement in overcoming them.

Before we proceed with our criticism, certain facts should be mentioned which are recorded in Thorndike's experiments, and are substantiated by other investigators. It can be shown, for instance, that animals which have already undergone a certain experimental training are better fitted to meet the somewhat varying conditions of similar tests, than other animals which are being experimented upon for the first time. This is undoubtedly to be explained in part by the fact that the new situation of being locked up in a box gradually loses its terrifying effect upon the animal; accordingly, as the animal becomes less excited, it makes fewer aimless movements. If we compare the time-curves of Fig. 7 with those of Fig. 8, which relate to the same problem, their difference may in part be attributed to this influence; because the first curve is that of an animal learning the act of turning a wooden bar in its first puzzle-box experiment, whereas the two other animals, the time-curves of which appear in Fig. 8, had already been tested in other boxes where the task involved striking, biting, or rubbing against a wire noose hanging some fifteen cm. above the floor [151].

In addition to the general effects of previous experience, certain more specific influences can also be demonstrated. Modes of procedure that prove to be unsuccessful, such as biting at the bars of the cage, or attempting to force the body through too small an opening, are less frequently employed as the animal becomes more experienced in the tests. All these facts can be readily understood in accordance with Thorndike's principles, and would naturally operate to shorten the learning-curve.

It is a different matter, however, when we come to consider another modification reported by Thorndike, namely, "that the animal's *tendency to pay attention to what it is doing* gets strengthened; and this is something that may properly be called a change in degree of intelligence" [152]. But how can this statement be reconciled with the assumption that animals have not the slightest knowledge that their actions have anything to do with their achievements? Why, we may ask, do they give attention; and above all why does Thorndike use the word *intelligence* in this connection?

The facts upon which his statement rests are highly significant. After having once learned to free themselves from the first box by striking at a noose hanging from the front wall of the cage, both cats and dogs were found to require much less time in freeing themselves from a second box in which the noose hung from the back wall. In the case of a particular dog replaced in the same box after a pause of a day or so—the noose being now hung considerably higher than it was before —the problem was virtually solved at once; the three first trials lasted but twenty, ten, and ten seconds, respectively. "After nine days he was put in a box arranged with a little wooden platform two and one-half inches square, hung where the loop was in the previous experiment. Although the platform resembled the loop not the least, save in position, his times were only ten, seven, and five seconds." We have, therefore, in these cases a true *transfer of training;* for the animal employed a procedure which was successful under certain conditions after these conditions had been altered, and he did so in a manner appropriate to the alteration. One might suppose that this would make difficulties for a strictly mechanistic theory of interpretation, but Thorndike believes these difficulties can all be set aside without altering his hypothesis in the slightest. Thorndike objects, quite rightly, to an obsolete psychology which would infer from such observations that the animal must possess "general ideas"; that he must have understood, for instance, that to strike at a loop would bring release, or that "this thing in my cage is a loop" (though, to be sure, the external form of the loop was altered in many of the tests without disturbing the effects of practice). It can not be supposed that the animal is able to infer that a certain object must be struck at, no matter whether it hangs in front or behind, high or low. To such an hypothesis one may rightly object, but at the same time Thorndike blinds himself to what such an achievement actually signifies as an evidence of transfer. Thorndike thinks, for instance, that the animal can not see the separate things of our world at all; that he possesses only a vague total impression of the situation. Thus, a bird diving into the yellow water of a stream, or into a pool, or into an ocean, would not be able to see the difference that we would see in these situations. Only the total situation " water " comes into consideration for the bird; consequently, in the experiments reported, "the loop is to the cat what the ocean is to a man when thrown into it when half asleep "[153]. On the other hand, when a human being is confronted with a task, the total situation is at once broken up into its elements, among which the important ones appear in the foreground. This reduction simply does not take place in animals. Instead, it is the total situation, including its undifferentiated parts, which connects itself with the impulse of response, and this connection is neither influenced when one adds elements to the situation nor when one subtracts them therefrom ; provided *only that something is left which is capable of arousing the impulse.* Hence, to Thorndike, the fact of transfer indicates, not mental progress, but, on the contrary, a very primitive and undifferentiated stage of development.

This is Thorndike's argument, but it is self-contradictory; for in the first place the total situation with all its elements is supposed to be connected with the impulse; while in the second place we are told that the situation can be enlarged or reduced at will, though, as indicated above by the phrase in italics, one element at least must remain unchanged, or the connection itself will be lost.

It is not our purpose to revamp the anthropomorphic hypothesis which Thorndike has so vigorously attacked. On the other hand, our conception of the primitive aspects of the phenomenal world can not be stated in terms of a number of separate phenomena, each clearly set off from every other ; but the facts of the case do not require that we should accept either this older theory or the one Thorndike has advanced. The vague total situation described by Thorndike is not at all what we have previously referred to as a configuration, however primitive ; for the primitive configuration as we conceive it is not a single vague total quality but a " quality upon a uniform ground." Neither do we find Thorndike's " vague total quality " applicable in the explanation of any true transfer of training. Indeed, if " stupid " errors such as we have described occurred more often than they do, the theory of the total situation would be in a better way. If the animal in a puzzle-box, with the loop now hanging behind instead of in front, were directed only in accordance with the vague total situation, it would be forced to strike forward in the direction where the loop previously hung ; and all the more so because its natural behaviour would prompt it to attack its goal directly, rather than turn aside as it must do in order to reach the loop which now hangs at the back of the cage.[154] Yet instead of following this natural tendency which would attract it to the front of the cage, the animal usually alters its behaviour to correspond exactly with the alteration of the most *important* feature of the situation. Is not the inference justified, that in so far as the animal has learned to free itself from the first box, it has also learned to reconstruct the situation in a definite and more or less detailed manner ? If so, the same configuration will again be effective, even when the loop is hung in a different position in the second box. And hence " stupid " errors, or responses carried out without reference to existing conditions (as when the animal strikes at a loop in a position where it no longer hangs), would appear to be essentially different from behaviour in which a real transfer of training is manifest. Thus it is not the " stupid " errors, but the efforts of reconstruction in similar situations, which indicate the higher degrees of capacity for achievement.

To explain a positive performance which happens to involve something more than one was led to expect of it in terms of an inherent deficiency, is always a questionable procedure. We ought, therefore, to proceed methodically and allow the experiment itself to determine whether the animal's performance is to be regarded as an evidence of inherent incapacity or progressive achievement. Even Thorndike's experiments seem to show that the animal not only experiences certain vague total situations, but that in the course of learning this total situation becomes organized. When the loop differentiates itself, it is not as though it were now seen as a circular or elliptical figure of definite magnitude and colour, it is merely "something to be struck at," or "something to be moved." As such, it comes to occupy the central position in the total phenomenal situation. This situation, however, is essentially characterized for the animal as a "situation from which I wish to release myself in order that I may get at the food which lies outside." If, now, the loop becomes the central feature of the situation, this shows that neither it nor the movements made with it are without significance to the animal; for the animal has in some way connected its action upon the loop with the food outside the cage. The theory of an entirely meaningless learning is simply untenable.

The phenomenal description of the loop as " something to be moved " recalls to mind a description employed in the preceding chapter when the distinction was drawn between a "transitional" and an "end-situation." The loop comes to possess this "transitional" character, and to it there accrues a certain definition of the kind and the manner of this transition. In other words, a new characteristic now attaches itself to a stimulus which originally led to quite another phenomenon ; for the loop which first of all was more or less vaguely involved in the total situation now, as a result of learning, gives rise to a new phenomenon. This transformation could not result either from mere association or from a mere increase in the permeability of an already existing connection. We shall soon have something to say in opposition to the principles underlying the entire associational hypothesis. A further discussion of this matter can therefore be deferred until we are ready to take up the question in greater detail. But we have already achieved an important result; for in as much as the loop has acquired a definite transitional character, something actually *new* must have occurred in the animal's experience; or, more generally stated, the learning accomplished in Thorndike's experiments has led to the creation of a new sensory phenomenon.

Even from Thorndike's own results we can see that the facts of the case have not been forced in order to make them fit our theory. Experimenting with seven cats, tests were made of a different sort from those previously described, and with quite different results. In these tests the animal was not allowed to free itself, but the box was opened by the experimenter as soon as the cat had either licked itself, in the case of four of the animals, or scratched itself, in the case of the other three. This experiment was also successful, and it is therefore of the greatest interest to know " whether the animals under these conditions behaved in any wise differently than they did in the other experiments, for here obviously is a kind of *experimentum crucis* " [155]. The behaviour *was* different. As Thorndike describes it, " there is in all these cases a noticeable tendency, of the cause of which I am ignorant, to diminish the act until it becomes a mere vestige of a lick or a scratch. . . . Moreover, if sometimes you do not let the cat out after this feeble reaction, it does not at once repeat the movement as it would do if it depressed a thumb-piece, for instance, without success in getting the door open. Of the reason for this difference I am again ignorant " [156].

Köhler points to this as one of the most interesting of Thorndike's results. We might describe it as follows: The behaviour of the animal is typically different when the movement by which its freedom is gained is objectively meaningless. When the act has no sort of internal connection with release, the behaviour is not the same that it is when the movement leads directly, even though in an obscure fashion, to its end. The difference in the animal's behaviour corresponds with the difference in the conditions imposed, indicating that in the two cases the critical act is introduced into the animal's experience of the situation in different ways ; which means that the act must somehow have something to do with the situation as the animal experiences it, and leads us to assert that with vertebrates, at least, there is no such thing as an entirely meaningless learning.

This conclusion is confirmed by one of McDougall's experiments.[157] Before the eyes of his dog, McDougall placed a biscuit in a box which he then closed. The lid of the box could be opened with comparative ease by pressing upon the handle of a lever. Later on the experiment was made more complicated, though all the complications were simpler in character than were the contrivances of Thorndike's puzzle-box. From these experiments McDougall infers "that while the dog's behaviour was from the first purposive ; . . . the goal, and especially the steps toward the goal, became more defined in the dog's mind as he became more expert in his task." Among the data upon which this conclusion was based, the fact is recorded that after having once learned the task, the dog never repeated a fixed habitual series of movements, but with widely varying movements always achieved the same end.

§ 5—*Ruger's Comparative Tests on Human Beings*

We can now continue our discussion of learning by trial and error, by asking how a human being would behave if he were to be confronted with a similar task. This question has also been investigated in America and it is easy to understand why H. A. Ruger,[158] who undertook the problem, should have been led to do so after an investigation of animal-behaviour which he had previously carried out under Thorndike's direction. Ruger did not need to confine his human subjects in cages in order to force them to exercise their powers by an urge for freedom and food. The good will which they brought to the solution of their problems, strengthened by a desire to solve them as well as they could, furnished an adequate substitute for the more elementary impulses which motivate lower animals. The problem in his case was to solve a mechanical puzzle. The observer received a wire-puzzle and was instructed to remove some part of it. The time was measured from the beginning of the test until the puzzle was solved. The experiment was then repeated, always measuring the time, until the solution took place at once. The puzzle consisted of rings or other devices of wire strung together, the experimental subjects being called upon to find out which element of the group could be released, and how this might be accomplished. In comparison with Thorndike's dogs and cats, these human subjects had a very great advantage, in as much as their problem was far more definite than that of the animal whose single object is to get out of the puzzle-box. Nevertheless, a considerable similarity exists between the two types of experiment; for in neither case was a comprehensive understanding of the mode of solution possible at the outset. This lack of insight was heightened by the fact that the puzzles were three-dimensional devices which most of the observers found themselves unable to fully comprehend. At the same time we know that man desires understanding, and that to him understanding is as much an end as the solution itself, whereas in the case of a caged animal the only desire is to be released. Despite all this the procedure adopted by human beings in solving these puzzles often paralleled very closely the methods employed by the animals of Thorndike's experiments. "The times for repeated success in a number of cases remained high and fluctuating, the time for later trials in a given series being often greater than that for the first success. . . . In practically all of the cases random manipulation played some part, and, in many cases, a very considerable part in the gaining of success." [159] Naturally, connected operations of thought also occurred, and these were accompanied by an abrupt descent in the time-curve, without a subsequent ascent. These, however, were not the rule, and indeed the behaviour could at times be so stupid that manipulations which led to no change at all in the situation were nevertheless repeated again and again. We can see from this how precipitate were Thorndike's inferences; for in as much as his chief argument is based upon the time-curves and upon the "stupid" errors, it ought to be possible to transfer his conclusions directly to human behaviour. On the contrary, untalented as a person may be for this sort of task, he must at least be credited with knowing that his movements have something to do with the solution of the problem at hand. Consequently, if human behaviour is in many respects similar to that of other animals, one has no right to draw the extreme inference that animals lower than man possess no insight whatever. The experiments with human beings have one great advantage over those with animals in that the subjects experimented upon can give information as to how the thing was done. We can thus obtain more or less complete information regarding the internal behaviour of the subject and are not solely dependent upon inferences. If we ask what, then, constitutes learning in these experiments, the answer is that in addition to the mere perfection of manual dexterity learning consists essentially in an *organization* of the whole procedure. Let us eliminate the few cases in which the solution was reasoned out, and follow this process of organization in the other cases. If a successful movement comes about by chance, the first consequence as a rule is this, that the region in which the work is being done, or the particular kind of movement that is being made, is now emphasized and becomes the focus of the whole procedure. In a large number of cases the solution, therefore, is almost entirely a matter of "place-analysis," that is, the subject now knows where he has to work. Thereafter a marked descent is recorded in the time-curve, without recurrent rise. Instead of the gradual elimination of irrelevant movements which had previously been carried out, we find the sudden exclusion of a considerable number of these. Ruger also remarks, quite justly, that many of the sharp nicks in the time-curves of animals may likewise be attributed to this same factor.

What was found true in this very simple case also appeared to be true in more complicated instances. New variations of movements which proved to be successful occurred much oftener unintentionally, by chance, than intentionally. Their influence upon the time-curve, however, depended directly upon the kind of consciousness given to these "fortunate variations"; that is to say, a new movement which brings success remains in the actual possession of the individual so that it can be applied a second time only when it has occurred in such a way that its significance has been recognized. The deeper the insight, the stronger is this influence; a result which, as we shall see, has no significance at all in purely motor learning, but is of great importance in passing judgment upon the behaviour of animals.

The nature of the subject's understanding is described by Ruger in detail. It is not at all a process limited to human ideas, but is one that can take place entirely at the level of perceptual phenomena; in which case the perceptual material undergoes a transformation, often sudden and profound, without in any way involving the introduction of *ideas*. The motor side of the performance is naturally influenced thereby, so that the activity becomes adapted to the newly formulated field of perception. Thus this organization includes both the perceptual and the motor sides of the behaviour; but the completeness of the organization may greatly vary. At the lowest level, the whole process remains but a series of arbitrary steps, one after another. The unity becomes closer when these steps follow one another rhythmically, and at the highest level the activity is unified from beginning to end in the sense that a task is being fulfilled.

We may infer from this description that some degree of organization is also present in the experiments with animals, and that animal - behaviour is not merely an objective succession of events.

In Ruger's cases "transfer of training," or the successful application of a method learned under certain conditions to other and different conditions, always presupposed understanding. One of Ruger's experiments substantiates this statement on the negative side. An observer was tested with a certain puzzle once, and then all the separate acts necessary to its solution were extensively practised in systematic order. The same puzzle was then given to the observer in the same way in which it had been given the first time; but failing to recognize that the practised movements had anything to do with it, the movements he had learned were not applied, and his results showed that he was no better equipped than if he had not had the practice at all. This experiment also indicates that the organization of the motor and the perceptual parts must be undertaken together.

On the other hand, it was frequently observed that a certain practised procedure readily broke into another procedure, even when the subject knew perfectly well that it was entirely irrelevant to his task. This "perseverative tendency" of certain methods deserves special consideration, not only in view of what has already been said, but also in connection with certain experiments upon animals which we are about to describe.

From Ruger's experiments we have gained some insight into the behaviour of human beings in situations which at first were more or less obscure. It has been shown that improvement in efficiency goes hand in hand with an increased insight into the nature of the task. We use this word, *insight*, without theoretical pre-suppositions, in the common sense in which everyone takes it. If one knows that he is to remove a ring in a certain puzzle, and that in order to do so he must first move this piece and then that, turn the puzzle over and do something else, his procedure will be said to possess a greater degree of insight than the procedure of another person who simply goes ahead without any plan at all. But if one also knows that the ring is con-nected in such and such a manner with such and such parts of the device, and that these are again to be turned so and so, his procedure will indicate still greater insight. The conditions of Ruger's experiments were intention-ally chosen so as to make them as like the animal-experiments as possible. For this reason insight entered into them only as a result of a behaviour which origin-ally lacked this quality, a behaviour which could lead to a successful termination of the test only by chance.

§ 6—*Intelligent Learning. Köhler's Experiments with Chimpanzees*

Can experiments be so planned that the animal's behaviour will show insight without the aid of a chance-discovery? When we consider what this means, it at once becomes clear that both animals and children are well adapted to such experiments. Adults, on the contrary, are not suitable subjects, because they bring to their tasks a set of ready-made methods which need only be transferred to the new situation. But how these ready-made methods originated, it is not at all easy to determine. If, on the other hand, the problem selected makes such a transfer impossible, it is hard to find a suitable test; for usually a task of this order is altogether too difficult for an experiment. Hence the study of insight in its incipient forms can best be undertaken with children and animals.

In experiments with animals one should begin with those species in which the relatively best performances may be expected in the problems to be solved. For this reason our choice unhesitatingly falls upon the anthropoid apes. It was therefore an event of scientific importance when the Prussian Academy of Sciences founded its station for the observation of apes upon the Island of Tenerife. While serving as Director of this station, Wolfgang Köhler devoted the major portion of his time to an investigation of this problem. His results are not only of great scientific value, but for a mere description of the life of the chimpanzee, as he observed it, they are also of such unusual interest that his book is worthy of detailed study by all who have anything to do with the investigation and guidance of human intelligence.[160] If chimpanzees are able to solve original problems, not merely by chance, but with insight, then the behaviour of these animals ought to throw new light upon the nature of insight; for modes of behaviour that have become a matter of course with us adults may be expected to appear in a more plastic form in the life of an ape. If the simplest acts of intelligence can in this way be brought under scientific experimental observation, the results must yield important data for theoretical purposes. With adult man, on the contrary, an investigation of the simplest acts of intelligence is no longer possible.

Since Köhler's experiments provide us with the kind of information we need, we shall find it worth while to examine them in detail. Indeed, they furnish us with a significant contribution to the solution of our chief problems, namely the nature of *learning* in general, and the origin of the first *problems of achievement* (cf. p. 152) in particular.

We therefore raise with Köhler this question: Do chimpanzees show insight in their behaviour? Köhler's general plan of investigation was as follows: "The experimenter provides a situation in which the direct way to a goal is barred, but in which an indirect way is left open. The animal is introduced into this situation which has been so planned that it is *fully comprehensible*. The animal is then left to indicate by its behaviour whether or not it can solve the problem by the indirect means that have been provided." [161] The criterion of insight is found in the animal's capacity to select the indirect way unaided. With reference to the words in italics, the experiments were so planned that, in contrast to the puzzle-box tests of Thorndike, the animal required no knowledge of human contrivances in order to select the indirect means to the goal.

But may not the selection of the indirect means still rest upon chance? And is not Köhler's criterion therefore a mistaken one? These questions are un-equivocally answered by the simple observation of what actually takes place; because the true and the chance-solutions are so entirely different from one another in their appearance that one has no trouble at all in reaching a decision as to which is which. In chance-solutions the animal runs now here, now there, each movement being independent of the preceding, so that only by a kind of geometric addition can we trace the curve of the path followed, beginning with the point of departure and ending with the successful attainment of the goal. A true solution is quite different; for the animal pro-ceeds by a single continuous curve from its original position to the attainment of the goal. To be sure, a true solution often follows after a perplexed period of trial and error; but in this case the difference is even more striking, for the animal suddenly gives a start, stops a moment, and then proceeds with a single impulse in a new direction to the attainment of the goal.

Examples of this sort will be given presently ; but let us first note that what holds for animals also holds for children, upon whom Köhler performed parallel experiments, which Bühler has since supplemented.[162] In the case of a child one can often notice the very moment when the right solution first dawns upon him by the way in which his face lights up. Such changes of expression were also noted by Köhler in his chimpanzees.

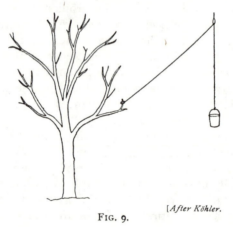

FIG. 9.

[*After Köhler.*

It was Köhler's rule to begin with the simplest problems, and to proceed systematically from these to the more difficult tasks. Only in this way can one be sure in a particular case which portion of the task was most difficult for the animal, and why this or that error was committed.

As his first test Köhler made the following experiment (see Fig. 9): An open basket containing fruit was suspended by a cord from wires crossing the top of the animal's cage. The cord passed through a ring, and the basket hung about two metres above the floor. The free end of the cord was then provided with a wide loop which was hung over a short branch of a neighbouring tree, the branch also being within the cage. This loop was about three metres distant from the basket, and at about the same height. As soon as the loop was removed from the branch the basket, of course, would fall to the ground. This may not seem to be an easy task, yet the situation as such is far more readily comprehensible than were those of the puzzle-box tests. As a matter of fact, the test proved much too complicated to begin with; for the solution of Sultan, the cleverest animal at the station, was made in the following manner: " After a while—the animal being very restless, as he was in all similar situations, particularly upon finding himself in unwonted isolation—Sultan suddenly went to the tree, climbed up to where the cord hung, and remained quiet a moment. Then, while glancing at the basket, he pulled the cord until the basket was drawn up to the ring at the top of the cage. He then let the cord loose and drew it up again, this time more forcibly, so that the basket tipped when it struck the wires above and a banana fell out. He climbed down, took the fruit, climbed up and again began to pull at the basket, but this time he pulled so powerfully that the rope broke, and the basket fell to the ground. Coming down immediately, he took both basket and fruit, and carried them off." [163] When the experiment was repeated three days later under slightly varying conditions, Sultan at once employed the last described type of solution.

We can not get very far with this result. To be sure, the animal has made use of the connection of rope and basket, but why no trace of the intended solution was indicated is not at all clear. Was it because the connection of rope and branch was not noticed, or was this connection incomprehensible to the animal? Perhaps the difficulty lay in the fact that the intended solution would have brought the fruit to the ground rather than into the hands of the animal, thus requiring the ape to employ an indirect means which at first would carry the fruit away from him, rather than towards him. That we can not answer these and other questions with any degree of certainty proves the inappropriateness of this experiment, and also the importance of the rule that one should proceed gradually from simple to more complicated tasks.

We shall now trace the course of Köhler's investigations, in order to review some of his more impressive examples which indicate what these animals can, and what they can not accomplish. Köhler began with a method which was literally one of indirection. Slight indirections, such as overcoming obstacles, are constantly met with in the daily life of these animals. For the purpose of investigating somewhat more difficult modes of indirection the following test was selected. In experiment No. 1 the basket was hung from the roof, but could not be reached from the floor. The experimenter then set the basket swinging near enough to a scaffold so that an animal who had climbed upon this could grasp the basket from his point of vantage.

In other experiments the connection between the animal and the fruit was made by an intervening link in the chain of behaviour. In the simplest case of this kind the connection was already provided by the situation—the question being: Can the animal make use of it? Thus in experiment No. 2, the fruit was placed beyond reach outside the cage, but a string was attached to it which came within the reach of the animal. In the next test (No. 3), the connection between the animal and the goal was not yet established, as it was with the string, but the situation included a stick within the cage as the only means whereby the animal could reach the goal. Similarly in No. 4, the goal was fastened to the roof and a box was placed in the cage which could be employed in order to reach it. A third variation of this method (No. 5), provided that the goal which was hung aloft could be attained if the animal would swing itself upwards by means of a rope which hung at a distance of two metres from the basket. All these experiments involve the *employment of tools*, by which we mean nothing more than the introduction of a mediating factor.

When reversed, this principle leads to the *setting aside of obstacles*. In experiment No. 6 the fruit lay outside the cage with a stick for reaching it conveniently at hand. Within the cage and directly opposite the goal a fairly heavy box was placed, which prevented the animal from employing the stick successfully, thus introducing a new difficulty. In order to attain the goal a tool is required which is not immediately available, because something else must be done before it can be used. This antecedent activity is introduced as a new intermediary which must be first dealt with before the animal can proceed from its original position to the attainment of the goal. This procedure can be described as the *fabrication of a tool*.

In experiment No. 7 the fruit was again placed out of reach in front of the cage, but neither a stick nor anything like a stick was at hand. In the rear of the cage, however, there was a desiccated tree, branches of which could easily be broken off and used as sticks.

In experiment No. 8 a swinging rope suspended from a bar for gymnastic purposes was slung over the bar three times in a manner easily comprehensible to a human being. In order to reach the goal this rope had to be used, but first it had to be uncoiled from the bar.

Experiment No. 9 was still more difficult, for the rope had been removed from its hook, and laid upon the floor; before it could be used it had to be re-hung.

In experiment No. 10, a box which must be placed under the goal in order to reach the fruit was filled with stones so that it was too heavy to move until the stones had first been taken out of it.

In experiment No. 11, two bamboo sticks were provided, each of which was too short to reach the goal; but one stick could be fitted into the other, and when thus put together the tool would be of adequate length.

In experiment No. 12, the "building" test, the goal was too high to be reached by a single box, but if two or three boxes were piled one upon another it might then be attained.

The indirect means to the goal were now elaborated. Before the original goal another goal was introduced which could not itself be directly attained. In experiment No. 13 the animal sat close to the bars of its cage,

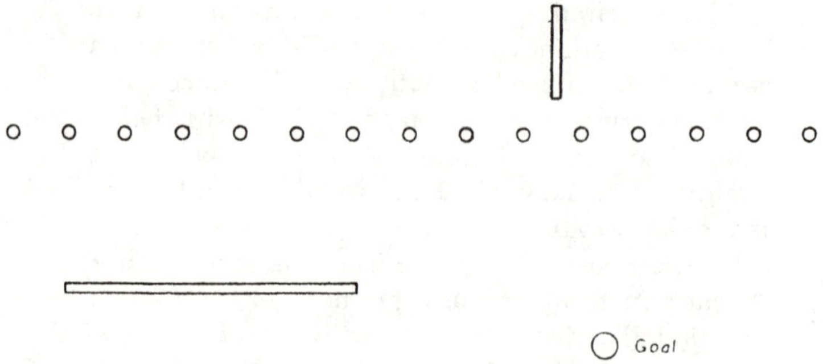

O Goal

[*After Köhler.*

FIG. 10.

opposite the goal which was outside. In the animal's hands was a stick, which, however, was too short to reach the goal. Outside the bars and some two metres to one side of the goal, but lying nearer the bars, was placed a longer stick which could not be reached with the hand, but could be reached with the aid of the shorter stick (see Fig. 10). In experiment No. 14 the stick with which the goal could be reached was hung from the roof, and could be attained only with the aid of a box placed under it. This experiment could then be still further complicated by having the box filled with stones.

The principle of indirection was then varied in two ways. (1) By indirection in the use of the tool: Is

186

the animal capable of finding an indirect means of employing the tool by which the goal is attained? In experiment No. 15, a device was employed which we shall call a "detour-board." The animal sat near the bars, and at a distance of about forty-five centimetres from a square drawer, with open top and lacking a rear wall, which was placed before it outside the cage (see Fig. 11). The fruit was then put in this drawer near the side toward the animal. The animal received a long stick in its hand, but in order to attain the goal the fruit must first be pushed away from the animal, which is contrary to the usual method of bringing the

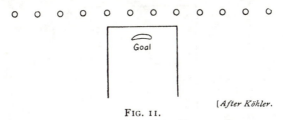

FIG. 11.                    [*After Köhler.*

food directly forwards. After the food had been pushed back until it was free of the drawer, it must then be pushed sidewards; only after it was completely outside the drawer could it be brought forwards. This detour involves an indirect procedure in the true sense of the word.

In experiment No. 16 a further complication was introduced; in order to obtain the food, the stick had first to be removed from the place where it hung by an iron ring, six centimetres in diameter, upon a vertical iron rod, thirty-five centimetres long, which extended from a box. Before making use of the tool, the animal had to remove it from this rod, which meant that the animal must turn ninety degrees away from the goal in order to secure the stick.

A second variation was as follows: (2) " In the course of using the tool the goal was brought into such a position that it could be attained only through an alteration of the animal's position." In experiment No. 17 (Fig. 12) the fruit was placed near the side wall (A) of a large cage which was closed with horizontally nailed boards. One of the upper boards was removed so that the animal could reach inside the cage, though not far enough to touch the floor where the goal rested. The opposite side of this cage (B) was provided with bars through which the animal could also reach, though not far enough to attain the goal when it was placed near A. A stick was then provided which could only

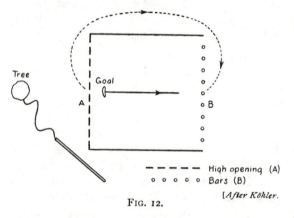

—————→ High opening (A)

o o o o o Bars (B)

[*After Köhler.*

FIG. 12.

be used on side A, since it was fastened by a rope to a tree on that side. In order to secure the fruit, what the animal had to do was first to push the goal with the stick towards side B, and then proceed to the B-side of the cage and procure the fruit by reaching with its hands through the bars.

The plan of all these experiments was to make them perspicuous to the animal. The later and more complicated tests presuppose that the simpler tests have already been successfully performed ; thus new factors were systematically introduced, in order to make the solution constantly more difficult. By this method it was easy to find out from the failures which occurred what the animal's difficulties were.

# INTELLIGENT LEARNING

The reader may ask if the chimpanzees were able to solve all these problems. Before answering, however, let it be stated that individual differences are so marked that one really ought never to speak of the capacity of a certain species. What one animal can do, another can not, and in all these experiments marked individual differences were both demonstrated and measured. With this reservation, the answer to the question is that only one of these experiments (No. 9), failed completely in the case of each animal tested. This was the test in which the rope had to be fastened to a ring in the roof. All the other problems were solved, and most of them as completely as one could wish, though in a few cases it was obvious that the limit of the chimpanzee's capacity had been reached.

By considering the concrete processes involved in the most important of these tests, we can give an account of the chief results. We shall begin with the experiments dealing with the employment of a tool. In this connection, No. 2 deserves detailed description. All the animals were able, without hesitation, to draw in the fruit when it was attached to a string, even when the string was very long; the test having been successful with a string as long as three metres. Nor was this task accomplished in the manner in which an animal might play with a string which it happened to find on the ground, and thus by chance come into possession of the fruit attached to the end of it; on the contrary, it was observed that the string was always drawn "quite literally with regard to the goal. Glancing toward the goal, the animal would begin to draw the string; the animal's behaviour being always directed upon the goal rather than upon the string." We might imagine this to be an obvious procedure for any animal, but when Köhler made a comparative test with a dog that had shown considerable capacity in other experiments involving ordinary features of indirection, he found that the dog was quite unable to carry out this act. Although taking the liveliest interest in the goal, the dog never took any notice of the string which lay beneath his nose [164].

This experiment was also varied with the chimpanzees, so that in addition to the actual connection of one string with the fruit, other strings were also placed near by, all leading in the direction of the goal. In this test it appeared that any string extending to the fruit might be pulled, whether it was fastened to the fruit or not, but that among a number of strings it was the shortest rather than the right one which was the more likely to be grasped. It would seem, therefore, that visual factors determine the behaviour of the chimpanzees in these simple tests, and that a visual connection may take the place of an actual connection—as when a notice-able visual characteristic, such as the shortest length, determines the choice from among a number of strings of different length.

Regarding the employment of sticks in experiment No. 3, attention may be called to the following details. This problem was also mastered by all the animals. Some animals, indeed, were already familiar with it when the experiments were begun. With other animals, where the experiment called for the use of a stick for the first time, it was observed that from the very start the animal would place the stick correctly behind the goal in order to fetch the fruit forward. The employ-ment of sticks can again be made more difficult by a simple alteration of the experimental conditions. The farther away the stick lies from the critical position, the more difficult it is for the animal to make use of it. It sometimes happens that sticks which the animals have previously used lose their significance when they are removed to a sufficient distance. If a stick is so placed that it is not visible when the animal's gaze is on the goal, or in the course of a wandering glance which is limited to the region of the goal, its employment may be prevented. Even if the animal occasionally looks at the stick, it does not necessarily employ the tool, because it can not see both the stick and the goal at the same time. In this respect, "one might say that the chance of a stick becoming a tool is a function of a geometrical constellation."[165] This limitation, however, holds only at the outset; for animals that have often been placed in such a situation soon overcome this difficulty, and thereafter the solution is no longer hindered by a visual separation of the goal and stick.

From this significant influence of visual factors we can understand the actual accomplishment of the animal in his employment of the stick; for it is not merely a matter of seeing or noticing an object such as a stick, because before it is employed the object must cease to be an isolated neutral thing to the animal, and become a member of the situation at hand. The object, must, in short, become a "tool." As a necessary condition for a correct type of behaviour an *alteration must occur in the object of perception*. What at the beginning possessed only the character of "indifference," or "something to bite upon," etc., now obtains the character of a "thing to fetch fruit with." It is thus easy to understand how a spatial separation of the stick and the fruit might render this process difficult; because an isolated thing can spring into a complex more readily when it can be viewed simultaneously with the complex than when it is spatially remote from it.

The difference between the behaviour of dog and chimpanzee in experiment No. 2 indicates that for the chimpanzee the string belongs at once to the complex of the goal, whereas for the dog the string remained an isolated object which does not enter into this complex at all.

The act of employing a stick seems to involve a transformation in the situation confronting the animal; for the stick, which at first was a matter of indifference to the animal, now becomes definitely related to the situation. What the animal has actually learned is to make an irrelevant object relevant to the situation, which is something quite different from an external connection between a certain stick in the field of perception, and a certain sequence of movements. If, for instance, a stick is not available in a situation that requires its use, something else may be employed, such as a piece of wire, the rim of an old straw hat, or a wisp of straw. In short, under these conditions, " anything that is longish and movable may become a ' stick ' in the purely functional meaning of a ' tool-for-grasping '." [166]. Indeed, one of Köhler's apes fetched its coverlet from its sleeping-room, and, pushing it through the bars, was able thereby to whip the fruit within reach.

These performances, like those referred to above (p. 169), also indicate transfer, and from the instances here described it may confidently be said that transfer can *not* be explained in the manner suggested by Thorndike. The chimpanzee's perception of the situation is by no means so obscure that, in a purely visual sense, either a handful of straw, or indeed a coverlet—which furthermore had to be fetched from another room, and did not originally belong to the situation at all—is identical with the stick which was first employed, or so like it that the animal can not apprehend a difference. On the contrary, only one conception of the performance is possible: that the animal has acquired an ability to introduce "tools" into certain situations. Nor is this ability limited to the particular thing with which it was acquired; on the contrary, it is an acquisition of a much more general nature. As Köhler expresses it, the stick as it appears in the field of vision has acquired a definite *functional value* in certain situations, and this effect is itself carried over to any object which may have certain general characteristics in common with sticks, even though these objects appear otherwise quite differently. What is going on in the phenomenal world of the chimpanzee's mind is made concrete to us by one of Köhler's observations. In watching an animal tantalized by the fruit which he can not reach until he has hit upon the employment of a stick or some other tool, Köhler remarks that "in consequence of my anxious expectancy, a transformation takes place in my own field of view, so that longish and movable objects no longer are seen as though they were mere things of indifference, static in their respective positions ; instead, they begin to appear as if in a ' vector,' and as if under pressure they were being drawn toward the critical position."

A transfer of learning from one thing to another results, therefore, from the sensible application of a certain principle of configuration. First, sticks, and later other things, come to acquire a place in the situation, and to enter into its configuration as members. The implication previously suggested (above p. 172)— contrary to Thorndike — with reference to primitive modes of transfer, attains a greater degree of probability in the light of these considerations ; and this behaviour signifies something more than a mere matter of attention. Bühler, however, seems to think that these cases of transfer in Köhler's animals can be explained by attention alone. Whenever we seek an object, according to Bühler, a dispositional state of observancy is aroused in us. Accordingly, if the ape sits "near the bars of the cage while an attractive morsel lies outside, the well-known act of fetching it with a branch is the idea which occupies the ape's mind ; and however vague this idea may be, if the ape chances to be moved by a restlessness to run about the cage—the goal always before him—sticks with which the fruit can be fetched will be the things which most readily emerge in his consciousness." [167] Bühler regards this explanation as in agreement with Köhler's idea of a functional value, but I must confess that what seems to me the most important thing about Köhler's hypothesis is altogether lacking in Bühler's explanation. To say that "things with which one can fetch fruit" emerge in the animal's mind misses the point. By an act of attention a stick or a coverlet may come into the focus of attention; but these articles remain what they were—a stick of wood and something to sleep under. Although they may also be "tools" suitable for fetching fruit, no mere act of attention can endow them with this phenomenal property. Attention, for which "seeking" is a natural condition, is only a secondary consequence of this process. The situation is unsolved, and presses for solution, and the animal's behaviour consists in transferring to certain things the characteristics of a "tool" which they did not previously possess.

Experiment No. 4, involving the employment of a box in attaining a goal which hung too high to be otherwise reached, throws some light upon the nature of the performance when it does not go smoothly at once. The animal in this case was Koko, the youngest ape at the station. At first he sprang and struck at the goal, then he went away from the wall upon which it was hung, but only to return again. "After some time and at a moment when he happened to be away from the wall, he approached the box and, glancing across at the goal, gave the box a slight push, without, however, moving it from the spot. His own movements had now become much slower than heretofore. At first he left the box standing, and took a couple of steps away from it, then he returned and gave it another push, *after again glancing at the goal.* But this act, too, was without sufficient force to indicate that he was really trying to move the box." The procedure was repeated, however, and the next time the box moved some ten centimetres towards the goal. The goal was then made more attractive by the addition of a piece of orange. A few moments later Koko again stood by the box, grasped it suddenly, and pushed it in one movement almost exactly under the goal. He then climbed upon the box, and snatched the fruit from the wall. "Enriching" the goal had strengthened the animal's

194

impulse sufficiently to bring about the solution. One can not say that the animal was at first too indolent to employ a solution he already knew; for a few moments later the experiment was repeated with the goal hung upon another part of the wall, some three metres distant from its former position, and this time the animal failed altogether. The first weak pushes which Koko gave to the box must therefore be regarded as steps preparatory to the true solution. Thus, although the box tended at once to enter into the situation, it was not evident at first how its entrance should be effected. "A single word is appropriate in describing the animal's behaviour during this period, namely, that the connection between the box and the goal was beginning to 'dawn' upon him."

The ape was unable to repeat the solution; for though tested again on the same and on the next day, and later on four different days with greater intervening periods, each trial was unsuccessful. On one occasion he placed the box so near to the wall that standing upon it he could almost have reached the goal. He did, indeed, climb upon the box at once, and reach as far as he could, but he made no attempt to move the box. Obviously it is not enough to bring the box into a general relationship with the situation; for a second point of importance is *how* this relationship shall function.

The experimenter was forced to interrupt these unsuccessful experiments, because the ape in his exasperation would end by rudely mishandling the box. After a pause of nine days—nineteen days after the first experiment — the test was renewed. This time the solution was fairly prompt, and could be repeated thereafter without hesitation. In the meantime the only noticeable after-effect of the first solution was that " something had to be done with the box." [168]

We have described this experiment in full because it furnishes some insight into the stage which intervenes between perplexity and a complete solution. The experiment shows how the direction of the solution was prepared for before the first success was achieved, and how thereafter all that remained was a kind of "place-analysis" which reminds us of Ruger's experiments (see above p. 177).

From another observation upon the employment of boxes, in a later and more complicated experiment, we can see what this behaviour involved. If an animal is unable to make use of a solution with which it is already familiar, the conditions that interfere often indicate what are the most characteristic features of the act. For instance, one of the animals, Chica, strove with all her might to attain a goal suspended from the roof, without ever using a box which stood in the middle of the room, although she had already mastered the use of boxes in similar tests. It could not be said that the box was overlooked, for the animal repeatedly squatted upon it when she was out of breath, and yet she made not the slightest effort to bring the box under the goal. During the whole time, however, Tercera, another ape, was lying on the box; when at length Tercera chanced to fall off the box, Chica grasped it immediately, carried it under the goal, and mounting it snatched down the food.[169] From this behaviour it may be inferred that the box upon which Tercera was lying was not an "object with which to fetch the goal," but "something upon which to lie." Consequently the box simply did not come into connection with the goal so long as it possessed a definite configuration of its own that made it inappropriate as a tool in another situation. To release a thing from one configuration, and transfer it by reconstruction into another configuration, would seem to be a relatively high-grade accomplishment. Nor is this difficulty confined to chimpanzees; on the contrary, it plays an important part in human thought. For instance, when you have need of a shallow dish, it might never occur to you that you could use the cover to a pot, unless such a cover happened to be lying before you on the table, away from the pot, in which case you would probably make use of it at once.

From the point of view of an adult human being, it is not easy to judge whether the problem of setting aside obstacles is simple or difficult for an animal. To us the obstacle-experiment, No. 6, would seem to be far easier than the application of a stick, or a box, as a tool. To a chimpanzee, however, the solution of No. 6 is rather more difficult; for not all the animals were able to accomplish it unaided. In general a chimpanzee is able to fetch a tool from a considerable distance, and bring it to bear upon a situation more readily than he can remove even a very simple obstacle from the same situation; the reason being that it is always hard to break up a definite configuration which already exists.

In the fabrication of tools we find examples in which a "reconstruction" of the situation was successfully carried out. In experiment No. 7, for instance, the achievement consists in seeing a branch as separate from the tree of which it is a part; that is to say, a thing which appears as a branch must be seen as a stick, and this proved to be a very difficult task for the less talented animals. It was noticed also that before a dead branch would be broken from a tree, the animal first tried to release a bar from its cage, because the bar was visibly a more independent object than the branch.

Experiment No. 8 indicates a new difficulty, and consequently a new aspect of the achievement. After experiment No. 5 had been successfully carried out, the test was repeated under the conditions of experiment No. 8; and the result was that every animal strove to pull the rope down from the bar into the normal position from which it could be used as a swing. Yet not a single animal solved the problem correctly by first uncoiling the rope. What the animals did was to grasp the rope any way, and pull it down as far as it would come. Only once in a while could the rope then be used to swing with, and only the best of the gymnasts could employ it successfully. The nature of this behaviour with respect to a coiled rope leads one to think that apes see these simple orderly coils, not as we do, but rather as a confusion of strands like a snarl, which we, too, are apt to attack without any definite plan, by grasping a strand at random and pulling at it. Though objectively a simple construction, a coil of rope seems to be something that a chimpanzee is incapable of apprehending as a clear-cut visual form ; instead, it seems to appear to him as a more or less chaotic figure, and this indicates a certain limitation in his capacity of achievement. This limit, however, is not unsurpassable ; for two years later, when two of the same animals were again confronted with this problem, one of them, Chica, solved it at once, completely and adequately, by uncoiling the rope as well as any man could. The other animal, Rana, although less successful, at least behaved with much greater assurance than she did before. Some development in the capacity of visual configuration and reconstruction seems therefore to have taken place in both these apes, although Köhler estimates the degree in which this capacity can be improved very slight.

Unusually impressive was experiment No. 11 with the double-stick. It was the cleverest animal, Sultan, who was here tested, and even he depended for his success upon the assistance of chance. For over an hour Sultan had laboured in vain, trying among other things the following procedure : one stick was first stretched as far as possible in the direction of the fruit, and then carefully pushed still farther by the second stick until the goal was actually touched. Thus, a contact was made with the goal, but unfortunately one that could not be used. This vain attempt at a solution was nevertheless fully carried out, so as to constitute a uniform configuration connecting the animal with the fruit. The experiment was then given up, and Köhler departed. Sultan, however, retained the two bamboo sticks, and the keeper remained at his post. It was the keeper who observed the animal, first sitting upon a box which stood near the bars, then rising, picking up the sticks, and after reseating himself on the box, beginning to play with them aimlessly. "In the course of this procedure it happened by chance that Sultan held one stick in each hand in such a way that they came into line with one another. He then placed the smaller one in the opening of the larger, sprang at once to the bars, toward which his back had previously been half-turned, and began to draw in one of the bananas with the double-stick. I called to the director, though in the mean time the sticks had fallen apart, because they had not been well fitted together; but the animal immediately replaced them." So runs the report of the keeper, and Köhler himself arrived in time to see the rest of the animal's performance of refitting the sticks together and securing the fruit[170]. After his first success Sultan repeated the act a number of times, without stopping to eat until he had fetched into his cage, not only all of the fruit, but also a number of other things. He appeared to enjoy the act, and he retained the method of solution so well that on the following day he was able to construct a still longer stick from three bamboo stalks. Although Sultan's solution depended upon the help of chance, chance operates here quite otherwise than it does in the experiments described by Thorndike; for it was not chance that led to the goal, nor did chance provide a practicable tool; instead it was the chance-situation when the two sticks were in line with each other, that favoured the correct solution. The solution itself was authentic, as the animal's subsequent behaviour proves. As soon as the two bamboo stalks were seen as one, they were likewise seen as the tool which had previously been lacking. Although a "fortunate variation" assisted in the solution, the solution itself is in no wise to be counted as having been one of chance. In order rightly to evaluate the assistance thus rendered, we must review the situation in the light of our own ways of thinking. While it is, of course, a greater accomplishment to be able to solve a problem by thinking it out, it is often difficult enough for human adults to make use of a chance circumstance as Sultan did where he passed from a type of behaviour without insight to an action which possessed this quality. Thus chance and insight are by no means opposed to one another, for insight frequently comes through the employment of chance.

Acts of building, as described in experiment No. 12, again furnish new data ; for in these performances the behaviour of the animals indicated very clearly that two different problems were involved. The one of setting a box on top of another box is no great task for an animal which already knows how to use boxes ; but the problem "of placing one box upon another so that it will stay there is extremely difficult"; this problem requires that a body of a certain form shall be united with another of similar form to produce a definite result —something which the chimpanzee never accomplished with insight, but only by trial and error. An ape will use structures so insecure that we would scarcely dare touch them with the finger for fear they might topple over ; yet the ape does not hesitate to mount them, and with his great bodily skill he is often successful in reaching the goal before the whole building tumbles down. Here again we have evidence that the animal's visual insight is limited.[171]

Experiment No. 13 was solved with insight by the more talented animals. What was demanded in this solution is again shown by the behaviour of the less talented apes, who, being unable to detach the shorter stick from the configuration involving bars and goal, could not compass the more complicated configurations leading from the shorter stick to the longer stick, and from this to the final goal.

Where problems requiring detours that involve independent, intermediate ends are correctly solved, the primary and secondary goals belong in such wise to the total configuration that they acquire very different kinds of value for the animal. This is again revealed by characteristic errors. In experiment No. 14 Koko was moving a box to the wall upon which hung a stick needed to secure the fruit; but on his way he had to pass by the fruit, and when he came near it "he was suddenly deflected from his straight course towards the stick, and began to use the box as if it were a stick with which to reach the fruit." Thus, influenced by the greater effectiveness of the fruit itself, when it was near at hand, the originally present and correct configuration of the solution was quite destroyed before it could be carried out.

The "detour-board" of experiment No. 15, in which the fruit had first to be pushed away from the animal before it could be seized, was in many respects informing. In the first place this problem was so extraordinarily difficult that even Sultan was unable to solve it completely. Only one animal, Nueva, after poking vainly at the fruit a great many times, suddenly reacted with the correct solution by shoving the fruit to the open end of the drawer—that is, at an angle of 180° away from herself. But even in her case, when the goal was almost at the open end of the box, a counter-action was suddenly made which brought the fruit back some five centimetres towards her, after which the problem was correctly solved. Counter-actions of this sort appeared again and again in later experiments, showing how difficult it was to overcome a strong contradictory tendency; and yet one would be inclined to think that, for an animal that makes detours so easily and so naturally as the ape, this one with the aid of a tool ought to be a very simple matter. On the other hand "even behaviour with insight which indicates intelligence must not receive an interpretation too highly intellectualistic." [172]

201

Sultan was the only other animal to succeed in this test; and he was aided by chance as he had been in the case of the double-stick previously described[173]. He was then able to accomplish the task of first pushing the goal at an angle of 180° away from himself; but the experiment had to be made easier for all the other animals. This was readily done by simply turning the drawer at a certain angle; whereby one could also measure the degree in which the test was made more easy, because as the detour-angle became smaller, it was found that animals hitherto unable to accomplish the task could now do so. Thus the size of the angle at which the problem was first solved could be taken as a direct measure of the accomplishment, and likewise of the intelligence employed. When the drawer lay parallel to the bars of the cage, so that the detour-angle was 90°, all the animals were successful. The rank attained by the animals in these tests also corresponded exactly with one which Köhler had previously estimated. Thus the detour-board proved to be an excellent test of intelligence.

Test No. 16 also indicated a limit to the ape's intelligence. To lift a ring from a nail was a performance which only the cleverest animals could carry out, and then only in their best moments. It was not merely by chance, however, but with insight, that the task was then accomplished. "The ring on the nail appears to present a visual complex to the chimpanzee which can only be completely mastered in case the conditions of attention are favourable at the moment. On the whole, however, there is a marked tendency to see the ring on the nail in a more obscure manner as soon as the animal falls short of the requisite degree of attentiveness"[174].

Considering all these tests together, we find the animals actually solving new problems which have been presented to them. Furthermore, the essential thing about these solutions is not a new combination of movements with which the animals were already familiar, but a "new configuration of the whole field." As has been shown by the previous discussion, the assumption that we are dealing with new combinations of old modes of behaviour can be maintained only if we accept chance as the creator of these new connections. To one who understands Köhler's experiments, it is impossible to assume that chance played any such part in them. This conclusion is obvious when we review the two chief arguments advanced by Thorndike in favour of the chance-hypothesis. Thorndike's first argument, derived from the form of the time-curve, must certainly be given up; for in view of the long periods of time which often intervened in these experiments before the animal found a solution to the problem, it is quite apparent that time-measurements of the chimpanzee's behaviour would not decide the question of chance-insight. These periods were always occupied, either by activities which had nothing whatever to do with the solution, or else by rest. During such a pause, however, Sultan "would scratch his head slowly, otherwise moving nothing but his eyes or perhaps his head, while he observed the situation about him in the most careful manner" [175]; which indicates clearly enough to the observer with what kind of behaviour the ape was engaged during these vagrant periods. As for the solution itself, it occurred typically as a single course of action without a break; and when the test was repeated the correct action would be almost immediately carried out. Thus, if one were to use time-curves at all, their evidence would be very strikingly against the operation of chance.

Thorndike's second argument based upon "stupid" errors appears to have as little weight as the other. Altogether Köhler observed but eight instances which might be called "stupid" errors; each of these was "an 'after-effect' of an earlier correct solution that had been frequently repeated, and had therefore acquired a

203

tendency to reappear without reference to the particular situation at hand. Furthermore, conditions favouring such errors appeared to be states such as sleepiness, fatigue, having a cold, and also excitement "[176].

Along with these "stupid" errors certain other mistakes occurred which have a special significance in understanding the behaviour involved. These other errors arise when one part of the principle of solution is correctly understood, while at the same time the problem involves some difficulty with which the animal is unable to cope. Thus, for instance, in order to increase the length of his stick, the animal would often seize two sticks and place them with the end of one touching the end of the other. This provided him with a longer stick, to be sure, but not with one he could use. It was this procedure that furnished the initial stage of Sultan's double - stick solution (see above, p. 198). To give still another example, the following behaviour was observed in the building - experiment. Chica found that with one box alone she could not attain the goal, no matter how high she jumped from it. "Suddenly she grasped the box with both hands and, pressing it with great force against the wall of the room, lifted it to the height of her head in the direction of the goal which hung above. If only the box had remained stuck to the wall her problem would have been solved; for then she might easily have climbed upon it and reached the goal "[177]. "Good" errors of this kind certainly can not be explained by chance; because the acts we have called "good" errors do not appear in arbitrary situations, but only under conditions where they signify something "good," that is, where they actually bring the animal somehow nearer its goal.

With respect to the problem of achievement considered at the beginning of this chapter, Köhler's experiments show that chimpanzees accommodate themselves to new situations, and solve new problems, by actually undertaking new modes of behaviour. As

Köhler has expressed it [178], the directions, the curves, etc., of these solutions may spring as *autochthonous* (and not necessarily "from experience") out of a stationary situation. This conception also supports the explanation given above of the animal-experiments reported by American psychologists. In the achievements of Köhler's chimpanzees we find new creations of a pure type occurring, in these experiments, quite free from chance. Instead of the solution first arising by chance, and thereafter becoming more or less "understood," understanding, or an appropriate transformation of the field, precedes the objective solution. We may therefore be permitted to call solutions of this kind intelligent performances of a primitive order. When a solution is found, the situation is altered for the animal in such a way that a gap in the situation is closed; that is to say, the desired but unattainable fruit has come within reach. We have here the characteristics of "closure" already met with in a previous connection (above p. 103); for when the problem is "solved" everything in the perceptual situation depends upon the total configuration. Likewise every movement has its place, so that the configuration, as we have called it, becomes unequivocally defined and complete. Dynamically considered, a configuration in time—and we now understand by configuration, not merely a plan in the field of perception, but the total process of the solution leading up to the attainment of the goal—has both a *beginning* and an *end*.

§ 7—*Other Interpretations placed upon Köhler's Experiments*

Before proceeding to evaluate the results thus far obtained, we must defend our position against certain objections that have been made to the conception of the chimpanzee's performance as a new creation, or as a sensible reconstruction of the situation with which he is confronted.

Bühler, for instance, who has considered Köhler's experiments in great detail, expressly recognizes both the value of the method and the far-reaching results obtained [179]. With respect to the interpretation of these results, however, he advances certain critical objections. Yet to my mind his objections appear to rest upon a failure to realize the precise bearing of Köhler's point of view upon the explanatory principles of psychology in general; for what Bühler attempts is to make the behaviour of these animals comprehensible in terms of the usual principles of psychology; whereas the results themselves seem to prove that these principles are inadequate, and must therefore be replaced by others. Summarily expressed, traditional psychology makes use of the following principles of explanation: *sensation* and *image*, *memory* (including the associative mechanism), and *attention*. Now Bühler belongs in the front rank of those psychologists who have recognized the incompleteness of this framework, particularly as regards the explanation of *thinking*. He has therefore supplemented these principles with others, although he still retains the older ones unaltered [180]. In a special case (p. 193 f.) we have already found it necessary to reject his elucidation of one of the chimpanzee-experiments, where he employed the principle of attention in explanation of a type of behaviour which appeared to us an outcome of the law of configuration. We shall now examine the nucleus of Bühler's ideas in greater detail, in the hope of being able to demonstrate the significance of the principle of configuration which we have adopted.

Bühler agrees that the behaviour of these chimpanzees must be sharply differentiated from what one calls instinct and training. By training Bühler means learning after the manner of Thorndike's animals, whereas Köhler's animals solve their problem with the aid of inner mental processes equivalent to those we call reflection. These inner processes can be regarded only as an equivalent, however, and are not at all identical with true reflection. In contrast to training, the behaviour of these apes may be designated as "discoveries," but according to Bühler, one must differentiate a true discovery from a discovery by chance, which only indicates the blind activity of an associative mechanism, without insight. Bühler endeavours, then, to show that the behaviour of these chimpanzees can be fully understood in terms of chance-discoveries, or at any rate that no evidence has yet been given of the existence of any higher accomplishment.

With this purpose in view Bühler employs a series of assumptions which he tries to support by reference to Köhler's descriptions. (1) "The principle of making a detour and the principle of fetching a fruit by pulling down a branch, or by tearing one off for this purpose" —these, he thinks, belong to the chimpanzee's instinctive dispositions. (2) The chimpanzee is able to *empathize*, or feel itself towards, the end-situation of attaining its goal; which is "not difficult to explain theoretically as a memorial after-effect of successful pursuits of a goal in the past." By these means, the ape can find his way to the goal, whether the way be conceived in the ordinary meaning of the term, or as providing an appropriate tool. (3) So far as material relations determine the behaviour of the animal, the assumption suffices that these relations are merely "noted," just as sensory contents are noted.

The third point is the more important; for from it Bühler infers that no real insight into the activity has been demonstrated. But what is implied by this statement that material relations are "noted"? In the first place, the statement refers only to the objective behaviour of the animal—for instance, that a connection between the stick and the fruit such as might be readily grasped by a human observer has likewise been employed by the animal. But "noting" is also commonly used as a description of inner behaviour, and Bühler also employs the term in this way. The latter usage would signify that along with the phenomenon in which this possible connection has been presented to the animal, there is added something else—the "noting" of it—which may or may not be represented phenomenally, and hence the previously unnoticed phenomenon becomes a noticed phenomenon, though otherwise it remains unaltered. A certain blue within the field of vision does not become another colour-tone through my noting it, and according to Bühler's argument this assertion of persistence without alteration applies both to material relations, and also quite generally to any relation whatsoever [181].

This hypothesis can be attacked from two sides. In the first place one can say [182] that a psychological description must limit itself, initially, to the determination of what is phenomenally given; whereas the employment of a concept like "noting" carries us beyond the phenomenal data of observation. When I say that I have failed to notice the difference between two colours, my statement is ambiguous and incomplete to a psychologist, because what he wishes to know is what I actually did note—what positive phenomena were present. In the case we have cited the answer might be: that the two colours were identical. But the psychological description (without noting) would then contradict the objective description (with noting); because it has been assumed that the noting of a phenomenon, whether of a sensory content or of a relation, leaves it qualitatively unchanged; whereas here in noting the phenomenon a relation of equality has been changed to one of inequality. At least I do not see how one can state the case otherwise from the point of view of Bühler's argument. If, however, the observer is unable to tell what the phenomenon was before he noted it, then, of course, we have the case for which this hypothesis of noting was put forward. But have we a right to substitute a noted for an unnoted phenomenon?

INTERPRETATIONS OF KÖHLER

Must we not rather ask upon what this ignorance of the so-called unnoted phenomenon depends? In other words, what is the positive, phenomenal characteristic of a complex so questionable that it calls forth a reply of ignorance as to its nature? An answer to this question is not so difficult: the phenomena which now appear as two colours were previously not there at all, even though their stimuli were operative. These stimuli would then provoke phenomena having the characteristics of what we previously called a *background*. Noting would then signify that a background-effect has been transformed into an effect of quality. Applying this interpretation to the experiment with the apes, the implication is that when the ape notices certain material relations he transforms the perceptual field in which these " material relations " were previously lacking into one in which they become central. Thus the field is altered so as to present a *new* configuration adequate to the problem. This, however, is what we have repeatedly referred to as being the essential feature of the animal's achievement.

The hypothesis of noting can also be tested in a second way, by asking what it can do in the explanation of a concrete case. Bühler assumes that the animals simply note the material relations that are given; but these relations in which the parts of a situation stand to one another, and to the situation as a whole, are innumerable. A stick, for instance, may be at the right of an animal and at the left of a tree; it may be nearer to the tree than it is to the bars of the cage, it may be longer than a piece of wire which is closer at hand; etc., etc. The theory must explain why, among all these innumerable relations, it is precisely the most important one that comes to be noted as the determinant of behaviour. What we should say is that an intelligent construction of the field takes place with respect to the goal, and that the solution is nothing else than the arousal of this construction.

209

Hence the problem of innumerable relations does not exist for us, because "innumerable relations" do not determine a meaningful configuration. If one wishes to eliminate intelligence, and refer to the event as the blind effect of an associative mechanism, one must be prepared to explain why it is precisely the significant rather than the insignificant relations that are noticed. It seems to me that Bühler has confused the issue by approaching it with a fixed definition of "insight," which presupposes a judgment involving experiences of certainty and assurance [183]. Since judgments of this sort have not been demonstrated in the case of chimpanzees, insight must therefore be denied them. But even if Bühler's description were appropriate to the behaviour of adult human beings when they act with insight, it would not at all follow that the simplest kind of behaviour with insight must likewise possess these characteristics of judgment. Thus Lindworsky, who has gone much further than Bühler in his criticism of Köhler's work, remarks that the apprehension of relations need not imply any assurance; this apprehension being "neither certain nor uncertain, but simply undoubted [184]." We should say that "significance" resides in the configuration, in the "noted material relations" themselves, whereas Bühler seems to assume that something new must be added to endow a content with meaning. Thus when we think it through, Bühler's third assumption seems only to lead us back again to our own hypothesis.

Let us now see how matters stand with regard to his two other assumptions. The first one, that detours are instinctive, would make it useless to try to give any explanation at all; because all instincts can be characterized by their goals, whether they be instincts of nourishment, of sex, of nest-building, or of anything else; yet such a characterization of instinct never indicates how a new path involving a definite detour can be determined merely by the situation at hand.

Again and again we have seen that instinct inhibits the ape from following a detour, and impels him to follow a more direct course; and even Bühler recognizes that the performances of Köhler's apes must be sharply differentiated from those of instinct [185].

The second assumption of placing oneself in the end-situation, and then finding a way back, is of no greater help, for it is altogether a matter of opinion whether or not one is justified in attributing any such capacity of projection to the apes [186]. Certainly Bühler has not demonstrated that this capacity must be granted them. Indeed, his data [187] would agree quite as well with an assumption that the animal really comprehends the achievements both of himself and of others of his kind. Nor can I see that anything has been gained by Bühler's assumption. Why should it be easier to find one's way from the goal back to the starting-point, than to find it in the opposite direction? The principal thing is the finding, and what the nature of this achievement must be we have seen in our discussion of Bühler's third assumption.

In order to be more concrete, let us see how Bühler conceives the associative mechanism to function.

"That the animal knows how to handle branches appropriately . . . does not astonish us, because this does not exceed the capacities of instinct and training. Certainly an arboreal animal must be quite familiar with the connection of branch and fruit. If, now, he sits in a cage before the bars of which a 'branchless fruit' has been placed, while within the cage there is a 'fruit-less branch,' the psychological achievement would be mainly to incorporate the two, so to speak, into one idea. Everything else is self-evident" [188]. The explanation requires no insight, because the assumption of a chance-discovery is sufficient. This interpretation is characterized by the employment of well-known principles of psychology, among which *memory* and *ideation* play a leading part. Yet I believe it can be shown that a true explanation is not thereby furnished us. Bühler states that before the bars a " branchless fruit " has been placed, while within the cage there is a "fruitless branch"; but actually we have only a fruit outside and a stick inside. In order to see the fruit without a branch, and the branch without a fruit, would necessitate an achievement in which an isolated thing becomes a member of a configural whole. The appearance of ease and obviousness, which this achievement seems at first to possess, arises only because we refer it to the animal's memory, upon the assumption that the animal has seen fruit on branches, and branches with fruit, so often in the past that now the appearance of fruit arouses the idea of a branch which should belong to it ; and similarly the sight of a branch suggests the fruit which ought to hang from it.

But surely this carries us into the realm of speculation, without any possibility of testing the validity of assumptions which demand a high degree of ideational ability [189]. In seeing a fruit lying upon the floor in the environment of its present artificial surroundings, we have to assume that an idea is aroused in the mind of the animal deriving from days long since past in the forest. Likewise, the animal is called upon to perceive a bare stick as a "branch" in order to be able to reproduce the fruit which should hang from it; whereas the branches upon which the animal formerly found its fruit in the forest must have had leaves ; furthermore they would not normally be seen as isolated parts, but as members of a tree or of a group of trees in which the animal lived. From his intimate knowledge of apes, Köhler concludes that their ideational material is at best very rudimentary, and that so-called " images " are virtually a negligible factor in their experience. Köhler also points out that images would be of little help to animals whose visual perception of relatively simple forms tends always to remain vague and confused. Even adult human beings must often strive to overcome a confusion of ideas, and this effort would presumably be hopeless in an animal whose perceptions are vague to begin with. Bühler accepts Köhler's opinion as well-founded [190], yet this certainly undermines his assumption that apes can reproduce their perceptions. Furthermore, if imaginal reproduction were frequent among apes one might expect that a real branch, still in the possession of its branch-function, would be more readily employed as a tool than a mere stick, or the rim of a hat. We have seen, however, from the relevant experiments of Köhler (No. 7 in our list above, pp. 185 and 197) that the result was just the opposite; since the ape found it very difficult to perceive a branch as something which can be torn loose from a tree; although, according to Bühler, it ought to be easier to imagine a fruit in connection with the branch of a tree than to imagine it associated with a stick lying upon the floor. We have interpreted the difficulty of the branch-experiment as indicating that it is very hard to destroy an already existing configuration, and we have applied this principle of configuration to the difficulty the animal finds in setting aside an obstacle. Here again the difference between our theory and Bühler's mode of interpretation is apparent; for Bühler explains the latter difficulty by saying that an arboreal animal like the chimpanzee seldom has any occasion to set aside an obstacle, and his achievements are merely a matter of memory.

A third objection to Bühler's ideational theory may be stated as follows: When an animal in its wild state wishes to attain a fruit hanging from a branch, it will usually bend the branch towards itself, or else break the branch off. But when one of Köhler's animals employed a stick for the first time as a tool, it placed the stick immediately behind the goal, and began to poke the fruit forward in the right manner. The essential feature of this performance obviously has nothing in common with the animal's behaviour in the forest.

The connection of the branch with the fruit in one idea presupposes a higher ideational level than we have any right to assume in the animal. Furthermore, the ideational supplementation of a fruit without a branch, or of a branch without a fruit, would at best provide nothing more than the idea of a fruit hanging from a branch. Since only that which has once been experienced can be "reproduced," the idea in this case would be nothing but a fruit on a branch; it could not indicate how the fruit seen at the moment might be brought into connection with the stick which is at hand, for this would involve a new achievement. I am therefore unable to understand how Bühler's assumption makes everything else "self-evident"[191]. As I see it, the problem is to bring the fruit and the stick together. But, disagreeing with Bühler, I find this connection to be: (1) not in the field of ideas, but in the field of perception; (2) I find it to be, not the reproduction of an earlier experience, but the apprehension of a new connection; and (3) I do not assume the opposed relations of a fruit without a branch, and a branch without a fruit to be present *before* they are united; on the contrary, all the perceptual situation contains at first is a desired but unattainable fruit together with a quite irrelevant stick. Consequently the stick could not be regarded by the animal as "lacking a fruit" until after it had entered into some sort of configural relationship with the fruit. Bühler's assumption is therefore superfluous; instead, we have a new configuration suddenly arising in which an irrelevant stick becomes a "bridge" in the situation of the ape's desire for the fruit. The sudden grasping of the solution which results is a process that runs its course in accordance with the nature of the situation, so that the complete solution of the problem takes place with reference to the configuration of the field of perception; and this is what Köhler maintains to be the criterion of insight. Indeed, this is the chief result of Köhler's experiments;

and it is a result which applies not only to our knowledge of apes, but also to the whole psychology of insight and of intelligent learning. The far-reaching implications of the principle of configuration are at once obvious. Not only are explanations based upon the theory of association unnecessary, but the principle of configuration denies the entire concept of association as it has previously been employed by psychology in terms of external and meaningless bonds of connection.

Yet Köhler's conclusion that chimpanzees show indications of insight has been attacked by P. Lindworsky in a far more radical manner than by Bühler. To Lindworsky insight begins with the apprehension of relations, which he denies to the apes. Instead, Lindworsky employs a number of explanations for the ape's behaviour which involve instincts and recollections of forest life, quite as Bühler has done. He then draws two important conclusions: First, in contrast with man, the anthropoid species, he says, has stood for thousands of years at a stationary mental level; consequently "the chimpanzees' mode of behaviour could not possibly show insight even though we should find ourselves unable to explain it in any other way." [192] Secondly, "the achievements of chimpanzees can not rest upon the apprehension of relations, for if they did we should be faced with the contradiction that in some acts a very large number of ready and relatively high-grade apprehensions of relations are observable, whereas in others we meet with the most remarkable absence of this capacity." [193]

I regard neither of these arguments as conclusive, but with reference to the second will remark that what is difficult, and what is easy, in the apprehension of relations is something that can be determined only by experiments such as Köhler has performed. Contradictions may exist between assumptions made regarding different achievements, and the results of the experiments, but certainly not between the difficulties

215

themselves and Köhler's contention that the animal's solutions involve an "apprehension of relations" with true insight.

## § 8—*Criticism of Köhler's Experiments*

We might conclude this discussion here were it not for the fact that Köhler's critics have attacked his work in still another way. Let us recall the experiments on choice-training which indicated the primitive nature of configural functions. In these experiments a test was made to find out whether training was a matter of an association established between a movement and an "absolute" sensory content, or if the bearing of one upon the other—that is, the configuration itself—determined the animal's behaviour. The connection between the achievement and the configuration is certainly quite arbitrary and meaningless when food is placed in either the brighter or the darker box, according to the will of the experimenter. It should also be remembered that in the critical test-experiments which followed after training, both boxes contained food. Under these conditions either the "absolute" or the "configurative" choice might have been expected, and either would have satisfied the animal's want. Since from our point of view a test of "intelligence" involves a configural function, it ought to be possible to place the animal under conditions where there would be an alternative between an "absolute" and a "configurative" choice, the "configurative" response being intelligent, whereas the "absolute" response would remain unintelligent. An experiment of this kind was developed from the test with the double-stick (cf. above p. 198 f.)[194]. In connection with this experiment it should be noted in advance that in fitting the sticks together the ape always placed the thinner one within the thicker one, holding the thicker one passively in the left hand and moving the thinner one towards it with the more skilful right hand. In a special series of experiments Köhler employed four tubes of different diameter so that No. 1 fitted into No. 2, No. 2 into No. 3, and No. 3 into No. 4. Two of these tubes, chosen in the serial order as given, were laid horizontally parallel before the animal, sometimes the thinner and sometimes the thicker being nearer at hand. No. 2 now became the thicker when paired with No. 1, while it was the thinner when paired with No. 3. Out of twelve trials Sultan grasped the thinner tube at once with the right hand, and the thicker with the left hand, eight times. In the other four trials, in which the sticks were at first grasped differently, they were changed " as quick as they were seen in the hands, without any testing, and always before the animal undertook the performance itself." In the majority of cases the animal picked up stick No. 2 with the left hand, or with the right hand, according as it was to be combined with No. 1 or No. 3. In other words, the ape handled the objects with reference to the configuration in which they stood to one another. Chica, who had previously acquired the double-stick method from Sultan, behaved likewise in these tests. Only once in the twelve trials was the thinner tube placed in the thicker one by the left hand.

In this behaviour Köhler finds a proof of insight into the solution of the problem, because the apprehension of the bearing of the two diameters upon each other determined with certainty the function of each tube. Thus Köhler contends that the manipulation of things with reference to their important material relations can be employed as a criterion of behaviour with insight—that is to say, of intelligence.

This conclusion is attacked by Lindworsky, who maintains that it involves a logical fallacy, because the same criterion can be applied to instinct. The only criterion of intelligence, he thinks, is " the manipulation of things with *complete insight*, or the manipulation of things in consequence of an insight into their material relations "[195]. I must confess I can find no logical fallacy in Köhler's procedure. What we have to determine is whether an observed behaviour shows insight or not, whether it is an intelligent performance or not; but the criterion by which this decision is reached must not itself include the concept of insight. Lindworsky's reference to instinct is inappropriate, because in purely instinctive manipulations the more important material relations are impotent just as soon as the situation varies to any considerable extent from the normal type of behaviour. This has been shown with remarkable clearness in the work of H. Volkelt [196] upon the behaviour of the spider. Volkelt observed that the spider will rush out of its nest and attack a fly which has been caught in its web. The fly is killed and fastened to the net; after which the spider returns to its nest, and proceeds to finish its meal upon another fly whose remains are still in its possession. Only after its meal is finished does the spider return to the web and bring the new prey into its nest. On the other hand, if one introduces a living fly into the nest, the same spider will react to it with the behaviour of flight and avoidance. Moreover, in the case of the chimpanzee, when the situation includes fruit beyond its reach and two sticks at hand, each too short for its purpose, we can hardly imagine an instinct which could guide the ape in putting these two sticks together.

Lindworsky inquires further, at what point in the act of the double-stick experiment does insight occur? But as soon as we have given up the idea that the performance consists of separate bits, and are ready to conceive it, instead, as a single total response of the type which we have described as a "closure," this question is quite irrelevant. Lindworsky, however, fancies he can detect three points at which insight might have occurred: (1) in the recognition as to which is the wider tube; (2) in the sticking of the smaller tube into the larger one ; and (3) in the employment of the lengthened stick. He then proceeds to deny insight at each of these three points ; believing that all three achievements can be otherwise explained. Taking up these points in the process in reverse order, No. 3 "explains itself as a chance-solution favoured by the pleasure which attaches to the desire for food, and thereafter made easy by self-training (Köhler)." But compare this description with the one given of the first experiment (cf. above, p. 199) ; and observe how Sultan, while first angling for the fruit, repeated the act of putting the sticks together immediately after they had fallen apart ; then observe how he continued to angle after many valueless things which he poked into the cage before he began to eat the fruit. Furthermore, let us not forget the difficulties we encountered with reference to the current theory concerning the influence exerted by pleasure upon learning, and likewise our discussion of the part played by chance, especially in this case (above p. 199). Chance-solutions, the favourable effects of pleasure, and self-training, all these terms are quite inappropriate to the actual conditions and results. According to Lindworsky, the second point in the procedure—the placing of one stick in the other—may well be an instinctive act. "In building a nest," he writes, "if it is requisite that a new twig should be introduced into the already plaited form, it is quite natural that the left hand of the ape should be placed at the opening while the right hand thrusts in the twig." The uniformity with which the animal always sticks the thinner into the thicker tube—never covering the thinner by the thicker —also the animal's passionate impulse to *poke things*, as described by Köhler—these are both regarded by Lindworsky as evidences of the uniformity characteristic of an instinct. But, I ask, what has poking at holes to do with the achievement of a lengthened stick? Nothing at all, except the quite irrelevant circumstance that in both instances we have a hole and a stick. Everything else in these two modes of behaviour is so vastly different, that analysis of this sort had best be avoided altogether. The lengthening of the stick offers no ground for inferring a stereotyped procedure. If the animal had varied its method by now poking the smaller stick into the hole of the larger, and again by covering the smaller with the larger stick, it might as well have been argued in a contrary fashion that the animal had no intelligence, because he only made movements of one kind and another until a result was finally achieved. With reference to the nest-building instinct, it may also be remarked that Sultan was not building a nest, and that putting two sticks together has nothing whatever in common with nest-building. Why, then, should just this particular part of the nest-building instinct have been effective in this case? What a curious idea it is, indeed, that the uniformly smooth course of the ape's performance, as it actually takes place, should be capable of analysis into such heterogeneous parts as the ones Lindworsky assumes are supplied by instinct, chance, and training.

Instead of deriving his hypothesis from the facts newly discovered by Köhler's experiments, Lindworsky attempts to explain everything that might occur in the ape's behaviour in terms of the simplest possible psychological concepts. Indeed, Lindworsky maintains that, even if we were quite unable to explain the animal's behaviour in any other way, there would still be no warrant for assuming that it involves insight. As to this conclusion, two remarks may be made: First, if the laws according to which animal-behaviour is determined are to be laid down in advance, of what use is it to carry out these troublesome experiments? And, in the second place, would Lindworsky's assumptions ever have led any one to perform experiments like those of Köhler? Certainly the connection between method and theory of investigation is far too close to permit an affirmative answer to these questions.

# CRITICISM OF KÖHLER

There still remains Lindworsky's first point, the recognition of the wider tube. Here we meet with a criticism directed against Köhler's theory of configural functions. Similar objections to those of Lindworsky have also been advanced by Bühler, while Jaensch [197], two years after Köhler's publication, has reported experiments made with hens, in which he employed a method similar to that of the Köhler-experiments (p. 138). Jaensch, however, has given his results a theoretical interpretation which agrees with the views of Lindworsky and Bühler, and is therefore, in principle, quite different from the interpretation given by Köhler. In view of the consequences drawn from Köhler's theory at the close of the last chapter we must now consider this other hypothesis in some detail.

We saw that after an animal had been trained to differentiate two things, A and B, in a certain way—say with reference to their brightness—so that B would always be chosen; if a test-experiment were then made in which B and C were presented to the animal, C differing from B in the same way in which B differed from A, in the majority of cases not B but C will be chosen. The results of these experiments were explained, in agreement with Köhler, by saying that the animal was not trained with respect to the absolute presence of B, but with reference to the *bearing* of A upon B; accordingly, the configuration which C possesses with respect to B remains the same as that which B possessed with respect to A. In other words, two colours adjacent to each other are not perceived as two independent things, but as having an inner connection which is at the same time a factor determining the special qualities A and B themselves. This statement agrees with the description of the phenomena in question, because under similar conditions introspection finds the most characteristic feature of such an experience the " togetherness " rather than the separateness of the two colours [198].

The negative side of this thesis—that " absolute "

training is less effective than "configural" training—is admitted by all investigators ; but the positive side, which regards the configural functions as very primitive processes, is denied and another explanation advanced in its place.

Schumann was the first person to observe certain unique phenomena v/hich accompany the process of comparison. Thus in the successive comparison of two circles, or lines of different length, an extension or a shrinking appeared in the field of vision according as the eyes passed from the smaller to the larger or from the larger to the smaller object. If one employed brightness- instead of magnitude-differences, this accompanying effect consisted in a "transitional experience" of brightening or darkening. The hypothesis we are now discussing concludes from the results of these experiments that the animals were trained with reference to these *transitional experiences*. " In training so that ' dark gray is forbidden,' while ' medium gray is allowed,' what the hen in truth learns is that it is allowed food whenever a transitional experience of ' brightening' occurs " [199]. In the test-experiments the animal chooses with reference to " configuration " rather than " absolute " colour, because the transitional experience from B to C is the same as it was from A to B. The main difference between this and Köhler's explanation is that this one holds to the old concept of sensation, supplementing it, in order to bring it into accord with the results of the doctrine of comparison, by the addition of the new concept of the transitional experience. It is the same procedure we have so often noted ; whenever any new facts reveal a defect in an explanation previously employed, instead of doubting the accuracy of the explanation — once it has become firmly rooted — something is merely added to make it adequate to the new facts.

Let us consider this particular addition a little more closely. Transitional experiences are added to " sensations," but the sensations are left quite untouched. The connections between the sensations remain completely objective, even though one can infer the relations between the absolute elements from the transitional experiences, as both Jaensch and Bühler do. Jaensch, to be sure, goes even further; for, employing an expression of Brunswig's, he declares that the transitional experience "hovers and reigns between the two objects, since it is a quality of neither of them" [200]. What this may mean, concretely, and what inferences can be drawn from it, unfortunately we are not told; yet here is a decisive point, because the doctrine of transitional experiences, in so far as it is actually distinct from the theory of configuration, can signify only that to the absolute experience of A and B, a transitional experience T is added as a third content to the two other contents; from which it might be inferred that T can undergo definite association just as well as A or B can. Indeed, the hypothesis is stated in just these terms by Lindworsky. But that T should ever "hover" between A and B, as Jaensch maintains, is something new; for then A—T—B becomes a uniform whole, the nature of which is itself in need of explanation. Is it, indeed, anything else than the "bearing of one upon another," the "togetherness" of the two, which Köhler has remarked?

It may be objected, however, that transitional sensations are observable data. But what of that? Nothing, so far as I can see, except that this "bearing," this step from one member of a pair to another, has been observed under the unnatural conditions of a laboratory experiment. When, however, the transition takes place in a natural manner, one can not "see" it; being intent upon finding "sensations," one "sees" only A and B, whereas transitional sensations emerge only under quite special conditions. But the question is a false one to begin with, because the description is psychologically incorrect. It is incorrect to maintain that nothing is given in a phenomenal pair of colours except one colour here and another colour there, just as it would be incorrect to describe the accompanying figure (see Fig. 13) as one vertical and one horizontal line. What we actually see in this figure is an angle, and in the case of a pair of colours what we see is a combination, a configuration, for which we require no transitional experience. And, indeed, any transitional experience that we may have always presupposes the existence of a configuration [201].

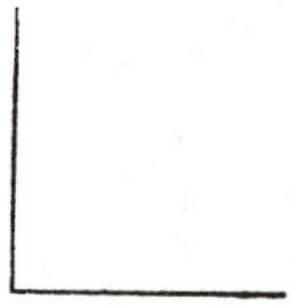

FIG. 13.

The following difficulty also appears to arise in connection with the doctrine of transitional experiences. These experiences are quite unknown to most persons, and it requires a " careful psychological analysis " before they can be apprehended. What right, then, have we to regard them as being the essential constituents of a comparison, even going so far as to attribute them to hens ?

In reply to this objection the advocates of the theory of transitional experiences reply that our judgments may be determined by sensory impressions which themselves are too weak to be noticed. In support of this hypothesis Jaensch refers to a well-known experiment upon the perception of depth. If one looks through a tube with one eye at a thread, one can readily recognize its approach or withdrawal. The image on the retina alters its width with the movement of the thread—the image becoming wider when the thread is nearer, and narrower when the thread is more distant. If, following Hillebrand's procedure, we replace the thread with an object whose displacement produces no such change in the retinal image—as, for instance, the sharp edge of a screen extending into the field of view—even considerable displacements will be quite unnoticed. From this Jaensch concludes " that in the case of the thread judgment can rest only upon the change in the magnitude of the retinal dimensions which accompanies the alteration of the thread's distance, and although this change is too small to be directly noticed as a change of magnitude, still it must determine the judgment of distance. The same is true of transitional experiences which . . . in spite of the very slight impression they make upon us, may yet serve as a basis of judgment "[202]. In this explanation we again find the inappropriate concept of "noticing." Otherwise the facts can be described as follows: A change in the breadth of the retinal image does not necessarily produce a change in the breadth of the phenomenon; for under certain conditions this change of retinal breadth may, instead, give rise to a phenomenal difference of *distance*. But the mediation of the judgment by a phenomenally unnoticed change of breadth is a mere hypothesis and, in addition, one which is in principle undemonstrable[203]. I can cite a quite analogous case where even Jaensch must recognize the validity of our interpretation. The enlargement of a retinal image may have the general effect of making the corresponding object appear larger. As a rule, however, the phenomenal enlargement is not proportional to the actual enlargement, but lags somewhat behind it; consequently the object seems to project itself towards us, and become clearer and more striking. Perhaps the best example of this is afforded by looking through lenses, such as those of opera-glasses; for the objects seen alter their apparent magnitude and distance very little, whereas their clearness undergoes a very striking increase. Yet in this case an analysis of the phenomenon into unnoticeable components which influence our judgment is quite out of the question. Jaensch, himself, has made notable contributions to the study of similar phenomena without recourse to any hypothesis of unnoticed sensations. It follows, therefore, that there is not the slightest occasion for introducing these hypotheses into the explanation of phenomenal magni-

225

tudes, and hence the argument for the necessary existence of transitional experiences falls to the ground.

We are also led to a like conclusion when we examine the argument Bühler employs. Transitional experiences, says Bühler, " are like hearing the overtones of a clang, which requires a certain practice before one can find these ordinarily neglected factors of experience " [204]. So-called clang-analysis, or hearing out the partial tones of a clang, has often been advanced as a striking demonstration of the existence of unnoticed sensations; yet Köhler has now shown that if one examines the facts precisely and without prejudice such an interpretation is unwarranted [205], because clang-analysis is an artificial production of certain tonal phenomena which occur only by reason of a special direction of the attention, whereas under normal conditions they do not exist at all. Although it is possible to practise this art of attention until overtones can be readily heard, there is nothing at all remarkable in this fact. Nor is any support given to Bühler's hypothesis by the fact that psychologists who, under experimental conditions, have practised seeing transitional experiences — such as those involving the comparison of distances—are able to find transitional experiences in their everyday lives. Helmholtz, indeed, found that for a time his enjoyment of polyphonic music was greatly disturbed by the insistence of the overtones which he had learned to analyse.

Thus a reference to clang-analysis does not overcome the difficulties of the hypothesis. Yet all these difficulties disappear when we consider, as proposed above (cf. p. 225), that under special conditions transitional experiences arise within the configurative phenomena themselves. For under these special conditions we do have a close analogy to the hearing of overtones; although the analogy now agrees rather than disagrees with the position we have taken. In other words, we can find no ground for assuming that transitional experiences exist where they are not observed, and even when they are observed the original experience—the configural phenomenon—instead of disappearing, remains unaltered, just as does the clang-colour of a sound when we listen to its overtones.

Our discussion is intended to convince the reader that there is no need of calling upon transitional experiences to explain phenomena in which these experiences are not observed; and in any event that a far simpler and a much more evident explanation can be given in terms of configural function. But the facts of the case are even more favourable to a theory of configuration than this statement might indicate; for with the progress of psychological investigation more and more instances have come to light in which the *effects* of configurations have been discovered where there was no possibility of referring them to transitional experiences. I need give but one example, similar to the previously cited case of two grayish colours of different brightness. Suppose we try to find out how much colour must be added to a certain gray of a definite brightness in order that it shall become just noticeably coloured. The minimal noticeable increment of colour is then called the colour-threshold. What we shall find is that the configuration of the whole phenomenal appearance exercises a marked influence upon this threshold; for the colour-threshold is dependent, not only on the brightness of the gray with which the colour is mixed, but also on the brightness of the uniformly gray background upon which the gray that is mixed with colour has been placed. We find, indeed, that the threshold is at its minimum, and the least amount of colour-admixture required, when both the gray and its background are of the same brightness. After adding to a medium gray upon a background of the same brightness the minimal amount of colour necessary to make it barely noticeable, the colour will immediately disappear as soon as the background is replaced by another which is either brighter or darker. This result can be stated as a law of configuration by saying that the greater the configurative difference between the brightness of a field and its background, the higher is its colour-threshold, and the more difficult is it to produce a colour-configuration.[206] Thus we see that colour - configurations are effective even where transitional experiences are altogether lacking.

The reader must pardon the detail in which this problem of the transitional experiences has been set forth, because its importance for systematic psychology is far-reaching[207]. Let us now apply the hypothesis of the transitional experience to the experiments with animals.

Two grays, A brighter than B, are placed before the animal. When the animal glances from A to B it will experience a darkening, and when it glances from B to A, a brightening. Since B is the colour which is to be allowed, training will consist in establishing a connection between a certain kind of behaviour and the experience of darkening. The transitional experiences of brightening and darkening ought, however, to occur in accordance with whichever direction is taken by the wandering gaze. The question therefore arises why one of these transitions should be preferred to the other. The answer to this question has appeared so obvious to writers on this subject that they have not taken it up at all ; and, indeed, the training-theory has but one possible answer. When the fowl has the transitional experience of brightening, both the eye and the head have been moved from B towards A. The head is therefore directed upon A and it should begin, wrongly, to peck at A. On the other hand, with the experience of darkening it turns from A towards B, and this time pecks at B and secures food. That is to say, the objective condition that the appropriate transitional experience finds the fowl's head nearer to the right gray than it is to the wrong gray is alone responsible for the fact that the fowl can be trained by this means. Again we are faced with a mechanistic interpretation of, the whole process, the validity of which is so questionable that I do not believe it can be made to agree with what is actually observable in these experiments with hens [208]. In the first place, we have to assume that the hen works like an automaton. Consider, now, the case of Sultan with his double-stick. How could "training" have effected his behaviour? For at the first attempt, without a single trial, Sultan took the thicker tube in his left hand and the thinner one in his right hand [209]. When, therefore, Lindworsky writes "that the first achievement (that is, the differentiation of the wider and the smaller tubes), in view of a possible explanation in terms of transitional sensations, can not be regarded as indicating any insight" [210], we may add that this "possible explanation" must not only be rejected on its own account, but that in this special case it altogether fails. Analyzing the experiment with the double-stick, Lindworsky found three places where intelligence might possibly have operated, and he believed he could exclude insight from all three. We have now refuted his argument point for point; our final consideration in regard to his first point having clearly shown the futility of his entire argument. To break up a performance into a number of separate, meaningless, components is an impossible hypothesis, when the very beginning of the act — the manipulation of the separate tubes in an appropriate way — is admittedly bound up with a definite apprehension of the situation.

But our criticism has accomplished even more than this end; for it has secured our conception of the original nature of these configural functions against further attack. We are consequently now in a position to refer in passing to a problem which faced us in a previous chapter. If configural functions are primitive, we ought also to find them in those original modes of behaviour described as instinctive; and, indeed, so we do. As already noted (above p. 97), the stimuli which

229

arouse instinctive action need not give rise to "simple sensations." If, for instance, a spider is put to flight by the approach of a bee, in no matter what position the bee may occupy with regard to the spider's eye, an explanation of this behaviour must be found in a very simple configural function which recurs in each and every one of these innumerable positions of the bee. The problem then is to find out what may be the characteristic features of these primitive configurations.

### § 9—Bühler's Stages of Development and the Principle of Configuration

We have demonstrated that learning always involves some new achievement, and our discussion has dealt with a kind of learning which can be said to involve insight. But there are also many achievements at a much lower level of development which likewise demand a similar interpretation.

Here we find ourselves again in opposition to Bühler; for although Bühler does not deny achievements with true insight, he advances a theory of stages of development. Below the upper stage of *intelligence,* described as a capacity to make discoveries, he introduces a stage of *training,* which involves mere associative memory, and below this still a lower stage of *instinct.* Bühler believes that instinct and training each has its advantages and disadvantages. The advantage of instinct is the certainty and completeness with which it works the very first time it is tried. The advantage of training is its adaptability to special conditions of life. Coupled with these, however, are the disadvantages of inflexibility in the case of instinct, and of "inertia" in the case of training — the latter being shown in the fact that learning by habituation is a slow process. The advantages of both the lower stages are united, however, in learning at the highest stage which he calls intelligent learning [211].

# BÜHLER'S STAGES OF DEVELOPMENT

Bühler's three stages afford a valuable insight into the course of mental development, and, after removing certain blemishes, we shall find his hypothesis altogether acceptable. First, let us ask what relation obtains between these three stages. It might be assumed that they represent three entirely distinct modes of behaviour, but this would signify that new functions are added to old ones in a manner difficult to comprehend. Despite all differences of opinion, the theory of associative learning and the theory of instinct must be intimately connected. At present the consensus of opinion seems to be that instinctive and habitual behaviour take place by virtue of connections between definite pathways in the central organs of the nervous system. These connections are regarded as fixed in the case of instinct, and modifiable in the case of habit ; a distinction sometimes thought of as evolutionary, so that the instincts are but the acquired habits of one's ancestors.[212] In conceiving intelligence as a distinct function, Bühler stands more or less alone. Attempts have been made to reduce intelligence to the effects of association, and although we must deny this hypothesis too, we do, of course, recognize the significance of a single principle which would enable us to avoid the necessity of assuming three entirely heterogeneous modes of response. This single principle, which always plays the chief rôle, whether it be in the explanation of instinct, habit, or intelligence, is for us the principle of configuration. Consequently, the behaviour itself, with its inner " closure " and its definite direction, becomes the essential feature in every explanation we shall have to offer, just as it has already served us in explaining the relation between instinct and reflex. The principle of configuration, which has proved its validity in explaining acts of intelligence, is simply transferred to the explanation of lower forms of behaviour. Although this is a complete reversal of the usual mode of procedure which has been adopted in explanation of the most primitive modes of behaviour, the principle of configuration must not be given an anthropomorphic turn—as though a dog, for instance, were only a very stupid man, which would be just as foolish as it would be to regard man as a very clever dog ; for only after we have worked out the common features in the behaviour of both dog and man, shall we be able to describe and define the difference between them. Having assumed that intelligence, habit, and instinct depend upon differently constructed functions of configuration, we shall now consider how these differences may be conceived, and how the distinctions drawn by Bühler can issue therefrom.

Let us begin with the "inertia" which Bühler attributes to habituation. How can we explain the fact that so-called mechanical learning requires so much more time than intelligent learning? Even Ruger's experiments (cf. p. 174 ff.), which were very like those of training, indicated a descent in the time-curve only when a performance achieved by chance was also understood. This agrees with Köhler's remark upon the choice-training of his animals: "If we attribute the time or the number of trials, in short, the 'work' done by the chimpanzees and hens in learning this kind of task, to the establishment of associative bonds (between a certain configuration and a reaction) our estimate of the essential achievement of the animals would not be high enough, because *the chief task of the chimpanzee in 'choice-training' is the discovery of the precise material connections involved in his behaviour.*" [213] This inference is drawn from learning-curves, that is, from the distribution of right and wrong responses. Although at the beginning right and wrong choices follow one another in a purely chance order, a change suddenly takes place, after which virtually no errors are made. In an experiment with Chica, for instance, among fifty choices before this change occurred, twenty-five were wrong, while after the change had taken place only four errors were made. Such behaviour, as it has also been described in the similar experiments of Yerkes, corresponds throughout with the characteristic appearance of the true solution in the tests of intelligence. Köhler's inference seems, therefore, to be justified. In addition, Köhler makes this further observation: " The greater the number of different choices Sultan had learned to make with a pair of objects bearing different marks, the quicker he would be able to master a new problem, the material of which was not too difficult; the same can be said of the other animals." [214]

The reason habituation requires so long a time is that the conditions of the external surroundings, or of the internal organization of the animal, exclude the possibility of immediately apprehending the configuration. Under such conditions the act must, indeed, be repeated again and again in order to bring the configuration out. Instead of serving to strengthen bonds, the chief function of repetition is to prepare the ground for the construction of an appropriate figure which first occurs as a result of chance. After the configuration has once been constructed, repetition serves to make the behaviour appreciably firmer and easier—but not before.

This assumption seems to agree better than any other with the known facts. We know, for instance, that, in a purely habitual achievement, like that of mechanically learning a series of nonsense-syllables, a " collective apprehension " [215] is requisite, in which the several members are bound together in a uniform whole. Usually this construction of a unity occurs in the form of rhythmical groups, but in general what we mean to say is that in order to be learned the material must first receive some kind of figure,[216] every facilitation in the construction of which is a facilitation of learning. Likewise the " moment of grasping," which Aall finds so essential to memory, can be understood without difficulty as the learner's application of certain familiar principles of configuration to his material [217]. Furthermore, the following interesting result was secured by A. Kühn in an investigation made in the psychological laboratory of the University of Berlin. It is a known fact that in learning a visually presented series of words or nonsense-syllables the learner never confines himself merely to reading the material over, but involuntarily soon begins to recite it. In this way he both anticipates what is to come, and reaches back for what has gone before. Whenever the observer is forbidden to employ recitation, he finds himself unable to learn the series, no matter how often the material is read over. Indeed, the accumulation of mere readings in these particular experiments seemed to be harmful to retention ; for the oftener the material was " merely read," the more repetitions by the " recitative-method " were thereafter required before it could be learned. The effectiveness of recitation rests therefore upon the fact that "*it leads to a more fundamental and more many-sided working-over of the material.*" [218]  Finally, K. Lewin, as a result of some ingenious experiments carried out in the same laboratory, reached the conclusion "that the learning-process can not be conceived as a connection between separate constructs. . . . Instead of learning 'syllables,' one learns 'to react to a given stimulus with a definite response'. . . . *The way is being practised which must be followed later in the reproduction.*" [219]

The "working-over," and the "way"—these terms are equivalent to what we have called the configuration. With reference to the facts revealed in processes of mechanical learning, we are therefore led to conclude that *all learning requires the arousal of configural patterns.*

Having thus set aside, as not basic, the presupposition of the principle of trial and error, which is the principle of "frequency," it follows that repetitions without the achievement of a configuration remain ineffective whenever they are not positively harmful. In the broadest sense, practice means the formation of a figure, rather than the strengthening of bonds of connection.

234

# BÜHLER'S STAGES OF DEVELOPMENT

Our conception of Bühler's stages of development can also be given an adequate physiological foundation. Again and again in this chapter we have met with the difficulty involved in a physiological theory of association (cf. above p. 157). In order to master this difficulty we have seen how the behaviourist has been led to reject the essential concept of association as a connection which is established by the individual in the course of his experience. Indeed, more than twenty years ago Von Kries pointed out that the arousal of associations can not be explained on the basis of a mere "pathway-" hypothesis which assumes that nervous excitations travel along fixed paths. We shall set aside the question as to whether an assumption of innumerable innate connections can be made to overcome the difficulties involved in the variable nature of the associations to be established, for, even so, there are still other objections which Von Kries has brought forward against the pathway-hypothesis, and upon which Erich Becher has enlarged [220]. According to Von Kries the pathway-hypothesis is inadequate, not only to the problem of establishing associations, but also to the problems of "associative effects" and "generalizations." With respect to the first of these Von Kries has particularly in mind the problem of spatial and temporal forms. Two lines which meet are called an "angle," while each line taken by itself is only a line. The associative effect of the two lines is therefore not the sum of the associative effects of each line taken by itself, and this new product the pathway-hypothesis does not explain. Under "generalization" Von Kries refers to a fact of learning which we have already discussed with reference to instinct; namely, the psychological similarity, both in appearance and in effect, of processes which physically are quite different. Having once seen a figure we are still able to recognize it after its position, magnitude, and colour have been so greatly altered that different pathways must now be involved, and the whole process must take place in quite a different

235

manner than it did before. As a matter of fact, no object is ever twice reflected in the eye in exactly the same way. Variations of this kind are so common that they apply to all learning. Von Kries's conclusion, which relates closely to our own, is "that in many ways learning can not be a matter of the development of pathways, which bring remote parts into connection, but must be something that can only be pictured as the formation of unified domains, facilitating the co-existence of various states"[221]. In carrying out this principle hypothetically Von Kries refers these phenomena to inter-cellular activities.

In his conception of achievement Von Kries approaches our position very closely; the main difference being his attribution of achievement in learning to separate cells, the processes of which can only be conceived as co-existent, though they are, of course, adapted to one another. We, on the other hand, find the essential feature to rest in the state of arousal, or in the course taken within the whole domain which is involved. Becher has pointed out the untenability of any hypothesis which would limit these functions to a single cell[222], and concludes that no adequate physiological theory of memory is possible. A way out of the difficulty has, however, been indicated by Wertheimer's hypothesis of a *configurative* physiological process, and in his book on physical configurations Köhler has recently shown that this hypothesis can readily be applied to our know-ledge of physics. Consequently, objections to a physio-logical theory of association no longer force upon us the acceptance of psycho-vitalism[223], but, instead, open to us a new way in which association may be explained in terms of the physical configurations of the nervous system. These configurations, having already served us in the explanation of instinctive activity, will now prove of special value in clarifying the achievements of intelligence. From all of which it follows that instinct, habituation, and intelligence, instead of being three different principles, are the expression, in different forms, of one and the same principle.

The difference emphasized by Bühler between intelligence and habituation, namely, the "inertia" of habituation, can now readily be explained, and we shall have occasion to describe it at greater length in the next chapter. The other criterion, possessed by habituation and intelligence together, in contrast with instinct—namely, the capacity of adaptation to external conditions—can easily be made to conform with our hypothesis. The criterion mentioned in the previous chapter, which has to do with the difference between inflexible and plastic dispositions, must therefore be taken as a peculiarity of the configural function itself, in accordance with which certain configurations are so definitely determined by conditions innate to the individual that they must necessarily be effective the first time they are called forth; whereas other configurations are not so definitely fixed. If and how plastic configurations arise will depend upon special conditions, in contrast with which instinctive configurations are essentially the same in all the individuals of a species. It is those types of configuration the conditions of which are less definite that give rise to the more pronounced individual differences.

# CHAPTER V

# SPECIAL FEATURES OF MENTAL GROWTH

## B. THE PROBLEM OF MEMORY: THE LEARNING OF CHILDREN

### § 1—*The Function of Memory and its First Appearance*

OF the two main problems of learning, we have already endeavoured to clarify one; namely, the problem of achievement. Before we proceed to consider in detail the acquisitions of the child, we shall take up the second of these essential problems, which is that of memory.

When one speaks of memory in everyday life, one thinks in general of remembrance—the fact that one can revive past events which are no longer present by "imagining" them. One thinks, for example, of a friend who has recently died; and sees him, as it were, in the "mind's eye"; while once again the familiar conversation with him is rehearsed. The characteristic of this remembrance is a phenomenon to which there attaches an *index of the past*. The experience we have imagined appears with an indication of the time at which it actually happened as, for instance, long ago in the time of our youth; but also in the same manner as before, and in the same spatial location—in the forest at N., or on the lake at Z., or somewhere in Berlin, in the Alps, or elsewhere. Descriptions such as these indicate that references to time and place can greatly vary in definiteness. These references may be relatively definite, as, for example, on the day of my examination at the door of the examination-room; or they may only

238

approximate the time, as during my student years in
J. But the reference is always definitely to something
previously experienced. We speak ordinarily of remembrance, however, even when these indications of time and
place are lacking. One may not be able to remember
Kepler's laws, and yet be able to solve a particular
problem. Remembering in this case means that one
can solve the problem without necessarily remembering
when and where he learned its laws. In short, we speak
of remembrance when, by reason of a previous experience, we are able to solve the problem or name the laws
in question without first reading them up in a book.

But remembrance is not the only way in which
memory can lead us beyond the present; for not only
the past, but the future, is also experienced. I see
lightning and await thunder; I hear the bell-signal in
the theatre and await the rise of the curtain. In expectancy we have still a further accomplishment of
memory. Our reason for not reversing this proposition,
and holding that expectancy must rest upon remembrance, has already been discussed in Chapter III, with
reference to the analysis of instinctive reactions (cf.
p. 100); and the conclusion there reached holds true
for intelligent reactions. The configurations to which
reference was then made included temporally extended
patterns. When an animal drags a box below a stick
suspended in the air, this act already implies progress
towards the goal, in the attainment of which a stick is
needed, although any previous experience of the sort
may be lacking. In the first solution of such a problem
each part-reaction is made as a member of—or with
reference to—the solution as a whole. Perceptual experience furnishes numerous examples of this; as, for
instance, in hearing an entirely new melody we soon
find ourselves expecting how it will proceed.

But remembrance and expectancy in the forms explained do not yet exhaust the faculty of memory.
Thus far we have considered the function of memory

in a certain independence of perception ; as the occasion
for " memory-images," or whatever one chooses to call
the non-perceptual phenomena of memory.  But still
another and no less important function of memory is
revealed in perception itself.  I go down the street, and
meet many strangers.  Yet here is a familiar face ; there
is my friend X ; and over there is the lady who stood
next to me yesterday in the street-car.  Thus memory
lends a character of familiarity to perceived objects,
which again may greatly vary in definiteness from a
mere quality of familiarity, as in the first instance above,
to the complete assurance of the second ; or again to a
familiarity possessing either the characteristic of remembrance, indicated by the lady of the street-car, or
of expectancy.

This perceptual accomplishment is not necessarily
restricted to an individual cognition—or " recognition,"
as it is called,—for when I apprehend a rose as a rose,
or a piece of chalk as chalk, my perceptual phenomena
also owe a considerable part of their essential character
to memory.  In order to understand this fact one need
but observe how in time an object such as a new piece
of apparatus alters its appearance—one might almost
say its physiognomy—as a result of handling it daily.
It is an indubitable fact that memory penetrates
throughout the entire range of our perceptions; and
certainly this effect of memory, in contrast with the
one previously referred to as a " memory - image," is
tied to the perceived object.

But the achievements of memory are not yet at an
end, for hitherto we have confined ourselves to the
inner aspects of behaviour—that is, to phenomena of
experience—whereas objective behaviour is also shot
through with memory.  I need only refer to an example employed in the last chapter.  If I do not drown
when I find myself in deep water, it is because I
learned to swim in my youth.  In this case memory
works altogether without the aid of any revived ex-

perience ; for long before I can think to reach a decision, my arms and legs are already carrying out their appropriate responses. After I succeed in coming to the surface and have again filled my lungs with air, it may occur to me that this or that particular stroke would be useful or skilful, and thereafter I can regulate my swimming accordingly. It is in this way that the phenomenal effects of memory have their influence upon motor behaviour. The achievements of memory are accordingly threefold:—

i. The participation of consciousness which may be more or less definite ;

ii. The relation of this consciousness to perception— that is, whether the "images" are free or tied ;

iii. Certain kinds and degrees of positional and temporal definition, which may be altogether perceptual.

With these distinctions in mind, let us consider the development of memory in the life of the individual. At birth the infant's behaviour shows that (i) memory-images participate but little; (ii) when they do they are tied up with perception ; and (iii) are without temporal or spatial definition. First of all, the infant completes some objective act of behaviour which soon comes to involve a true component of learning, however slight may be the degree of consciousness necessary to it. On the phenomenal side, this achievement of memory indicates a quality of familiarity ; and perhaps even earlier, a quality of strangeness. If one brings an infant into a strange room before the completion of the first half-year, its behaviour alters noticeably. The infant looks around the room with a wide-eyed "astonishment," which disappears as soon as the child is returned to its usual surroundings. The effect of the memory of its usual surroundings is indicated here by an impression of strangeness ; but the basis for this impression must already have existed, because its memory would have

241

been the same had it never been taken into a strange room.  How is this effect of memory to be understood? Perhaps the best answer has already been found in the distinction drawn between the "background" and the "quality" of primitive phenomena.  The effect of memory derived from accustomed surroundings will then be this: that the "background" of consciousness acquires the peculiar character of a relatively fixed level upon which separate phenomena make their appearance. "Astonishment" follows, therefore, whenever this level is altered.  The conception of the *level* is of such considerable importance in psychology, that it is always a matter of interest whether a change of environment involves the level or the qualities which emerge therefrom.

Within the first six months of a child's life one can also observe signs of smiling when the infant sees its mother or some other familiar person; and, on the other hand, signs of avoidance and displeasure when the infant is brought in contact with strangers.  Here the participation of consciousness is apparently greater; because, on the one hand, the response is no longer determined by the background alone, and, on the other hand, a negative reaction to strangers is opposed to a positive reaction to persons with whom the child is familiar.

The next step, I should say, is one that adds to the character of familiarity a temporal definition which it did not previously possess—this being an expectation directed towards the *future*.  Stern insists [224] that a reference to the future takes place earlier than a reference to the past; but I think he infers the independence of memory from perception too easily when he calls these first expectations "ideas."  Let us take an example.  Stern's daughter Hilda, as early as the age of five months, put out her lips when the spoon with which she was fed was offered to her; although at first it had been very difficult to accustom the child to eat with a spoon.  Instead of speaking of images of expectancy, this behaviour should, I think, be described as follows: The child had learned to comprehend the process of feeding as a configuration in which the spoon played its definite part as a "transitional phenomenon." That is to say, the spoon as a phenomenon contained within itself a characteristic which carried beyond itself, just as a dark cloud appears not only black, but "threatening," without our having actually to imagine the oncoming thunderstorm.

Expectation, as a consciousness that something is missing, has as little need of "free" imagery as have the corresponding phenomena of familiarity and strangeness. Miss Shinn reports of her niece at three months that "she was much interested in a guest, a lively girl, and not only followed her movements, but would look for her when out of sight (89th day)." Stern concludes from this that the impression must have lingered afterward in the fainter form of an image [225], but I doubt it. In view of the very early age at which this observation was made, the existence of images, or phenomena independent of perception, seems to me very improbable. A more adequate description, I think, would be that a very vivid situation suddenly disappears and in its place there comes another which has as its chief phenomenal characteristic, a "blank," or a "lack of completeness."

It is not at all certain when the first "free" images are employed. Remembrance unquestionably occurs at the beginning of the second year, and with it the first definite relationship to the past. But whether remembrance is at first connected with perception, as seems to me probable, can not be decided from the factual data at hand.[226] It is equally difficult to decide whether the first "free" images are images of expectancy. Certainly the first references to the past are extremely indefinite and become definite very slowly; so that even for a four-year-old child a definite remembrance of yesterday is difficult, and one of the day before yesterday, impossible. At this age there exists a vague impression of happenings long past, likewise a rough distinction between before and after, and occasionally one between to-day and not to-day. The characteristic of place is better developed than the characteristic of time—"that was in Berlin"—"that was in London," etc. All remembrances are, indeed, members of larger complexes, and they carry their membership characteristics along with them.

Images without temporal and spatial relations, such as we use to aid us in our thinking, might be expected to occur very late in the course of development. I prefer not to consider the so-called "images of fantasy" in this connection. When a child understands a story and relates it—and the story-age begins with the fourth year [227]—the images that occur can scarcely be called non-temporal, because their employment is hardly different from that of images referring to the child's own distant past. These images of fantasy, however, mark progress to the extent that instead of going back to individual experiences, they are first called into being by a story; otherwise they seem very like memory-images in their nature.

The memory of children also develops so as gradually to span ever-increasing periods of time. This subject has been thoroughly investigated by Clara and William Stern, who find that progress is shown in recognition as well as in what may more precisely be called remembrance. Recognition has precedence, thus disclosing the fact that it is a more primitive type of behaviour than remembrance [228]. Furthermore, it has been shown that the motives for remembrance undergo development; for at first remembrance attaches to perception, and only later to "images." In the beginning the child is passive with respect to his remembrances, but gradually he learns to control them so that voluntarily, or upon being questioned, he can recall to mind definite events [232].

Reference should be made finally to a peculiarity of youthful memory which Jaensch and his students have made the occasion for an extensive series of valuable studies [230]. Youth often shows a capacity for a visual and also, though less often, for an auditory type of image, which is unique in quality, in as much as a sensory impression can be voluntarily reproduced with full sensory clearness after a shorter or a longer period of time. Among 205 boys, ranging from ten to fifteen years of age, this capacity was indicated in 76, or 37 per cent. At what age this "eidetic" disposition, as Jaensch calls it, appears we do not yet know, but the investigations thus far made lead us to think that appropriate experiments can be undertaken successfully with very young children. Among the many different results Jaensch has secured, we shall mention but a few. Even "sense-memory does not retain the material presented without a selection having taken place. The achievement in this respect is not dependent, for instance, merely upon the frequency of presentation and the insistency of the object, but rather upon a selection which is directed from a definite point of view." One of these "points of view" is that of *objectivity*, which in many individuals is so strong "that in the investigation of colours we must give up the usual expedients of scientific optics, and rely rather upon such things as *flowers* for our stimuli; because these, rather than homogeneous papers of the same colour, give rise to the most definite images" [231]. Furthermore, it appears in these experiments that the perceptions of eidetic individuals may be influenced in a manner interpreted by Jaensch and his followers as a fusion of the perception with the eidetic image. Yet even when there is no fusion of the two, when the perceptual and the imaginal objects are separately distinguishable, a reciprocal influence of an assimilative sort takes place which is the greater the more similar the perception and the image are to one another [232].

Since we have denied that association operates as an external bond between independent parts, we can no longer accept the law of association as it is usually stated: namely, that if the phenomena A, B, C, . . . enter consciousness several times together or in immediate succession, and one of them appears thereafter alone, it brings with it a tendency to reproduce the others; special laws being derived which regulate the strength of the tendencies which lead from one factor to another in the association. We now find it necessary to restate this law so that it may read somewhat as follows: If the phenomena A, B, and C . . . have been present once or oftener as members of a configuration, and if one of these reappears while still possessed of its " membership - character," it will have a tendency to supplement itself more or less definitely and completely with the remainder of the total configuration. What is meant by the limitation of " membership - character " relative to reappearance can be made clear by the following example: Suppose one were asked to name a tree which begins with " will," and should answer " willow." This would be quite easy. However, if the membership-character of this syllable " will " as the beginning of a word were lacking, and we were reminded instead of a single monosyllabic word, it might be difficult to proceed from the word " will," to the word " willow."

But reproduction can also take place in quite a different manner. In our example " willow " may result, not only because " will " as an initial syllable supplements itself to form a complete word, but also because an attempt is being made to construct a word out of " will " in accordance with some appropriate form of the language. Here again reproduction occurs in such a way that the total configuration is produced from the initial member. It is therefore unnecessary that the completed form which is produced should have been previously experienced. It is precisely in this way that many "false" constructions appear in a child's speech, which do not belong to the language at all, and which the child has never before heard. These "words" are freely formed by the child in accordance with certain principles of construction with which he is familiar. From the mass of material upon this subject which the Sterns have collected, we may select the following examples: Hilda Stern, 3·8—*vergurtelt* = to fasten with the aid of a girdle; the same child, 3·9 — *metern* = to measure with the aid of centimetre stick; Gertrude Stern, 3·10 — *maschiner* = a locomotive engineer; the same child, 4·4 — *dieben* = to steal; S.S., 2·6 — *es glockt* = the bells ring [233].

This kind of reproduction, which has even less in common with the older form of association than the first which we mentioned, is very important in the development and progress of thinking. It may also be remarked that Otto Selz has stated the law of reproduction in a manner similar to the one we have adopted. In the experiments which he carried out, as well as on the basis of other well-known facts, Selz has shown that an explanation in terms of the "constellation" of numerous independent associations is entirely inadequate to the facts [234].

The older doctrine of association embraced not only the law of association, but also reproduction by *similarity*. To be sure, one often spoke of association by similarity, along with association by contiguity, but association then referred to the process of recall rather than to the bond established between ideas. Since the term *reproduction* has been introduced, one should no longer speak of association by similarity; because the principle maintains that an idea A can reproduce an idea $A^1$, without a previous connection, provided that $A^1$ and A are sufficiently similar. And hence this principle does not rightfully belong to the theory of association, because similarity is not an external but an internal material connection ; consequently a law which replaces all internal connections by bonds which are merely external would here be violated.  Consequently, there has been no dearth of attempts to exclude reproduction by similarity altogether from the explanation in reducing everything to association by contiguity.  The facts, however, do not warrant this procedure, and L. Schlüter [235] working at Göttingen under the direction of G. E. Müller—one of the chief representatives of the psychology of association—has recently found additional proof of the existence of effects which must be attributed to similarity.  In addition, the work of Rosa Heine [236] in the same laboratory shows that recognition can not be explained in terms of mere "bonds" of association.  Indeed, it has been thought for a long time that some connection must exist between recognition and reproduction by similarity, and I myself have considered both achievements as special cases under a more general law [237].

It is very difficult to explain these facts by the theory of association, and especially by reference to its physiological frame-work.  We have already seen that other results attributable to similarity have been made the chief objection to the theory of association by Von Kries.  On the other hand, a theory based on "configurations" encounters less difficulty because "similar configurations" are also found in physics ; and the law of similarity need only mean that configurations once present will furnish conditions favourable to the appearance of others like or similar to them.

We are therefore led to characterize the chief facts of memory as follows : When a new configuration arises under fixed objective conditions, this behaviour of the organism is somehow preserved.  Upon repeating the objective conditions, the configuration will accordingly arise much easier and much swifter than it did the first time.  It will also return when the external conditions change and are no longer so favourable as they were at first, even though the conditions are so incomplete that they would of themselves give rise only to a part of the whole configuration.

## § 3—*Motor Learning: The Parts Played by Maturation and Learning in Walking*

Having cleared up some of the preliminary, theoretical, questions, we may now consider the development of the child himself, taking our examples from the four directions differentiated at the beginning of the preceding chapter (cf. p. 143).

We shall not repeat what we have said in general about the learning of movements (p. 145), but begin with the concrete instance of learning to walk. The first attempt at walking, and the first success in walking alone, are subject to great variation in the time of their appearance. The eighth month is usually early and the fourth half-year very late for beginning to walk. One says that a child *learns* to walk and, of course, he does learn many things in the course of his varied attempts at walking. But does he actually learn *walking?* If a child, ready to make his first attempt to walk, were hindered for a few weeks, as James has proposed, would he at the end of this time, when at last permitted to make the attempt, behave as clumsily as he does when he is not so hindered? It is highly improbable that he would; although the psychologically interested widower, upon whom James set his hopes that this experiment might be tried, has not yet been found. Superiority at the later date would then depend solely upon maturation, and the clumsiness of the child's first attempts must therefore in part be due to the fact that the centres from which the movements of walking are controlled, have not yet fully developed. Awkwardness also results from the as-yet insufficient development of bones and muscles. Walking seems, therefore, to be an inherited type of behaviour; a conclusion which agrees with the fact that birds, too, are able to fly safely and fairly well when first they leave the nest. To be sure, the act becomes more complete with practice, and we should hardly maintain that a child who, without injury to his muscles, were prevented from walking up to his sixth year, could then upon his first attempt run as well as his companions of the same age. But this in no wise leads us to assume that walking is altogether a matter of learning; for maturation itself requires a stimulation which can only be had through the activity of the parts which are maturing.

The facts in the case are indicated by an investigation of Breed on the development of pecking among chickens. If one understands by *pecking* the entire process of food-taking—the striking, seizing, and swallowing of food — a marked development in this complicated activity seems to go on during the first days after hatching. Beginning with the second day small grain was presented to the chicks, and from day to day it was carefully observed how many attempts at pecking were successful. Among fifty such experiments in one group of chicks, the average of successful attempts was as follows: In the first-day trials, 10.3; in the second, 28.3; in the third, 30; in the sixth, 38.3; and in the fifteenth, 43.2. For comparison other chicks were tested which had been artificially fed for several days and then allowed to peck their food for the first time. The result was that although their performances at the start were no better than the performances of the control-group, improvement followed much more rapidly. One chick which began its pecking four days after the normal group, exceeded their performance on the next day. From these results it would seem that maturation without stimulation can accomplish very little; yet I believe that a large part of the improvement must still be attributed to this source, in as much as all the chicks were about equally efficient after the sixth day, although individually they varied greatly in the amount of practice they had had. In order to be effective, however, maturation requires stimulation through the functioning of the act itself[238].

That in learning to walk there is still something actually to be learned, is clearly indicated by an observation of Binet, who found that the older and weaker of two sisters—a first child—walked alone at an earlier age than the younger child ; the reason being that the older one gave her whole attention to the matter ; carefully choosing her objects of direction, and then proceeding to march with the greatest seriousness from one object to another. The younger child, on the other hand, was very vivacious, and would strike out without considering or attending to what she was doing[239]. This observation upon the influence of attention on learning to walk indicates that something was actually being learned, although we do not know precisely what. We may assume, however, that it was less the movements of walking themselves, than the inclination towards the goal, and the adaptation of means to this end.

### § 4—Continuation : Grasping and Touching ; Motor Configurations

Movement-complexes of grasping and touching, which we shall now undertake to consider, are learned even earlier than walking. Exact observations upon the development of this behaviour have been made by Preyer, by Miss Shinn, and more recently by Watson[240]. The development takes a very complicated course and passes through numerous stages. The original touch-organ of the suckling is not the hand, but the mouth. After the fourth week, everything that comes to the mouth is not only sucked, but worked over with the lips and tongue. This behaviour is no longer directly connected with the taking of nourishment ; for if one places his cheek to the mouth of a suckling, the child if hungry will begin to suck ; otherwise he will lick the cheek with his tongue.

Touching with the mouth assumes a growing importance until all kinds of things are brought to the mouth by the hand. But this development does not take place all at once. A stage precedes at which the suckling brings only its hands to its mouth (according to Miss Shinn this stage begins with the third month). It is interesting to note that at first this movement is not carried out by the hands alone; but as the hand is raised, the head is also lowered, so that the movement is visibly one of bringing hand and mouth together. The child is not carrying out certain definite hand- and arm-movements, but is merely uniting hand and mouth. From Watson's experiments it would seem that an essential component of this early behaviour still persists after the child is able to bring other objects than his own hands to the mouth. Watson reports that on the 101st day a baby raised a stick of candy that had been placed in her hand and poked it far back into her throat, which seems to indicate that the behaviour was completed only after the fingers had touched the mouth, rather than by the contact of the candy with lips and tongue.

The advent of grasping with the hand was observed by Miss Shinn during the twelfth week. If by chance an object came in contact with the hand it would be grasped and lifted, and then, after a time, let fall again. It was also observed that the mode of grasping depended upon the position of the hand with reference to the object touched. The eyes seemed to play no special part in this behaviour; for the child neither looked towards the object touched, nor towards her hands. At first the development of this behaviour seemed to be purely a matter of touch; though in the course of these movements, objects held in the hand frequently came by chance in the neighbourhood of the mouth. On the 86th day, Miss Shinn's niece tried for the first time to put a rattle into her mouth. On the next day this attempt was continued, the rattle being first raised to any place on the face and then directed toward the mouth. After reaching the mouth, the rattle was then sucked in. It was noticeable, however, that the child could put her thumb in her mouth much more readily than she could the rattle. And yet almost three weeks earlier, upon her 48th day, a pencil which had been placed in her hand was carried six times to her mouth and energetically sucked by lips and tongue. From then until the 86th day, however, the child made not the slightest attempt to repeat this behaviour. Mention is made of this fact because *anticipations* of acts at a very early date, which only later are performed with facility, are a common characteristic of the development of young children, and are also of the greatest interest.

The achievements described are slowly perfected. The head also co-operates at the beginning; for instance, if the rattle chances to hit the nose, instead of lowering the hand, the head is raised to bring it to the mouth. Yet the act always begins with a chance-contact of the object with the hand. If both hands happen to be touched, both are employed in raising the object, although this does not imply any true co-operation of the two hands; for if the two hands themselves chance to come into contact with one another, the one will be grasped and conducted by the other to the mouth.

After the 99th day the participation of vision in grasping was observed for the first time. Miss Shinn's niece then glanced down at the object while she was grasping it. In contrast, the direction of gaze toward a sound takes place at a much earlier date. As early as the 45th and 57th days, Miss Shinn reports her niece as looking around towards the keyboard of a piano which was being played; but it was not until the 87th day that she glanced at the rattle which she already held in her hand, and whether the sense of contact was the occasion for this direction of her gaze remained uncertain. Apparently the gaze is directed much earlier by the ear than it is by the hand; provided Miss Shinn's observation is not susceptible of quite a different interpretation, which we have previously suggested (cf. p. 83). At a still later date, the eye begins to direct grasping; a long period ensues in which the eye confines itself to looking at the hands or at the object grasped, and the development of the behaviour of grasping something seen is very gradual. On the 113th day, Miss Shinn's niece looked at her mother's out-stretched hand, and with her gaze thus directed made awkward movements with her own hand until the mother's hand was touched, grasped, and conducted to the child's mouth. How important the mouth is in this whole course of behaviour, is shown by Preyer's relevant observation at this same stage of development: namely, that the mouth would be opened before, or immediately after, the object was grasped— an observation since confirmed by Watson. In this way grasping after something seen is for a long time the first stage of an undertaking to bring a seen-object to the mouth. This stage continues for a long time with a characteristic awkwardness and lack of adaptability. The fingers, for instance, will be spread out in no position for grasping; the position being taken only after contact. During the hand-movements, the gaze is directed fixedly upon the object. In a certain sense there recurs in this part of the act the same type of behaviour which has already taken place in the simpler endeavour to introduce a felt-thing into the mouth; though now the act is concerned with the adjustment of the object to the hand, rather than to the mouth.

Even after this behaviour has been practised, touch by the hand must still be substituted for touch by the mouth. At the age of seven months, Miss Shinn's niece played with an object for the first time without carrying it to her mouth, but such behaviour was rare up to the end of her eighth month, and even far into the second year objects were occasionally brought to the mouth. Artificial means must be employed with many children even as late as the third year in order to wean them from this habit, especially if it be thumb-sucking. The direction of the hand by touch is attained very slowly—much more slowly than direction by grasping.

Taking this phase of development as a whole, it appears that a relatively complicated behaviour arises out of much simpler activities. And yet we are unable to agree with Preyer's statement that learning consists in nothing else than a partial isolation and re-combination of already existing movements; or in other words that learning is only a matter of *training* as this term is commonly understood. Bühler, for instance, regards learning to grasp as being entirely dependent upon training. We now see why it has been necessary to indulge in such a long theoretical argument as to the nature of this form of learning; for, writes Bühler, "the entire acquisition of innumerable manipulations and activities which the child learns to master in his early youth are executed in accordance with this principle of training, beginning with positional movements of creeping and walking, passing through the stage of grasping-movements, and culminating in the technical and artistic performances which constitute training in the narrower sense of the term" [241].

On the other hand, Bühler points also to the similarity between grasping and gazing; for he tells us that just "as the eye-movements which bring the image into the clearest field of vision are released reflexly by means of peripheral light-stimuli, so the arm-movements which bring the object to the mouth as the place of most sensitive touch, are released by means of the pressure sensations of the skin" [242]. This statement refers to a stage of development in which seeing does not yet participate in grasping, and Bühler's explanation is given in terms of the formation of bonds between the pressure sensations of the hand and the kinæsthetic

255

sensations of bending the arm. But we have already rejected this hypothesis in the case of eye-movements of fixation, and have replaced it with another. Can we do the same with reference to the development of grasping and manipulation?

Quite apart from the general considerations of the previous chapter, there are, in fact, a series of data which contradict explanations based upon bonds of connection. In the first place, the same objection can be raised against this hypothesis that has already been raised against the similar hypothesis in the case of visual fixation: namely, that the number of connections would need to be enormous. The hypothesis takes its departure from the fact that an individual has learned to attain a certain result by movements which are explained in terms of connections, without first demonstrating that all the connections necessary for such an explanation actually exist. Von Kries attacks the hypothesis on these grounds[243]. Taking writing as an example, he points out that the innervation of the muscles required in writing even a portion of a letter involve the greatest variability, according as we write large or small letters, quickly or slowly, energetically or easily, with this or that position of the arm, to the right or to the left, above or below on the paper. Von Kries also finds in this variability a decided objection to the "pathway-hypothesis." Furthermore, how can this theory of bonds explain the "anticipations" already referred to (p. 253)? An infant was observed to place a pencil in its mouth correctly, six times. This, to be sure, might be explained by bonds of connection between the several movements, provided we assume that the act started each time with the same position of the arm. It might, therefore, be said that this sequence of acts occurred first of all by chance, and was retained during the brief period of time in which the performances were being repeated. But this description is contradicted by Miss Shinn[244], who reports that after placing the pencil in the resting hand of the child, "the hand closed on it at once (the thumb correctly reversed) and carried the pencil to the mouth. I had no idea that this could be more than an accident, but pushed the hand away from the neighbourhood of the face, lest the pencil-point should do harm in some aimless movement. To my surprise, the baby *six times* carried the pencil directly back as I pushed it away, and as she did so she put out her lips and tongue toward it eagerly, with sucking motions, much as when about to be put to the breast." This is the description of a good observer, and from it one must conclude that the same movement was not repeated each time in any such manner as would allow the same connections to function again and again. On the contrary, the behaviour was of a kind that would attain the same result each time it was repeated. Indeed, the process appears to be entirely embedded in an instinctive mode of behaviour ; for the child put out her lips and tongue toward the pencil with the same sucking movements that followed when she was about to be put to the breast.

Reserving this observation of Miss Shinn's for further consideration at a later time, let us consider another argument against the hypothesis based on bonds of connection. The hypothesis maintains that a movement originally carried out instinctively, or in any other way, enters as such into a subsequent performance which is being learned. Regarded as a movement, any unit must remain the same afterwards that it was before being incorporated into a subsequent process of learning, which presupposes that the course of behaviour is made up of separate and isolated parts, a presupposition which has its exact analogy in the sensory domain, where perceptions have been likewise conceived as a number of separable sensations. Our theory of configuration supplants this view, against which we shall have still further proofs to bring in this chapter. It may therefore be noted at once that an hypothesis which has failed to satisfy our needs in the sensory field, can hardly be expected to agree with the facts adduced in the case of movement.

If a young baby imitates the movement of an adult by carrying out an action, which he is otherwise able to do spontaneously or instinctively, the imitative action is found to differ from the similarly constituted spontaneous action by a marked degree of awkwardness. Compayré notes this difference [245], and the Sterns report of their daughter, that " if one says to the child when she is well disposed, ' erre, erre,' these syllables which she otherwise utters involuntarily and easily, will be repeated, but only after an apparent effort, which often lasts several seconds " [246]. This difficulty can not be explained in terms of piecing part-movements together; for if that were the case the action ought to occur quite independent both of the result and of the total situation.

In America numerous experiments have been undertaken to study the learning of new acts; such as throwing a ball at a target; striking at a punching-bag; writing on a typewriter, or a somewhat more simplified act of the same order. Tests have also been made of writing under difficult conditions, as with the left hand, or so that one's own writing is only visible in a mirror. The results of all these investigations indicate, as noted in the previous chapter, that the learning of a certain type of movement is not simply a motor affair, but that sensory components are absolutely essential to it. A further and generally confirmed result is the following: The more strictly motor a task is, the less has consciousness to do with learning it, and the more must the learner be directed upon the result, rather than upon the activity itself. Whenever one throws a ball at a target and gives attention to the throwing rather than to the target one is quite sure to miss the mark [247].

In learning more complicated movements, as for instance, writing ten words always in the same order on a typewriter, the course of learning is as follows: In the beginning each letter is sought and written for itself, that is to say, a mode of perception which we may call *seeking* becomes the centre of the whole action. This complicated process alters as superfluous movements are eliminated ; but, above all else, as the act is learned a complex unity supersedes an unconnected mass of particulars[248]. In this unification a " movement-melody " composes itself. The visual search for single letters disappears and attention is thereafter directed only upon the entire course of the procedure. Indeed, any special consideration of details always introduces difficulties. How far the visual aspect of learning may disappear is shown in an example given by Betz[249], who had acquired a considerable practice in typewriting, and always used the same machine. Once, however, when he tried to see if he could write down from memory the picture of the key-board of his machine, his attempt was a failure. Not only had he the greatest difficulty in reaching any decision at all as to the appearance of the keys, but although in writing he never looked at the key-board, he made many gross errors in reproducing the order of the letters. In doing what we are accustomed to do, we are aware only of the errors we commit ; then the wrong movements spring forth "as not belonging to the melody."

If we ask further how a movement-melody can develop out of a summation of movements, the answer is that it does so of itself whenever attention is rightly directed upon the goal, which is an object of the outer world. Thus the movements constantly vary in the direction of a better formation, which is achieved in a manner similar to the achievements in efficiency described in Ruger's experiments. Although in Ruger's experiments improvement in learning was effective only when it was understood, here the case is different, at least in so far as the finer adaptations are concerned ; for although these adaptations may occasionally be reflected in consciousness, this has no influence upon the efficiency of learning, and to direct attention upon them only disturbs the performance. As early as 1889, Müller and Schumann found that a movement-melody (they called it a "motor adaptation") can be composed without the participation either of volition or knowledge. Ordahl has since shown that attention is influential even in learning very simple movement-melodies [250]. If one lifts many times in rhythmical succession a lighter and a heavier weight, a motor adaptation is gradually built up, in as much as the lifting of the pair of weights becomes a process in which the lighter weight is followed by a more energetic lift, so that the two liftings taken together have an iambic rhythmical character. The existence of this motor adaptation was proved by tests made after the practice-experiments were over, in which the normal weight was paired with other weights within the same range of heaviness. On account of his motor adaptation, the observer found that if he lifted two equal weights, the second seemed much too light; and only after it had been made considerably heavier than the first weight, did the two appear to be equal. The observer, of course, knew nothing of this adaptation, which nevertheless made the second impulse to lift so much more forcible than the first that the corresponding weight seemed to be much too light.

Two different methods of arousing motor adaptation were tested by Ordahl. In one the observer's attention was distracted from the practice of lifting the two weights —one of which was twice as heavy as the other—by reading to him an interesting story, the content of which he was afterwards required to relate accurately. As a complementary experiment the observer's attention was directed upon the weights. In the practice-tests a weight twice as heavy was employed as the second member of the pair, and also two slightly heavier and two slightly lighter weights. The observer was then called upon to decide in each case whether the second weight was twice as heavy as the first, or more or less heavy. Under these conditions the adaptation was, in fact, notably stronger than under the conditions of the distraction-experiment. We may also recall, in this connection, Binet's observation that attention contributes its part to a child's effort in learning to walk (see above, p. 251).

Taking these results together, our conclusion seems to be that in learning a more or less complicated movement a movement-melody must be composed; that is to say, a formation after the manner of our "configuration" takes place which does not consist of independent parts, but is an articulate whole. The motor adaptation itself, which is explained by its discoverers in quite a different way—namely by association—is nevertheless in evidence as to the correctness of our assumption. Consequently, a motor adaptation arising under the conditions of a strictly rhythmical lifting of weights, regulated by the beats of a metronome, presupposes a configuration for the same reason that it has been found impossible to learn nonsense-syllables without constructing them into a configural complex. The relation of motor to sensory learning is also indicated by the fact that many of the laws of sensory learning have been found applicable to motor adaptations, especially in the experiments of Lottie Steffens—a pupil of Müller—and hence it can not be supposed that motor and sensory learning are derived from two quite different sources. The improvement in a performance ought therefore to consist in the construction of better and more complete configurations. Certainly such an improvement is not an intelligent performance. To know beforehand how we must perform the act avails us nothing; for these configurations do not originate as "intelligent" configurations do. Their seat must chiefly lie in other centres. And yet some connection must exist between them and the centres of those processes which are accompanied by a high degree of consciousness. In beginning to learn, the phenomena of perception must be present and the learner must have a fixed purpose. The configurative formation is then influenced by these components. Practice, or continual repetition, is requisite, and it is very apparent that repetition contributes essentially to the fixation of the behaviour. One has only to think how a musical virtuoso has to practice in order that his "fingers may not rust." It is equally apparent that repetition has still another object; since it must create conditions favourable to the arousal of the new configuration. In learning by repetition, the concept of chance—in the sense in which it is used in the theory of trial and error—will not suffice. Chance may help, but it seems to me extremely doubtful if each new advance is really haphazard; especially when one considers how "wise" are the nervous centres which have nothing to do with consciousness, and how promptly and exactly they function in the face of sudden danger.

But a closer argument in support of this point of view would lead us too far. It is enough to note that new configurations are also attributable to these lower centres; as is demonstrated by the fact that the practice-curve improves by leaps which occur in learning new movements, as well as on the "good day" which Ruger speaks of; furthermore the influence of a "good day" is likewise felt in intelligent behaviour; the most difficult problems requiring intelligence being solved only under these conditions (see above p. 202).

Finally, it appears from the observations of Köhler that "a correlation exists between the intelligence and the manual skill of the chimpanzee"[251]; a fact which would be very singular if a relationship did not exist between these two kinds of behaviour. Intelligence and dexterity are also both subject to great individual variations. The construction of a "motor configuration" is specifically differentiated from an act of intelligence, chiefly in that a projection of the configuration prior to its performance is impossible. In this respect a motor pattern resembles the construction of a configuration in what is called "training," though it may far surpass the results of training in its refinement and precision. Acts of skill are often referred to as achievements of training, and there can be no objection to this description so long as one conceives training as we have done without mechanistic implications.

Returning to the child's learning to grasp and to touch, these are also acquisitions of new configurations, and indeed all behaviour in which sensory and motor components work together is closely related to the experiments we have described. We can now explain *anticipations*. The configuration takes place when the objective conditions happen to be unusually favourable, and since these conditions do not repeat themselves, the configuration can only reappear when a change in the internal conditions has taken place ; in which event the external conditions may be even less favourable than they were upon the first occasion. This statement will also account for "anticipations" such as those described above in connection with Köhler's experiments upon intelligence (see p. 195).

The question now arises : How far are we here concerned with true learning, and how far with mere maturation? Since the behaviour of grasping and touching is acquired by every normal child, these achievements must somehow be foreshadowed in the child's predisposition. Preyer and Shinn both call grasping an instinctive act, but we now see how difficult it is to draw a strict line of differentiation between innate and acquired activities because the boundaries are not absolutely fixed. Individual experience and the special behaviour to which each individual is subjected, each plays an important rôle in grasping ; yet the transition between maturation and learning is explicable only when maturation and learning both lead to the same end, which is the formation of new configurations [252].

§ 5—*Sensory Learning: The Development of Colour-Vision*

With the aid of a few significant examples we shall now try to follow the course of development in the perception of the child, in order to see how a picture of the world as we know it gradually arises out of the primitive and diffuse configurations of early experience. It is a truism to us adults that our perceptual world is the sum-total of our experiences. The question is: *How has experience brought this about?* We must not forget, for instance, that the problem of experience involves *achievements* as well as *memory;* and furthermore, that the possibility of components attributable to *maturation* must always be kept in mind.

We shall begin with the investigation of colour-perception, in which great pains have been taken to accumulate a wealth of interesting results of great importance for a general theory of colour-vision. A large number of methods have been thought out in these investigations; some depending entirely upon speech, while others are more or less free of linguistic aid, and can therefore be applied at an early age prior to the development of speech.

### A. *Methods involving Language*

1. *The Word-Sign-Method:* two colours are placed before the child and named for him. He is then asked to point to red, to yellow, etc. When the names of two colours have been learned, a third is added, and so on.

2. *The Naming-Method:* (*a*) as directed by the investigator, in which the child is shown separate colours to which he responds with their names; (*b*) as *spontaneous*, in which the child selects colours from a box and names them himself.

3. *The Symbolic Method:* the child is told a story, a definite colour being shown him for each of the persons involved, with the remark that "this is the father," "that

is the mother," etc. When the story has been related several times the child repeats it, and at the same time points out the colours belonging to each character.

### B. *Methods without direct Linguistic Aid*

1. *The Method of Arrangement :*

(*a*) By *Names.* A number of colours are placed before the child and he is told to pick out all the red ones (or blue ones, etc.).

(*b*) By *Samples.* A colour is placed in the child's hands and he is told to select from a pile all colours like the sample ; or, one shuffles the sample in with the other colours and lets the child find it again. The method of arrangement requires language only to the extent of explaining the problem to the child.

The last two methods, which follow, are copied from experiments with animals, and are applied entirely without speech.

2. *The Method of Preference :* in which several different colours are placed before the child, and one observes in a large number of cases which ones he grasps, or toward which he glances.

3. *The Method of Training :* By means of rewards, one seeks to persuade the child to select a single colour, from among a number that are shown him. If the training is successful, the existence of a *sensory* achievement is thereby demonstrated.

In early infancy colour-impressions, although occasionally they give rise to strong feelings of pleasure,[253] play but a very slight rôle (the colour of anything being as yet unimportant as a means of recognition). Thus, Miss Shinn's niece did not react at all in her seventh month when a white pacifier was given to her instead of the customary black one. Reactions may however, be called forth by colours. Very early the child turns toward bright objects, and begins to react differently to light and darkness. In this connection it should be noted that light and dark are not really colour-designations, such as black and white, but instead indicate differences in the "level" of the surroundings. All that we can properly say is that a bright object may stand out readily from its "background" at a very early age. One also finds at this early date that saturated colours are preferred to those which are achromatic (black-gray-white). Miss Shinn reports this distinction at the end of the third month, while Valentine, investigating with the method of preference, in which the child was tested by the direction of his gaze, confirms this finding in the fourth month. Valentine's experiments show, too, that colours are not all of equal value; for he was able to obtain the following series in order of preference: yellow, white, pink, red, brown, black, blue, green, violet [254]. This series indicates two things: (1) that the bright colours come before the dark ones—white before black, pink before red; and (2) that the long-wave "warm" colours are much preferred to the short-wave "cold" colours. One might almost suppose that in the white-black series, not black but an intermediate like dark gray is least attractive, because otherwise it is hard to understand why blue, green, and violet all followed after black.

Holden and Bosse [255] employed the method of preference in an ingenious way by placing coloured squares on a gray ground of the same brightness as the colours, and observing whether or not the coloured squares were grasped. The result of their experiments was that the colours from red to yellow were grasped promptly by children seven to eight months old, but that the infants must be from ten to twelve months old before they would reach for the colours from green to violet. What can we infer from this result? It is clear that if a child grasps at a coloured square he must have seen something on the gray background which was different and worth striving after; and this difference could not have been one of brightness alone, because the conditions of the

266

experiment excluded this possibility. But neither can we infer that the child saw *red* and *yellow*, for we do not know that anything different was seen in the test with the red square than was seen in the test with the yellow square. And what shall we conclude from the negative results obtained in the eighth month with the "cold" colours? This much, at least, can be said; that the child did not perceive anything that was at once different from the background and worth grasping. Since these same colours were grasped a few months later, it is at least very improbable that this negative result involved seeing a difference, though without any desire to grasp the colour; for on such an assumption it would be difficult to understand why so sudden a change in the desire for these colours should have taken place. The most probable explanation is that at first only the "warm" colours stand out against the achromatic shades; the "cold" colours being added later on.

What colour-phenomena are experienced by the child at this stage of development? Putting the matter as simply as possible, the child experiences configurations of gray and not-gray; not-gray being like none of the colours we know and recognize, though it differs from gray in the same way in which we find that all variegated colours differ from those which have no colour at all. By the customary usage of speech *colour* means just those tones which we have designated as variegated—white, gray, and black being commonly referred to as "uncoloured." We conclude, then, that during the first three-quarters of the child's first year of life no configurations of colour arise other than this primitive chromatic-achromatic distinction; and, indeed that this configuration comes into being only when objectively "warm" colours chance to lie upon a colour-less background, or, we might add, upon an objectively "cold" ground of the same brightness.

Now when a colour-configuration is also established for the short-wave colours, the question arises whether this phenomenon is like the one determined by the long-wave rays, or whether, in its distinction from this configuration, it also possesses the phenomenal characteristics of the "cold" rather than of the "warm" colours. This question can not yet be answered with any degree of certainty, but, as we shall see, there soon occurs a stage in the child's life when this distinction between the "warm" and "cold" colours is made. I am inclined to believe, however, that at the beginning the "cold-figures" appear merely as undifferentiated "colour-figures." Several facts seem to support this view. Learning the names of the colours is at first very difficult and generally comes much later, unless the child has been influenced by some special training. Names of colours may occasionally be employed, but quite promiscuously; whereas a colourless object is never given a colour-name. The Sterns report of their daughter that "at the age of three years and two months Hilda called bright and dark things *white* and *black*; otherwise she pointed with assurance only to the colour *red*. But the accuracy of the word *red* was obviously quite accidental, since *all variegated colours were likewise called red*"[256]. As Winch has noted, it often happens that variegated colours are distinguished from neutral tones by giving them all the same name, which indicates that all variegated colours have a common characteristic in contrast to the achromatic tones, and that this common factor must therefore be much more influential than any differences seen between the variegated colours themselves.[257]

With some reserve I may note the following observation upon myself. Being "colour-weak"[258], I see red and green only under favourable conditions. There are certain colours which I recognize immediately as "coloured," yet they are always very distasteful to me, simply because I am unable to classify them. I am tempted to call them brown, though they easily slip over into red, or even into green. Yet they possess, as I have said, a quality which makes them unsuited to belong with any of the other colours. Still, these colours are chromatic beyond a doubt.

Turning now to the experiments which involve the use of language, the numerous results of Preyer, Binet, Shinn, and Winch [259], among others which are available, seem at first glance to be quite contradictory. It is impossible to give an explanation covering all these observations with any degree of certainty, because we are not sure of the exact nature of the colours with which the individual investigators have worked. Future workers in this field should consider this point and take care that in all examinations of colour-vision differences which may be attributable to brightness and saturation are rigidly excluded.

An important material cause of the varying conclusions reached by different investigators may be found in the fact that the result of an experiment depends so largely upon the *method* employed. Word-sign-, naming-, and arrangement-methods give quite different results, as Binet and Miss Shinn have already pointed out. In each method, too, the number and selection of colours to be combined are of the utmost importance in determining the results of the test.

I may refer to Binet's experiment as an example. He began his investigations with a little girl two years and eight months old, placing before the child at first only red and green strands of wool (the Holmgren test). Examination by the first two language-methods produced 100 per cent. correct reactions. Yellow was then added, the result being that yellow and green were constantly confused. When the yellow was removed, all the reactions were immediately correct ; as soon as it was included, the errors began again. If the green was now taken away the word-sign-method indicated no errors ; but with the naming-method there were 100 per cent. mistakes, since yellow was always called green. On a day when the naming-method sti·l ind.

269

cated a complete confusion of yellow and green, the arrangement-method (Bl*b*)—in which a certain strand already shown was selected from a pile containing three strands each of red, yellow, and green—was carried out with no errors at all.

Up to the present these results have almost always been interpreted as indicating errors which consisted solely in attaching the wrong names to the colours. This explanation, however, appears to be insufficient; for why should naming have been so difficult? Apparently there are difficulties here which do not exist in learning other words. Furthermore, we have already seen that the names black, gray, and white are never employed for variegated colours, provided the colours are sufficiently saturated.[260]

Other results indicate that frequent confusions of colour occur in the case of blue-green, green-white, yellow-white, violet-blue, red-blue (according to Miss Shinn), all pale colours with gray or white, and all dark colours with black. Finally, Winch performed a large number of experiments with the naming-method which previously had furnished only the most unfavourable results. Winch sought to eliminate the defects of this method by testing children who already had been taught the names of the colours in the kindergarten, where all the colours were practised equally. According to Winch, a difference in the serial order of the correct word-usage must then depend altogether upon a difference in the colour-phenomenon itself; provided, of course, that phonetic difficulties attaching to the particular names of the colours have been taken into account. The individual variations were now considerable; but on the average the following series was indicated: red, blue, green, yellow, violet, orange. Meumann gives exactly the same series; while Garbini found the following series, both in naming and in discrimination: red, green, yellow, orange, blue, violet.

In considering results such as these, it is easy to

assume, as most investigators have done, "that what we have here is the development of certain modes of apprehension, but not the development of a sensory capacity or, in physiological terms, the development of reactions of the 'visual substances' in the sense of Hering's theory "[261]. The principal grounds upon which investigators have been led to this view are the following : First, the great variation in the results obtained from different observers. Secondly, the great individual differences. For instance, Miss Shinn's niece could name red, yellow, and blue things at the end of her 73rd week. Experiments were then begun in the 79th week, and were at once successful in the case of these three colours. With Preyer's son, on the other hand, it was impossible for him to learn two colours at the end of the 87th week, and the experiments were for the first time successful in the 108th week. Thirdly, the dependency of the performance upon the nature of the test. Bühler finds support for this conclusion in an instance of anticipation observed by Mrs Woolley. The child observed in its sixth month indicated by grasping-tests a definitely graded preference for colours : "warm" being preferred to "cold," and dark to bright. This preference then disappeared altogether, and for many months no differentiation on the basis of colours was in any wise indicated. It is Bühler's opinion that "it would be without rhyme or reason to assume that the sensory capacity had undergone any retrogression." Bühler's argument, however, is based upon a presumption which we have already several times declined to accept ; namely, the "constancy-hypothesis," according to which a certain sensation always corresponds to a certain stimulus just as soon as ever the capacity for the sensation in question has been attained. It is only on the basis of this assumption that Bühler's inference is valid ; otherwise one might say that the conditions for the appearance of colour-phenomena in the case of Mrs Woolley's child were especially favourable in the

271

sixth month—a possibility which even Bühler makes note of. The grasping-tendency is at this time in the ascendant, and if a number of coloured papers are placed before the child it glances frequently from one to the other before it grasps. As development proceeds further, the child is no longer restricted to grasping, but begins to undertake new types of manipulation with things; in consequence of which the colours become entirely irrelevant. In other words, since the conditions are no longer favourable for the appearance of colour-phenomena—or, better, of colour-configurations—the phenomena themselves fail to appear.

Whatever may be said against the special argument based upon anticipations such as Mrs Woolley has recorded is also applicable to this entire mode of thought. We simply can not be satisfied with a description which states that the child experiences the colour-sensations correctly but is not yet able to apprehend or discriminate them. We should rather ask: What is now the actual nature of the child's phenomena? Indeed, the case is the same as it was when we argued against " unnoticed relations " (cf. above p. 208 f.). From our point of view the assertion that a colour-difference is apprehended signifies that two colours have entered into a definite kind of union ; in other words, there arises a configuration of two colours, in which the colours appear as they stand in this configuration. The development of colour-perception is therefore the gradual construction of new colour-figures; accordingly the conditions for the arousal of such figures may readily become less favourable than they were at some previous time. Thus the anticipations which have been described in so significant a way by Mrs Woolley, and which have also been observed by other investigators, are in fact a demonstration of the validity of our theory; for we have already shown (p. 263) how anticipations may be understood as configurative processes arising under exceptionally favourable external conditions.

Regarding the results in this way, their dependency upon the method employed is also readily comprehended; as can be shown by reference to Binet's experiment which we described above. If the configuration red-green has been acquired, and yellow is then added, the confusion which takes place in naming may be looked upon as an indication that now the same configuration is operative; namely, that of red—not-red. In agreement with this interpretation, the word-sign-method indicated no errors for red and yellow, whereas by the naming-method all the results were wrong. If, on the other hand, the arrangement-method was employed, the red configuration was no longer involved when the child was tested with a yellow or a green. The "relational system" having been changed, so to speak, everything now depended upon the configurations of yellow—yellow, or of green—green, or again of yellow —not-yellow, or green—not-green. The arrangement-experiment teaches us, indeed, that variants of this kind actually occur without in any way contradicting the results obtained in the other experiments.

It is apparent that future investigators will have to take these configurations more into account than they have done in the past. Both the kind of colours, and the ground upon which they are exhibited, must be systematically varied.

A discovery of Köhler offers further support to our theory. In his investigation of chimpanzees he arranged some tests of choice-training in which he selected colours A, B, C, not from the black-white series, but lying somewhere between red and blue, or between red and yellow. His results correspond exactly with those previously reported. One observation, however, is of particular interest. A, B, C, D, E,—E being the reddest —were five different colours lying between red and blue, whose nuances were easily distinguishable by man. Taking the pair B C, the chimpanzee was required to learn to react to the markedly reddish C. This attempt was a failure. The interval was then increased, and the investigation continued with the pair B D. The selection of D was then rapidly learned. When thereafter the pair B C was again offered, C was chosen correctly without an exception ; and some time later, D was selected without an exception in the interval C D [262]. This result is very important to us for the following reason : At first it was impossible to construct a definite configuration of B C, although occasionally it proved effective; but the configuration of B D took place at once, and thereafter both B C and C D were effective. Here, then, is a case which corresponds exactly to our law of memory as formulated on p. 248 f. A configuration arising under favourable objective conditions reappears also when the conditions are less favourable.

The following hypotheses concerning the development of colour-vision seem to me justified by the results we have cited. First of all, a configuration takes place with reference to colour and non-colour, and this occurs earlier with the long-wave colours than with the short-wave colours. Consider now the developmental series of Winch and Meumann in contrast with the one obtained by Garbini (cf. above p. 270). If we omit the position of orange in Garbini's series, the difference is much less than at first it appears to be. After red there follows in each series a " cold " colour, then a second " warm " and a second " cold " colour—although in inverted order —and finally an " intermediate colour," violet ; followed in the series of Winch and Meumann by orange, which appeared earlier in Garbini's series. Since the methods of testing and learning were different in all three cases, one could hardly expect a closer correspondence ; yet in my opinion this much, at least, can be provisionally inferred from these results : that after the stage of colour—non-colour, described above, there follows a period in which " warm—cold " and probably also " warm —colourless " and " cold—colourless " configurations arise; which would account for the confusion of blue and green, these being configurations achieved by the intermediate zone of the retina, such as are indicated in cases of red - green colour - blindness. How intimate this connection with colour - blindness may be, the material at hand is too incomplete to determine.

In the next place we may suppose that a differentiation takes place within the "warm" and "cold" colours, causing the four principal colours, red, yellow, green, and blue to appear. More exactly, we can say that in opposition to the colourless experiences, colour - configurations are constituted in four directions. Here, too, I have been able to find an analogy in a case of defective vision. The last step would be a differentiation leading to the appearance of the intermediate colours, and although the development is essentially one of maturation, practice influences it very markedly. Thus, the considerable difference in the reactions of Miss Shinn's niece and the Stern children may, in large part, depend upon their respective environments; for the latter children grew up in the stony surroundings of Breslau, whereas Miss Shinn's niece lived in a country house amid the luxuriant landscape of California.

According to this view, the learning of colour-names depends upon the possibility of arousing accurate colour-configurations. The connection between colour-configuration and name has never, perhaps, been so strikingly observed as by Stumpf in the case of his own child. This boy (as we shall have occasion to note at the close of the chapter) spoke a language of his own up to his fourth year—a language which contained but two colour-names: *ä* and *weich*. "Every colour in contrast with white was called *ä*, and in contrast with black, *weich;* or speaking more generally, the darker of any two colours was *ä* and the lighter *weich*" [263].

To us, the configuration is the primary characteristic, the name of the colour being secondary. But this point of view has been completely reversed by Peters in a work written with great insight upon the basis of certain experimental distinctions which he made for the purpose of elucidating some of his data. Peters regards the confusions which children make, not only in naming but also in arranging colours, to be a result of the influence exerted by their names upon the apprehension and comparison of the colours themselves [264]. He confines himself to the confusion of intermediate and principal colours, blue and violet, red and purple, etc., and deduces five consequences from his thesis which he then attempts to prove experimentally.

(1) Children who possess no definite colour-names, ought to commit no errors in arrangement; (2) neither should they commit any errors when the correct names are introduced. (3) On the other hand, such children must commit errors whenever one introduces the same name for both *principal* and *intermediate* colours. (4) Children who are already able to name the intermediate colours correctly, should make no errors in arrangement. (5) Children who at first commit errors in naming and arranging should correct these errors as soon as they have learned to name the colours correctly.

Peters believes that he has demonstrated all five of these inferences. He concludes, therefore, that the development of colour-perception in older children has nothing to do with sensory functioning, or with its morphological substratum, but depends altogether upon the constitution of the so-called higher intellectual processes of apprehension, reproduction, and thinking with respect to these sensory capacities. Apprehension is not altogether determined by sensation, since a knowledge of the colour-names may, under certain circumstances, be of greater significance than the sensory component; yet, but for the naming of the colour, no errors at all would ever be made. " A child who attaches the same name, blue, to both blue and violet, does not merely apprehend violet as something which looks so-and-so, but at the same time, as being an object which is called blue. . . . The colour-name which thus influences apprehension—one might speak here of a verbo-perceptive influence—is in both colours the same, and the knowledge of this common term has the obvious effect of altogether setting aside any difference in their appearance, so long as this difference is not too great "[265]. We have directed our argument so often against the employment of such concepts as "apprehension," etc., that the reader will at once be able to formulate for himself our objection to this particular interpretation. We have only to show how Peters' experimental results appear after we have set aside the distinction which he has drawn between the sensory and the higher intellectual functions, as though they existed separately and along side one another, in order to indicate what may be their real value.

Let us therefore consider these experiments in detail. Backward children were made the subjects of the investigation, and since all possible stages of colour-mastery can be found among these cases, they furnish exceptionally good material from which to obtain an answer to the question raised. The subjects tested ranged between 6·10 and 12 years of age, while their mental ages varied from 5 to 9·4 years. In determining mental age, these children were classified in comparison with normal children by means of the Binet-Simon scale of tests. This is not the place to discuss this method of testing, but one should not expect to find by such means anything more than an approximate characterization of mental age. That a backward child of a certain mental age is not at all the equivalent of a normal child of the same chronological age was shown in these experiments ; for Peters remarks of his backward children that a momentarily successful practice in naming colours lasted only for a brief period of time. (Cf. also the observations on p. 33 f.)

The investigations themselves were experiments upon the arrangement of coloured samples. A coloured skein of wool was laid before the child, who was then given the task of selecting " all the others that look like this wool here " from a pile of thoroughly mixed skeins consisting of seventeen different nuances; three skeins having been provided of each of six colours.

The child was then taught to name certain colours. These separate colours were again shown in a constantly changing series and, with the aid of pointing the finger, the names were again repeated.

Peters did, indeed, find support for each of the five inferences stated above. Unfortunately, he found only one case in which the child originally possessed no definite colour-names, and hence, in accordance with the first inference, made no errors in his arrangement; although this child did place some skeins of brighter and less saturated blue along with the blue sample. A boy who possessed an almost perfect understanding of the colour-names—so that he even called violet colours *lilac*—misnamed only the purple, which he called *red*. Yet in the arrangement - experiment this same boy reacted differently when he received a red, than when he received a purple sample; for although he made no errors in the first instance, when he was afterwards given the purple sample he selected not only all the purples but also the reds. Peters does not make allowance for this striking behaviour; but concludes from the experiment in which a correct arrangement had previously been made with reference to the blue sample, that when the names of intermediate colours were known there were no errors; but when only the names of principal colours were known, errors of arrangement occurred. Peters' second inference, however, is further-reaching than the experimental report with which we are now dealing: namely, that errors of arrangement occurred only when the intermediate, and *not* when the principal colours were used as samples [266]. A behaviour of this kind was

278

partially duplicated in another experiment. The name red for red and purple tones, and the name blue for both blue and violet tones, were taught to a boy who knew no colour-names, and therefore did not confuse the colours at all. After instruction, this boy placed all the blue and violet tones with the blue sample; with the red sample, however, he placed no purple tones at all, but only the red ones. Unfortunately, no experiment was made with the purple sample as the standard of comparison.

The experiment with a little girl who, among all the colours, named only red and blue correctly, went very prettily (cf. our discussion on p. 274 above). With the red sample she placed red, purple, and lilac; and with the blue sample, blue, violet, and lilac. The name *violet* was then suggested to her, and no more errors were made with the blue or purple samples; though she repeatedly selected the wrong skeins, either violet or blue, from the pile and after comparing them with the sample laid them back again. Peters thinks that this hesitancy may have had some connection with the child's previous habit of calling violet objects blue; but the same behaviour was observed in a boy who named only the principal colours correctly, although he committed no errors in his arrangements.

The experimental results which have now been reviewed seem to demonstrate that Peters' theory is at best incomplete. Yet the experiments also indicate the direction in which we must seek for an explanation of the discrepancies we have noted. Let us begin with the data last mentioned where no actual errors in arrangement were made. A wrong skein was often rejected only after it had been selected for comparison with the sample. There are two points of interest here: (1) Why was the wrong colour taken from the pile at all; and (2) What does this comparison signify? The second question can be readily answered. When colours are held side by side—the sample and a differently

279

coloured skein—they exist together as members of a configuration which, since the comparison led to rejection,
proved to be a configuration involving a *difference*.

Peters has a theory to cover the first question, but we
have already seen that his theory fits the facts only in
special instances, and not generally. Apart from these
special instances, Peters' theory depends upon the
soundness of his entire hypothetical structure. If we
can get along without his theory, we may say that
the wrong colour was picked up because the stimulus
for such an act was afforded by the colour itself; in
other words, the colour was chosen for comparison with
the sample - colour because the stimulus involved an
*index of uncertainty*. One result of name - learning
would therefore be that colours acquire indices of uncertainty; which leads us to the main problem—What
takes place in learning of this type? According to
Peters, learning is solely a matter of the connection
between a sensation and a word. But we have already
seen that connections of this sort are not the primary
achievements of any systematic training. The important
thing is that the child shall "see the point" of the tests.
If a child, to whom blue skeins of wool are named as
being blue, while violet ones are called violet, intends
to learn this fact, he must first understand, however incompletely, why colours, which until then have borne
the same name, should now be named differently. This
means that in the process of learning the child must
acquire a new colour-configuration. He must learn to
see something different when blue appears on the background than when violet is there. This is the most
natural thing in the world to me—a partially colour-
weak person. When a child I never could understand
why adults often called "blue" things "lilac." I have
since learned why, though rather incompletely; for I
now know that a blue can be reddish, and I therefore
try to reconstruct the colour as a red. This is often
difficult, and sometimes impossible. But if I can lay

a blue colour alongside of one which is doubtful, such as violet, my doubt is removed ; for in the colour-pair the one which was just now bluish and very " doubtful " becomes strongly reddish, often, indeed, quite purple. When, therefore, a child is taught to give the same names to principal and intermediate colours, whereas previously he had made no use at all of colour-names, the child must learn, for instance, when to say blue, and when to say red. Thus he undertakes to construct the *same* configuration for blue on a background that he does for violet on a background (and likewise for red and purple). The fact that principal and intermediate colours are not named differently until much later is, from our point of view, a sign that the blue and red are originally formed by the intermediate no less than by the principal colours. Although we are here dealing with a " verbo-perceptive " influence, its effect must be quite different from the one Peters refers to.

We can now understand, not only Peters' five inferences, but also the facts which he did not explain. I do not need to go into details, but would like to point out that during instruction the child has figural experiences of colour and ground, and that in the selection which takes place the figures are complicated by heaping the colours together and thus mixing the different strands of wool. This is undoubtedly the principal reason why wrong colours are so often placed beside the test-colour for comparison ; leading, finally, to a figure for comparison in which an intermediate colour is contrasted with a principal colour. In the matter of differentiating principal and intermediate colours in incorrect arrangements (cf. p. 278), the following may be said : Psychologically, an arrangement of colours with reference to a red standard is not the same as an arrangement with reference to a purple standard, even though the same name is attached to each standard. Since purple against a background gives the same kind of figure as red against a background, when the relational system has purple as its standard, all reds will belong in this system. Consequently, the figure in which purple is differentiated from red does not come into consideration, because the standard, with reference to its background, already possesses the characteristic of red. On the other hand, when the standard is red, the purple figure can easily arise in opposition to the red; and this opposition may be carried in the memory so that purple will be rejected; again indicating that the principal colours have an outstanding position.

Peters has, in point of fact, demonstrated the influence exerted by names upon the apprehension and comparison of colours, but we need not take "apprehension" and "comparison" to be processes of a "higher" order that are merely added to a lower order of unchanging sensory processes. Instead, these are all configurative processes determining the quality of their membership, including the so-called "sensations." In this respect Peters' experiments bring a valuable support, as well as a deeper insight, into the development of our theory.[267]

The untenability of Peters' hypothesis is indicated by an argument which he advances in its support. The influence of knowledge upon perception is often remarked in the case of adults; especially with reference to colour. For instance, a white lying in a shadow does not look black, neither does a gray in full illumination look white, so long as one is able to survey the spatial arrangement of each. Hering was the first to call attention to these phenomena, which he termed *memory-colours*, although Hering's theory differs from that of Peters. Katz,[268] who has made a thorough investigation of these phenomena, found that the apparent whiteness of an achromatic tone maintains its relative independence of the amount of light reflected from its surface into the eye, even when no knowledge at all is given concerning the "actual" nature of the colour. On the other hand, he found that this "reference to the illumination"—this *transformation*, as Jaensch has called it—is bound up with the fact that the colour appears as the *colour of an object*, and not merely as an extended coloration, such, for instance, as that of the blue heavens. This discovery has been substantiated, and given greater precision, by Gelb's observations upon pathological cases.[269] Katz, however, regarded these colour-transformations as effects of memory ; that is, as products of experience.

By means of choice-experiments, of a kind we already know, Köhler[270] has been able to show that colour-transformations occur with chimpanzees, and even with hens. The hens experimented upon varied in age from seven to fifteen months. One-half of them were trained to eat from a white surface and the other half from a black surface, the two surfaces being placed side by side in the same illumination. It was found that the influence of this training remained without alteration, even when the white surface was shaded to such an extent that it reflected less light than the black surface—the black surface in some cases being objectively 12.4 times as bright as the white. Not only is knowledge or any "verbo-perceptive" influence here excluded, but likewise any effect of experience whatsoever ; for, if the word "experience" is to have any meaning at all in the explanation of human behaviour based on perception, it is certainly not applicable to the experience of a seven-months-old hen (and the same experiments can be made with even younger fowls).

Since in these transformations the bearing of one colour upon another is always involved, we can not be accused of anticipating the development of our theory if we again apply the operation of configural functions to our explanation ; especially when we consider that Köhler's selective trainings all depended upon such configurations. Consequently, the facts Peters adduces in support of his theory, as well as his own experiments, both lead back to our own theory of the development of colour-vision. How very young children would behave under similar conditions has not yet been investigated, but the problem is one well worth undertaking.

### § 6—*Continuation : Spatial Factors*

We shall now select for consideration a few of the more important problems involved in the development of visual space-perception. In the beginning the infant's field of vision, considered as an area within which visible objects arouse reactions, is very limited. At first the child sees only what lies directly before him ; objects which appear but slightly to one side, above or below, being practically non-existent. Similarly, visual depth is very slight. Stern calls this perceptual limitation *near-space,* and reckons it as approximating a half-sphere about the head with a radius of perhaps a third of a metre. Whatever lies beyond is not seen with any specific quality, though it may contribute to the general background of visual experience. This limit of a third of a metre is not inflexible, however, but depends upon the kind of object seen ; indeed, a general variability of this sort obtains throughout the entire field of vision. Thus bright objects can be perceived at greater distances from the centre than dark objects, whether with reference to height, breadth, or depth. Compayré reports on this point as follows : " Place a lighted candle two or three metres from a child fifteen or twenty days old ; he will look at it fixedly ; if you place it three, four, or five metres from him, it will become evident that the child has lost sight of the light, and you will be sure from the uncertainty of his glances that he no longer perceives anything." As regards the absolute magnitude of the distance, reports of observers vary considerably [271].

Attempts have been made to explain these facts on the ground that a restricted field of vision depends upon a later development of functional capacity in the peripheral than in the central portion of the retina ; while

284

inability to apprehend visual depth has been attributed to an original incompleteness of eye-movements, especially those of accommodation and convergence. But this cannot be an adequate statement of the case; because in certain ways these characteristics of visual space, as found in early childhood, recur again in adult life. The peripheral portions of the field of vision, as well as the remote distances of visual space, are always at a disadvantage in comparison with the nearer regions; and this is true for perceptions of colour as well as for those of form and magnitude. Analogous to the results obtained with children, the degree of this disadvantage depends upon the nature of the object selected for the test [272]. This latter circumstance, in particular, contradicts the all too simple nature of the explanation which has been offered. We must think of development in terms of a process of maturation in the course of which certain regions of the nervous system attain the capacity of forming fixed configurations which at first they do not possess; this process of maturation being dependent upon functional employment. From numerous pathological observations we know that even an adult is able to develop such an ability through practice, when the practice is needful to him. Biological importance attaches at first only to what is near at hand; and to be able to see at great distances is for most living beings of no importance whatever. That a dog, for instance, should be able to see the mountains which enclose a valley, seems to me, from personal observation, highly improbable.

I am inclined to believe that a connection exists between the extension of the field of visual space and still another of its properties. To us adults the "apparent magnitude" of an object—that is, how great a thing looks—is relatively independent of the actual magnitude of its retinal image. When a man removes himself from a distance of one metre to a distance of four metres from us, he does not suddenly appear to be one-quarter as large as he did before, even though the retinal image must have undergone diminution to this extent. As a matter of fact, we see no change of magnitude at all. Thus, within a certain distance we never confuse a small object near at hand with a large object farther off. Yet this independence of retinal magnitude is not absolute; for when I find myself at a considerable distance from the man, he suddenly appears very small indeed. A village seen from a mountain top may look like a toy which came out of a box, and even a very high mountain peak when seen from another peak at a great distance may look like a minute point. On the other hand, there is a certain adequate distance, a zone, as it were, within which the "actual magnitude" of an object is best apprehended, and this distance is different in apprehending a thimble than it is in apprehending a man, and is again different in apprehending a mountain [273].

These phenomena have usually been explained in the way indicated by Helmholtz; thus Stern speaks of an involved association between the impression of distance and that of magnitude; while Bühler points out that the relative independence of apparent magnitude from the retinal image "must first be acquired and practised by the child" [274].

Unfortunately, we know almost nothing about this acquisition and practice on the part of children. Helmholtz reports an undated remembrance of childhood, when human beings seen on a church-tower in Potsdam looked to him like dolls. I can also recall a very similar experience. On the victory - column in Berlin cannon-barrels are placed at different heights, and I remember quite well that I could scarcely believe my father, with whom I often passed by this column, when he told me they were all cannons; for while the lower ones did appear like short rifles, the higher ones seemed like small pistols. Although they no longer look that way to me, the upper ones still seem smaller than the lower ones, and no amount of knowledge has sufficed to alter this sensory impression, which is in direct contradiction with Helmholtz's explanation from experience, signifying an association of sensations with ideas and judgments.

The experiments in choice-training which Köhler carried out with chimpanzees have again shown that the relations here involved are similar to those of colour-transformations, with which phenomena the relative constancy of apparent magnitude possesses a consider-able objective likeness.[275] Köhler trained his animals to choose the larger of two boxes having front-boards of different size, the boxes being at like distances from the animal. The larger box was then so far removed that the retinal image of its front became smaller than that of the smaller box. All necessary precautions were taken into consideration, and yet the effect of training persisted. Even the behaviour of a four-year-old chim-panzee indicated the constancy of apparent magnitude within a certain zone of distance ; which shows that the usual hypothesis referring the constancy of selection to experience is highly improbable, if not impossible. All the facts otherwise known concerning apparent magnitude, such, for instance, as the effects of clearness, impressiveness, the configuration of what is seen—that the smaller the apparent magnitude, corresponding *ceteris paribus* to a definite retinal image, the greater the clearness attaching to it [276] — all these point toward dependencies which involve the total configuration.

The development of this capacity which, as Köhler points out, can be investigated by choice-training with very small children, is in all likelihood more a matter of maturation than of learning ; although the process is obviously of such an order that it can not go on inde-pendent of the employment of the organs concerned [277]. That is why I have suggested above that a connection must exist between the development of an apparent constancy of magnitude, and the development of spatial

287

extension. And even at a relatively late period of life this development is not yet at an end, as was demonstrated both by the observations of Helmholtz and myself; since mine certainly extended back into the sixth, if not into the seventh year of my life. These observations, however, do not mean that constancy of magnitude may not already have been established for shorter distances than those here referred to.

The following observation of Stern does not aid us at all with our problem: Once when the baby was eight months old, while waiting for his bottle, he was shown, by way of a joke, a doll's bottle about one-fifteenth the usual size. " He became greatly excited and snapped at the bottle as though it were the real one." As Stern rightly points out, this demonstrates how small a part size actually plays in the recognition of things during this period of life ; but it does not indicate, as Stern also infers, that a constancy of magnitude, in the sense in which we have employed the term,[278] must have been lacking.

An hypothesis based upon experiments with eidetic images (cf. p. 245), which has been advanced by Paula Busse to explain the as yet uninvestigated cause of development in the constancy of magnitude, seems to me likewise untenable. Her idea is that the eidetic image of an object when seen at close range ought to fuse with the perceptual complex of the same object when it is more distant, thus maintaining the constancy of magnitude[279]. There is nothing to question in her observations, and they are interesting and important enough in themselves, but just how they relate to the constancy of magnitude and its development is a matter which must first be investigated in greater detail. For instance, in a demonstration made by Jaensch before a scientific gathering at Nauheim in 1920, a remote object was so influenced by the constitution of the eidetic image that it appeared to be enlarged beyond its actual limits, as previously determined by the points of a compass. In a case like this, the matter is extremely complicated; the factors in the configuration upon which the apparent magnitude depends may exercise a different influence upon the eidetic image than they do upon either the perceptual, or the after-images. Nor is there any reason to suppose that one of these influences is more original than another, so that the others must be derived from it.

The perception of *form* confirms the suitability of our general principle of explanation. We have previously referred to the fact (cf. above p. 133) that it is not the simplest of geometrical forms, but those biologically the most important, which are first evident in infantile perception. From her 25th day forward, Miss Shinn's niece took an interest in human faces, which in her second quarter-year she was able to distinguish as familiar and unfamiliar. To teach the child "simple figures" is possible only at a much later time. Miss Shinn, to whom we owe a number of good observations on this subject, was able to impress her niece with the printed letter *o* in the beginning of her twelfth month. From her 343rd day the child pointed out the *o* correctly, while in the thirteenth month her behaviour showed marked independence of the absolute magnitude of the letter. On her 382nd day the child found an *o* printed in small type; and thereafter would occasionally confuse *o*'s with *c*'s. This behaviour is very instructive, because sensory-wise *c* and *o* are quite different, but as a figure a *c* may be taken for an "incomplete" *o*. At the end of her 21st month, the names of the forms which the child had learned from a toy consisting of small and variously shaped pieces of cardboard, were for the first time applied to things in her environment. Thus, for instance, the folded edge of a man's collar was called a triangle. This should not be understood to mean that the collar-edge simply reproduced the name *triangle* on account of its similarity with the triangular cardboard, but rather that the triangular con-

289

figuration which was acquired in the use of the toy now entered into the perception of a man's collar. That is to say, the progress which the child had made was not merely in naming, but essentially in perceiving.

At the end of her 22nd month, after the child had acquired a remarkable facility in dealing with and in recognizing plane figures, experiments were performed with simple geometrical solids. These solids gave the child considerable difficulty, especially in learning to use the word *cube*, instead of which she always said *square;* although she learned very readily to employ the word *ball* for a *sphere*. This difference also indicates a peculiarity of perception. From the start, the figure of a cube is very closely related to the figure of a square, whereas a ball is evidently something new, as compared with a flat circle.

In consideration of what has previously been said, these achievements are relatively late; moreover, children are able to recognize pictures of persons at a much earlier date. They also take pictures for actual things; fear, for instance, was shown by Miss Shinn's niece on her 293rd day when the picture of a cat was placed before her. The behaviour of a child towards pictures is also like his behaviour towards things; the child will put his finger into the eyes of a portrait, just as he would into those of a living being. Miss Shinn's niece recognized large portraits as those of human beings in her tenth month, and she recognized individuals, such as " mother," " father," etc., as early as the beginning of her second year. Even small photographs were recognized, and the father was found among a group of other persons. A child of nine months takes pleasure in his picture-book, and actually knows the pictures. According to Stern, the crude outline at first determines recognition, while an equally crude filling-in of the surface holds the second place in his interest; the finer details, however, attain importance very gradually. Stern tested the significance of the outline by a neat method which he calls the method of "evolution." This method consists in "constructing a drawing before the eyes of the child, ceasing at the moment the child is able to name it"[280]. Some of these tests are here reproduced, and crude as the drawings are, they were recognized at the age 1·10 (Fig. 14).

These experiments prove that the figures of early infantile perception may be readily aroused, though they are still very crude, and possess little in the way of internal structure. The internal structure, however, becomes constantly more definite as the child develops. And hence, figures which a child recognizes at an early age are sometimes not recognized later on. Hilda

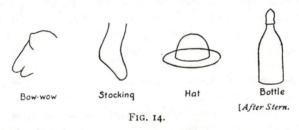

Bow-wow     Stocking     Hat     Bottle

[*After Stern.*

FIG. 14.

Stern, for instance, who recognized the bottle in the above figure at the age of 1·10, was unable to recognize the same picture two and one-half years later. Binet also experimented upon a little girl of 1·9 with simple outline drawings. From his results we may note the following: Expressions of smiling and weeping and the direction of the gaze were recognized in faces where the achievement would have been considerable if one were to think of it in terms of the geometry of drawing, since the differences of expression were determined by fine differences of internal structure. This result, therefore, would seem to contradict Stern's conclusion as to the primary significance of the outline; though the facts agree very well with data reported concerning the recognition of photographs, where Stern himself calls attention to this contradiction. Binet's experiments, however, are also in direct contradiction with the otherwise quite improbable explanation offered by Stern, who states that the recollections a child has of his parents must be much more detailed than his recollections of other objects. Yet since the child can distinguish fine nuances of expression in quite unfamiliar faces, this fact can only be explained in agreement with our previous results when we regard expression as a part of these quite early phenomena, so that what the child recognizes in the picture is the expression itself rather than the configuration of a surface. Indeed, what the child recognizes in the face of his father is not the colour, the size, the distance between the eyes, the form of the nose, mouth, chin, etc., but those essential characteristics which enable us to differentiate a good photograph from a poor, though geometrically correct, one—that is, those properties of a picture for which we have no special name in our language.

Another of Binet's results is no less interesting. When presented severally, the child fails to recognize the isolated parts of objects which he would recognize without hesitation were they exhibited in their proper relations. Thus an ear, a mouth, or a finger was not recognized in Binet's tests, even when the test was repeated nearly three years later (at the age of 4·4); which shows very clearly that quite different phenomena may correspond to the same objectively given thing (the outline of an ear, for example), according to its context. To employ two expressions coined by Wertheimer, a familiar "whole-part" or a completely unfamiliar "part-whole" may correspond to the same objectively given thing. What is indicated by these examples may be expressed by saying that phenomenally, to a child, a man is not made up of his members, but the members belong to the man. Close ethnological parallels of this fact can be found. Thus, in many languages it is impossible to say merely "hand," because hand is always the hand of a particular person.

If, for example, an Indian were to find an amputated arm, he could not say : " I have found an arm," but he must say, " I have found of someone his arm " [281].

Stern has pointed out a further peculiarity of infantile perception [282] ; namely, that to a child a form is much more independent of its *absolute spatial position* than it is to us adults. Children often look at their picture-books upside down without being in the least disturbed, and investigators have shown that pictures turned at an angle of ninety, or even one-hundred-and-eighty, degrees are as easily recognized as those in a normal position. This peculiarity continues for a long time. Even at the beginning of the school-period it may be noticed that many children copy the letters given them, not only in the right position, but in all possible positions ; as for instance in mirror-writing, or upside down. Teachers who, at my request, have made observations upon this subject, have reported that certain children can read mirror-writing at first just as well as they can ordinary writing ; which shows the difference between children and adults ; for an adult finds it no easy task to read mirror-writing. Originally, then, a figure is in a high degree independent of its position, whereas for adults the absolute orientation of the figure is a very powerful factor. Right and left, above and below, become characteristic properties of the different members of the configuration ; and consequently of the total-form. A closer investigation of the development of this positional factor in children's perceptions would certainly prove a stimulating and a valuable undertaking. One might suppose, for instance, that the well-known over-estimation of a square standing on a point, as compared with one of the same size lying on its side (Fig. 15), would not exist for children whose forms are as yet independent of spatial positions.

This independence of figure and spatial position may be connected with the independence of figure and magnitude which has already been mentioned. The

293

varying possibilities of formulating the perceptual world
of an adult, according to form, magnitude, position and
colour, all entering into one configuration which is
determined in many ways, are to a child still more or
less independent of one another. But we must not
forget that even with us the connection is not so close
as it would appear to be from a purely rational and
logical consideration; for it would be too much to
suppose that we adults complete all the configurations
named, simultaneously and with the same degree of
distinctness. On the contrary, we see in general much
less in things than we might; and hence it is quite
possible to see something large and dark, without being

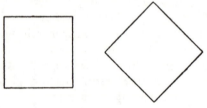

FIG. 15.

able to specify its form or indicate its colour. To give
a common, everyday example, one sees a man with
very friendly little eyes, and yet has not the faintest
notion whether they are blue or brown.

As a final problem in the perception of form, the
things in our environment may be seen from very
different points of view, and in very different aspects,
so that the same thing may be reflected upon the
retina in a multiplicity of ways; yet just as in the case
of colour and magnitude, the actual phenomenon as it
is given to the naïve individual fails to follow these
changes; but instead a certain thing always appears
with the same configurative qualities that are most
characteristic of it. When I see a chair in such a
position that only a corner of its seat is visible, and
that this corner, when drawn in its true perspective,

294

would not be a right angle, still my perceptual phenomenon is not at all that of an acute angle; for what
I see is the corner as a part of the rectangular seat.
One finds this to be true whenever one experiments
with any sort of figure with which the observer is un-
acquainted before the experiments are made. One also
finds that the perceptual phenomenon does not follow
the "aspect," but shows a marked tendency to be seen
as it actually is; that is, in a manner corresponding to
its orthogonal appearance, with an orientation at right
angles to the line of regard. This effect, like that of
the constancy of colour and magnitude, is of such
enormous importance in the construction of our perception of the world as to justify us in calling it a *constancy
of form*. Bühler finds here an analogy, which I think
to be correct, between the perceptual constancy of form
and the nature of our concepts [283].

From children's drawings we can infer that this
constancy of form becomes the child's mode of perception at a very early age. If the child is called upon
to draw a cube from memory, or from a model, or even
from a plan in perspective (according to Katz), what he
actually draws, as a rule, is a number of connected
squares. Many adults, too—as for instance the author
and his wife—if called upon to draw things which are
not quite easy, like a chair, will do exactly the same
thing; a fact which has been demonstrated experimentally by J. Wittmann [284]. Again and again one tries to
draw the back and seat of the chair as rectangles, and
when the drawing fails to look right, one resorts to all
manner of intellectual tricks; because to perceive only
a certain aspect of any thing is a task which can be
achieved by many persons only after the greatest effort
and practice. It is different with those who possess some
talent in drawing; for they learn with relative ease, some
perhaps even without external aid; yet a correct apprehension of the *appearance* of a thing is certainly neither
a natural nor an original propensity. At first each thing

has actually but one phenomenal appearance or, perhaps, in some cases a small number of appearances; and these succeed in maintaining themselves despite all changes of perspective. This prominent aspect of a thing is very "simple," and perspicuous [285]. The question then arises: How does it happen that this simple form is maintained even when the objective conditions do not favour its arousal? One has been accustomed to call upon memory for an explanation; thus Bühler states that a child is unable to extricate its immediate impressions of form from the influence of previous experience [286]. That would seem to mean that without previous experience the child ought to see a thing exactly as it appears, and not *orthoscopically*, as Bühler calls it. Wittmann, too, thinks that under these conditions we apprehend, first of all, the actual objective appearance [287]. I would suggest, however, that the explanation is not given by memory, or at least not primarily, but involves the laws whereby configurations are aroused, which indicate that certain forms are favoured from the start and that these forms are at the same time geometrically "simple" and physically significant [288]. Only in this way can one actually explain orthoscopic forms, because the instance in which a view in perspective furnishes an exact correspondence between just one face of the body and its orthoscopic appearance is so very infrequent that, strictly speaking, its probability is zero—one favourable instance as compared with an infinite number of unfavourable instances. The presumption then is that an object is first of all apprehended, that is to say, instead of remaining chaotic, it arouses a phenomenal configuration, whenever it happens to be seen in a way which favours orthoscopy. Thus a cube would be apprehended as such only when one happens to stand more or less parallel with its front; accordingly it will not be apprehended as a cube when one corner happens to be slanted forwards. After the orthoscopic configuration has once been aroused, however, it maintains itself with reference to quite different aspects, where the problem of configuration is more difficult; but even then the case is not one of simple memory; for the objective aspect must also be reckoned with, especially when the appearance varies considerably from the orthoscopic view. And hence the object itself still exerts an influence upon the phenomenal configuration, so that either the orthoscopic form appears in an oblique position, or else a new form arises which stands between the orthoscopic and the perspective appearance. The constancy of form, therefore, just as in the case of the constancy of magnitude, is not at all absolute.

In the investigation of perception we have met with the same kind of functions in the constancy of colour, magnitude, and form. In all three we have rejected an explanation based on individual experience in the sense that experience means either the formation of new connections, or determinations having recourse to "apprehension" and judgment. We have found, instead, certain laws of configural functions developing on the one hand through mere maturation—though not, to be sure, without stimulation—and on the other hand being recast, or newly created. These processes of recasting and creation may be called experiences, but experience in this sense becomes a concept which transcends the dispute over Empiricism and Nativism. In the adult a configural function is, in its phenomenal aspect, a *perceptual*-experience in its own right; for it is neither a mere judgment, nor a mere apprehension of sensations. The development of these configurations can not be conceived as a simple combination of sensations, or as the outward manifestation of a juxtaposition of repeated sensations. On the contrary, we must either think of the configural function as a process which alters, refines, recentres, and enriches the configuration throughout its entire make-up—a procedure in which maturation participates very largely—or else we must regard it as the arousal of an entirely new configuration for which a "dispositional readiness" was previously present in the individual. These brief indications may suffice to supplement the ideas we began to develop on p. 81.

§ 7—*Continuation : The Categories of Perception*

Finally a very important group of problems can be mentioned, more by way of reference than for detailed discussion. These problems have to do with the formation of categories of perception. We adults perceive before us numerous things possessing the most varied properties, which stand in manifold relation to, and exert reciprocal influences upon, one another. How is it in the case of the young child? One answer to this question we must deny at the outset [289]. The experience of a thing, with its significant features, and the processes which refer to cause and effect, can not be explained, as Hume maintained, as a mere conjunction of unrelated sensations. We have excluded these unrelated sensations altogether from our psychology. What we have to deal with, then, is the arousal of particular kinds of configuration, and the real question, though at present we are unable to answer it with any degree of certainty, is how and when these forms arise. Stern believes that he can ascertain a development which takes place in three stages. "The different points of view from which the world is mastered are not acquired simultaneously by the child, but they appear successively and in a cumulative fashion, so that what is old remains and becomes enriched by the new that is added to it. . . . The first stage of thinking is 'substantive': from the chaos of unreflective experience the substantial is the first to work itself out into independently existing persons and things, as separate contents of thought. This stage is followed by a stage of 'action,' in which the activities of persons and things are isolated in thought so as to attract special interest. But not until the third stage, that of 'relations' and 'properties,' does the child develop a capacity to separate from the things themselves their inherent characteristics, and the varying relations which obtain among them "[290]. According to Stern, these stages recur in each new kind of mental operation, so that a child may occupy simultaneously a high level with respect to an earlier accomplishment and a lower level with respect to a later one. Three such accomplishments which succeed one another, each having the same course of development, are : learning to speak, describing pictures, and remembering pictures.

The first point to be noted in this citation is the ambiguity of Stern's "chaos of unreflective experience." If he means a chaos of unrelated sensations, he has made an assumption which we have already found reason to deny. It is also obvious that Stern's categories do not apply to "thinking" alone ; for without a doubt they occur first of all in *perception*. It is improbable that Stern means anything else, though it may be well to preclude a possible misunderstanding on the part of the reader.

Aside from this point, however, there are certain objections to Stern's position, although his work is undoubtedly based upon a large number of observed facts. For instance, Bühler remarks that the sequence of categories in later achievements can not at once be likened to the sequence of earlier accomplishments [291].

It must also be remarked that "properties" and "relations" belong with different configurations. A "property" or distinguishing feature is an evolution of the thing-pattern ; as a thing emerges from its background it acquires internal articulation, without thereby losing anything of its unity or totality. The relation, on the contrary, refers in general to several already isolated wholes, and often quite directly to distinct things. And hence, there arises a larger whole which includes these separate things, so that in a certain sense we may consider the relation as the internal articulation within this larger whole. But the question still remains: How closely are these two principles of configuration—property and relation—dependent upon each other?

We must also question, whether the substance-stage truly precedes all the others. "We know," writes Bühler, "that from the beginning the attention of the child fastens directly upon movements and changes. . . . Is the comprehension of activity actually retarded in the child's development?"[292] I might also add that although the child's first speech-sounds, exclusive of interjections, have a substantive character[293], nevertheless, as Clara and William Stern themselves have pointed out with special emphasis, "the child's units of speech do not belong to any particular word-group, because they are not separate words, but sentences." For this reason, Stern characterizes the first expressions of a child as "one-word sentences." "The *mama* of a child can not be translated into ordinary speech by the unit-word *mother*, but only by a complete sentence such as, 'Mother come here,' 'Mother give me,' 'Mother put me on the chair,' 'Mother help me,' etc." Stern also observes that a modification in speech takes place when it becomes apparent to the child that each thing has a name—a process of development which we shall take up at the close of the chapter. It is here that the substance-stage first makes its appearance, apparently in consequence of the *name-function.* Previously the state must have been different; for the active connection of objects and persons must have been given without any definite discrimination of things and their effects. The first configuration of order, then, is undoubtedly that of things; in this respect Stern's three stages are justified, with the provision, however, that they do not arise from "unreflective chaos," but from a kind of data which, though very primitive, are yet already formulated to the extent that both conscious things and their effects are contained within them.

One must not suppose, however, that a "thing" means exactly the same to a young child that it does

to us; for to a child a thing and its effect can not be
so sharply separated as they are in our thought. A
mother, for example, is not only something which
"looks so," and "is so," but more exactly something
which "does this," "assists thus," or "punishes so."
Nor does the effective side of a thing disappear when
the child has attained the substance-stage of thought;
for even causal connections which to us seem quite
difficult, may be recognized early in the life of a child;
although causality to a child is, of course, something
quite different from what it is to us. For examples, a
little girl of 1·11 remarked that "The wind make
mamma's hair untidy; Baba (her own name) make
mamma's hair tidy, so wind not blow adain (again)"
(Sully); and a small boy of 2·7, holding his fingers
before the sun, remarked that the "sun made his fingers
bloody" (Scupin). We do not leave the field of perception here any more than we do in the perceptual
configuration of an object. It would be quite mistaken
too, I think, to say that in the first example the wind
was perceived as one thing, and the moisture as another;
or, in the second example, to say that the red appearance
of the fingers and its connection with the sun was
"thought out." From the point of view of a child
these effects are described as simple facts of perception,
just as if there were a single object with all its characteristics. The category of causality, however, is a configuration which soon transcends perception. This
change takes place when the child sees a thing, or
some one of its characteristics, *as* an effect, and is thus
led to ask after its cause. In this sense we shall have
to concern ourselves with the category of causation
later on.

§ 8—*Sensori-motor Learning: The First Achievements
of Training and Intelligence*

Since we have studied the problem of achievement
in the previous chapter, we need here consider only a

few examples selected from infantile development. As an example of sensori-motor learning we have already referred to the maxim that a "burnt child shuns the fire." In this case the matter seems to be much simpler than it is in cases where a positive achievement must be attained; for here one might suppose it possible to explain the result without reference to the problem of achievement. But as a matter of fact that is not true, for this case is only a significant representative of many infantile accomplishments, all of which must be treated exactly as we have treated other instances of learning; a conclusion which becomes apparent as soon as we consider that a burnt moth does *not* shun the fire. What we have called a "first achievement" is here an understanding that pain comes from fire, and that the flame which was at first so attractive and so desirable may become, through painful experience, something "dangerous" and "to be avoided." A mere connection between sense-impression and reaction, or even the destruction of any such original connection, would be an insufficient hypothesis; because a constructive achievement is here necessary, however little it may seem to demand of the individual. Consequently, if a child running about in a state of excitement should by chance get burned, he would learn nothing from his painful experience; because, without the participation of attention, learning does not take place. The chief function of pain in these experiences is to arouse attention and thus furnish favourable conditions for the construction of a new configuration. The withdrawal of the burned hand is naturally reflexive, but what is learned is not to withdraw the hand, but to avoid fire in the future; and in a state of inattention nothing at all is learned.

This interpretation of the facts is also confirmed by the experiments Watson has made upon the acquisition of this reaction. For a long time (from the 150th to the 164th day of life) touching the flame, which caused a reflexive flexion of the fingers and a withdrawal of the hand, had no effect of teaching the child to avoid the flame. On the 178th day the reaction was for the first time modified, and seemed to be distinctly inhibited ; but only on the 220th day had the transformation, which we have described, been fully accomplished. Then, instead of grasping for the candle, the child slapped at it, and after this new reaction had appeared, the child grasped at the flame but a single time [294].

It is in this way that we must understand the simplest achievements of learning by animals ; as, for example, in the instance previously described of the chick which learned to avoid pecking at evil-tasting cinnabar cater- pillars. K. Lewin in his war experiences has vividly described how things undergo a quite analogous change in us adults [295] ; how, for instance, the "homogeneous" landscape becomes "limited" and "directed" as one approaches the firing-line ; and how a transformation again occurs as one leaves a position behind him, so that suddenly what was just now a "position" becomes merely an acre of ground. These are analogies of the process as it presents itself in a most primitive form. In the initial stages of its development the child learns a tremendous amount ; much, indeed, at the level Bühler calls training or "drill," though from our point of view we must always presuppose a certain degree of understand- ing. This statement is also true of accomplishments for which one might perhaps more appropriately reserve the term "training," since they are essentially meaning- less to the child. We refer here to types of behaviour instigated chiefly by adults for their own amusement. For instance, one asks a child to do something, or to "say please," or to "tell us how big you are," etc. Configurations of this sort are quite vague. A certain child, who had been trained to respond to the sentence : "Bring the butter," by fetching the dish, did so at the age of 1·4 when the father said, "That's a butterball." A still younger child of six to eight months who had

learned to turn his head in response to the question
" Wo ist das Fenster ? " made the same seeking-move-
ments when the question, "où est la fenêtre?" was
asked in a similar tone of voice [296]. It is not the total
sensory complex with its complete membership which
constitutes these configurations, but only a significant
accent, or perhaps the crude total form.

Soon, however, problems arise in the everyday life of
the child similar to those which Köhler's chimpanzees
were required to solve. One may therefore inquire
when and how the first actual achievements of intelligence arise. Köhler himself has reported a few
observations made upon young children in experiments
like those he employed in his tests of apes. Bühler has
likewise followed with experiments of this order. Bühler
began his tests when his child was nine months old, by
a clever employment of the child's playful grasping [297].
The infant sat upright in his bed and grasped at everything within reach, in order that he might bring it to
his mouth. The behaviour of grasping was then made
systematically more difficult. A piece of rusk was
placed slightly out of reach, with a string attached to
it which came within reaching distance. In another
experiment an ivory ring with which the child was
accustomed to play was placed over an upright rod
about as large as one's finger, from which the child had
to lift it. The principles employed in these experiments are already familiar from the description given
of Köhler's procedure. At the beginning of his ninth
month the child was unable to make use of a string
connected with an object ; instead he always " stretched
his arm directly towards the biscuit without observing
the string. If, by chance, the string was grasped in
the hand, it was either let go or pushed aside. Only
in two sittings did he appear to comprehend the connection, which enabled him to perform numerous correct
solutions promptly one after the other. I still think
that the child did comprehend the situation on these

two occasions, though at the following sitting all had been forgotten." Not until the end of the tenth month did the child really "comprehend" the situation well enough so that one could let the string lead out in any direction, and still he would immediately grasp it and fetch the biscuit. Bühler was able to exclude the possibility of this behaviour being an accidental achievement. The result, therefore, is of interest in several respects. We may call particular attention to the *anticipation* involved in the first two instances of success; an example of which has also been given in connection with the investigation of apes (cf. p. 195). Similar anticipations have been frequently observed in cases of "sensori-motor" development, and we have already emphasized the theoretical significance of this concept (cf. above p. 263).

In harmony with Köhler's results, the child found the removal of a ring from a peg a much more difficult task. The act was not successful until the middle of the second year, but the comprehension of the act was then so complete that a key was immediately taken from a nail, and a hat from a cane.

Köhler performed the detour-experiment with a little girl of 1·3 who had been walking alone for only a few weeks. The child was placed at the end of a blind alley two metres long and a metre-and-a-half wide. Beyond the restraining partition lay an attractive object, in plain sight but not within her immediate reach. "The child first pushed as close to the object as the wall would allow; then after looking slowly around, examining the whole length of the alley, she suddenly gave a satisfied laugh and in one trial made the circuit around the wall to the goal" [298].

With children, as well as with chimpanzees, it is much more difficult to make a detour with the aid of a tool. Köhler used the detour-board (in the normal position—the open side of the enclosure being at the greatest distance from the child—cf. above p. 187) in an experiment with a boy aged 2·1, who had shown that he could readily make detours in his bodily movements. But the boy, who was of average intelligence, was unsuccessful in his performance with a stick. Like the chimpanzees under similar conditions, he gave vent to his desire for the unattainable object, by throwing both his stick and his belt at it [299].

Köhler also found a correspondence between the behaviour of young children and chimpanzees with respect to building operations and the handling of a coiled rope (cf. p. 197). In building, children have at first the same difficulty chimpanzees have in putting one thing upon another, and they fumble about in the most curious manner. At the close of the third year, however, a child will have learned to comprehend the simplest of these achievements, whereas apes make scarcely any real progress even after abundant practice. Since the correct manipulation of a rope may be attributed to a visual achievement, the awkwardness of children, which can be observed up to the fourth year, and even later, may therefore depend in part upon the fact that a wound-up rope does not yet constitute an adequate visual configuration for them.

A pretty incidental observation made by Preyer furnishes from child-life an analogy to the "employment of a box" by apes. Preyer's seventeen-months-old child was unable to reach his playthings from a high cupboard, so "he ran about, brought a travelling bag, got upon it, and took what he wanted" [300].

It is to be hoped that these methods of investigation, which have now been perfected in principle, will be systematically employed as a means of penetrating more deeply into the development of infantile achievements.

### § 9—*Continuation : The Problem of Imitation*

Most of the child's achievements are acquired, not in the artificial isolation of an experiment, but in connection with an environment which already dominates the achievements themselves. It is here that we meet with the important problem of *imitation*. Few questions have been so much disputed as this one. While many investigators of imitation concede it a dominant position among the influences affecting the child's development, others would exclude it altogether. It is impossible that this disagreement should arise from different conceptions of imitation; because the concept has been analyzed very thoroughly and in many different ways. American writings in particular are full of different classifications of imitation which bring out all its characteristic aspects. (A few of the investigators of this subject are: Lloyd Morgan, Thorndike, Berry, Watson, McDougall, and Stern.) To state the problem as I see it, imitation involves (1) configurations already belonging to an individual's equipment which are made to function by the performance of an act of the same kind on the part of another individual; (2) imitation may also be the arousal of a *new* configuration in an individual when he perceives some one else acting in a certain manner. Both types can be subdivided. Under the first type we can distinguish (*a*) instinctive, and (*b*) acquired configurations; and under the second type we can define the level of the achievement demanded by the new configuration. To illustrate: (1*a*) A bird, seeing danger, emits a cry of warning, and this cry is repeated by other birds to whom the original cause is not perceptible. (1*b*) A familiar melody which one has heard may be involuntarily repeated. Performances at a low level of type 2 are those of repeating words never before heard—or, indeed, making any responses of an essentially motor nature. A performance at a higher level would be that of comprehending from a model how to solve a problem. In this connection we might think of the problems in Köhler's experiments. Extreme variations are possible in the perfection of these new achievements, because the new configuration aroused in imitation may be far less complete than its model; it may be far less precise; or it may even miss the point of the imitated action altogether.

It seems to me that this classification includes the important differentiation with respect to the nature of imitation which Lloyd Morgan has pointed out. We can perhaps characterize this difference by saying that imitation may either be of a movement or of a series of movements, or it may be of a purposive action. For a long time animal-psychologists have looked only for the first of these types, and when they failed to find it, have concluded that there can be no general capacity for imitation. Thus, as an argument against imitation, Thorndike cites the case of a cat which pulled the loop with his paws, whereas the cat "(whom he saw) pulled the loop with his teeth." Berry, however, points out the fallacy of this argument, since it holds only for the imitative repetition of the movement [301].

The distinction we have now made is, of course, subordinate to the main division previously drawn; because the higher the type of configuration arising through imitation, the more readily can the imitation be characterized with reference to the end sought. On the other hand, the more superficial the configuration is, the more the imitation is apt to be characterized as merely one of movement. The differentiation in configurations which here comes into consideration was discussed in the last section of the previous chapter (cf. p. 230 ff.). Just as drill-performances differ from intelligent performances, so the imitation of a highly significant action will differ from one of lesser significance. The more a performance is of a purely motor nature, and the more it depends upon inherited, or instinctive, configurations, the more it will appear to be a mere imitation of the movements being made. Yet even here, if one compares the movement imitated with its imitation, it is the integrated movement-melody of each which stands forth as being the common element. A photographic reproduction of the separate movements involved is never found. If an organism attempts to flee because it sees other organisms flee, what it imitates is the act of flight as a whole, and not the movements of the limbs themselves. In like manner, when I yawn quite involuntarily upon seeing some one else yawn (an example of the most primitive type of imitation), I open my mouth in my way, not in his way ; for what I imitate is *yawning*, and not the movements of the other person's jaws. Hence the difference emphasized by Lloyd Morgan turns out to be, not a difference in kind but in degree, both of precision, and of the complexity of the configuration. It is, therefore, a difference whose importance is greatest when we are dealing with the question of learning by imitation.

Hitherto, whenever one spoke of instinctive imitation, one meant something quite different; namely, the connection between the perception which initiates the movement, and the movement carried out. How does it happen that a bird will repeat a cry of warning? This reaction has been considered an instinctive disposition by Lloyd Morgan and Stern ; whereas other writers, such as Groos and Thorndike, refuse to accept this explanation, though they are unable to furnish a better one [302]. The problem of imitation for Thorndike is naturally quite unsolvable, because he has built his entire explanation of behaviour upon the theory of neurone-connections. A common imitative disposition, then, would require a web of neurone-connections so highly complicated that Thorndike feels justified in rejecting it as altogether improbable. Groos also rejects the imitative disposition for similar reasons. Thorndike accepts, however, the instinctive release of a whole series of single movements, all of which would fall under our Group 1*a*.

Since we have rejected a theory of behaviour, including instinct, in terms of connections between neurones, to assume now an instinct of imitation as being a direct arousal of a movement by means of perceiving the same

309

movement, would be only one way of avoiding any explanation at all. I do not think we need be so sceptical. At the beginning of this chapter we became acquainted with a law of reproduction which indicates that a configuration once given provides favourable conditions for the arousal of the same or of a similar configuration ; and the behaviour of infants is altogether consistent with this law. Stern, following Baldwin, regards self-imitation as the first type of imitation to appear. A child will repeat the same reaction in end-less monotony, whether it be a new manipulation or a vocal utterance. Since, according to Stern, this reaction starts as a purely motor mechanism, a connection is gradually formed between the movement and its per-ceptual result, so that in time the result itself will arouse the movement, thus giving rise to what Baldwin calls a circular activity : R—P—R—P, where R is the move-ment of reaction and P the perception of this movement, or its result. On this hypothesis self-imitation is reduced to an associative connection. The fact that deaf children babble shows that utterances may occur altogether with-out the aid of hearing ; yet the ear soon begins to play an important part in this behaviour, as indicated by the fact that the deaf babble less, and do not modulate their babbling like normal children [303]. It is highly improbable that the connection between hearing and utterance is acquired only by an external association. The de-pendency of our speech-apparatus upon hearing is actually much more direct. Many years ago Köhler called attention to the human capacity of singing a tone after it is heard ; a capacity which is possessed to a remarkable degree by adults, and also by children at a very early age—having been observed even before the close of the first year of life. At the same time, Köhler sketched an explanatory hypothesis to cover the origin of this capacity. The following examples will indicate its early appearance among children. Preyer reports a little girl who could sing a tone struck on the piano correctly in her ninth month, and who, together with two of her sisters, sang before she could speak. Stumpf also tells of a little daughter of the well-known composer, Dvořák, who, at the age of one-and-a-half years, could sing melodies with piano-accompaniment quite correctly, even when they were rather difficult; and who in her first year began to repeat the march from " Fatinitza " after her nurse [304].

That the relation of hearing to vocal utterance can not be a matter of mere associative connection, is also shown by other vocalic imitations. Long before they understand speech, children will imitate words more or less clearly which they have not yet spoken spontaneously; and we have already called attention to the fact that vocalizations which occur spontaneously may be imitated at a very early age. (Cf. above p. 258.) Stern's daughter repeated *papa* at nine months for the first time, although this vocalization had not before appeared in her babbling monologue. In general, however, imitation at this age is practised more frequently with inarticulate noises: smackings, crunchings, and vocal cadences. In this connection we have an observation of Humphrey, reported by Preyer: "When about four months old the child began a curious and amusing mimicry of conversation, in which she so closely imitated the ordinary cadences that persons in an adjacent room would mistake it for actual conversation." The articulation, vocalic organization, etc., was of course very incomplete.[305] The performance is in some ways analogous to the repetition of true melodies, and certainly can not be explained in terms of associations previously acquired. At the time when speech is being learned, there begins a period of *echolalia* in which the child repeats with tireless continuation all the words or sentences it hears; either completely, or else their closing cadences [306]. This practice, and the direction it takes, are also very characteristic; for the child tries to make his imitations more and more like his models. In order to explain this behaviour, Claparède finds himself constrained to postulate an "instinct to conform" [307]; but this explanation carries us no further than the assumption of an instinct to imitate. The facts recited have a general bearing, however, for parrots utter sentences chiefly with reference to their typical cadential characteristics, and one can also notice that they practise until their imitations become more and more perfect.

If we could but assume an immediate structural connection between the perception and the movement, all these facts would be readily understood. The perceptual configuration would then reproduce the configuration of the movement, because of their inherent similarity; and the movement would then be a phenomenal copy of the perception, since the connection between these two distinct configurations (perception and movement)—which we have described as the reproduction of one by means of the other—must also involve a more or less definite and intimate structural connection. This connection, too, is shown by the fact reported above (p. 258), that an act which a child is able to carry out spontaneously, is made with much more trouble, and with much less completeness, when it is aroused by imitation. When the whole structure has attained a certain degree of firmness, this will be indicated by the stability of its separate members. The child then hears the spoken sound as something which is to be imitated, and he speaks in order to imitate the sound, hearing his own voice "as a more or less good replica of what he has heard." If the replica is "less good" it has the characteristic of incompleteness—of something lacking—an idea already familiar to us, and which of itself indicates that the performance is not yet over; that the organization can not stop here, since an end is attained only when the spoken sound has become a good copy of its model.

312

# THE PROBLEM OF IMITATION

In this way the configuration of a model and its imitation attains a state of equilibrium. There appears to be no need of a special instinct to explain this adaptation; because we are able to refer it, not only to the general laws of Psychology, but also to the laws of Physics [308]. Furthermore, this connection between perception and movement is of the same order as that which enables us to perceive the nature of the mental processes of others (cf. p. 21).

We have assumed the possibility of a configurative connection between perception and movement, and we have conceived this connection in terms of relatedness, or similarity. It may, however, be of quite a different sort. When any one is solving a problem in my presence, I am able to imitate him if I understood the solution. In other words, if the perceptual configuration is properly aroused, so that, for instance, something previously indifferent now becomes the focus in which I apprehend the whole figure, the solution of the problem is immediately possible. There is nothing mysterious in the fact that a proper sequence of movements will follow upon such a perception. That is to say, we find here no special problem apart from the general one; how a voluntary act takes place at all—which we shall not now undertake to decide. I will give an example of this type of response. In a game of forfeits, which children like to play, one child receives a spoon from another and passes it on to his neighbour with the words, "Lirum-Larum Löffelstiel, wer das nicht kann, der kann nicht viel." The game is to receive and to pass the spoon along just as it was passed by the one who first held it; for instance, the spoon should be received with the left hand and passed on with the right. Whoever makes a mistake must give a forfeit. It is very interesting to observe how children, who do not yet know the game, learn it; the point being to find out what it is all about. This is the sole difficulty; as soon as the trick is comprehended, the problem is solved. The connection between the perceptual configuration and the movement to be made is therefore not itself a problem of imitation; because the imitation is essentially achieved as soon as the perceptual configuration arises in observing the other's behaviour. The problem with which we are here engaged does not involve our second form of imitation at its higher level; because the movement was already intended before the behaviour of the other person had been seen. A chimpanzee who attains its fruit by imitation is already intent upon attaining it before the other animal has shown him how the act can be done. Similarly, when playing a game of forfeits the child is from the start intent upon doing the right thing. But there are also instances of another sort in which the perception of the response calls forth an intention to carry it out; as, for instance, when a child of 0·11 dusts off a chair after seeing some one else do so. Yet even here we have nothing incomprehensible; because in grasping completely what has taken place, the connection of the result with the movement is at once apprehended, and consequently the perceptual configuration will itself lead to an imitation of the movement. One can explain this behaviour from different points of view. In the first place, the procedure has a certain similarity to the configurative supplementation spoken of at the beginning of this chapter; the movement is carried out because it is a part of the configuration. This would also explain the fact that it is so difficult to pass by a piano, a letter-box, or a door-bell, without striking a key, opening the box, or pushing the button. Such a law, when applied to perceptual configurations, would constitute the factual content of a law formulated by James, Wundt, and others—the so-called ideo-motor law which Groos employs as the chief principle in the explanation of imitation, and which Thorndike, in turn, has so energetically opposed. The law states that every idea involves a tendency to movement, and is therefore itself capable of producing its appropriate response.

But one might also suppose that the impulse to carry out a copied action involves another law of configuration, which has to do with a tendency towards precision and fixity.

In reality this group of intended responses seems to stand between the two types of imitation previously discussed. In "intelligent" imitation, the model serves only to make possible the arousal of a correct perceptual configuration. The transformation into movement requires no explanation, because the intention to perform the act was present independently of the model. In the first type of imitation, however, which may be illustrated by babbling, the model not only arouses the perception but also the impulse to imitate; and the transition from the perceptual to the responsive configuration is thus problematic. In the case mentioned of dusting a chair, the model furnishes both the perception and the impulse, and the transition from perception to movement requires an explanation no more than it did in the first type, because it belongs to the "understanding" of the act to be imitated. Since the question of imitation itself is no longer involved, what is done is not directly an imitation of the movement made by another, but falls under the direction of the configuration perceived.

If a baby in its thirty-eighth week can strike two spoons together after seeing its mother do so,[309] we shall have to assume that the infant's comprehension of the mother's action is sufficient to call forth the appropriate movement ; which is certainly no more of a riddle, and also no less of a riddle, than intelligent imitation.

With respect to the most primitive type of imitation we must therefore conceive the connection existing between the perceptual and motor aspects of the entire configuration as being of a peculiar intimacy. That we may and must accept this hypothesis for verbal and tonal imitation, has already been pointed out [310]; and there is no essential difference between these and other modes of behaviour. At first, imitation has to do with expressive movements. In the middle of the child's first year of life he can be made to smile by smiling at him, and likewise made to cry by appearing to cry before him. Even Thorndike recognizes an immediate and authentic imitation in the case of these expressive movements ; including, indeed, a large number of others of the same sort, among which may be mentioned pursing the lips, which was imitated by Preyer's son at the close of his fifteenth week. We have noted, however, in an earlier chapter that the emotions and their expressive movements must somehow be very intimately connected (cf. above p. 117), so that the transition from perception to movement must also rest upon this intimacy of the configurations involved.

Although we have not solved our problem, we believe we have indicated where the solution is to be sought, and how the connection takes place between lower and higher types of behaviour. The problem of imitation has thus been reduced to a very general problem of configuration ; namely, how any perception can issue in movement. It is possible that the law of configurative supplementation, as well as the law of the repetition of figures, are both effective here. But there may also be other laws or peculiar emphases involved.

Since an intention to imitate can have various causes, we are led to the differentiation of two sets of problems: first, the necessity of imitating, and secondly, the ability to imitate. The whole problem of imitation has sometimes been considered as though imitation were compulsory ; but that is a very one-sided view, for the essence of imitation is to be found in ability to imitate. It is no criterion of imitation to say that its intention arises entirely from perceiving the act of another. When a child learning to speak imitates everything he hears, this is certainly not a matter of " compulsory " imitation, because it is only *what* he says that is determined by the acts of another. Of course it is important to realize that a compulsion to imitate also exists, but this should be understood as something which arises from ability to imitate. To be able to imitate means that a perceptual configuration may acquire a definite influence over a certain type of action; while the impulse to do anything at all may arise from some other source. It is clear that the more primitive an organism is, and the fewer factors there are to determine its acts, the greater must be the influence exerted by the configuration of what is perceived. There must therefore be a gradual transition from an ability to imitate to the necessity of imitating; for at best the model imitated is only the strongest among a number of other factors which might determine an impulse to act[311]. Even in quite primitive cases of simple "susceptibility," this is true. When I am fresh I can quietly observe another person yawning without feeling obliged to yawn myself, but when I am tired his yawning not only determines *what* I shall do, but also *that* I shall do it. If I am very angry or very sorrowful I am less susceptible to another's laughter than I might otherwise be. It therefore seems to me that the problem of compulsory imitation is of less importance than the problem of ability to imitate.

Let us now pass from the general problem of imitation to the special one of learning by imitation. Here we have two possibilities. In the first, the individual learns by imitation to perform an already familiar act in a new situation. Imitation would then take the form 1*a* or 1*b*, and would occur without comprehension, being understood only after the movement was made. But imitation may also occur in accordance with the second form we have distinguished, in which case the imitation itself introduces a new configuration. It would appear from the facts as we know them that learning by imitation is essentially of this second type. At the lower stages babbling and verbal repetitions are clearly of this order. But even in other respects learning by imitation seems to be of this kind. The results which bear upon imitation in animal - experiments are not altogether in agreement, yet this much at least may be said with assurance : that although imitation is infrequent, when it does occur it is highly significant. Many of the negative results obtained in experiments on imitation are probably attributable to the fact that the investigator was looking in vain for an imitative performance at a very low level. Berry points out that his cats imitated only when they understood the act to be copied; and Köhler writes as follows : " If once in a while an animal, before whom a solution has been carried out, is suddenly able to accomplish the task without having previously indicated any conception of what was to be done, one can hardly refrain at that moment from estimating the animal's intelligence very highly. Unfortunately one sees this very rarely, even in the chimpanzee, and then only when the situation and its solution fall approximately within the same limits that circumscribe the animal's spontaneous behaviour"[312].

Observations made upon children seem also to point in this direction. Mrs Moore expressly states that the boy whom she observed did not imitate to any extent until he had begun to understand other peoples' actions, and similar indications are given in Stern's observation that the continual repetition of speech only begins after an interest in, and a comprehension of, speech has already taken place.

Learning by imitation is, however, easier than spontaneous learning, and certain accomplishments like speaking and writing could not be learned at all without the aid of imitation. Somehow the situation is "improved" by the presence of a model ; both because the point of attack for the solution is emphasized, and also because the individual becomes more attentive to things which were not previously connected with the situation. Imitation becomes much easier when the action to be copied can be presented with the aid of language, so that its essential features can be pointed out and clearly perceived. But it is no art to imitate movements which have already been learned or comprehended ; as Köhler remarks, chimpanzees also imitate without difficulty under these conditions.

In this sense, imitation is a powerful factor in development. Most of the things we learn are acquired, not through our own discovery, but through the comprehension of models or, in later years, by means of instructions expressed in language. Apprehension in this way constantly becomes an easier achievement ; though in the beginning imitation is scarcely less difficult than a new discovery. Despite these difficulties, man never learns so much in the same period of time as he does when a child ; and in childhood learning is always an achievement of a high order. Therefore one should not speak thoughtlessly of the actions of a " mere child," but ought rather to respect the period of childhood on account of the extraordinary fullness of its achievements.

§ 10—*Ideational Learning : The First Use of Language and its Problems*

We turn now to the final aspect of learning, which we have called ideational. Perhaps the greatest number of problems, and certainly the most difficult ones, fall under this heading ; for it is through ideational learning that man frees himself from the perception of things present to his senses, and thus attains his mastery over the world. We shall consider here but a few problems that can be set within the framework we have already constructed. Many questions arise in this connection which, though they have been hotly debated, have not been satisfactorily explained by general psychology. We shall avoid these controversies as far as possible, referring the reader to the seventeenth chapter of Bühler's book for a statement of the points at issue.

319

# THE PROBLEM OF MEMORY

Our consideration may be prefaced by the following remark: The distinctions we have drawn, in order that we might trace the course of learning through individual performances, are so fluid that even when we are speaking of ideational learning we are always in the closest contact with learning of the perceptual and sensori-motor types. As we have already seen, the most important categories appear first in perception.

We have now to consider the child's progress in learning to speak, for language is our most important material of thought. With language we can transcend the present; with its aid we recall the past and anticipate the future. What do we know about this development which carries the human being so far? Unless observations have deceived us, there is a time about the middle of the second year of life—subject to considerable individual variation—in which the child's vocal expression undergoes a sudden development. Previous to this time, single words have been spoken as one-word sentences with a wish- or affective-character, although for several months the child's primitive vocabulary may not have increased very noticeably.[313] Now a sudden increase is noticeable in the number of words employed by the child, in connection with which the "name-question" appears as a typical phenomenon. The child points to all kinds of objects, asks "Wa's 'at?" and is satisfied when their names are told him. The name-question seems to be the more important factor and the one upon which progress is chiefly based, for it may happen—as in the case of Stern's son—that an interval of some months will elapse between the appearance of these definite name-questions and the child's own use of the names which are given him in reply.

The progress here taking place has been characterized by Clara and William Stern in the following way: The child now makes *the most important discovery of his life; which is that everything has a name.* Bühler also emphasizes this conclusion, regarding the performance as a "discovery," whose real nature he then proceeds to analyze [314].

Still a third peculiarity of this period may be mentioned, which differentiates it from the preceding period, and which shows conclusively that a transformation has occurred in the child's mode of relating the *word* to the *world*, or more particularly, the *word* to the *thing*. The general content of the one-word, and later of the multiple-word, sentence, which originally was but an expression of desire or emotion, is now itself altered. Along with these affective expressions, "material" determinations appear ; that is, most of the child's talk is concerned with *naming* things. This is evidenced, first, by the fact that the use of interjections develops but little during this time, whereas the substantives, employed in these "objective" appellations, undergo rapid growth. The change is also manifest in the following displacement : Whereas substantives were previously employed as expressions of volition, interjections and words of demand are now used as substantive designations. "The word *please* gradually became for Hilda a designation for the material object ' roll,' even when the object was not asked for. Similarly, the exclamation *siete* (look), which had often been connected with the gesture of the out-stretched index-finger, finally came to serve as a name for the hand in this position. (At 1·9 our daughter cried, *lauter siete* [much look] when she saw a number of hands so depicted in an advertisement.[315]) " This citation from Stern indicates the transition to the real *substance-stage*, of which we have already made note.

At this period of infantile development, the word frees itself from the wish-affective-relationship and enters into a new relation with *things*. Things must have been present in the form of relatively firm and fixed configurations even before this time ; for no one would or could assume that thing-configurations develop only in connection with their names. The behaviour of the child during his pre-lingual period would certainly not warrant such an assumption. To be sure, naming is not without its effect upon the thing-configuration. If the question is asked how the first perception of a thing arises in the child, we may answer negatively that it would be wrong to suppose that the "thing" is nothing but a mere connection of various visual, gustatory, and auditory attributes resulting from frequent repetition; as, for instance, that the thing "mother" is a conjunction of the different "views of the mother" plus the impressions which the child gets from feeling its mother, and from hearing its mother's voice. On the other hand, we can say positively that "thing" means a definite kind of configuration in which the world appears to the child; a configuration whose connected membership is much firmer, much more intimately bound together, and the whole much more definitely particularized, than any mere set of external connections would allow. It is also a feature of the thing-concept that its configuration should have a core, or centre, to which the members of the configuration adhere in a definite manner; in other words, a thing has its attributes. It has often been remarked that nothing remains of a thing when its attributes are removed. But the inference that a thing is nothing but the *sum* of all its attributes would be just as false as the assertion that a forest is nothing but the sum of all its trees. Just as in the case of the forest, the essential factor is the community of life; so, too, in the category of things it is a peculiar kind of cohesion which counts most; and this can be described psychologically in no other way than by stating that these variable attributes adhere to a stable core. We are therefore led to assume that the thing is not constituted or constructed in the course of development out of previously existing attributes, but rather that the arousal of a thing-configuration means that a definite "figural core" enters into the child's phenomenal world. Certainly,

322

the core is more original than the sum of its attributes, and since the organization of the thing takes place gradually, its separate attributes must appear very slowly. Therefore, the thing does not originate in "non-thingness," but rather replaces "non-thingness." In answering the question how a given datum may first appear as a thing, we should assign an important rôle to frequency of repetition. A frequent recurrence of the same, or of a very similar, datum will result in causing this datum to emerge sooner from the original chaos as a specific figure. This much can be gathered from the investigation of Brod and Weltsch [316]; but the influence of repetition here implied is quite different from the one which we have previously denied.

Once a thing-configuration has arisen, it may recur under entirely new conditions. When the child can see its mother as a thing, he will also see a stranger who frightens him as a thing. When the child is able to comprehend his milk-bottle as a thing, he can also comprehend in the same way a new rattle which he has just received as a gift. The case of causality is a similar one, and Bühler has pointed out [317] that the causal relation develops, not from uniformities, but from whatever excites wonder. During the period of time in which this enormous progress in the development of speech occurs, the thing-configuration must already have developed to some extent; so that the child already possesses certain stable configurations having definite but shifting members which correspond to the variable attributes of one and the same thing.

The naming of objects is a discovery or invention of the child; and Bühler stresses the point that this is a perfect parallel to the inventions of chimpanzees [318]. Since we have already recognized invention as an act of configuration, it follows that naming can also be regarded as a configurative achievement; accordingly, we may infer that the word enters into the thing-pattern just as the stick enters into the animal's situation of

323

"desire-to-get-fruit." It is then quite easy to assume that a word acts like any other member in incorporating itself into the pattern of a thing ; or in other words, that the name becomes an attribute of the thing—a possibility which Bühler has also considered. The name would then become a definite attribute of the thing, though it is at the same time a "variable"; because the thing can also be seen without hearing or seeing its name. So, too, are the mother's eyes a shifting attribute of her face, since they become invisible when her head is turned. This variability holds true for unsophisticated adults; for a blue dress retains its blueness even when its colour can no longer be seen in the darkness. Yet the name is a peculiar kind of attribute, in that anything may possess it. Thus, a child can supplement anything with a name, and the name will then become the most pronounced character of the thing. In this way the ascription of a name may prepare the way for a further organization of the thing's attributes.

Even in our adult experience the fact that the name is an attribute of a thing, is not so strange as might at first be thought ; for object and name do not always stand in such an external relationship as they do in cases where we call the mass $m$, the velocity $v$, etc. A little joke will best explain what I mean by this. In a conversation on the value of different languages, Mr Y finally says : "The English language is the best, and I can prove it to you. Take the word *knife ;* the French call it *couteau*, the Germans *messer*, the Danes *kniv*, while the English say knife, and that's what it really is"[319].

Certain facts from folk-psychology may also be cited in support of the hypothesis that a name is primarily the attribute of a thing. In primitive society the name given to a child is neither arbitrary, nor is it left to the fancy or discretion of the child's parents. Indeed, the name is not *given* at all; for since the child is only the

324

reincarnation of a defunct ancestor, it already has a name when it comes into the world. But among many primitive peoples a man acquires in the course of his lifetime other and more important names than this one. With each significant event of his life, such as the ceremonies at puberty, at marriage, at killing his first enemy, and at entrance into a secret society, he receives a name which is a mysterious symbol of the new "participation," of the new and mystical connections which have arisen within him. And what happens to real names also happens more or less to all words, since in these primitive communities the distinction between individual and general terms is never so great as it is among civilized people. The speaking of words has magical effects, and for primitive people words occupy positions in the world-pattern quite similar to those of other objects and properties [320].

The naming-age of childhood raises many questions for discussion. If everything has a name, how does the child acquire all the different words needed? Apparently the child employs other methods of finding names for things, beside that of asking questions.

1. Some names seem to occur as true inventions, about whose origin we know nothing in detail. Mrs Moore reports quite a number of such names. One of Stumpf's observations has perhaps a considerable significance in explaining how these names come about. His son gave the name *marage* to a building-stone of a peculiar shape, and he was able to remember it when he was seventeen years old, and give as the reason for his use of the word that "*the stone looked just the way the word sounded, and still does.*" In this instance we have a very odd kind of inner connection between the object and its name; origins of this sort should furnish a very stimulating field of study [321].

2. Words originally learned for a definite thing gradually extend their range of application. A thing whose name the child does not yet know may be given a name

325

which is known to belong to some other object. As these transferences are of great theoretical interest, we shall give a few examples of them. One of "Hilda Stern's earliest words, employed even before the end of her first year, was *puppe*. Although used for the first time in connection with a real doll, the word was soon applied to her other playthings, like her cloth dog and stuffed rabbit; but for a silver bell, one of her chief playthings at this period, the word was never used." At the age of 1·7 this same child called the tips of her parents' shoes *noses*. "She then liked to pull our noses, and discovered the possibility of pulling likewise the tips of our shoes." To a certain boy of 2·3, "*lala* first meant song or music; later, when he had heard a military band, it meant soldier, and finally all kinds of noises, including any unmusical sounds like claps and thuds" [322]. Many such transfers have been described. They appear long before speech has arrived at the stage of naming indicated in our first example, as is shown by Preyer's observation that his son uttered the word *atta* at the end of his eleventh month whenever anything disappeared—either when a person left the room or when the light was turned off. These transfers, however, maintain themselves during the naming-period, which again throws light upon the nature of naming itself. It does not appear that everything must have its own special name; for if this were so, these transfers would not take place. It seems to be sufficient if a thing possesses any kind of appropriate name. Mrs Moore reports, to be sure, that with the impulse to name things, both the number and the extent of these transferences decrease; but it seems to me that further observations are requisite before we can determine what influence the naming-tendency exerts upon the number and form of these transferences.

How can we understand the nature of these transferences? Bühler is right in comparing them with the transferences of chimpanzees; for instance, when the

animal employs the rim of a hat as if it were a stick.[323]
A direction of inquiry is thus indicated from which an
explanation may be sought. In no case dare we assume
that the child confuses things for which he employs
the same name. Mrs Moore makes this point very
clearly, by showing that behaviour towards different
things bearing the same name may be quite distinct.
So, for instance, her child called all little girls, Dorothy,
but she showed signs of pleasure only in the presence
of the particular Dorothy whom she knew, and from
whom the name had been learned [324].

When Clara and William Stern write that at this age
"the child's apprehension of its impressions is still so
poor and confused that differentiations are passed over
which no adult could overlook" [325]; this is certainly an
incomplete statement of the case. When a new thing
is given an old name, we should interpret that fact by
saying that the new thing enters into a configuration
which was acquired with something else. The new
thing does not need to be identical with this other thing,
but only to possess certain characteristics which agree
with the older configuration. What we must try to
investigate is the configuration of each separate instance
in which a thing and a name stand together. When
we previously assumed that the name is added as an
attribute of the thing, this is to be understood only as
the general outline of an hypothesis to be filled in by
further investigation; for as Wertheimer has indicated,
the characteristic configuration of a thing may greatly
vary. "So, for instance, *red* in the statement that 'the
wall is red' is quite different from red in the statement
'blood is red'" [326]. These are problems for an investigation into infantile thought and speech to which, for lack
of personal experience, I can only refer.

3. Finally, the child creates new names by combining
old ones. Bühler recognizes the importance of this
fact and demands its systematic investigation. Pretty
examples of this kind of naming are furnished by

Stumpf's son, who until the fourth month of his fourth year employed only his own language—a language essentially made up of these combinations [327], as may be indicated by the following samples :

> *hoto*, horse ; *papn*, to eat ; *hoto-papn*, milk-wagon ;
> *loh*, to run ; *hoto-loh*, mail-wagon ;
> *ei*, egg ; *hopa*, to raise, to take up ; *ei hopa*, tea- or egg-spoon ;
> *wausch*, flesh ; *wausch-hopa*, fork ;
> *kap*, broken in two ; *wausch-kap*, knife.

We adults would call this procedure something like a description, such as we might make use of when we do not know how to name a thing or event ; but in the early stages of development these words have a true naming-function, in as much as the name is not yet a " mere " name. This primitive naming-function gradually undergoes a change, as is indicated when a child describes butterflies as " pansies flying " [328] ; for here we seem to be at a much later stage of development where description and naming are no longer so much alike as they are at the beginning. The procedure, however, has not altered. The combinations which the child employs are also very instructive in understanding the configurations of thing and name. On the one hand they indicate that the name does not connect itself with the thing in a purely external manner, as the old theory of association would have us believe ; for in that case one could find out the names of things only by questioning. Instead, the configuration tells how the thing should be called, so that one can see its name in it. On the other hand, it is interesting to note how the activities and the effects of things are employed in their naming. A thing is in no wise isolated from its effects ; for its effects belong essentially to its being. A fork, for instance, is not a metal object with four tines, but " something to eat with." This conclusion regarding the effect of the thing is borne out by the investigations which have been made of children's definitions. The extensive observations of Binet upon his two daughters ($2\frac{1}{2}$–$3\frac{1}{4}$ years, and $4\frac{1}{2}$–5 years) are of especial value in this connection [329]. The younger child, as well as the older one, always answered questions of: What is that? (for example, a knife, roll, snail-shell, etc.) with a statement of purpose or action. This is also found to be true of children just entering school. To the child, therefore, a thing is not a completely isolated fragment, since the effective power and purpose of the thing adhere to it as a part of its essential nature.

Thus far we have considered language used during this period of greatest speech-development only as a process of naming. Our conception of naming must thereby be adapted particularly to the facts involved. Yet this period of development should not be regarded too schematically; for though naming plays an important rôle at this time, language also serves other purposes. Even in addition to the retention of interjectional and volitional words, statements are also made by the child which transcend the naming of things, and indicate that even at this early age language may enter into relations with other configurations. The following is an example from Taine reported by Compayré [330]. A little girl eighteen months old greatly enjoyed the game of "hide-and-seek," in which her mother or nurse would hide behind the door and then call *cou-cou*. The same child had been told, *ça brûle* when her soup was too hot, when she came too near the fire, and when her hat was put on in the garden as a protection against the burning sun. One evening, on the terrace, when the sun was seen disappearing behind a hill, the child said: *a bule cou-cou*. Here a process of uniting two event-configurations into one is indicated. The transference from a one-word to a many-word sentence is carried out; not, as Major reports in his observations, by making the child repeat two words which are somehow connected, but in a manner indicating a new and important achievement on the part of the child. At present how-

329

ever, as Bühler remarks [331], we are not able to set forth the exact psychological significance of such a performance. The problem is difficult, but its solution is nevertheless worth attempting.

Finally, Bühler has pointed out the following characteristic of the early language-period [332]. Very soon in the development of childish language there occur such general words as *this* and *one* (in the sense of "something"). Bühler observed these words when his child was 1·7, and they were not merely used in place of a definite name for something, but were correctly employed. "We had always the impression," he reports, "either that the more definite word did not occur to the child at the proper time, or that, for unknown reasons, he was not concerned to find a more definite name." Bühler's interpretation seems a reasonable one. Using our own terminology it may be stated as follows: To the child a thing is something which has a name belonging to its thing-character. Not only does the name *dolly* belong to the doll, and the name *mama* to the mother, but the naming-configuration is operative even before the name is given. The configuration demands supplementation, but this demand may be satisfied in other ways than by the particular name of the thing, so that under certain conditions a general word like *one* is quite sufficient. A word of this kind then becomes a sign for the completion of the general configuration of thing and name. In the previous case of the child's question: "What's that?" (cf. above) the word *that* does not perform this function, but merely indicates the incompleteness of the configuration; hence the *that* of the question is to be replaced by the name given in response. In the present case, however, *this* or *one* may take the place of a name for something which already has a name, and through this process of assigning names the thing-category is itself made clearer and more vivid.

Quite analogous is the usage of the word *machen* (to do) which Bühler frequently observed as early as 1·5

330

in all kinds of combinations such as *snell machen, kaput machen, lala machen* (to sing), and quite generally in *so machen*. These are expressions for the relational configuration of happenings, just as *this, that,* or *one* are expressions for the configuration of a thing including its name.

We have already indicated that causality soon comes to play an important rôle. Again and again it is evident that causal relations not only exist between " things frequently experienced in succession," but also that unusual events which stand out from the commonplace appear distinctly and immediately in a causal order. As an effective means of relationship, causality soon penetrates the entire thinking of the child, assuming, at times, highly amusing forms. I can illustrate this fact with a few stories which came to me directly from parents. A four-year-old child who had been put to bed for the night said to his mother who sat by finishing a bit of sewing : " But you can't see anything ; for I have my eyes closed." A little girl, also four years old, who was travelling with her father on the railroad cried out when the train entered a tunnel and everything became dark : " Father, I have gone away "—an observation which clearly indicates a difference between the child's categories of comprehension and our own. The third example, of a little girl of 4·10, shows that causality may also affect things by virtue of its own nature, thus leading to a definite " philosophical " consideration. One day this little girl asked her mother, from whom she had learned that the dear Lord made everything : " Then who made the dear Lord ? " And when her mother answered : " He made Himself," she objected : " He couldn't do that because He wasn't there."

Further observations are, of course, requisite in matters of this kind ; but they will not be in vain, for in this way we can obtain glimpses into the origins of our most important categories.

§ 11—*Continuation : Number-Configurations*

We shall single out in conclusion one more category, in order to demonstrate how *different* are primitive configurations from those employed by adults; and how the attributes originally essential to a configuration may disappear, and be replaced by others entirely foreign to the original pattern. We refer here to *numbers*—the forms of thought which science has so highly developed. In a work of the greatest significance to the psychology of categories, Max Wertheimer has investigated the kind of ideas employed by men who do not possess our developed number-system, in tasks where we would use numbers[333]. Wertheimer deals in the main with primitive peoples, but he gives some examples from infantile development, and he has also been able to demonstrate that even our "common-sense" numbers often differ in radical ways from the numbers of mathematics.

It is characteristic of our thinking that we are able to carry out thought-processes abstractly, with any sort of material, quite independent of the natural relations of things. This is not so in earlier stages of development where the things themselves determine what kind of thought-processes shall be carried on with them. Here is an interesting example: "If one asks for the class-concept of two terms in this way: 'What are both $x$ and $y$?'—it often happens that among a number of 'right' reactions, a break suddenly occurs, and instead of classifying dog and cat as domestic animals, they are called *enemies*[334]." In a large measure this dependence upon the things themselves is also found in operations and constructions which are used in place of our numbers, and which we may call "pre-numerical constructs." While our counting is transferred to whatever objects we may choose, and yet always remain the same; order, natural modes of grouping, natural relationships of members and materials, remain more or less relevant to the pre-numerical constructs. Such a construct is the pair: as a pair of eyes; but a dish and a table are not a pair, neither are a stalk and a blossom. A pair is comprehended as being made up, not of "equal things, but of things that belong together"; thus, for example, man and wife are a pair, called a married couple. The same holds true for a group of three members: two adjacent trees and a third one farther off are not necessarily a natural group of three. Bühler cites a pretty example from the investigations of Decroly and Degand,[335] where a child of 4·9, who had learned to comprehend a group of four members, was asked how many cherries there were when a pair was hung over each ear. The child always replied: "Here's a pair and there's a pair." The Sterns[336] also cite the case of two children of the ages 2·7 and 2·10, investigated by Major and Lindner, who were able to understand and make use of "two apples," but not of two eyes, two ears, etc. This observation may appear singular, because paired members form so natural a group to us adults; and Decroly and Degand found that their child knew and understood the twoness of eyes, legs, stockings, and gloves at the age of 2·2. The paradox is explained, however, when we consider that pre-numerical con-structs do not have the same characteristics that our numbers have. With numbers, two is always the same, but with "two eyes, two boards, and . . . two fighters, each pair gives rise to a different configuration of two."[337] Consequently, when the child has learned the twoness of apples it does not follow that he is now able to transfer this configuration to pairs of quite a different constitution. In this connection Wertheimer observed that for children three single nuts have the designations of one, two, three; while three objects which lie in a certain order have another designation; namely, that of the form in which they are arranged. Thus, children are often greatly astonished to find that the five-spot domino corresponds to the quantity five, and we ourselves reckon apples by the bushel and years by the score.

To how slight an extent numerical constructs are transferable is shown by the following observation of Friedrich, reported by the Sterns. A child 4·3½ was asked by his grandfather: "How many fingers have I?" to which the child replied: "I don't know, I can only count my own fingers." This is not an instance of mere mental incapacity, but is largely a result of natural factors which oppose the transfer of an operation from one material to another. When a pot is broken in two, it is unnatural to say that two things have been made out of one; the natural thing is to say that the pot is in shards or fragments.

Long before the first number-words are properly employed, pre-numerical constructs play a part. The following experiments can be made in the first months of the second year: when a child plays with two or three identical objects, such as beans or coins, no distinction is made between them; but if one of them is taken away, while the child's attention is diverted, its absence will be noticed immediately, even when the order of those remaining is also changed. On the other hand the removal of one from a large number of objects will not be noticed. As Wertheimer maintains, the formation of natural groups and conglomerate constructs is genetically prior to counting.

Counting is a supplemental process, occurring first as a serial arrangement about the beginning of the second year. Apples, blocks, fingers—always things of the same class—are arranged in series and the child says *one, another one, still another one*, etc., or *button, another button, still another button;* but never simply apple, apple, apple [338]. When we recall what was said about the first use of the word *one*, it will be clear that serial words, such as "another one," etc., stand for things seen and employed as members of a series

334

already present or in course of construction. This implies a step in the direction of counting and the conception of numbers. But serial construction and group - construction remain different processes, even after the child has learned to count properly. The Sterns give the following example of their daughter, Hilda, aged 3·7. When five fingers were held out before her, and the question asked how many fingers there were, she would count them correctly. " If, however, the question was asked over again; ' How many fingers are there?' she would begin to recount them each time the question was asked. The last finger was indeed the fifth, but the total number of fingers did not yet mean to her the sum of five "[339]. Thus, as Wertheimer has pointed out, many peoples use other number-words in counting than the ones they use in naming sums.

The pre - numerical constructs of children are, of course, constantly influenced by association with adults; and hence they do not become stable enough to show their capacity in performance as they do with primitive people. Wertheimer says of the constructs employed by primitive people, that they are both less and more effective than our logical constructs. " Less, in that certain operations of thought commonly employed by us are altogether excluded from consideration; more, in that the thinking itself is in principle more intimately concerned with real things." The release from reality, which is both possible and easy to our mode of think- ing, is a specific product of our civilization. The child must go a tremendously long way in a short time in order to learn to think as adults do, in a manner which is not at all natural to him. To lead him along this way, so that his advancement may be vital to him, this is the difficult though grateful task of the teacher.

CHAPTER VI

# THE WORLD OF A CHILD

IN this brief concluding chapter I shall try to indicate
some of the important features of the child's world, as
contrasted with the world familiar to us adults. The
child's sphere of interest has been called a world of
*play*, a world of irresponsibility, in which unreality
reigns supreme. These characterizations merit a closer
scrutiny.

The problem is not identical with that of understanding children's play; for real play, in its very
beginnings at least, occurs so early in life that we can
not yet speak of a conception of the world, even in the
simplest literal sense of the word. On the other hand,
there appears in later types of play only one aspect of
what we really have in mind; for the distinction we
adults draw between play and serious endeavour is
certainly quite a different matter to the child. Even
if the child does not really play all the time, as
adults do occasionally, still his world has some of
the characteristics of play. In other words, certain
peculiarities which belong to the play of children, and
likewise in some degree to the play of adults, may be
found in the internal and external behaviour of children,
even when they are not playing. We must not forget
that the child grows up in a world controlled by adults,
in consequence of which he is constantly being subjected to their influence. We have to deal, therefore,
not with a set of conditions which remain unaltered for
a long period of time, but rather with a view of the

336

world which is constantly undergoing a process of transformation; sometimes more rapidly, and at other times more slowly. This fact must be borne in mind when we try to set forth the characteristics of the child's world.

I choose the following example as a starting-point for our considerations. A child may play with a stick of wood and treat it like his "dear baby." Yet a short time later, after being diverted from his play, he will break the same stick of wood, or throw it into the fire, without any compunction at all [340]. How can these two different types of behaviour toward one and the same object be reconciled? Superficially considered they seem to be altogether incompatible; for the first action is carried on no less seriously or intently than the second, which makes it impossible to suppose that when acting as though the stick of wood were a living being, the child is only playing, whereas in destroying the stick he has taken into consideration the real character of his plaything. In many ways it is apparent that the matter can not be so simple as this. One can see that a child manifests a deep and genuine feeling for his playthings; for intense emotions can be provoked by interrupting the play-situation. Sully has given numerous examples of this fact [341]. "One little boy of three and a half years who was fond of playing at the useful business of coal-heaving would carry his coal-heaver's dream through the whole day, and on the particular day devoted to this calling would not only refuse to be addressed by any less worthy name, but ask in his prayer to be made a good coal-heaver (instead of the usual 'good boy'). On other days this child lived the life of a robin redbreast, a soldier, and so forth, and bitterly resented his mother's occasional confusion of his personalities."

We must conclude from this statement that the child takes his play very earnestly. And it is apparent that we can not merely set off play from its usual anti-

337

thesis of earnestness and work; but must try to find some other distinction.

It is characteristic of much of the play of children (most typically in their play with dolls) that inanimate objects are treated like living human beings. This observation is generally confirmed and applies to behaviour in a much wider sense than we have attributed to play. "That is to say, the child sees what we regard as lifeless and soulless as alive and conscious"[342]. Sully gives some pretty examples: The little boy twenty months old who had a special preference for the letter W and always used to speak of it as "dear old boy W"; and the youngster of four who drew an F by mirror-writing and then putting the correct letter to the left of it, ꟻ F, cried out: "They're talking together."

Miss Ingelow remembered that when she was two or three years old she "used to feel how dull it must be for the pebbles in the causeway to be obliged to lie still and only see what was round about. When I walked out with a little basket for putting flowers in I used sometimes to pick up a pebble or two and carry them on to have a change: then at the farthest point of the walk turn them out, not doubting that they must be pleased to have a new view." It seems to me quite incorrect to speak of a propensity for *personification* in this case, meaning that children first have perceptions like our own, and afterwards endow them with life by inference from the analogy of their own experience. Such a view, however, has long been held in folk-psychology; and the theory of animism advanced by English investigators, and confirmed by an immense amount of material, rests upon this basis. The universal animation which primitive peoples find in nature has thus been taken to be an explanation of facts based upon rational inferences from human behaviour to the behaviour of things. To-day this theory is assailed on many sides, and in what follows I shall cite some of the chief objections which Lévy-Bruhl advances in his important work on the subject. I may refer the reader, also, to the excellent and easily accessible little book by K. Th. Preuss [343].

Animism can not be conceived as an "explanation" of the world, for in the first place the life of primitive man is such that he could not take any interest in theoretical explanations. In the second place, primitive man needs no explanation; because the disconnected things which the philosophy of man has slowly exposed to view, do not exist for him at all. The theoretical exponent of animism seeks to give a plausible explanation of the facts of folk-psychology by imagining how he would himself come upon such ideas if he were at the same level of civilization, and placed in the same surroundings, as primitive man. But in so doing the theorist makes the mistake of identifying primitive man with himself; an error which is like that committed by a well-known biologist who, having succeeded with the aid of a microscope in perceiving a retinal image in an insect's eye, concluded that what he saw was what the insect must have been able to see [344]. The error here made is as clear as day to a psychologist. What one sees through the microscope are only the objective factors which may be effective in the insect's vision; but what the insect actually *sees* when it has this definite retinal image, it is quite impossible to observe. The same is true regarding the theory of animism. The environment of primitive people and their peripheral sense-organs are approximately known to us, but we can no more draw conclusions from this knowledge than we can in the case of the insect; because our perception is a product of development and, as we have seen, the child perceives things differently than we do. The development of perception depends upon the total environment, the milieu, and above all, upon the sociological conditions of this milieu. Lévy-Bruhl attaches a special importance to the last point, and for this reason: Man grows up as a member of society—and with primitive people

339

internal social connections are much stronger than with us—so that man's entire development, including, of course, his perceptions, is dependent upon society. To give a rather weak analogy, we have found that language —which is a *collective* factor—plays a very important rôle in the first development of perception.

There is really nothing to explain ; for "primitive people do not perceive as we do." Our "natural things" do not enter into their perception at all. Before the characteristics can arise which are all-important to us, the primitive mind finds other and *mystical* character- istics in things, by means of which they are perceptually connected. The connection itself is, therefore, not a problem, but something given ; and the question which arises is how development has been carried on so as to loosen these originally fixed connections.

Since everything that exists for a people at this stage of civilization possesses mystical qualities which are much more important to them than "natural" characteristics, our distinction between the living and the dead, the animate and the inanimate, can have no meaning to them. Rivers, clouds, winds, even the main directions of space, to mention but a few examples, all have their mystical powers. The distinction, therefore, between animate and inanimate, is a product of develop- ment ; at the beginning no such question could possibly arise, since every thing, even including directions, names, and words in general, possesses its active principle as an immanent attribute.

When we return now to consider the child, it is evident that this view can be carried over directly to him. We should not suppose it "natural" that a child would first be able to see dead things which he later endows with life ; for the original situation is, rather, one in which the characteristic of effective activity belongs to every- thing alike. The discussion of the thing-category in the preceding chapter has already led us to this con- clusion, and Bühler also comes to it when he says : "The child knows absolutely nothing of life and mind, but is acquainted only with purposive events." Unlike the poet, a child is unable to breathe life into a dead thing [345]. He must gradually learn to make the distinctions we make, and these become an acquisition to his perceptual categories.

If we ask what are the criteria employed in deciding whether a thing has life or not, we can answer only by investigating the behaviour involved; for the answer depends upon the kind of place a thing occupies in a larger course of events, or in a more comprehensive dynamic structure. Consequently, when the child learns the distinction between the animate and the inanimate, this more extensive structure must still be involved.

There is a similar process in the development of such categories as "mere appearance," which we can already trace to some extent in certain cases of children's activities. As pointed out in an earlier connection, after the child has learned to reach for an object seen, this object possesses certain visual and tactual characteristics belonging to its configuration as a thing. The child is, therefore, constantly grasping at spots of light, shadows, and the like, and must gradually learn that there are things which may be seen, but which can not be grasped or touched. The behaviour of children in response to reflections in a mirror is of especial interest. Preyer describes his son's development in this respect very thoroughly. At first the image was not seen at all, later it was smiled at and grasped at, then it was apprehended as if it lay *behind* the mirror, and finally movements of avoidance were observed; for the child looked away when the mirror was held up before him. At this stage of development the reflection apparently frightened him, as something which did not fit into any of his patterns. Dogs probably never get beyond this stage. I have observed this behaviour in my own dog, and up to this point it coincided perfectly with Preyer's observations. The first time the dog came before a large mirror standing on the ground he ran up to his image barking loudly, and with a great show of excitement. Later he ran to one side of the mirror and stuck his head between the mirror and the wall. Since that time he has taken no notice of reflections in the mirror, and, like Preyer's son, he turns away his head whenever I hold him in front of a mirror. But development proceeds rapidly with a child. In two weeks' time after the sixtieth week of life all shyness before the mirror had been overcome by Preyer's son, and some preparation, at least, had been made for a correct understanding. Yet the child still grasped for and, indeed, struck at, his image. But soon this behaviour also ceased and the child employed the mirror thereafter just as we do [346]. Cases of an opposite sort have also been observed, in which a child demands to see something invisible that has been felt; as, for instance, in the case reported by Sully of a little girl not yet two years old who wanted to see the wind.

The original thing-phenomenon in which the visual and tactual are closely related, must therefore be broken up in certain instances and new patterns formed in which there may be only visual, or only tactual, constituents. Something similar must take place in drawing the distinction between animate and inanimate; except that this process is much more complicated and difficult, since the configurations involved are themselves much more extensive. It is not to be wondered at that this process goes on for a long time before it is complete enough to afford a clear-cut differentiation. And, even after the basis for this distinction has been crudely laid, this will not prevent the old undifferentiated pattern from re-appearing again and again. I would even go so far as to say that vestiges of these old patterns are still frequent occurrences in the everyday life of adults; and not merely in the form of superstitions, either.

If it be asked what kind of a pattern this is which gradually enables us to distinguish the dead from the living, one might frame an answer in terms of the original "expression" of perceptual phenomena. Although, at start, all phenomena are expressive, they are not all expressive in the same degree—a fact which we have found to be influential in the development of perception (cf. p. 291 f.). It is possible that the distinction between the living and the dead arises from this difference in degree of expressiveness; for certainly a pencil has very little of this quality, whereas a snake, even though stuffed, has very much of it. In other words, along with the progressive evolution of perceptual configurations goes the differentiation of their expressive qualities, so that the distinction of the living from the dead would proceed directly from the development of single percepts.

In addition, I might venture to assume that this distinction is also gradually drawn from the consequences of the child's behaviour with the things in question; for gradually, though very gradually, of course, the child will notice that things react in very different ways. On the one hand, he will experience contradictions in "living" things; he must approach them and shape his reactions to them quite differently than with inert things. On the other hand, the learning of this distinction may be made more difficult by the fact that "living" things conform more than inert things to the wishes of the child; thus displaying, in a certain sense, an opposing behaviour. Two examples from Sully illustrates this point: A little girl of five one day stopped her rolling hoop and exclaimed: " Ma, I do think this hoop must be alive, it is so sensible: it goes where I want it to." In another example this pattern of connection was "falsely" employed; or, as we should say, cause and effect were interchanged. A little girl scarcely two years old said to her mother during a rainstorm: " Mamma, dy (dry) Babba's hands, so not rain any more " [347]. The distinction may also involve emotions, since one can bring pain to the animate, but not to the inanimate. Thus the child notices that his little brothers and sisters react to ill-treatment quite differently than does his doll. All the same, it seems to me a tenable hypothesis that this distinction is facilitated by these consequences; and that the child must learn to consider his behaviour with respect to its consequences, and in this way come to look upon his conduct as the *beginning* of a series of interrelated events.

We see now why development must proceed so slowly. A child's ability to bring the present into relation with the past and the future is quite inadequate, as Stern has pointed out[348]. Even after a beginning has been made, the total connections of the world and of life are by no means grasped at once; for smaller and more limited relationships must first be built up which, as we shall soon see, can exist in relative independence of one another.

Returning again to the problem from which we started out—namely, the question as to the nature of childish play—it seems to me that we can best understand play, psychologically, by considering the activities of the child from the point of view of the larger configuration of events in which play occurs. We have, at the beginning, a situation in which the child can form no temporal patterns at all which go beyond the activities just performed. Here all separate act-complexes must be independent of one another, every one being of the same sort and of the same worth. From the child's point of view, there is not as yet anything at this stage that can be called play or not-play. From an adult's point of view, however, childish behaviour at this stage can be characterized as *playful*, provided one accepts Groos's definition of play as an activity which is enjoyed purely for its own sake.

But gradually the child perfects his temporal patterns, and it becomes a characteristic of these that many of them can exist side by side without influencing

344

each other very strongly. I believe that the two systems first to arise have to do, one with undertakings, processes, and things which relate somehow to adults ; while along-side of these a second system is developed which is independent of adults. Thus to a child the world of adults separates itself slowly, and at first indistinctly and obscurely, from his own child-world. The world of the adult makes itself gradually felt through the un-pleasant consequences of certain acts of behaviour. In the adult's world the child is not free, but instead meets with compulsion and opposition which are lacking in his own world. So long as the connection between the child's world and the adult's world is still a loose one, motives for drawing new distinctions, such as that between the quick and the dead, are doubtless found to be stronger in the adult's world than they are in the child's world where no such requirement is made. If a child finds himself in his own world, these categorical analyses are largely lacking from both his external and internal behaviour ; therefore he acts the same towards both animate and inanimate things.

But we must proceed still further. The relative independence of different patterns from one another refers not only to the two great groups constituting the child's world and the adult's world, but is likewise valid in the individual connections within each of these worlds. But while the adult's world, by virtue of the same principle which distinguishes it from the child's world, soon forces itself to be comprehended as a *totality*, so that the independence of individual actions, one from another, gradually disappears ; it is quite different in the other world where, to-day, the child may be a coal-heaver and to-morrow a soldier ; and where a stick of wood that has just been cuddled may the next minute be thrown into the fire. Yet these different actions do not interfere with one another, because they have no more connection with one another than they have for us when we are at play. The jack of diamonds may be a tremendously important card—"the right bower"—when I am playing euchre, but it is only a relatively unimportant card when I am playing bridge. With us adults, of course, there is always a conformity to the "rules of the game," which are fixed and valid in each kind of game; whereas a child's play is not bound by any such extraneously determined rules. Yet the lack of connection between plays is the same in both cases. The fixed and rigid connections that pervade our world are but a result of the domination of our non-play life; whereas to a child this domination is not originally present, and only gradually introduces itself.

Finally, the illusion indicated by the child who plays with a mere stick of wood as though it were a doll, can also be explained in terms of our principle. As a general rule the "illusion" will be no greater when the plaything is more nearly true to nature. Favourite dolls are not necessarily the costliest products of the toy-shop, but may be the simplest, rudest, and often more or less damaged specimens. This would seem very remarkable if one were to identify the child's world with that of the adult; seeing each separate thing in the position which it occupies in the general and all-inclusive relationships of life. Yet adults have reasoned in this way; that because a doll is so very different from a living child one must therefore make it just as like a child as possible. Accordingly, we have dolls fitted out with mechanisms which close the eyes when they are laid down, and which produce vocal sounds when they are squeezed. We have dolls which are beautiful, with hair genuine or deceptively similar, and with clothes correct in every detail. To a child, however, a doll is never a part of the adult-world, or, at any rate, it becomes so only after it has been taken away from the child for protection or as a punishment; and since the doll does not occupy any such fixed position among definitely regulated things, the entire assumption upon which dolls are usually made is a false one. To the child it is sufficient if something is there to satisfy a present want; and the thing, whatever it be, will then have all the characteristics necessary for this purpose. Since a stick of wood can be caressed, it becomes at once a baby to be loved and cuddled. The fact that it does not have certain other character-istics belonging to a real baby, does not come into consideration at all; because the need of harmony with the rest of experience is simply not felt. To a child there is as yet no *single* world-all in which particular objects have each a manifold of relations.

Ethnological analogies to this interpretation are also available. For example, primitive peoples do not know anything about a single world-all which binds everything together. What is right for the white man may be altogether wrong for them. If a white man shoots an invulnerable fetish-bird, this does not destroy the bird's invulnerability in their eyes, but only shows that different charms work for the white man. This primi-tive view of the world not only lacks the criterion by which we endow with reality only such things and processes as are perceptible to *everyone;* but, in addition, those things which are visible only to the chosen few — the medicine - men — are considered to possess a peculiarly magnified and important reality.

Finally, as we have already pointed out and can now confirm by examples, the characteristics which are important in the world of primitive peoples are entirely different from those that are important in our own world. This is apparent in primitive drawings and their relation to reality. Here we enter a sphere which, externally at least, is very similar to the peculiar nature of the child's world which we have described. Spencer and Gillen made the following observation in Central Australia, where the natives maintain that certain drawings are made only in play and have absolutely no meaning; yet *precisely the same* sketches have a very definite significance when they are attached to objects found on consecrated ground. The explanation of this phenomenon, and of the wonder and mystery which it has for us, lies in the fact that while our standard of judging the relationship between image and reality is their likeness, to primitive people it is their common participation in the same mystical power. For this reason it is quite impossible for us to interpret these drawings. Parkinson reports from the South Sea Islands that a drawing which had been taken for snakes really represented a pig; and that another figure, which might perhaps have passed for a face, was really a club. The natives were greatly astonished that one should ask them about the meaning of these drawings; for they could not imagine how anyone could fail to understand the drawings at once [349].

It is, therefore, not unheard of that a thing should first derive its being and its significance from the relationship in which it exists. So long as no larger connection binds everything together, a stick of wood may very well be a trifling thing at one moment, and a dear dolly the next.

To say, then, that the child experiences no genuine illusion in his play means, according to our view, that the object under consideration is perceived in an illusory manner only so long as the child is in his own world. But he may slip over from this world into the world of the adult, and then the object will be treated differently. But it cannot be said when the child is absorbed in his play that any part of this other pattern of the adult-world must also be present to him. Groos emphasizes this distinction by remarking that "if we may not assume consciousness of the illusion in complete absorption, nor yet any true alternative with reality, we are forced to the conclusion that the appearance produced by play differs essentially from the reality which it represents, and is incapable of producing genuine deception" [350].

What is most characteristic of the child is his own

child-world, which to him is more important and more dear than the world in which the adult dwells. For a long period of time the child makes no less progress in his own world than he does when he comes under the influence of the adult-world. Furthermore, when the distinction between these different worlds begins to be known, when the child himself begins to speak of playing, this play-world becomes all the more vivid to him. A stimulating anecdote reported by Sully illustrates this fact. "One day two sisters said to one another: 'Let us play being sisters'"[351]. Since the sister-configuration comes from the adult-world, or at least belongs to that stage of development, what was here proposed was to take this pattern over into the child-world in order to give it a quickening reality.

The instance of Stumpf's son, who spoke his own language for a whole year, and could not be broken of the habit by any admonition, is a good example of the fact that occasionally even performances which bring the child into relation with adults, and which are of special importance in the construction of the adult's world, may originally be carried over entirely into the sphere of the child's world. Stumpf writes of his son: "When we corrected him and said: 'This is called snow,' or 'this is called milk,' he would still answer: 'Ich kjob,' 'ich prullich'" (these being his expressions for the same things).

We have already mentioned the sudden transition to normal speech, which Stumpf explains in the following way: "The psychological motive was very simple; the child had grown tired of the game. He may also have felt, finally, that the deviation of his language from the vernacular, and its incompleteness, were both disturbing and humiliating"; which was no doubt true. The adult's world had become so powerful that it was now the child's ambition to attain it, rather than make use any longer of the possibility of remaining in his own world, which had now assumed a somewhat contemptible

349

character. Thus, after a time, the child became ashamed of his own language.

Another modification in the boy's speech appears to me to have been a harbinger of this transformation. For a long time the boy called his brother Rudi, *olol*, and himself *job*. But there came a time, even while he yet spoke his own language with reference to everything else, when he avoided these names and would only say, and give heed to the names used by adults. "*Job weg, liki da*" (Liki being the name which adults called him — an abbreviation of Felix); "*olol job ä— rudi liki haja,*" meaning that Olol and Job are bad names, while Rudi and Liki are nice[352]. An encroachment upon the child's world by the world of the adult is manifest in this instance; which Stumpf describes very pertinently by saying that the old name *job* no longer seemed *worthy* to the child. Slowly the child-world must give way to the world of adult, and the case of Stumpf's son gives us a good insight into this process.

There is, however, one sphere of interest which children learn from adults that has a very close and intimate relation with the child's world; and that is the sphere of religion. To a child, religion is something tremendously serious; perhaps, indeed, truly "holy"; and yet despite, or better still, because of, this, it is completely incorporated into the child-world. As the adult sees it, the child *plays* with religious things. The Christchild; the Christmas-eve manger with its figures of men, angels, and beasts—these are realities corresponding to the child's world; for they are things to which the customary laws of the adult-world apply no more than they do to any other playthings.

Mrs Else Roloff has carefully observed and reported upon the religious play of her two little girls[353]. The plays, which centred about the Christmas festival, were of outstanding significance. "Before the festival, Eva was 'the Christchild.' She flew through the room with outstretched arms bringing gifts to all the children. . . .

The little one also claimed an office, and was promoted to the position of the 'angel choir,' to sing and mingle with them. After Christmas eve the holy persons were represented by building blocks. . . . In Heaven—a stage-like structure with stairs leading up to it—stood the Saviour, the Lord Jesus, the 'Guest,' and the Christchild. The relation between the Christchild, the Saviour, Jesus, and the Guest, was remarkable. The children knew very well that the Christchild was called Jesus and that He grew up to be the Saviour, yet they maintained that *their* Christchild was always small. They knew, too, that at our meals we 'pray that Jesus may be our *Guest*'; but this did not hinder them at all from attributing separate personalities in their play to all these names."

This last observation is of especial interest; for it illustrates a peculiarity of childish thinking that may extend far beyond the province of religion; a peculiarity which is brought out so clearly in this instance, only because the material was especially well adapted for it. This peculiarity is related to a characteristic which has already provided us with a key to so many features of the child's behaviour: namely, the relative independence of different configurations. Jesus, the Saviour, the Christchild, and the Guest can be united in the structure of a single personality, although it is doubtful whether a configuration possessing all these separate properties (for the names are properties) could be experienced simultaneously by a child. Nevertheless, the smaller constellations of the main configuration may be entirely self-sufficient, and exist side by side without disturbing one another; indeed, they may exist in the same form in which the total configuration exists. To us, such a procedure would mean a logical contradiction, but, as Mrs Roloff has shown, there is no such contradiction in the child's mind. Here the author refers quite properly to analogies from folk-psychology; for neither does this contradiction of thought exist at primitive levels of civilization. A thing can have two forms at the same time and can also occupy different places. That it is the *same* thing despite these, to us, incompatible circumstances, derives from the fact that the total configuration in which the identity is contained is quite different from the one we know. The development of our whole- and part-configuration is based upon the principle of non-contradiction; but in the case of other civilizations and, as we now see, in the case of our own children as well, the process is different. For the principle of contradiction is irrelevant; such things as liveliness, active power, and mystical characteristics being of much greater importance. Thus the fact that three objects, which were once but the names and attributes of a single personality, should nevertheless become three different and independent beings is in no wise disturbing to the primitive mind.

In tracing this development still further, it appears that the configuration of the adult-world constantly assumes a greater extension, so that the complete independence of different worlds is no longer possible. The school acts as a very important agent in this process; for in school there is both work and play. What was once a world of equal rank with the adult's world, gradually becomes a mere matter of play. Before this takes place, the real world occasionally forces itself into the child-world, so that even in his play the child is now and then conscious of the fact that there is another world beside his play-world; one in which his play is not to be taken seriously. At this period the stimulus to play may even be heightened by the fact that the play-world is devoid of all responsibilities. Groos describes this behaviour as follows: "Think, for instance, of the laughter of romping boys which serves to reassure the combatants by its implication that, in spite of appearances to the contrary, the fight is only playful " [854].

Yet play always remains a sphere relatively shut off

from the rest of the world, and for a long time illusion
—as we have employed this term—retains its power.
What the child will do only with the greatest reluctance
when he thinks he is working, he will do with burning
zeal in play.

But the opposite may also occur; for play itself can
be so directed that it becomes closely related to the
rest of life. The play-character then disappears almost
entirely. One may take part in a game of chance
simply because one is in a mood to play, and then
suddenly notice that in the course of the play one has
become so deeply involved that to lose the game would
be a very disagreeable experience. Thenceforth the
play-mood is all gone, and the progress of the game
becomes a serious decision of fate.

This example has been chosen, not from the life of
a child but from the experience of an adult; yet I
believe that the chief feature of an adult's play is that
it still belongs to a "world-apart," and that whenever
we play we step out of the usual relationships of life.
(Thus professional gamesters can not be said to "play.")

This development, as we have here sketched it, is
characteristic of *our children;* but play is to be found
in every other type of civilization, and likewise among
animals. Our theory, however, can not at once be
carried over to these other manifestations of play,
because the distinction of the two worlds, which to us
is so marked, either does not exist at all, or is quite a
different affair in the lives of animals and primitive
men. An investigation into the psychology of these
other kinds of play is not a part of our task. Nevertheless, we shall complete our sketch with a few words
upon the biological significance of play in order to
bring it more closely into connection with certain
things that have previously been discussed.

We have noticed that the child acquires many, and
not the least significant, of his accomplishments from
his child-world. When he lives in this world he does

what we objectively designate as *play*, in accordance with the definition already given (cf. p. 344). Now Groos has advanced the opinion that the play of children is of tremendous biological value in preparing the child for serious endeavour. "I find this value," he says, "in the *indirect* benefit, both physical and mental, which must be ascribed to play by way of practice and preparation"[355]. In the second chapter (page 40) it was stated that childhood is the time for learning; and that the longer the period of infancy, the more the individual has to learn. Groos's theory is in perfect harmony with this idea. If play is of service to living, then, according to Groos, one should not say that animals play because they are young and joyous; but rather that animals enjoy a period of youth in order that they may play. In both of his excellent books on play Groos has supported his views with a great mass of material, so that the theory has now become universally acknowledged.

Yet I must warn the reader against an over-estimation of this theory. Not only must one guard against a false pedagogical application of play by smuggling artificial and foreign aims of instruction into the child's world (to this Bühler has already referred in the conclusion of his larger work), but one must also remain unprejudiced by theories of play, both as applied to children and to animals. Instead, these intensive expressions of vitality should be taken into account as they are, without considering any aim whatsoever. Play is but one type of behaviour among others. While a relationship of course exists between all kinds of behaviour, a procedure which brings all behaviour under the single head of practical utility is distinctly one-sided, and has led to many errors which have been sponsored by the rationalistic utilitarianism of the last fifty years.

The question has also been asked what are the effective causes which, in any particular instance, lead an individual to play. No explanation based on tele-ology is a real explanation, but at best an indication of the direction in which an explanation may be sought. The child knows nothing of the end which is being fulfilled by his play. Many theories of the reason for play have been constructed, of which the most famous is the Schiller-Spencer "surplus-energy" theory. In addition to this, the "recreation" theory of Lazarus has played its part. The main points of these theories can easily be gathered from the names that have been attached to them, and an exhaustive discussion of the subject will be found in the works of Groos [356].

Bühler contributes a new suggestion by pointing to the fact that, aside from any consequences whatsoever, all activity brings *pleasure*. I would modify this state-ment by adding that a *successful* activity—that is, an activity which brings something I desire, or one that achieves what it should—brings me pleasure, whether the end attained be itself pleasurable or not. We have already met with examples of this fact; I may recall, for instance, Köhler's experiment with the double-stick which Sultan fitted together, and continued to employ even after he had brought all the fruit within reach. Bühler regards this "functional-pleasure" as the motor which drives a disinterested activity of play [357]. I find here a very suggestive idea, but one which has yet to be developed into a theory; for it is certainly no easy matter to comprehend theoretically the transition from pleasure to action. Nevertheless, there can be no doubt that the pleasure taken in an achievement operates as an incentive to new achievements.

It is not my intention to give a classification of children's play; for that can be found in the works of Groos, Bühler, and Stern. Accordingly, our discussion of the subject ends at this point.

In this book I have tried to give an introduction to the study of child-psychology by pointing out the principles in accordance with which the behaviour and development of the child may be comprehended. But the reader must not conclude from my book that all the riddles have been solved, and all the questions answered ; for this would not be true. The general aim of my book has been but to point out a way in which the solution of these numerous problems can be attained. The nature of mental development as it has been revealed to us is not the bringing together of separate elements, but the arousal and perfection of more and more complicated configurations in which both the phenomena of consciousness and the functions of the organism go hand in hand.

# NOTES

List of Books frequently referred to in these Notes

Becher, E., *Gehirn und Seele*, Heidelberg, 1911. Referred to as *GS*.

Bühler, K., *Geistige Entwicklung* (Full title on page 36). Referred to as *GE*.

,, ,, *Abriss der geistigen Entwicklung* (Full title on page 36). Referred to as *AG*.

Claparède, E., *Experimental Pedagogy and the Psychology of the Child* (Full title on page 36).

Compayré, G., *Intellectual and Moral Development of the Child*, Parts I. and II. (Full title on page 36).

Edinger, L., *Vorlesungen über den Bau der nervösen Zentralorgane der Menschen und der Tiere*, Vol. I., 8th ed., Leipzig, 1911. Referred to as *Z*.

Groos, K., *Seelenleben* (Full title on page 36). Referred to as *SK*.

,, ,, *Die Spiele der Tiere*, 2nd ed., Jena, 1907. English edition, *The Play of Animals*, New York, 1898. Referred to as *PA*.

,, ,, *Die Spiele der Menschen*, Jena, 1907. English edition, *The Play of Man*, New York, 1901. Referred to as *PM*.

James, W., *The Principles of Psychology*, 2 vols. (1890), New York, 1905.

Kafka, G., *Einführung in die Tierpsychologie auf experimenteller und ethologischer Grundlage*, I. Die Sinne der Wirbellosen, Leipzig, 1914.

Köhler, W., " Optische Untersuchungen am Schimpansen und am Haushuhn," *Abhandlung d. K. Preus. Ak. der Wiss.*, Jhrg. 1915, Phys.-math. Kl., Nr. 3. Referred to as *OU*. (Separate edition).

,, ,, " Intelligenzprüfung an Anthropoiden," I. *ibid.*, Jhrg. 1917, Nr. 1. Referred to as *I*. (Separate edition). Also in book form : *Intelligenzprufüngen an Menschenaffen*, Berlin, 1921, 2nd ed. Page references to the book are given in parenthesis. (Eng. transl., *sub. tit.* 'The Mentality of Apes,' will be published in the autumn of 1924 by Kegan Paul & Co. (New York : Harcourt, Brace & Co.) ).

,, ,, " Nachweis einfacher Strukturfunktionen beim Schimpansen und beim Haushuhn. Über eine neue Methode zur Untersuchung des bunten Farbensystems," *ibid.*, Jhrg. 1918, Nr. 2. Referred to as *StF*. (Separate edition).

,, ,, *Die physischen Gestalten in Ruhe und in stationären Zustand. Eine natur-philosophische Untersuchung*, Braunschweig, 1920. Referred to as *PhG*.

357

# NOTES

Lévy-Bruhl, L., *Les Fonctions Mentales dans les Sociétés Inférieures,* 2nd ed., Paris, 1912.

McDougall, W., *Outline of Psychology,* New York, 1923.

Moore, K. C., " The Mental Development of a Child," *Psychological Review Monograph Supplement,* Nr. 3, 1896.

Morgan, C. Lloyd, *Habit and Instinct,* London and New York, 1896.

Preyer, W., *The Mind of the Child,* Parts I. and II. (Full title on page 35).

Shinn, M. W., " Notes on the Development of a Child," *Univ. of California Studies,* Vol. I., 1-4, 1893-99.

Stern, W., *Psychologie der Kindheit* (Full title on page 36). Referred to as *PsdK.*

,, ,, *Person und Sache, System der philosophischen Weltanschauung.* I. " Ableitung und Grundlehre," Leipzig, 1906. Referred to as *PS.* II. " Die menschliche Persönlichkeit," Leipzig, 1918. Referred to as *MP.*

Stern, Clara and W., *Kindersprache* (Full title on page 37). Referred to as *Sp.*

,, ,, ,, *Erinnerung,* etc. (Full title on page 37). Referred to as *EA.* (Separate edition).

Stumpf, C., " Eigenartige sprachliche Entwicklung eines Kindes," *Ztschr. f. päd. Psychol. u. Pathol.,* 3, Heft. 6, 1901. Referred to as *SpE.* (Separate edition).

Sully, J., *Studies of Childhood* (Full title on page 36).

Thorndike, E. L., *Animal Intelligence, Experimental Studies,* New York, 1911. Referred to as *AI.*

,, ,, *Educational Psychology,* I., *The Original Nature of Man,* New York, 1913. Referred to as *EP.* (The third volume of this work was not available for my use).

Volkelt, H., " Über die Vorstellungen der Tiere. Ein Beitrag zur Entwicklungspsychologie," *Arb. z. Entwicklungspsychologie,* edited by F. Krüger, *1, 2,* Leipzig and Berlin, 1914.

Watson, J. B., *Behaviour, an Introduction to Comparative Psychology,* New York, 1914. Referred to as *B.*

,, ,, *Psychology from the Standpoint of a Behaviourist,* Philadelphia, 1919. Referred to as *PB.*

358

## NOTES TO CHAPTER I

(1) This holds also for the principle of convergence advanced by Stern and frequently employed by him in child-psychology (cf. p. 51). The principle is derived from more general considerations, as may be seen from Stern's philosophical works (cf. especially *MP*, p. 95 f.).

(2) Of course we should not deny the existence of the most intimate connection between behaviour and experience ; on the contrary, that is precisely our view, but here we are dealing only with the systematic question of awareness.

(3) I have recently discussed this problem from the point of view adopted in this book. Cf. " Zur Theorie der Erlebnis-Wahrnehmung," *Annalen der Philos.*, III., pp. 375–399.

(4) This conclusion can not here be more definitely established, but in my opinion it excludes the possibility, not only of mensuration, but also, contrary to appearances, of any true enumeration of the phenomena.

(5) In the sense employed on page 8.

(6) We can altogether disregard the problem how we know anything of the consciousness of our fellow-creatures. Our previous criterion was simply the possibility of communication.

(7) Compare the following also with G. Kafka's discussion, p. 6 ff.

(8) But consider again what was said in note 2. Rubin reports the converse proposition, that one can follow the contours of a figure without making eye-movements, as, for instance, on an after-image. In this case the impression is always given that eye-movements are actually being made. Cf. Rubin's book referred to in note *115* on p. 365.

(9) We must decline to enter here into a criticism of psycho-vitalism. The argument of the text is directed less against this theory than it is against many other current modes of explanation in psychology. In my opinion the difficulties with which a psychological theory of consciousness has previously been burdened are now overcome, so that one of the main stays of psycho-vitalism has fallen away.

(10) Thorndike, whose position is in many ways close to that of the behaviourists, also employs the term behaviour, as we do, so as to include the phenomenal aspect of conduct.

(11) Cf. my *Erlebnis-Wahrnehmung* (note *3*).

(12) Cf. W. Köhler, Die Methoden der psychologischen Forschung an Affen, *Handbuch der biol. Arbeitsmethoden*. Edited by Abderhalden, Abt. vi. Teil D, p. 69 ff.

(13) Fundamentally their physiological theory is only a translation into physiological terms of the psychological atomism which

they have rejected, as I have pointed out in my review of Watson's Psychology (cf. *Psychologische Forschung, 2,* 1922, p. 382 f.). No physiological theory can be independent of psychological theory. This does not imply an explanation in the sense attacked above, but simply an adequate treatment of the facts. Thus, the analysis of consciousness into sensations would be a psychological theory even if one proceeded to explain the isolated sensations physiologically ; and likewise it would be a psychological theory if one were to deny the concept of sensation, and substitute another, for which a physiological explanation would then have to be sought.

(14) Köhler, *I,* page 70.

(15) *Ibid.,* page 71.

(16) Meantime Köhler has attacked this problem in all its bearings in the article cited in note *12,* and has indicated the direction in which we must look for its solution. Scheler, also, in his book on *Sympathy* treats of the perception of another person's mind, his views being in some respects the same as our own. (Cf. M. Scheler, *Wesen und Formen der Sympathie ; Die Phänomenologie der Sympathiegefühle,* 2nd ed., Bonn, 1923).

(17) It may be objected that we are now defending a procedure which we have just denied ; namely, the inference from functional to descriptive facts. In reply, I would say that I have opposed such an inference on account of the false conclusions which have been drawn therefrom. Here, however, our conclusion is drawn from functional observations which terminate in functional activities, though by the roundabout way of descriptive concepts. This functional inference can, however, be tested ; therefore the descriptive middle-term can do no harm, and may be of the greatest benefit in reaching an explanation. Cf. also Köhler's discussion with reference to consciousness in animal-psychology. *OU,* p. 56 A.

(18) *Z,* p. 58.

(19) To be sure, now one part and now the other, is more strongly developed according to the living conditions of the animal. Cf. Edinger, *Z,* p. 59.

(20) *Z,* p. 507.

(21) Under certain conditions experimenter and observer may be the same person.

(22) Cf. with this, Chap. IV., p. 234.

(23) Cf. Bühler's discussion, *GE,* p. 53 ff.

(24) In Chap. IV., p. 193, an application of this procedure to animal-psychology is described.

(25) Detailed instructions for planning and keeping child-diaries are given by Stern, *PsdK,* p. 13 f.

(26) O. Külpe, Psychologie und Medizin. *Ztschr. f. Pathopsychologie,* I., 1912, p. 12 of the separate edition.

# NOTES

## NOTES TO CHAPTER II

(27) Cases are not here considered in which the conditions of life of an individual or of a species suddenly undergo a marked change.

(28) Cf. in this connection, Lloyd Morgan, p. 16 f.

(29) *PS*, pp. 299–300.

(30) Bühler has recently spoken of the " chimpanzee-age " of the child. *GE*, p. 77.

(31) *I*, p. 75 (66). Cf. also his description of the animal's behaviour when touched with an electrically-charged wire, *I*, p. 65 (58).

(32) R. A. Acher, " Spontaneous Constructions and Primitive Activities of Children Analogous to those of Primitive Man," *Amer. Journal of Psychology*, 1910, *21*.

(33) A clear and straightforward presentation may be found in the *Naturphilosophie* of E. Becher, *Kultur der Gegenwart*, Leipzig and Berlin, 1914.

(34) Claparède, p. 188.

(35) According to Claparède, p. 188, note.

(36) *Sp*, p. 263.

(37) Cf. Groos, *SK*, p. 8.

(38) *PsdK*, p. 224.

(39) In other places Stern advances other views which 1 can not list here. He finds the inner essence of human unity in recapitulation, and speaks of the common heritage of the entelechy-character which passes from the species to the individual. But these conceptions can be understood only in relation to his philosophical system, and are consequently outside the range of our discussion. Cf. *PS*, p. 324 f., *MP*, p. 110.

(40) Cf. Claparède, p. 188 f.

(41) *PsdK*, p. 18. Cf. also *MP*, p. 95 ff.

(42) Most of the psychological text-books—and especially the large works of Ebbinghaus, Wundt, and Watson—contain detailed descriptions ; as does also Becher's *GS*.

(43) Edinger, *Z*, p. 46.

(44) *Z*, p. 522. Some time ago I discussed Edinger's views in a brief paper entitled : " Ein neuer Versuch eines objectiven Systems der Psychologie," *Ztschr. f. Psychol.*, *61*, 1912.

(45) *Z*, p. 523.

(46) L. Edinger and B. Fischer, " Ein Mensch ohne Grosshirn," *Archiv. f. d. ges. Physiol.*, *152*, 1913.

(47) Cf. l.c., p. 27.


## NOTES TO CHAPTER III

(48) Soltmann, " Über einige physiologische Eigentümlichkeiten der Muskeln und Nerven der Neugeborener," *Jahrbuch für Kinderheilkunde*, *12*, 1878.

(49) Cf. M. Gildemeister, " Über einige Analogien zwischen der Wirkung optischer und elektrischer Reize," *Ztschr. f. Sinnesphysiol.*, *48*, 1914 ; also P. Cermak and K. Koffka, " Untersuchungen über Bewegungs- und Verschmelzungsphänomene," *Psychol. Forschung*,

1, 1921, especially p. 100 f. The term *fusion* which is used in the text corresponds with customary terminology, but tells us absolutely nothing in regard to the theory of the phenomenon. A theoretical discussion will be found in the second article cited above.

(50) This number is dependent upon so many factors that we shall here be obliged to content ourselves with an approximate statement.

(51) With very rapidly moving motion - pictures a different phenomenon appears. Motion is again lost, and one sees the moving object multiplied. For example, a gymnast jumping over a horse may be seen, during the jump, with six stationary legs. The same phenomenon of multiplication is well known with alternating beams of light—as produced, for example, when the hand with out-spread fingers is moved rapidly back and forth.

(52) Cf. Preyer, I, p. 44, Bühler, *GE*, p. 97, and Moore, p. 57.

(53) It is not denied that experience may be involved in the development of seen-movement, but the question is *how ?*

(54) The authors do not draw this conclusion, but are very cautious in expressing themselves on this point. Cf. *op. cit.* p. 1.

(55) *Ibid.*, p. 4. Also, when Preyer asserts (I, p. 214) that a child born without a cortex produced crude sounds when his back was rubbed, this does not seem to have been an altogether normal reaction.

(56) Preyer, I, pp. 196–7.

(57) *PsdK*, pp. 31–2.

(58) As Preyer points out, such movements may of course under certain conditions be directly harmful. Thus a child may during sleep open one eye with a movement of its hand and go on sleeping with this eye open.

(59) The same state of affairs is naturally to be found in the sensory field, where it is referred to as the " law of specific sense-energies " (Johannes Müller). Also, the processes which take place in the sensory centres of the brain as correlates of the pheno-mena of sense-perception are the specific processes characteristic of distinct domains. The reader will find a brief presentation of the data on this subject in an article by W. Nagel, " Die Lehre von den spezifischen Sinnes-energien," *Handbuch der Physiologie*, edited by W. Nagel, *3*, 1905, p. 1.

(60) For an orientation into the complicated subject of eye-movements, which can only be touched upon here—and also for the facts concerning space-perception in general—the following book is recommended : St. Witasek, *Psychologie der Raumwahrneh-mung des Auges*, Heidelberg, 1910. References to other original sources will be found in subsequent notes.

(61) Ewald Hering, *Die Lehre vom binokularen Sehen* (first part). Leipzig, 1868, p. 22 and p. 3.

(62) H. v. Helmholtz, *Handbuch der physiologischen Optik.*, 3rd ed., revised by Gullstrand, Von Kries, and Nagel, *3*, Leipzig, 1910, p. 48.

(63) Cf. with this, Hering, *op. cit.*, p. 18 ff.

(64) *Ibid.*, pp. 22–23. Köhler has observed the same relations in the co-ordinations of chimpanzees, *I*, p. 189 (173).

(65) Cf. Von Kries' statement in Helmholtz's book cited above, p. 514 (note).

(66) *Ibid.*, p. 511 ff.

# NOTES

(67) Cf. *PB*, p. 243 f.

(68) Cf. Bühler, *GE*, p. 95 f.

(69) Bühler, *GE*, p. 97. The italics are mine. Bühler reaches no decision whether the connection is inherited or acquired, and whether it is brought about by maturation or by experience.

(70) This last behaviour is designated as the *principle of the greatest horopter*. Cf. with this, E. Hering, *Beiträge zur Physiologie, 4*, Leipzig, 1864, p. 261 ff.

(71) Hering's principle of avoiding illusory movement, *ibid.*, p. 265 ff. Helmholtz's related principle of easiest orientation (*op. cit.*, p. 55) which Hering attacks, shows by its name the close relation between seeing and eye-movements.

(72) *PhG.*

(73) Cf. Köhler, *PhG*, pp. 27, 201–2, 262–3. Investigations which A. Marina published, first in 1905, and then in revised form in 1910, are in full agreement with Köhler's point of view. Marina operated upon apes, first by exchanging the medial rectus and lateral rectus muscles of an eye, and later so as to substitute the superior rectus for the lateral rectus. In the first case, therefore, the eye was moved outward by the previously inward-moving muscle, and *vice versa*. In the second case the muscle moving the eye outward was eliminated and its place taken by a lifting muscle. If a definite impulse were conducted from the centre through the pathway to each muscle, the animal must have made the most remarkable eye-movements after the wound had healed. But, instead, the voluntary and automatic sideward movements of the eyes were carried out in a normal manner as soon as the cicatrization was complete. From this and other results the author concludes " that the anatomical association-pathways from the centres to the eye-muscles are not fixed," and that the *conduction pathways have no predetermined function*. Considering the results of other operations of transplantation, he seeks to justify his attribution of a very general significance to this conclusion, and demands a new foundation for the physiology of the brain. The validity of his inference and its bearing upon brain-anatomy and physiological psychology is also admitted by Ziehen in a review of one of Marina's investigations, though out of respect for the older theory Ziehen thinks that certain errors have probably been made in the experiments. Cf. A. Marina, " Die Relationen des Palaeencephalons (Edinger) sind nicht fix," *Neurol. Centralbl.*, *34*, 1915, pp. 338–345, and the review of this article by Ziehen in the *Zeitschr. f. Psychol.*, *73*, 1915, pp. 142–3.

(74) Cf. Preyer, I, p. 79 ; Shinn, I, p. 22, 109 f., and 129.

(75) Cf. Thorndike, *EP*, p. 48 ; Preyer, I, p. 256 ; Watson, *PB*, p. 241.

(76) Preyer, I, p. 259.

(77) According to Compayré, I, p. 83–4.

(78) Cf. above all, Lloyd Morgan, then Preyer, I, p. 236 ff., and James, II, p. 383 ff.

(79) Morgan, pp. 122–4. A similar observation may be found in James, II, p. 400.

(80) James, II, p. 385. James' chapter on instinct is written with all the charm of his vivid style of presentation. Although I

cannot subscribe to his theoretical conclusions, I recommend the reading of this chapter most highly. A brief statement of the history of the concept of instinct may be found in Groos, *PA*, p. 25 ff.

(81) p. 106.                                    (82) Thorndike, *EP*, p. 1.

(83) *EP*, p. 123 ff.                        (84) *EP*, p. 134, repeated from *AI*, p. 35.

(85) *GS*, p. 397 ff.

(86) Cf. Köhler, *I*, for example p. 51, (46), and elsewhere.

(87) In a recent paper H. C. Link has reached conclusions similar to those appearing in the sequel of our text. Cf. *Amer. Journal of Psychology*, *33*, 1922.

(88) Cf. Groos, *PM*, p. 146.

(89) W. McDougall, "Use and Abuse of Instinct in Social Psychology," *Jour. of Abn. and Soc. Psychol.*, *16*, 1921-2, pp. 293, 325, 330; *Outline of Psychology*, 1923, pp. 110, 128; Lloyd Morgan, "Instinctive Behaviour and Enjoyment," *British Journal of Psychology*, *12*, 1921.

(90) *PhG*, p. xiii. Counterparts of our concepts of end- and transitional situations are found by the vitalists in the morphologico-physiological domain. Thus Driesch distinguishes between "completeness" and "incompleteness,' and defines the former as "allowing no sequential processes to take place from *internal* causes without a co-ordinate disturbance of form." Cf. H. Driesch, *Die organischen Regulationen, Vorbereitungen zu einer Theorie des Lebens*, Leipzig, 1901, p. 84.

(91) M. Wertheimer, "Experimentelle Studien über das Sehen von Bewegungen," *Ztschr. f. Psychol.*, *61*, 1912, p. 251 f. (Frankf. Habil-Schr., p. 91).

(92) These conditions, which I have omitted from the text, in order not to confuse readers who are not proficient in natural science, have been formulated by Köhler as follows (*PhG*, p. 250): "In every process which issues at all in an end-situation, independent of time, the mode of distribution shifts in the direction of a minimum of configurative energy." The last-mentioned considerations in the text all follow Köhler's book. The next citation in the text being from p. 257.

(93) In the article referred to in note *89*, McDougall also vigorously refutes the hypothesis that instincts may be explained in terms of connections between neurones, but he is less radical than we are, since he leaves the existence of motor mechanisms unquestioned. According to McDougall an instinct employs divers motor mechanisms on different occasions. *Op. cit.*, p. 116 f. Our considerations are based upon instinctive activities which lead to an immediate conclusion, such as nest-building, etc. Aside from these there are others the successful termination of which is only felt a long time after the performance has taken place, and sometimes only by the organism of the following generation. For these instances, our discussion is inadequate, as one of my critics has rightly pointed out (*Psychologische Forschung*, *3*, p. 203). It is certainly of importance, though it would be a difficult task, to extend our hypothesis, so that it might be adequate to cover all these instances.

(94) Bergson has devoted a detailed investigation of the philosophy of nature to the relation of instinct and intelligence. For him instinct and intelligence represent two different and equally

364

attractive solutions to one and the same problem. Cf. *Creative Evolution*, New York, 1911, p. 135 ff., viz. especially p. 143. Recent discussions of the problem of instinct have led to the expression of many ideas similar to those of this text ; for instance Lloyd Morgan's article cited in note *89*, and I. R. Kantor's " The Psychology of Reflex-Action," in the *American Journal of Psychology*, *23*, 1922.

(95) *GS*, p. 401.

(96) *PsdK*, p. 34.

(97) *A G*, p. 46.

(98) Cf. Morgan, p. 41.

(99) Cf. Kafka, p. 466.

(100) This conclusion is also maintained by McDougall.

(101) Cf. Watson, *B*, p. 125 f.

(102) *I*, p. 64 (58).

(103) *I*, p. 75 (68).

(104) Thorndike, curiously enough, thinks it probable that ornamenting, tatooing, etc., are modes of behaviour acquired by successful achievements. Cf. *EP*, p. 140.

(105) Quoted from Thorndike, *EP*, p. 159 note.

(106) Cf. Köhler, *Methoden* (note *12*), p. 75 ff., especially 79, and 100 ff.

(107) Bühler, *GE*, p. 86.

(108) The ear seems to furnish an exception, since at birth the middle-ear is filled with fluid instead of air so that no transfer of tone-stimulation to the sense-organ within the inner-ear can take place. All new-born infants are therefore deaf, but they react to sound as soon as the fluid has disappeared from the middle-ear.

(109) *PsdK*, p. 37.

(110) To my knowledge it has not yet been demonstrated whether the protective reflex-action of the *tensor tympani* (the drum-membrane muscle) is already functional ; and such a demonstration might be difficult to make, but probabilities favour the conclusion that it is functional.

(111) *GE*, 1st ed. (1918), p. 355.

(112) *EP*, p. 301 ff.

(113) Cf. with this the discussion of Volkelt with reference to " learning capacity " and " incapacity to learn," p. 120 ff.

(114) I, p. 295.

(115) Cf. in this connection Köhler, *PhG*, pp. 52 ff., 192, 207. The phenomenal and functional differences between figure and ground have been treated in detail in a monograph by E. Rubin : *Synsoplevede Figurer*, Köbenhavn og Kristiania, 1915. (German ed. : *Visuell wahrgenommene Figuren*, Copenhagen, 1921).

(116) The assertion of the existence of these simplest elements does not necessarily include the assertion of their temporal priority. (Cf. Stern, *PsdK*, p. 56). But even Stern's own view seems to me insufficient. It is not enough to recognize the mere diffuseness by which he characterizes the original state. See the little paper by Wertheimer on the principles involved in these matters which has just appeared : " Untersuchungen zur Lehre von der Gestalt. I, Prinzipielle Bemerkungen," *Psychologische Forschung*, *1*, 1921.

# NOTES

(117) This fact is emphasized particularly by Mrs Moore. For example, p. 51.

(118) Stern, *PsdK*, p. 61.

(119) *StF*, p. 49 (note).

(120) Cf. Scheler, *Sympathie* (note *16*), p. 275.

(121) Cf. for example Stern, *PsdK*, p. 38.

(122) Cf. Lévy-Bruhl, p. 27 ff.

(123) M. Brod and F. Weltsch, *Auschauung und Begriff*, Leipzig, 1913, p. 6.

(124) So Wertheimer reported at the 5th Congress for experimental psychology in Berlin, 1912.

(125) The method employed by Katz and Révész, in which the " grain denied to the fowl " was simply glued fast to the plate, can not be employed with large and powerful birds, which are able to tear the grain loose. Cf. Köhler, *OU*, p. 58.

(126) Köhler, *StF*, pp. 12–13.

(127) *StF*, p. 24.


## NOTES TO CHAPTER IV

(128) Cf. for example Thorndike, *EP*, pp. 25, 201.

(129) Exact descriptions of the conditions of the experiment may be found in Thorndike, *AI*, and in Watson, *B*.

(130) An arrangement of the opposite kind is also possible, where the food is in the box and the animal outside ; but this does not in any way alter the principle. Cf. Watson, *B*.

(131) p. 165.

(132) *GE*, pp. 5, 113.

(133) *GE*, p. 209.

(134) *AI*, p. 108 f.

(135) *GE*, p. 6.

(136) *AI*, p. 108 f.

(137) Watson, *B*, pp. 186, 259–60.

(138) Cf. the following with Watson, *B*, p. 262 f.

(139) Cf. Thorndike, *EP*, p. 185 ff.

(140) Cf. Watson, *B*, p. 257. In his second book, Watson expresses himself with greater restraint. After discussing four theoretical possibilities, he recognizes the hypothetical character of the whole matter and refrains from accepting any one of them. *PB*, p. 294–5.

(141) Thorndike subsumes under this law two groups of facts : that a bond is strengthened by use, and that it is weakened by long disuse. *EP*, p. 171 f.

(142) *GE*, p. 113.

(143) According to Stout, in *A Manual of Psychology*, 3rd ed., London, 1913, p. 382. Cf. in general, Stout's keen criticism of Thorndike's theory. Examples like those cited in the text will also be found in Thorndike, *AI*, p. 72.

(144) *EP*, p. 188 f.

(145) *EP*, p. 172 f.

# NOTES

(146) *EP*, pp. 281–2.

(147) *AI*, pp. 43–4.

(148) Lloyd Morgan, pp. 152–3.

(149) *AI*, p. 119.

(150) Cf. with this Köhler, *I*, p. 19 f. (16 f.).

(151) Not all the curves have been reproduced. One of an animal which was first tested in the wooden-latch box appears more like the second curves reproduced by us in Fig. 8.

(152) *AI*, p. 48. The italics are mine.

(153) *AI*, p. 119.

(154) Cf. with this *AI*, p. 117 f. ; and Köhler, *I*, pp. 10 (8), 142 (130).

(155) Köhler, *I*, p. 20 (17).

(156) Thorndike, *AI*, p. 48.

(157) McDougall, *Outline*, p. 196 ff.

(158) H. A. Ruger, " The Psychology of Efficiency," *Archives of Psychology*, Nr. 15, 1910.

(159) *Ibid.*, p. 9.

(160) Köhler, *I*.

(161) *I*, p. 5 (3).

(162) Recently also J. Peiser, " Prüfungen höherer Gehirnfunktionen bei Kleinkindern," *Jhb. f. Kinderheilkunde und physische Erziehung, 91,* 1920.

(163) *I*, p. 9 (6, 7).

(164) *I*, p. 22 (19). The same results were obtained in similar experiments made by W. T. Shepherd. Dogs and cats can not make use of string-connections (or even simpler relations), but Rhesus monkeys—which do not belong to the anthropoids—have no such difficulty. Cf. " Tests on Adaptive Intelligence in Rhesus Monkeys," *Amer. Jour. of Psych., 26,* 1915.

(165) *I*, p. 31 (28).

(166) *I*, p. 28 (25).

(167) Bühler, *GE*, p. 21.

(168) Köhler, *I*, p. 33 ff. (30 ff.).

(169) One can not interpret this behaviour as indicating merely that the box was previously too heavy for the animal, because in an earlier experiment the ape had actually pushed a box upon which Tercera was lying ; but the problem then was only one of removing an obstacle. Cf. *I*, p. 141 (128 f.).

(170) *I*, p. 100 f. (91 f.).

(171) *I*, p. 105 ff. (96 ff.).

(172) *I*, p. 181 (166).

(173) Cf. also *I*, p. 191–2 (175).

(174) *I*, p. 197 (180).

(175) *I*, p. 151 (138).

(176) *I*, pp. 153–4 (140 f.). Cf. with this also the above mentioned results of Ruger (pp. 127–8).

(177) *I*, p. 123 (112).

(178) *I*, p. 186 (170). According to the general plan of his work, Köhler leaves the decision open between the explanation we have

# NOTES

made in the text and some other possibility. But after his later publications, *StF*, and *PhG*, there can be no doubt as to which possibility he really accepts.

(179) *GE*, p. 9 ff. ; *AG*, p. 16 ff.

(180) Cf. with this *GE*, p. 390.

(181) Cf. also Bühler, *Die Gestaltwahrnehmungen*, I, Stuttgart, 1913, p. 16 ff. I do not believe that Bühler still maintains this doctrine in all strictness ; although other passages in *GE* (p. 358), besides the one cited, indicate a like tendency. In still another chapter Bühler develops quite a different theory of perceived relations, which can not be here considered. Köhler refutes it, however, in a recent article, " Zur Theorie des Sukzessivvergleichs und der Zeitfehler.," *Psychol. Forschung, 4*, 1923, p. 125 ff.

(182) The doctrine of unnoticed sensations, which finds its classical expression in the first volume of Stumpf's *Tonpsychologie* (1883), was attacked by Cornelius in his *Psychologie als Erfahrungswissenschaft* (1897). More recently Köhler has written a paper bearing directly upon this subject : " Über unbemerkte Empfindungen und Urteilstäuschungen," *Ztschr. f. Psychol., 66*, 1913. Cf. also my paper : " Probleme der experimentellen Psychologie," in *Die Naturwissenschaften, 5*, 1917, Nos. 1 and 2.

(183) *GE*, pp. 350, 354 f.

(184) *Stimmen der Zeit, 95*, 1918, p. 391.

(185) Cf. especially *GE*, pp. 17, 25.

(186) I must, indeed, express doubt as to whether this can be readily explained as an after-effect of memory. (Cf. above p. 206).

(187) *GE*, p. 14 f.

(188) *GE*, p. 22.

(189) Bühler speaks (*GE*, p. 25) of a (relatively) vivid impulse of imagining.

(190) Cf. Köhler, *I*, pp. 210–11 (192) ; and Bühler, *GE*, p. 312.

(191) Thorndike's criticism is directed against the formulation of just such hypotheses.

(192) *Op. cit.*, p. 288.

(193) *Ibid.*, p. 391.

(194) Cf. the following with Köhler, *StF*, p. 56 ff.

(195) *Stimmen der Zeit, 97*, 1919, p. 66. Meanwhile J. Lindworsky has published a clearly written paper upon his general psychological theories, with special reference to his theory of relations. (Cf. " Unriss-skizze zu einer theoretischen Psychologie," *Zeitschrift für Psychologie, 89*, 1922). This theory of relations is critically examined by Köhler in the article cited in note *181*.

(196) Cf. Volkelt, p. 15 ff.

(197) " Einige Allgemeinere Fragen der Psychologie und Biologie des Denkens, erläutert an der Lehre vom Vergleich," *Arb. z. Psychol. u. Phil.*, edited by E. R. Jaensch, I, Leipzig, 1920. Apparently Köhler's publication was unknown to Jaensch, since he does not mention it.

(198) Köhler, *StF*, p. 13. We have already given the full quotation on p. 140.

(199) Jaensch, *op. cit.*, p. 24. Cf. Bühler, *GE*, p. 174, and the similar statements of Lindworsky, *Stimmen der Zeit, 97*, p. 64 f.

# NOTES

(200) Jaensch, *op. cit.*, p. 21.

(201) According to Jaensch (p. 20), transitional experiences are " of the same kind as the phenomena of movement described by Linke, Wertheimer, and Koffka." But these phenomena of movement are from our point of view only typical phenomena of configuration. Cf. also Wertheimer's work cited in note *91*.

(202) *Op. cit.*, p. 28.

(203) Cf. with this Köhler's discussion in the work cited in note *182*.

(204) *GE*, pp. 177–8.

(205) Cf. Köhler's " Akustische Untersuchungen," especially III and IV, " Vorläufige Mittlg.," *Ztschr. f. Psychol.*, *64*, 1913, p. 99 ff. and III, *ibid.*, *72*, 1915, p. 121 ff. This conclusion has now been fully confirmed by the investigation of M. Eberhardt performed in Köhler's laboratory, which reduces clang-analysis to quantitative terms. Cf. " Über die phänomenale Höhe und Stärke von Teiltönen," *Psychologische Forschung*, *2*, 1922.

(206) This law cuts across another ; viz. that *ceteris paribus*, the colour-threshold is lower for a dark field than for a bright one. The fact reported in the text was first pointed out by Stumpf (" Die Attribute der Gesichtsempfindungen," *Abhdlg. d. K. Preuss. Ak. d. Wiss.*, Jhrg., 1917, *Phil.-Hist. Kl.*, Nr. 8, p. 84 f. which includes references to earlier investigations of the subject). I myself reported an investigation before the *Naturforscher-Versammlung* at Nauheim (1920) which substantiates and supplements Stumpf's conclusions, and I employed then the point of view of the psychology of configuration. These experiments have since been carried forward in my laboratory, and published in the *Psychologische Forschung*, *5*, 1924. Even the differential threshold for brightness is dependent upon the brightness of the field surrounding the surface to be tested, and the threshold is minimal when background and surface tested have the same degree of brightness. This was demonstrated by F. Dittmers in the Göttingen laboratory (" Über die Abhängigkeit der Unterschiedsschwelle für Helligkeiten von der antagonistischen Induktion," *Ztschr. f. Sinnesphysiol.*, *51*, 1920). But to find here a configurative uniformity does not mean that an exact physico-chemical explanation must be given up, and the advantages of the Müller colour-theory abandoned ; for configurative uniformities are also physico-chemical —a statement which is hardly necessary to readers of Köhler's book on physical configurations.

(207) Cf. also the discussion of transitional sensations in Köhler's paper cited in note *181*.

(208) Certainly it does not agree with the description Köhler gives (*OU*, pp. 59–60) of learning in hens.

(209) Köhler, *I*, p. 101 (92).

(210) *Stimmen der Zeit*, p. 66.

(211) *GE*, p. 2 ff. Cf. also p. 390.

(212) Cf. Bühler, *GE*, p. 4.

(213) Köhler, *StF*, p. 51.

(214) *StF*, pp. 85–6.

(215) Cf. G. E. Müller, " Zur Analyse der Gedächtnistätigkeit und des Vorstellungsverlaufs," I, Erg.-Bd. *5*, d. *Ztschr. f. Psychol.*, 1911, pp. 332 ff., 372.

(216) *Ibid.*, III., Erg.-Bd. *8*, 1913, p. 210 f.

# NOTES

(217) Cf. A. Aall, " Ein neues Gedächtnisgesetz," *Ztschr. f. Psychol.*, *68*, 1913, p. 43 f.

(218) Cf. A. Kühn, " Über Einprägung durch Lesen und Rezitieren," *Ztschr. f. Psychol.*, *68*, 1914, p. 396 ff., especially pp. 443, 473 f.

(219) Cf. K. Lewin, " Die psychische Tätigkeit bei der Hemmung von Willensvorgängen und das Grundgesetz der Assoziation," *Ztschr. f. Psychol.*, *77*, 1917, p. 245 ; and " Das Problem der Willensmessung und das Grundgesetz der Assoziation," *Psychol. Forschung, 1* and *2*, 1922.

(220) Cf. Von Kries, *Über die materiellen Grundlagen der Bewusstseins-Erscheinungen*, Tübingen und Leipzig, 1901 ; and Becher, *GS*, p. 161–327.

(221) *Op. cit.*, pp. 41–42.

(222) *GS*, p. 284 ff.

(223) The complacency with which the American behaviour-psychologists ignore this criticism is truly astounding.

## NOTES TO CHAPTER V

(224) *PsdK*, p. 64.   Cf. also Groos, *SK*, p. 34.

(225) Shinn, I, p. 22, *PsdK*, p. 62.

(226) Cf. also Bühler, *GE*, p. 302.

(227) Bühler, *GE*, p. 319.

(228) *EA*, p. 3 ff. :   *PsdK*, p. 139 ff. :   Bühler, *GE*, p. 299 f.

(229) Cf. Stern, *PsdK*, p. 156.

(230) Cf. E. R. Jaensch, " Die experimentelle Analyse der Anschauungsbilder als Hilfsmittel zur Untersuchung der Wahrnehmungs- und Denkvorgänge," *Sitz.-Ber. d. Ges. z. Bef. d. Ges. Naturwiss,* zu Marburg, 1917, No. 5.   The same : " Zur Methodik experimenteller Untersuchungen an optischen Anschauungsbildern," *Ztschr. f. Psychol.*, *85*, 1920.   Paula Busse, " Über die Gedächtnisstufen und ihre Beziehung zum Aufbau der Wahrnehmungswelt," *Ztschr. f. Psychol.*, *84*, 1920.   A vast amount of work has since been published by Jaensch and his students, a comprehensive view of which may be had from Jaensch's " Über die subjektiven Anschauungsbilder," *Bericht über d. VII. Kongress f. Exper. Psychol. in Marburg*, Jena, 1922, p. 3–49 ; from O. Kroh, *Subjektive Anschauungsbilder der Jugendlichen*, Göttingen, 1922, and from my critical report in the *Psychol. Forschung, 3*, 1923.

(231) Jaensch, *Sitz.-Ber.*, pp. 64, 5.

(232) Busse, *op. cit.*, p. 43 ff.

(233) *Sp*, p. 362 ff.

(234) O. Selz, *Über die Gesetze des geordneten Denkver aufs*, I, Stuttgart, 1913.

(235) L. Schlüter, " Experimentalle Beiträge zur Prüfung der Anschauungs- und Übersetzungsmethode bei der Einführung in einen fremdsprachlichen Wortschatz," *Ztschr. f. Psychol.*, *68*, 1914, p. 103 f.   Cf. also the chapter on association by similarity in my book *Zur Analyse der Vorstellungen und ihrer Gesetze*, Leipzig, 1912, pp. 343–360.

# NOTES

(236) R. Heine, " Über Wiedererkennen und rückwirkende Hemmung," *Ztschr. f. Psychol.*, *68*, 1914.

(237) In the book just cited, p. 344 ff., which also contains a bibliography. Cf. also Wertheimer, *op. cit.*, p. 252 (note).

(238) Cf. Watson, *B*, p. 138 ff.

(239) Cf. Compayré, I, p. 287 f.

(240) Preyer, I, p. 241 ff. ; Shinn, I, p. 306 ff. ; Watson, *PB*, p. 275 ff.

(241) *GE*, p. 113. Cf. also p. 8.

(242) *GE*, pp. 102–3.

(243) *Op. cit.* (note *220*), pp. 21, 32 f.

(244) Shinn, I, pp. 306–7.

(245) Compayré, II, p. 9 f. Cf. also Preyer, I, p. 283 f.

(246) *Sp*, p. 15 ; *PsdK*, p. 47. Cf. also Bühler, *GE*, pp. 205–6.

(247) L. E. Ordahl, " Consciousness in Relation to Learning," *Amer. Jour. of Psychol.*, *22*, 1911, p. 189.

(248) E. C. Rowe, " Voluntary Movement," *Amer. Journ. of Psychol.*, *21*, 1910, p. 331.

(249) W. Betz, *Psychologie des Denkens*, Leipzig, 1918, p. 48 f.

(250) *Op. cit.*, p. 181 ff.

(251) *I*, p. 139 (126), note.

(252) With reference to the very interesting observations made by A. Gelb and K. Goldstein on a patient with high grade optical agnosia and a total loss of " visual imagery," special attention should be called to the following statement : " The co-operation of vision in the act of grasping develops in such a way that the grasped object is first seen, but only later is the seen object grasped.' Cf. *Psychologische Analysen Hirnpathologischer Fälle*, I, Leipzig, 1920.

(253) Cf. Stern, *PsdK*, p. 121.

(254) C. W. Valentine, " The Colour Perception and Colour Preferences of an Infant during its fourth and eighth months." *British Journal of Psychology*, 1914, *6*, p. 363 ff.

(255) W. A. Holden and K. K. Bosse, " The order of Development of Colour Perception and Colour Preference in the Child," *Archives of Ophthalmology*, 1900, *29*, 261 ff.

(256) *Sp*, p. 229. The italics are mine.

(257) The Sterns write (*Sp*, p. 229) " that the difference between variegated and non-variegated colours is much more striking and important to the child than the difference between the different colours themselves." Their explanation in terms of attention and lack of interest, instead of in terms of sensory factors, is refuted in our text.

(258) Of the protanopic type (red-weak).

(259) Cf. A. Binet, " Perceptions d'Enfants," *Rev. Philos.*, *30*, 1890, and Winch, " Colour-Names of English School Children," *Amer. Jour. of Psychol.*, *21*, 1910.

(260) Preyer also recognizes (I, p. 21) that this can not be altogether a matter of naming.

(261) Bühler, *GE*, p. 184.

(262) Köhler, *StF*, pp. 67–72. With the pair AB, B was chosen

# NOTES

19 times out of 20, and with the pair DE, E was selected in each of the 21 trials.

(263) Stumpf, *Spe*, p. 20.

(264) W. Peters, "Zur Entwicklung der Farbenwahrnehmung nach Versuchen an abnormen Kindern," *Fortschr. d. Psychol.*, 3, 1915, pp. 152–3.

(265) *Op. cit.*, pp. 161–2.

(266) The first part of the conclusion has not been completely demonstrated either, since no tests were made with violet samples. The erroneous classification of purple occurred only with the purple and not with the red sample. An analogous behaviour with the violet sample would therefore be *a priori* possible.

(267) According to a report which K. Goldstein made before the Psychological Congress at Marburg (April 1921), it appears to me possible, if not even probable, that another and more direct relation exists between speech and colour-perceptions than the one assumed in the text. Goldstein's publication should bring evidence on this point.

(268) D. Katz, "Die Erscheinungsweisen der Farben und ihre Beeinflussung durch die individuelle Erfahrung," Erg.-Bd., 7, d. *Zeitschr. f. Psychol.*, 1911.

(269) A. Gelb, "Über den Wegfall der Wahrnehmung von 'Oberflächenfarben.'" In the collaborative work cited in note *252*, p. 408. (Also in *Zeitschr. f. Psychol.*, *84*, 1920, p. 247).

(270) *OU*, p. 39 ff. ; and "Die Farben der Sehdinge beim Schimpansen und beim Haushuhn," *Ztschr. f. Psychol.*, 77, 1919.

(271) Cf. Compayré, I, p. 104 ; Stern, *PsdK*, p. 70 ff.

(272) Details concerning these facts may be found in both of Jaensch's books, Erg.-Bde., *4* and *6* d. *Ztschr. f. Psychol.*, 1909 and 1911 ; and also in M. Jacobson's "Über die Erkennbarkeit optischer Figuren bei gleichen Netzhautbild und verschiedener scheinbarer Grösse," *Ztschr. f. Psychol.*, 77, 1917.

(273) Cf. Katz, *op. cit.*, p. 97.

(274) Cf. Stern, *PsdK*, p. 72 ; Bühler, *GE*, p. 336. In another place (p. 146), to be sure, Bühler expresses himself much more cautiously.

(275) *OU*, p. 18 ff. A theoretical discussion is also given here.

(276) Cf. here again Jaensch's books cited in note *272*.

(277) That stimulation of the eyes by light is necessary for the development of the optical centres is shown by Claparède's report (pp. 126–7), that the visual centres of cats whose eyelids were sewn together at birth were arrested in their development. Cf. also Becher, *GS*, p. 177 f.

(278) *PsdK*, p. 72.

(279) *Op. cit.* (note *230*), p. 59. Cf. also my critique cited in note *230*.

(280) *PsdK*, p. 120. The perception of simple geometrical forms can be tested systematically with the aid of outlines, instead of by Miss Shinn's method. According to Preyer's statements (I, p. 65) the results might then be quite different and more favourable. Thus at the end of the second year a child called a sketched circle a "ring," a square a "window," a triangle a "roof," etc.

It may also be mentioned that in an investigation which

# NOTES

Groos made with a five-year-old girl he found that regularly formed figures were preferred to irregular figures—a result which deserves further investigation. Cf. *PM*, p. 62.

(281) Lévy-Bruhl, pp. 188–9.

(282) *PsdK*, p. 123 f.  Cf. also W. Stern, "Über verlagerte Raumformen," *Ztschr. f. angew. Psychol.*, *2*, 1909 ; and Bühler, *GE*, p. 148.

(283) *GE*, pp. 368–9.  Cf. also the statements by Betz, *op. cit.*, (cf. note *249*), p. 50 f.

(284) J. Wittmann, *Über das Sehen von Scheinbewegungen und Scheinkörpern.*, Leipzig, 1921.  Tables 5 and 6.

(285) Cf. Wittmann, *op. cit.*, p. 171 ff.

(286) *GE*, p. 254.

(287) *Op. cit.*, pp. 162–171.

(288) Cf. Köhler, *PhG*, p. 253 ff.

(289) Stern and Bühler do the same.

(290) *Sp*, p. 212 ; *PsdK*, p. 131 f. ; cf. also *EA*, pp. 9, 16.

(291) *GE*, p. 129.

(292) *GE*, p. 130.

(293) Cl. and W. Stern, *Sp*, p. 163.  Cf. the following with *ibid.*, p. 164 ff.

(294) *PB*, p. 278 f.

(295) K. Lewin, "Kriegslandschaft," *Ztschr. f. angew. Psychol.*, *12*, 1917.

(296) Cf. Bühler, *GE*, pp. 208–9 ; Stern, *Sp*, pp. 155, 269.

(297) *GE*, p. 77 ff.; *AG*, p. 50 ff.

(298) *I*, p. 13 (10).

(299) *I*, p. 193 (176).

(300) Preyer, II, p. 12.

(301) Cf. Thorndike, *AI*, p. 89 f. ; and Chas. S. Berry, "An Experimental Study of Imitation in Cats," *Jour. of Compar. Neurol. and Psychol.*, *18*, 1908, p. 24.

(302) Cf. Morgan, p. 168 ff. ; Stern, *PsdK*, p. 48 ; Groos, *SK*, p. 52 ; Thorndike, *EP*, p. 108 ff.

(303) Cf. with this and with what follows, Stern, *PsdK*, p. 47 ; *Sp*, p. 148 ff. ; and J. Mark Baldwin, *Mental Development in the Child and the Race*, New York, 1895.

(304) Cf. Preyer, I, p. 90 ; Stumpf, *Tonpsychologie*, I (1883), p. 293 f. ; II (1890), p. 553 ff.

(305) Cf. Preyer, II, p. 257.

(306) Stern, *Sp*, p. 153.

(307) Claparède, p. 142.

(308) In the meaning of Köhler's book, *PhG*.

(309) Cf. Moore, p. 18.

(310) A confirmation of this principle is found in the behaviour of Stumpf's son who suddenly repeated four short prayers correctly and " almost faultlessly " after he had been speaking only his own language for years with never a word of the mother tongue.  " That he should utter the words almost faultlessly after talking a strange language, so to speak, up to this time, is certainly noteworthy," writes Stumpf.  Cf. *SpE*, p. 22.

# NOTES

(311) Cf. with this the statements of Groos, *PM*, p. 286.

(312) *I*, p. 176 (161).

(313) Cf. Stern's summary, *Sp*, p. 158 f., and with what follows, *ibid.*, p. 175 ff.

(314) *GE*, p. 374 ff. ; and also simpler and clearer, I think, in *AG*, p. 58 f.

(315) Cf. Stern, *PsdK*, p. 243 ; *Sp*, p. 178.

(316) *Op. cit.* (cf. note *123*), p. 17 ff.

(317) *GE*, pp. 386–7.

(318) *AG*, p. 59.

(319) Cf. also Sully, pp. 76–7.

(320) Cf. Lévy-Bruhl, pp. 407 ff., and 198 ff. ; also a similar observation upon children by Sully, pp. 76–7.

(321) Moore, p. 125 ; Stumpf, *SpE*, p. 25. (The italics in this quotation are mine). Cf. also Sully's remarks upon " colour-hearing " in children, p. 33 f.

(322) Stern, *Sp*, p. 172 f. ; cf. also among others, Preyer, II, p. 86, and Moore, pp. 140–1.

(323) *GE*, p. 375 ; *AG*, p. 59.

(324) Moore, p. 123.

(325) *Sp*, p. 172.

(326) Cf. G. von Wartensleben, *Die Christliche Persönlichkeit in Idealbild*. Kempten and München, 1914, pp. 2–3 (note).

(327) Stumpf, *SpE*, p. 6 ff.

(328) Sully, p. 30.

(329) *Op. cit.* (cf. note *259*), p. 600 ff. ; cf. also Bühler, *GE*, p. 405 ff.

(330) Compayré, II, pp. 41–2.

(331) *GE*, p. 222.

(332) *GE*, pp. 396–7 ; *AG*, p. 143 ff.

(333) M. Wertheimer, " Über das Denken der Natürvölker. I. Zahlen und Zahlgebilde," *Zeitschr. f. Psychol.*, 60, 1912.

(334) *Op. cit.*, p. 329.

(335) *GE*, p. 195.

(336) *Sp*, p. 250.

(337) Wertheimer, *op. cit.*, p. 327.

(338) Stern, *Sp*, pp. 428–9. The procedure is quite analogous in other languages.

(339) *Sp*, p. 251.

## NOTES TO CHAPTER VI

(340) Cf. Bühler, *GE*, p. 310.

(341) pp. 38, 47.

(342) Sully, p. 30.

(343) Lévy-Bruhl, Introduction and chapter I, K. Th. Preuss., " Die geistige Kultur der Naturvölker," *Aus Natur. u. Geisteswelt*, Nr. 452. Leipzig and Berlin, 1914.

# NOTES

(344) Cf. Volkelt, pp. 26, 43.

(345) *GE*, p. 389.

(346) Cf. Preyer, II, p. 197 ff. Cf. also the reports on chimpanzees which Köhler has recently published, showing how they behave before a mirror. (" Zur Psychologie der Schimpansen," *Psychol. Forschungen*, 1, 1921, p. 35 ff. English translation, *The Mentality of Apes*, in this library).

(347) pp. 96, 80.

(348) *PsdK*, p. 250.

(349) Reported by Lévy-Bruhl, pp. 59, 62, 124 f. The citation is from p. 127.

(350) *PM*, p. 387 f. This whole book is pertinent to the questions under discussion, pp. 380 ff., 385 ff. ; cf. further *PA*, p. 287 ff. ; *SK*, p. 205 ; Bühler, *GE* p. 310 ; Stern, *PsdK*, p. 181 f.

(351) P. 48.

(352) *SpE*, pp. 18, 22, 16.

(353) Else Roloff : " Vom religiösen Leben der Kinder," *Arch. f. relig. Psychol.*, *2–3*, 1921, p. 194 f.

(354) *PM*, p. 387.

(355) As Groos remarks, Spencer had already expressed the same idea, though Groos came to his theory independently of Spencer. Cf. *PM*, p. 374 f. ; *SK*, p. 70 ff.

(356) Groos, *PA*, p. 1 ff. ; *PM*, p. 361 ff. ; *SK*, p. 64 ff.

(357) *GE*, p. 434.

# INDEX

Aall, A. : 233, 370
Abderhalden : 359
" absolute " choice : 141, 216
absolute magnitude : 284, 286,
289
accommodation of the eyes : 71,
79, 146, 285
Acher, R. A. : 361
achievement, problem of : 152,
181, 204, 238, 301, 302
achievement-test : 25, 32, 33
adornment, instinct of : 43, 114,
115
adult-world : 345, 346, 349, 350,
352
after-image : 289, 359
age-data : 50
anencephalic infant : 126, 150
animal-experiments : 167, 318
animal-psychology : 2, 3, 12, 19,
22, 137, 155, 308, 360
animal-stupidity : 163
animism : 339
anthropomorphism : 22
anticipation : 253, 256, 263, 271,
272, 305
apparent magnitude : 285-7,
289
arrangement-method : 269, 270,
273, 278
association : 127, 128, 132, 133,
155-7, 165, 173, 215, 216, 223,
230, 231, 235, 236, 246-8, 261,
286, 287, 311, 328, 363, 370
associative mechanism : 206,
207, 210, 211
atavism : 44
attention : 193, 194, 202, 206,
226, 251, 259-61, 300, 302
attraction (instinctive) : 110,
121
audition : 121
auditory nerves : 82
auditory perception : 26
auditory stimuli : 82, 83
autonomic system : 23
avoidance (instinctive): 110,
118, 121, 145, 218, 242, 341
axis-cylinder : 53

babbling : 310, 315, 317
Babinski-reflex : 83, 84, 150
background : 131, 209, 227, 228,
242, 266, 299
Baldwin, J. M. : 33, 310, 373
Becher, E. : 108, 235, 236, 357,
361, 370
beginning-situation : 107
behaviourism : 12-22, 27, 28, 91,
359
Bergson, H. : 364
Berry, C. S. : 113, 114, 307, 308,
318, 373
Betz, W. : 259, 371, 373
Binet, A. : 33, 34, 251, 261, 269,
273, 277, 291, 292, 329, 371
Binet-Simon Scale : 277
biogenesis : 44
" bond " : 92, 109, 123-5, 146,
164, 215, 232-4, 246-8, 255-7,
366
brainless child : 55-7, 65, 85, 86,
126, 150
Breed, F. S. : 250
Brod, M., and Weltsch, F. : 136,
323, 366
Brunswig, A. : 223
Bühler, K. : 33, 35, 36, 61, 75,
77, 110, 118, 123, 124, 156,
160, 162, 182, 193, 206-14,
221, 223, 226, 230-2, 235, 237,
255, 271, 272, 286, 295, 296,
299, 300, 303-5, 319, 320, 323,
324, 326, 327, 330, 333, 340,
354, 355, 357, 360-3, 365,
367-75
building-tests : 186, 200, 204, 306
Busse, Paula : 288, 370

centrifugal fibres : 53, 54, 70
centripetal fibres : 53, 54, 70
cerebellum : 23, 58, 59
cerebrum : 23, 55, 65, 126
Cermak, P. : 63
Cermak and Koffka : 361
chained reflexes : 90-7, 108
chance : 199, 200, 202, 203, 205,
207, 219, 220, 232, 233, 256,
262

# INDEX

# INDEX

# INDEX

# INDEX

"non-closure" : 103
"non-thingness" : 323
"nothing" : 207–9

object-colour : 283
odour : 110
"old" brain : 23, 52, 54, 55, 57, 64, 74
olfactory lobes : 23
one-word sentence : 320, 321, 329
ontogenesis : 44–7, 57
Ordahl, L. E. : 116, 260, 371
orthogonal appearance : 295
orthoscopic form : 296, 297
overtones : 226, 227

pain : 120, 121, 302, 343
Palæ-encephalon : 23
Parkinson : 348
partial tones : 226
pathway-hypothesis : 235, 256
pecking : 87, 88, 107, 111, 112, 250, 303
Peiser, J. : 367
perception : 63, 64, 72, 149, 156, 178, 191, 192, 212–4, 224, 240–3, 245, 257, 259, 261, 264, 282–5, 290, 293, 295–9, 301, 309, 312–4, 316, 322, 338, 340, 362
perception of form : 285, 289, 294
perseverative tendency : 178
personification : 338
Peters, W. : 34, 276–83, 372
phenomena : 8, 13, 17, 30, 31, 79, 82, 102, 119, 128–31, 133–7, 140, 142–6, 148, 149, 171–3, 177, 208, 209, 221, 222, 225, 226, 236, 238, 240, 242, 243, 268, 272, 282, 287, 292, 294, 295, 320, 342, 343, 348, 356, 362, 369
photo-tropism : 111
phylogenesis : 45–7
physical configuration : 236, 369
"place-analysis" : 177, 196
plantar reflex : 83, 84, 150
plasticity : 122–5
play : 45, 336, 338, 344, 346, 348, 350, 352–5
plaything : 337, 346, 350
play-world : 349, 352
pleasure : 156, 159, 160, 219, 265, 327, 355
practice-curve : 262
pre-lingual period : 322

pre-numerical constructs : 332–5
Preuss, K. T. : 339, 374
Preyer, W. : 35, 65, 66, 82, 85, 86, 110, 116, 119, 120, 126, 145, 251, 254, 263, 269, 271, 306, 310, 311, 316, 326, 341, 342, 358, 362, 363, 371–5
primitive drawings : 347
primitive man : 339, 353
primitive mind : 340, 352
primitive peoples : 324, 325, 332, 335, 338–40, 347, 348
problem of achievement : 152, 181, 204, 238, 301, 302
Prussian Academy of Science : 180
psychological atomism : 359
psychological method : 29–31
psycho-physical method : 25, 28–30
psycho-vitalism : 104, 236, 359
pupillary reflex : 111, 112, 121
pursing the lips : 118, 316
puzzle-box experiment : 167, 168, 171, 174, 175, 183

quality : 82, 131, 135–7, 141, 142, 171, 209
questionnaire-method : 45

reaction : 232, 265, 284, 302, 303
recapitulation : 44, 45, 48, 361
recognition : 240, 244, 248, 265, 288, 290, 292
"recreation" theory : 355
reflex : 68, 69, 71, 76, 78, 79, 81, 82, 84, 86, 87, 90–2, 98, 100, 103, 107, 108, 110, 112, 125, 231
reflex-arc : 69, 70, 92, 149
reflex-arc theory : 93
reflex-mechanism : 69, 77, 108
reflex-system : 67–70
religion : 350, 351
remembrance : 238–40, 243, 244
repetition : 233, 262, 322
reproduction (imaginal) : 29, 213, 214, 246–8, 276
retina : 63, 71, 76, 81, 275, 284, 294
retinal image : 79, 97, 225, 285–7, 339
Rhesus monkeys : 367
rhythm of development : 49, 50
Robinson, L. : 84
Roloff, Else : 350, 351, 375
Rothmann : 56

# INDEX